Praise for *Mormons on the*

"People the world over are flocking to the Internet, (discovering the Church of Jesus Christ of Latter-day Saints. LauraMaery Gold has captured the essence of each and has melded them together in this book. I heartily recommend it as must reading for anyone interested in religion and/or the Internet."

—Arthur Wilde, LDS Section Leader, the CompuServe Religion Forum

"I thought I was pretty knowledgeable about LDS Web sites, but Mormons on the Internet *has opened my eyes to a vast universe of LDS resources and online communities. This book has now created a problem for me: to express it in bumper sticker vernacular, So many LDS Web sites, so little time!"*

—Robert D. Starling, LDS Film/TV Producer, Founder, Associated Latter-day Media Artists (ALMA)

"At last, someone has done it all and done it right! Moses was enabled to see everything in the universe; when it comes to the universe of the World Wide Web, this book does the same."

—Chris Conkling, Author of *A Joseph Smith Chronology, Lord of the Rings* (United Artists screenplay)

"This book will become an incredibly valuable resource for all Latter-day Saints who have found the helpful wonders of the Internet."

—Robert J. Allen, M.D.

"Mormons on the Internet is a great way for members of our worldwide church to stay linked. LauraMaery's book is not only a font of information, it's a lot of fun. This is a must have book for anyone hooked up to the Internet."

—Michael Rutter, Author of *Run of the Arrow and The Corporate Edge*

"This is the resource you've been looking for—a friendly, step-by-step guide to all things Mormon on the Internet. LauraMaery Gold is irresistible, combining a strong business and Internet background, a wonderful writing style, and a lifetime of service as an active Latter-day Saint."

—Cathy Gileadi, Author of *Homeschool Genesis* and *Everywoman's Herbal*

"Finally—a computer book I not only understand, but find exciting. LauraMaery Gold gives us an explosion of righteous ways to use technology to bless ourselves and others."

—Joni Hilton, Author of *As The Ward Turns* and other LDS bestsellers

"A timely and useful guide for LDS internet users, and a convenient 'phone book' of like-minded friends."

—Christina Nibley Mincek, LDS Director of Public Affairs for North Florida/South Georgia

"An excellent resource. I was introduced to many useful Web sites I wasn't previously aware of."

—David M. Brown, Idaho Boise Mission President

"LauraMaery Gold has a pithy, intelligent style that's a delight to read—and she knows her Net!!"

—Kristen Randle, author, MLA Best Book of the Year 1997

"I knew that the Internet was a fertile field for members of the LDS Church, but until reading this 'Book of Modem' I had no idea how entrenched we are in it. This is fascinating and informative reading."

—Kathryn H. Kidd, moderator of Nauvoo.com and author of *Paradise Vue*

"LauraMaery Gold is one of the outstanding writers and contributors to the Internet. Her book is filled with valuable information for all Internet users, and her helpful advice provides a step-by-step guide to finding and using that information. I heartily recommend Mormons on the Internet *to all Latter-day Saints."*

—Craig Anderson, Professional software developer and long-time Internet user

"LauraMaery Gold's vivacious and spirited presence has been a joy to the LDS on-line community. Mormons on the Internet *will be an invaluable resource, containing both helpful advice for the novice and beneficial information for the experienced LDS Internet participant."*

—Robb Cundick, Former CompuServe LDS Section Leader,
Member of the Mormon Tabernacle Choir

MORMONS
ON THE INTERNET
2000–2001

LAURAMAERY
GOLD

PRIMA PUBLISHING
3000 Lava Ridge Court • Roseville, California 95661
(800) 632-8676 • www.primalifestyles.com

PRIMA PUBLISHING and colophon are trademarks of Prima Communications Inc., registered with the United States Patent and Trademark Office.

Library of Congress Cataloging-in-Publication Data
Gold, LauraMaery.
Mormons on the Internet, 2000–2001 / LauraMaery Gold.
p.   cm.
Includes index.
ISBN 0-7615-1568-2
1. Mormons--Computer network resources Handbooks, manuals, etc.
2. Church of Jesus Christ of Latter-Day Saints--Computer network resources Handbooks, manuals, etc. I. Title.
BX8638.G655   1999
004.67'8'088283--dc21   99-41660
CIP
01 02 03 DD 10 9 8 7 6 5 4 3 2
Printed in the United States of America

How to Order
Single copies may be ordered from Prima Publishing, 3000 Lava Ridge Court, Roseville, CA 95661; telephone (800) 632-8676. Quantity discounts are also available. On your letterhead, include information concerning the intended use of the books and the number of books you wish to purchase.

Visit us online at www.primalifestyles.com

CONTENTS

FOREWORD

By Keith Irwin

About 12 years ago, I stumbled across a group of Latter-day Saints talking to one another on CompuServe, at that time a relatively new computer network. Living in the rather lonely world of the frequent business traveler, I was intrigued that, on a daily basis, I could post messages that would be read and replied to by Latter-day Saints not only from different parts of the United States, but from around the world.

I thought I was a pretty typical Latter-day Saint. I grew up in the Church and have served as a bishop and on several high councils. But these were people whose experience was different from my own. One member lived near the Arctic Circle. Another had left the Church years earlier over his inability to reconcile some doctrinal issues. Still another was a bishop in Utah Valley. Yet another lived in an inner-city ward in the Midwest. Still another was actively RLDS. Several had struggled with substance abuse and marital problems. A disproportionate number were proficient musicians. Many had lived outside the United States. These differences made for wonderful, nearly addictive conversation. I found myself hurrying through my work each day so I could log on and see what my newfound cyberfriends had to say.

Today, technology has enabled nearly anyone to connect to the Internet and join in the global conversation. The growth rate of Internet users has been astronomical, and it is certain that the number of users interested in discussing the Mormon experience is likewise growing dramatically. This creates great opportunity for Latter-day Saints, but it is not without some serious challenges.

The hazards of the Internet have been well publicized. All the vices are there: gambling, pornography, scams—even stalkers and child molesters. I often tell inquiring friends that the Internet is a reflection of the world. Anything you can find in the world, regardless of its merit, can be found somewhere on the Net. I pass on a maxim of a former mentor, Bonner Ritchie, "You can't make the world safe for people; you have to make people safe for the world." Indeed, I doubt if it is even possible to control the content of the Net, given its global configuration. But by taking the same precautionary measures you would take when you leave your home, your trips into cyberspace will likely be as safe as your walks down the street. You wouldn't walk into an "adult" bookshop. Neither should you wander into an adult Web site (most of which are well marked). You wouldn't give your address to a stranger. Neither should you give your phone number or street address over the Internet to someone you don't know. You wouldn't let your children wander around without knowing where they are. Neither should you let your kids wander around the Net without knowing what they are doing.

The most "hyped" feature of the Internet is the World Wide Web. A search using services such as Yahoo www.yahoo.com[1] or AltaVista www.altavista.digital.com will turn up hundreds of sites that deal with Mormonism. Many are simply lists of other Web sites. Others are adversarial. But some are truly extraordinary. Take a look at Nick Literski's temple Web site www.vii.com/~nicksl or Dave Crockett's pages on Mormon History www.indirect.com/www/crockett/history.html. There is enough information on these pages to bring new life to any Gospel Doctrine lesson. Not to be missed is LDS-GEMS, www.lds-gems.com, a service that distributes news of the Church, inspirational stories, and glimpses of history via e-mail.

Though slow to develop, the official LDS Church Web site, www.lds.org now offers conference talks, church announcements, and current public affairs information. The Church's genealogy Web site www.familysearch.org offers the most comprehensive family history database online.

The commercial use of the World Wide Web has not been overlooked by Mormon businesses. Interestingly and fortunately, their marketing approach seems to focus on creating a significant set of resource pages for Latter-day Saints, only part of which is promotion of their products. Infobases www.ldsworld.com has an

---

[1]Editor's note: Internet sites described in this book are listed along with their addresses, or "URLs." URLs appear in a special typeface (e.g., www.writerspost.com/mormonnet); e-mail addresses appear italicized and within angle brackets (<mormonnet@writerspost.com>). If you're new to the Internet, see page 44 for information on using the addresses.

enormous Web site with pages for all aspects of Mormonism. Deseret Book www.deseretbook.com uses a similar strategy. In each case, Latter-day Saints end up with terrific databases of information.

I've often lamented the inefficiency that takes place when Latter-day Saints exert tremendous time and energy preparing the same lessons. The computer connection to Latter-day Saints around the world is changing that. Think of the possibilities for a seminary teacher, for example. Each day a thousand or more seminary teachers struggle to find new and interesting ways to present the same lessons. Now, though, when a new idea is conceived, it can be instantly shared with others via the seminary mail list or on Web sites with pages devoted to seminary. Similarly, seminary teachers can discuss the challenges of their callings as well as rejoice in their successes with others sharing the same experience. With similar lists now online for Primary, Sunday School, Young Men/Young Women, and High Priest group leaders, no teacher in the Church should ever feel that he or she is without support.

The global connection of Latter-day Saints creates new challenges as well. In pre-Internet days, the Mormon rumor mill may only have extended from Logan to St. George, with occasional telephone forays into the rest of the country. Now a juicy tidbit that has some face validity can spread from Alberta to Auckland in a matter of minutes. About six months before the recent combining of lesson manuals for the Relief Society and Melchizedek Priesthood, a general authority attending a stake conference in the Midwest briefly mentioned it in a talk. A member who heard the news immediately posted it to the Internet, where it became the subject of discussion by members around the world. Another member saw the report and decided to check it with the Church Curriculum Committee in Salt Lake. An astonished Church employee replied that this information was not officially released. When told that it was already on the Internet, he was speechless.

The ability to manipulate the online community is best illustrated by the "Great April Fools Prank" played out in the early days of the Internet on LDS-NET, the very first LDS mailing list. Freewheeling discussions featuring many unorthodox positions were a frequent staple of LDS-NET. Early on April first, one of the members posted that he had been at a social where Church employees mentioned that the General Authorities were monitoring the LDS Internet mailing list discussions. Several replies reflected astonishment and mild paranoia. Then a co-conspirator in the prank posted that his stake president was calling in people who were participating in Internet discussion groups. This report generated a furor in which people asked if they could edit their prior posts out of the archives. Others blasted the General Authorities for "spying." Still others took themselves off the list. This cacophony of anxiety and anger was not put to rest until nearly midnight, when the originator of the discussion posted "April Fool."

More recently, a bogus news story about a Brigham City, Utah, school board received such wide circulation that it made the national news. Another equally fraudulent story about BYU archeologists working at Adam-Ondi-Ahman and a concurrent Mormon land rush in Missouri also made the rounds. Sorting information, misinformation, and disinformation may be one of the greatest challenges any Internet user confronts.

The most valuable feature of the Internet is not the plethora of information in the Web sites, but the interactive features such as mail lists and newsgroups. These features allow the creation of communities where ideas and experiences can be exchanged and great learning can take place. When CompuServe asked me to lead the LDS group several years ago, I felt it important to set parameters on discussions so the group would have a focus. Messages, for example, should obviously have something to do with Mormonism. But what other guidelines should there be?

Some LDS groups had set pretty strong rules, ensuring orthodoxy among their members. Others with no parameters degenerated into slug-fests between LDS and Evangelical Christians.

Seeking to create something different, I pondered what it might be like in my ward if all the people we say we want to come to Church—nonmembers, former members, less actives, and others—actually showed up and said what they really thought. The thought was a hilarious mental feast. But I could see it reaching the point of raucous debate where orthodoxy was up for grabs and anarchy reigned.

There would have to be some simple guidelines for engagement. What if people were required to treat each other with civility? What if inquiry was as valued as advocacy? What if respect for others' beliefs was required behavior? These became the parameters of our community. The gates were open wide. We welcomed anyone interested in discussing Mormonism, be they active, inactive, former, liberal, conservative, straight, gay, LDS, RLDS, polygamist, or monogamist—but the content and tone of all posts had to be respectful of people and their beliefs. I also set discussions of the specifics of temple ordinances off limits, but any other topic was fair game.

The result was the most savory mix of conversations I have yet experienced in cyberspace. People not only talked rationally about their agreements and differences, but after some time, discussions began to demonstrate that people genuinely cared about each other. Soon conversation about our personal lives became as common as esoteric theological debate. While there were a few who could not tolerate the presence of "the unfaithful," most found it a unique and valuable community. I know of no one who became estranged from the Church as a result of interaction with this diverse group, but I do know of several baptisms and many reactivations that came, at least in part, from our association.

I once related this experience in a talk in stake conference. After the conference, the visiting member of the Quorum of the Twelve, L. Tom Perry, challenged me to "keep that group going." As a result, I sometimes refer (tongue in cheek) to the LDS group on CompuServe as the only one with an apostolic mandate.

Unfortunately, there are too few broad-based LDS discussion groups where civility is the rule. The lack of civility, in my opinion, has led to a specialization of discussion groups. ZION is decidedly conservative. MORMON-L has a reputation of being a liberal free-for-all. JOSEPH is a moderate and quite orthodox list that avoids discussion of political or social issues. LDS-NET still exists as a general purpose mail list, though it is currently home to a fairly small group of people. I'm hopeful that other "general purpose" mailing lists will develop, and communities will evolve where inquiry is more valued than advocacy, and where genuine dialogue about differences can take place. Orson Scott Card's Nauvoo Web site www.nauvoo.com has an interactive feature that seems to be in this tradition. And the newsgroup *soc.rel.mormon* has a similar aim.

There are many other terrific lists that specialize by interest rather than by philosophical outlook. AML-LIST is a very active group focusing on Mormon literature. EYRING-L focuses on science and religion. My own list, LDS-BOOK-SHELF, is devoted to collectible Mormon books. I'm certain that a trip through this book will turn up a list devoted to your interests. But if it doesn't, it's easy to start one of your own.

For Latter-day Saints, the possibilities of the Internet are just beginning to emerge. Distance learning technology using the Internet could easily be translated into virtual wards in remote areas of the world. General Conference can be brought into every home and possibly even made interactive! One can only begin to ponder the changes that might come from instant two-way communication between the Church and its membership. I don't know for certain how this technology is going to change our lives, but I do know for certain that it will.

Keith Irwin
San Jose, California
<*kirwin@wenet.net*>

ACKNOWLEDGMENTS

There are so many Latter-day Saints who helped with this project that I couldn't even begin to name them all. Well, OK, I could begin. There's Jamie Miller, my editor and new Best Friend, who spearheaded this entire project. Thank you, Jamie, for your enthusiasm and your confidence. And my thanks also to Andi Reese Brady, for jumping in to help with the editing process of the first edition. Thanks, too, to the good people at Argosy, who sorted through the usual assortment of typos and blunders. You were all a joy to work with.

There's the irresistible Keith Irwin, who made my first foray into the Mormon online community so delightful. Several years ago, when I was going through a rough patch in life, Keith appointed himself my electronic home teacher and saw me through. Keith's perspectives on the power of online communication have been invaluable in informing my own thoughts on the matter. Thanks, Ellen, for letting him loose.

My thanks go to Elder Jeffrey R. Holland, who took the time from his packed schedule to talk with me about the future of the Internet as a missionary tool. Thank you, Elder Holland, for that and for many years of your inspired and inspiring counsel. I'm only a face in the bleachers, but the Lord has spoken to me many times through your words.

To all the Mormon Internetters who responded to my questions and were generous with their time and their insight: I appreciate your kindness in taking the time to share.

I am indebted to the "five horsemen" of the Internet: Clark Goble *<cgoble@fiber.net>*, Kent S. Larsen II *<klarsen@panix.com>*, John Walsh *<mormon@mormons.org>*, Dave Crockett *<crockett@goodnet.com>*, and David Kenison *<dkenison@xmission.com>*, who have among them thoroughly indexed the Mormon Internet. More than that. They have, in large measure, created and defined the entire LDS online experience. They are the brightest lights among the hundreds of Latter-day Saints who have built and maintained a Web of faithful Internet sites.

My appreciation also goes to Infobases, creator of the delightful LDS Collectors Library, and the source of many of the quotes found in this text. If you don't have your own copy of Collectors Library, you're missing out. Stop by the Infobases Web site www.infobases.com to place your order.

To Carol James, my visiting teaching companion and dear friend, who patiently picked up the slack for me month after month: Thank you. Thank you very much.

To my grandpa and grandma, Stan and Vera Zielinski, who gave me the foundation to be whatever good thing I am today: I love you and miss you.

And then there are saints of an entirely different stripe. To Andrew Zack, my Jewish agent who laughed when I described him as a Gentile: Thanks, Andy, for negotiating the hard part of the work.

To all the rest of the editorial staff at Prima, you have my gratitude for working through tight deadlines, bizarre technological glitches, and a manuscript full of unfamiliar ideas.

And most of all, to my wonderful husband—the best man in the world—who watches over me, takes care of me, and raises our babies when I'm glued to a keyboard: Danny, I love you more every day.

INTRODUCTION

A Community of Mormons

It was in the early 70s at a youth conference in the Seattle area that I first caught the vision of technology's role in the future of the Church of Jesus Christ of Latter-day Saints. A large group of young people gathered in the stake center to hear our Stake Patriarch talk to us about the growth of the Church, and about our role in that growth.

In awe I listened to this venerable, inspired man describe a Church growing so fast that we'd one day have temples in operation in every corner of the globe, general conferences broadcast to the world via satellites, a missionary effort that would go not to dozens of people, but to thousands of people at one time. As we come ever closer to the time of Christ's return, he told us, the work of the Lord will proceed at an ever more rapid pace, and God will give us the knowledge we need to make that work go forward.

It all seemed too fantastic to a young girl whose entire exposure to computers had been the panels of blinking lights on *Star Trek* reruns. But for the past quarter of a century, I've kept the memory of that prophetic declaration in the back of my mind, looking forward to a day—perhaps near the end of my life—when I would live to see those words fulfilled.

I grew up in the middle of a communications revolution, oblivious to what I was experiencing. In 1978, as a young journalist at the *Daily Herald* in Provo, Utah, I watched stories spool out of the wire service machines on machine-readable punched strips of yellow tape. The decoding process was so complex, though, that the miracle of the transmission itself was obscured.

I first went online in 1982, when, as a student at BYU, I got access over a 300-baud modem from my home computer to a gigantic mainframe computer on campus. I used the connection to print school papers on a room-sized laser printer.

Over the years, I used online connections to send stories from my home in Taipei to my editors in Hong Kong, and later to build an electronic bulletin board for readers of the computer magazines I edited in Singapore, Malaysia, and Hong Kong. Still, I couldn't envision the complicated BBS technology evolving into anything bigger.

Imagine my delight when, in mid-1994, I discovered a thing called the World Wide Web, the part of the Internet that allows anyone to publish anything they want to say and make it available to readers anyplace in the world. Within a year, the Web software and Internet connections had evolved to the point where it became practical for Just Plain Folks to get online. Within days of an Internet service provider setting up shop in my calling area, I was on the Internet and building my own Web page. In honor of my Patriarch, I began collecting testimonies, conversion stories, temple experiences, and missionary experiences for publication on the Internet—my own missionary effort being broadcast to the world, as in the vision of that Patriarch, via satellites.

We Mormons have an awesome world view. We see God's hand in every good thing. From the Reformation to Columbus to the United States Constitution, we see a world directed by a God who wants us back. And at the same time, we see the malevolent work of an anti-Christ, a Satan who can use those same tools to bring about the destruction of mankind if we're not vigilant.

I see God's hand in the technology revolution taking place in the world today. I see communities of like-minded Latter-day Saints coming together from their homes and offices in every little village in the world to inspire one another, to support one another, to work out the programs of the Church in their own ways. I see Scouting Saints working together to share ideas. I see single Saints extending the hand of fellowship and support to one another. I see conservative Saints discussing politics, and liberal Saints discussing conservative Saints. I see Latter-day Saints struggling with same-sex attraction acting as support and help for one another. I've seen Saints struggle with every kind of trial, and receive kind words, loving advice, and cyber-pats on the back as they worked through their difficulties. I have seen miracles take place in the lives of members—and nonmembers—of the Church through the friendships they've found in online LDS communities.

I've also seen the opposite of every one of these good things. There are places on the Internet rife with contention, filled with slurs against everything Latter-day Saints hold true and sacred. I've seen true hatred, vicious lies, half-truths, and unwarranted attacks. I've seen sacred things held up for public ridicule. I've seen slanted points of view, the expression of fringe opinion, and cloaked requests for "information" that turned out to be nothing more than bait for later attacks.

In the words of my cyber-hero, Keith Irwin, who for many years moderated the LDS section on the CompuServe Religion Forum, "You can find anything in Cyberspace that you'd find in real life." It's just easier to find it on the Internet.

Isn't it comforting to know, when you do find things that send you to the stacks for further research, that there's also a community out there of intelligent, thoughtful, well-educated Latter-day Saints who are eager to discuss them with you?

This, then, is the Mormon Internet: An eclectic collection of Web sites, chat rooms, e-mail lists, discussion forums, and newsgroups operated and populated by people who love the Church and the gospel, and who want to share their joy with anyone willing to participate.

And as an enthusiastic cheerleader for all who share the vision of a worldwide community of Latter-day Saints, I stand at the gates of a New Jerusalem, and bid you enter.

Author's Introduction to the Second Edition: Mormons on the Internet 2000–2001

The LDS Internet has exploded! In the first edition of this book released late in 1997, we reviewed some 500 sites and included almost anything that had an address. In this edition, we had to sort through more than 6,000 LDS Internet sites, only a third of which made it into this book. That's a lot of online time spent categorizing, rating, reviewing, and updating sites. The good news: owners of this book will have full access to our Web site at www.writerspost.com/mormonnet, where you can search all 6,000+ links, add additional resources, and sign up for the *Mormons on the Internet* newsletter.

New to this edition are Hotlinks—the very best resources in each category of this book. You'll also find a completely new chapter on Internet safety: what parents need to know to keep their families safe on the Internet. Also new to this edition are sections for senior Saints, teaching resources, health and fitness, and more. The top twenty list has grown to 25, along with a list of honorable mentions that are well worth bookmarking.

And you'll also find lots of resources for building your own Web site. Look for instructions on getting free Web space and site-building tools, along with lots of advice for budding LDS Webmasters.

Whether you're an Internet novice, or an experienced Webmaster yourself, you'll find information here to amuse, educate, inspire and edify. Welcome to the online community of Latter-day Saints!

LauraMaery Gold
Kent, Washington
<*mormonnet@writerspost.com*>

PART ONE

BUILDING A COMMUNITY

1

LATTER-DAY SAINTS ONLINE

Welcome to the world of the Mormon Internet, a vast fellowship of Latter-day Saints, our e-mail lists, our discussion groups, our Web pages, our chat areas, and our community.

The LDS online community includes people of every description—active members, less-active members, even nonmembers. It takes in members from the Pacific Rim, Europe, and South America.

It includes the devout, the skeptical, the missionary-minded, the disenfranchised, the young, the old, the married, the single. It includes the brilliant, the clever, and the distressed.

Members of the community participate at every level: from those who should be in a 12-step program for their hourly involvement in chat areas and newsgroups, to people who barely have time to check their e-mail every couple of weeks.

What they all have in common is this: access to an online connection, and a fascination with the Church of Jesus Christ of Latter-day Saints.

WHAT YOU'LL FIND IN THIS BOOK

This book does more than tell you how to get on line. And it's more than a directory of LDS sites on the World Wide Web. Here you'll also find reviews of many of those Web sites, along with ratings that will help you find your way around with a minimum of wasted effort. Compiled here, for the first time, is the fascinating story of the development of the Mormon Internet—perhaps the major LDS pioneering effort of our age. The book also features interviews with the people who have contributed to the LDS online community. They explain, in their own words, their vision for a world in which Latter-day Saints in every condition . . . in sickness, in health, in poverty's vale, or abounding in wealth—ahem, in every circumstance can find joy in one another's fellowship.

HOW THIS BOOK IS ARRANGED

This book is arranged in three parts: Building a Community, The Mission of the Church, and Living a Latter-day Saint Life.

Part 1 describes the Mormon online community, the Church's Web site, the process of getting on line, and the first steps in getting around the Internet. You'll also find a new chapter on Internet safety.

Part 2 addresses the threefold mission of the Church, showing how Latter-day Saints are using the resources of the Internet to Proclaim the Gospel, Perfect the Saints, and Redeem the Dead.

In Part 3, Living a Latter-day Saint Life, you'll find a guided tour of Internet sites related to the following areas:

- **The Living Church.** International sites, events and activities, news and LDS publications, units of the Church, and a multitude of broadly focused discussion areas.
- **Auxiliaries.** Priesthood, Primary, Relief Society, Seminary, Single Adults, Sunday School, and Young Men and Young Women.
- **Interest Groups.** Youth, seniors, dating and courtship, fulfilling callings, women, professional groups, home schooling, health resources, Saints dealing with same-sex attraction, and commercial sites.
- **Pursuit of Excellence.** Personal scripture study, Mormon arts and letters, humor, and emergency preparedness.
- **The Glory of God Is Intelligence.** Resources on Church history, research groups, science and religion, the Church in society, doctrinal issues, and comparative theology.

Finally, you will find an overview of the top 25 LDS sites on the Internet, along with suggestions for getting involved in building a meaningful contribution of your own.

WHAT'S CHANGED FROM THE FIRST EDITION

If you bought the first edition of *Mormons on the Internet*, you've already seen some changes. OK, well, the cover's different. But there's more!

- **New contributors.** Several readers generously contributed stories about their families and their Internet experience to this new edition of *Mormons on the Internet*. You'll enjoy reading about how they've solved problems.
- **A new chapter.** Worried about bringing the monster into your home? A new chapter on Internet Safety should ease your mind. Learn about software that will protect your kids from predators, pornography, and violence.
- **New Internet resources.** Hundreds of them.
- **New format.** Web browsers have gotten smarter. Now our Internet addresses are easier to read.
- **A new companion Web site.** You'll never have to worry about links in this book going out of date. Our completely rebuilt Web site lets visitors add links to new LDS Internet sources directly to the page. And we'll regularly update the site to alert you about missing sites, new addresses, and significant improvements.
- **Hot Links.** A quick guide to the hottest LDS sites on the Internet.
- **Icons.** Helpful graphic pointers throughout the book will point you to cautions, reminders, and helpful hints.
- **Mailing List.** Readers can sign up for a low-volume newsletter describing important LDS Internet changes.

WHAT YOU'LL FIND IN THIS CHAPTER

This chapter provides an overview of the power of the Internet in the LDS community. You'll first meet a member, a former Baptist minister, who joined the Church because of his online experience. You'll be introduced to some of the pioneers of the Mormon Internet, and will learn what motivated their decisions to contribute their resources to the community.

After that, you'll find a section on how Latter-day Saints use the Internet, in which a large number of Latter-day Saints who frequent the online communities of the Internet talk about why they're there. These members explain for themselves what they find on the Internet that helps them in their families, their work in the Church, and their daily lives.

At the end of the chapter, you'll find a description of the system used throughout this text to rate Internet resources. You'll want to keep a finger in that final page.

THE POWER OF THE INTERNET

There's no question but that the Internet is a powerful force. How powerful? It's a forum for discussion. A repository of information. A facilitator of friendships. But it's even more than that. It is, in fact, a whole new paradigm for spreading the gospel. There are already countless new members of the Church who credit their Internet experience as a significant factor in their decision to be baptized. Some investigators encounter the Church as a result of friendships they develop over the Internet. Others use the resources of the Internet to research the Church and its teachings, and only later make friends with Latter-day Saints.

Over the past few years, I have run across a number of Latter-day Saints who affirm that the Internet played a role in their conversion. A member of my own ward was introduced to the Church through an online acquaintance. Pam was baptized last summer, and though she's moved to another town to finish school, she keeps in contact via e-mail.

Another friend, whom I know only through years of online discussions, worked through some doctrinal issues in online conversations with loving Latter-day Saints and rejoined the Church years after he'd asked to have his name removed. He's since seen other members of his family come back to the Church they'd once left behind.

Another Latter-day Saint says his Internet discussions have made the difference in his ability to remain in the Church, despite the loneliness he sometimes feels in his own ward.

Other Latter-day Saints tell of inactive or former members that came back to full membership because of encouragement they'd received from online friendships.

Ronald Conrad Schoedel III, a Latter-day Saint living in Ontonagon, Michigan, credits the Internet as the single most significant factor in his conversion. Brother Schoedel <schoedel@up.net> had a Baptist upbringing, and was ordained a Baptist preacher and practiced in the ministry for about three years. "As you may know, members of that faith are responsible for some of the more ludicrous anti-Mormon literature and propaganda," he writes, "so for most of my Baptist life, those falsehood-filled books shaped my opinion of the Church."

Ironically, though, Brother Schoedel believed and taught for a number of years that Christ visited the Americas, that prophecies in the Bible pointed to a gathering of His people in the Western hemisphere, and that Christ would return to the Americas.

After leaving the Baptist church over some differences of doctrine, he remembered hearing that the Book of Mormon addressed some of those same issues.

He located a copy of the Book of Mormon, and read it carefully. He says he "was convinced more or less right away that it was the Word of God. Of that I had no doubt; but still, with all the anti-Mormon propaganda I had been exposed to for so long, I had a hard time thinking that the Church could be God's true Church."

He went to the Internet to try to "objectively" find the Truth.

I searched everything. All the anti-LDS works one could find on the Net (of which there are plenty!) as well as all the sites put together by faithful Mormons, which detailed information about their faith and their Church. I began comparing the materials on each side, and saw many, many falsehoods in the anti-LDS literature and Web sites. About the time that I had come to the conclusion that *maybe* the Church could be correct, I contacted the Church and had some discussions with the missionaries. But still I focused most of my time and efforts on independent and individual study, to arrive at the conclusions I arrived at . . . which led me to be baptized and join the Church.

The Internet played a *huge* role in my finding true LDS doctrine, which I found basically in agreement with what I had believed and taught for years. But had it not been for the Internet, I don't believe I would have bothered to research the issues as intently as I did. I give much credit to those faithful Saints who have gone through the effort and time to set up Web sites sharing their faith, for those sites were instrumental in me gaining a true and correct picture of what the Church actually believes and teaches. By allowing individual Saints to publish their articles on line, the Internet cut through the lies and deceit that big-money publishers have put out against the Church. The Internet allows all Saints to share their faith in a manner that can effectively combat the lies that abound. The Internet did it for me, by allowing me to find the Truth. Of course, all credit goes to Heavenly Father for allowing this.

A community has power—the power to draw together, to support one another, to respond to questions, and to help in times of trouble. The Internet community also provides fellowship unavailable in any other forum.

With that power comes responsibility. A responsible member of the LDS community behaves while on the Internet at least as well as he would IRL—e-mail shorthand for "in real life"—with the knowledge that his words, which seem ethereal in their electronic form, are being recorded not only in electronic archives, but in the hearts and minds of readers who may be searching for strength.

The following letter by author Craig J. Patchell of Orange County, California, appeared on AML-List, a literary e-mail list distributed by the Association of Mormon Letters. In his message, Brother Patchell <patchellcj@aol.com> describes the elements that create a community. While he speaks to writers of LDS fiction, his thoughts on building a community apply equally to Latter-day

Saint writers who publish their thoughts in other forums—notably on the Internet. (Excerpts from this letter are reprinted with the author's permission.)

. . . One of the prime purposes of literature, which is the modern day successor to the bardic storytelling tradition, is to build community. One of the most direct devices for doing that, especially among a geographically and culturally diverse people, is to invoke the commonality of shared experiences. Our lives are intensely personal experiences, and, in a day when we have to a large extent lost the close-knit communities and inter-connectedness that was the rule only two generations ago, we often suffer from perceived isolation.

The writer . . . can bond hundreds and thousands of people into a kind of meta-community, unhindered by geographic dislocation.

Mormons are a meta-community in and of themselves through their religious experience, but what happens to us beyond the chapel walls is the compelling and defining experience. . . .

It's a heady feeling of power, knowing that what you say can be heard not only by your small family, or even your large ward, but by hundreds, thousands, even millions of readers, at every level of faith, everywhere in the world.

The Internet makes everyone a publisher. "The Internet pulls down the walls or glass ceilings so that anyone may publish words, music, video, or art, and have anyone get access to their material," says Grant Johnson, a Latter-day Saint from Fair Oaks, California. "Wrong or right, that is what the Internet does. Personally, I think it is right. How *many* good ideas and products never see the light of day because some person in power rejected the idea for any number of reasons (personal, religious, political, or economical)."

What the Net allows, says Brother Johnson, is the ability to bypass the traditional roadblocks. Brother Johnson *<webmaster@new-jerusalem.com>*, Webmaster at the New Jerusalem Web site, calls the Internet "a champion of the 'little guy.'"

Don't Forget

What are LDS Internet users excited about? Their own Web sites and lists, of course. Developing these resources takes ambition and energy. They're also talking about inspirational sites, resources that help them with their callings, and genealogy aids. Latter-day Saints on the Internet want you to remember:

"The e-mail list I've started for LDS parents of special needs kids. It's *<LDSspecialones@onelist.com>*. Register at www.onelist.com/subscribe/LDSspecialones. I really think there's an audience out there that could use this. It's only been going on for a couple weeks now, and there are just 10 subscribers, which is good, but I do think there are more out there who can use the support such a list can provide!"
—Cathy Lemmon, Gresham Stake, Troutdale, Oregon
<lemmon_j@juno.com>

"Mormon-L *<mormon-l@catbyd.com>*. It's one of the oldest discussion forums for LDS on the Internet. Includes members and nonmembers. All subjects are allowed. Bashing the General Authorities or the Church is discouraged. Anti-Mormons are not allowed."
—Susan McMurray

For the Internet to have any real power over the lives of the Latter-day Saints, however, will require taming that urge to use words as weapons. It requires abiding by the counsel of the Lord that "the powers of heaven cannot be controlled nor handled [except] upon the principles of righteousness. . . . We have learned by sad experience that it is the nature and disposition of almost all men, as soon as they get a little authority, as they suppose, they will immediately begin to exercise unrighteous dominion" (D&C 121:36–39).

In abiding by correct principles, members of the Church leave open the door for the Lord to work miracles in the lives of people they meet in every part of the world.

Brian Phelps, a Saint from Livermore, California, sees the Net as more than a missionary tool. He believes the resources of the Internet can be useful within the Church itself. Brother Phelps *<btphelps@ netwizards.net>* says the Internet has the potential to positively influence the Mormon community worldwide, making Gospel-centered information more readily available. Brother Phelps runs the LDS Internet Resources FAQ Web site at www.netwizards.net/ ~btphelps/mormon. He anticipates a time when the Net will be an integral part of the administration of the Church. "Ten years down the road, I'd bet every meeting house will be plugged in, and Conference will be broadcast via the Internet instead of TV satellite."

Latter-day Saint Mark Cheney from Prescott, Arizona, has a similar vision. He foresees a time when the Internet will be used for e-mailing church reports of all types. "We already use computer modems to communicate between the wards and Salt Lake. But member locating service applications could be taken over the Internet. And much genealogical research is already being done and shared over the Net."

Another Internet user, Ken Burton from Murray, Utah, thinks that day is close at hand. Brother Burton says he gets the sense that leaders of the Church know that this communication medium will have a profound effect on the Church and the world. He

Don't Forget

"Don't forget FamilySearch.com, Cyndislist, any Genealogy Links!"
—Pam Gonder, Ocean Springs Ward, Biloxi, Mississippi *<pjgond@webtv.net>*

"Don't be afraid to use the Internet! It is a great resource! There are precautions that can protect us from those things that would do us harm, but it is like medicine! If used wisely, there is no end to what it helps with or what miracles can be wrought. If used unwisely, it can be dangerous!"
—Melinda S. Ema, Granite City, Illinois, Branch, O'Fallon Stake *<mindysue@ primary.net>*

"Latter-day Saints' Resources on the Internet www.erols.com/jdstone. More hits than any site except for the official church page."
—John Stone, Springfield, Virginia, Annandale Stake *<jdstone@erols.com>*

"Betty Pearson's missionary mom Web page and e-mail group."
—A reader in Salt Lake City's Wells Stake

"Mormons-Only. The new full URL is www.geocities.com/Heartland/ Lake/4765/, but the redirected URL is simply talk.to/mormons-only."
—Philip L. Musgrave , Kailua, Hawaii, Third Ward, Kaneohe Stake *<musgrave@e-mail.com>*

sees both apprehension (as seen in the church's slowness to take advantage of the technology and the occasional warnings from general authorities) and excitement. "Those who have a true understanding of the mission of the Church are willing to embrace any technology that can be used to further that mission," says Brother Burton. "Caution is warranted, but eventually the distribution of Church information will be instantaneous throughout the world—much like conference reports and the LDS-GEMS [a widely distributed e-mail list of Church news and other information] mailings."

HOW THE INTERNET PROVIDES A NEW MEANS OF SPREADING THE GOSPEL

The Internet provides a whole new way of reaching our brothers and sisters. Not only does it open the possibility of talking with people who are geographically diverse; it also clears the way to people who are reluctant to talk with members in all the traditional settings. If you find yourself uncomfortable approaching coworkers, neighbors, and your seatmate on the airplane about the gospel, you'll find that your inhibitions quickly disappear in the anonymity of the Internet.

In the same way, people who are resistant to speaking with missionaries on their doorstep or in public grocery stores have no such hesitation when it comes to speaking to member missionaries in the nonthreatening environment of the Internet.

Craig S. Matteson, a computer professional from Ann Arbor, Michigan, acknowledges that the technology permits anonymity and the possibility of falsifying identities, but says his experience there has been one where he's found "a real opportunity for emotional intimacy and openness." Because the contacts are not face-to-face, but person-to-person, he says, the friendships are real and lasting. He's right. I met Brother Matteson years ago in an online discussion forum, and we continue to keep in touch, though we've never met in person.

The Internet creates opportunities for learning and understanding that would never occur in any other setting. I met Jeffrey B. Winship, a member of the Reorganized Church of Jesus Christ of Latter Day Saints who lives in Independence, Missouri, through an online discussion group. When I moved to Missouri the following year, Brother Winship and another participant in that group who lived in Missouri were instrumental in helping me get acclimated. Later we had a chance to sit down together and discuss our differing views of the restoration and the gospel, a discussion that forever changed the way I see the world and live my life. Brother Winship's Christ-like example often set the tone for tolerance in that discussion group, so his thoughts on communicating in an electronic medium are worth reading. "People are more open to sharing their real feelings and understanding of principles, knowing that in few cases will they ever meet those with whom they are interacting," he writes. "They can be honest without being confrontational." Most significantly, he says, "the form of communication gives people the opportunity to think before they speak—very important when sharing testimonies with other people."

HOW LATTER-DAY SAINTS USE THE INTERNET

There are hundreds of reasons Latter-day Saints use the Internet. They find it helpful in building their families, finding solutions to problems, keeping up to date on the news of the Church, fulfilling their callings, and learning Church history.

Interviews with dozens of LDS Internet users about their online experience generated responses that form a pretty accurate picture of the best ways members of the Church make the Mormon Internet a part of their learning and growth. In this section, LDS Internet users describe how they use the Internet.

To Participate in a Community

Internet users say the online experience gives them a sense of community, a feeling of belonging even when they're far away.

Jim Picht has lived in Kyrgyzstan, on the Western border of China. He says that for six months, the Internet was his only link to the Church. "My mom's home teachers have been in touch with me by e-mail, as have friends from her home ward. I have no formal contact with even the international mission, but the AML-L and EYRING-L mailing lists have provided me with some interesting conversation with members, which has been very helpful to me." (See chapter 8 for more on mailing lists.)

Brother Picht occasionally spent Sunday mornings browsing the LDS-oriented Web sites—which passed sometimes as his Church activity for the day—and reading resource materials for Sunday School teachers and articles on scripture topics. "The Internet provides me a sense of LDS community, the only one I have," he says, "and if it hasn't made my testimony grow, it's probably kept me thinking about it more than I would have otherwise."

Ardis Parshall, a Saint living in Orem, Utah, doesn't suffer from geographic isolation, but says the ideological isolation can be just as difficult. "Oh, all right," she says, "I'll finally admit that I've been completely inactive for several years, for social rather than doctrinal reasons. My contacts with Church members on the Net over the past year have been overwhelmingly positive, and I finally feel like I fit into the community somewhere." Although the Internet is not an "official" resource, she finally has met some people she can actually talk to as friends about gospel topics.

Thom Duncan, who also lives in Orem, is much more blunt. "The LDS online community is the only community in which I feel comfortable," he says.

There are other kinds of isolation that the Internet community helps resolve. Author Benson Parkinson, from Ogden, Utah, works at home, "with preschoolers for company." Brother Parkinson says the Internet has made a "huge" difference in his life. "My e-mail box is like the church foyer and a faculty room rolled into one." Brother Parkinson operates AML-List, an e-mail discussion group for writers and fans of Mormon Literature. "My particular interests are relatively rare, even in the Church, and that's even more the case for people outside Utah. Fans of Mormon literature are one to an office and two to a city. Our discussion group gathers about 200 readers and writers of Mormon literature from around the country and world, many of whom have never had anyone to talk to their interests about outside their families."

That sense of community is shared by AML-List participant Scott Parkin, from Pleasant Grove, Utah. "The AML-List has been especially important to me in developing a sense of community. Because of AML-List, I have become quite interested in Mormon literature as one face of our faith, and that interest has led me to a more thorough investigation of Mormon literature, history, critical thought, and simple storytelling. The more I think about it, the more I become convinced of the reality and importance of the restoration and the modern Church."

People further away from the main body of Latter-day Saints say they find support in the discussion groups they find on line. Craig Anderson, who lives in Seattle, has been an active participant in online discussion groups for many years. "On CompuServe it felt like a family," he says. But the Internet is different. "On the Internet, there's a bit of [an] 'It's us against them, boys' sort of feel. Kind of like circling the wagons for mutual protection." But there's an up side. "Whenever I've encountered a situation where I had something in common with another Latter-day Saint, it's been nice to reminisce. For instance, I encountered on the Net a fellow I had met briefly in the Germany South mission."

The sense of community on the Internet is very strong. Dean Macy, from Peterborough, New Hampshire, wonders, in fact, if the LDS community isn't the mainstay of the entire online community. "Since I deal with LDS businesses, I have sometimes wondered if the LDS links take up most of the Web," he writes. "I feel a strong community presence."

Interestingly, some of the people participating on the Mormon Internet aren't even Latter-day Saints. One of the most active, Jeff Needle *<jeff.needle@ general.com>*, explains his fascination with Mormonism:

I can't tell you how many times I'm asked why I've spent nearly 10 years studying and corresponding and writing on Mormonism. I guess it's time to actually put it down on paper.

I first became interested in Mormonism about ten years ago. I was making a transition from the Seventh-day Adventist church (I was born and raised Jewish, by the way). Although Mormonism was an attractive option, I found myself reluctant to make the step in—there was something puzzling about that I couldn't quite figure out.

I visited the local (San Diego) Deseret Book outlet, and explained my predicament. The clerk gave me a phone number to call, and I visited a local fellow who was a rep for Sunstone. When I expressed an interest in the more esoteric aspects of Mormonism, he handed me a pile of past issues and said, "Everything you want to know about Mormonism can be found in here."

A bit much, as you know. But this really represented my first involvement in Mormonism. I began attending, and then presenting, at Sunstone symposia. The main topic I'm asked—"Why aren't you a member?" Imagine, being proselyted by Sunstonistas!

I also began volunteering at the local Deseret Industries store, their one and only book volunteer. Hundreds of LDS books come through here each month. I've been very fortunate in finding some old, valuable books, which are now part of my collection. A complete hardback set of the Journal of Discourses, for example, and a bound volume of the entire run of the Evening and Morning Star.

I find the Mormon story particularly compelling. Even the correlated versions of the Church's history are filled with excitement and true devotion. Mormonism is a unique American phenomenon, and I wanted to learn more and more about it.

The same man who gave me the Sunstone magazines (who is now a very close friend, and lives in Salt Lake City, and with whom I stay on each trip to Utah) got me involved on Mormon-L. I'm now on about a dozen LDS lists, and have started several myself, including mormon-spec, a list devoted to the discussion of speculative Mormon theology.

And this, after all, is where my interest really is. Reading the JD and many of the early LDS authors, I'm struck with the diversity and pure imagination of the folks who lived out that history. They had an idea, and that idea bore much fruit. Some of it has fallen by the wayside, but the record remains as a testimony to the fertile minds that moved this Church in its early days. While the general principles of the Restoration, which continue to direct the Church today, are firmly based in scripture and revelation, early Mormonism enjoyed a period of theological reflection that produced some very interesting ideas. They were, after all, charting new territory—reverently exploring the spiritual world, free of the boundaries of the creeds of the churches.

Involvement on the Internet has enabled me to ask (and nowadays, answer) many questions. As you know, the Internet is filled with all kinds of folks from all parts of the Mormon spectrum. I really have neither an agenda nor an investment in any of this, so I can appreciate the discussions as the "consummate outsider."

Tell you a little side story: my last trip to Utah (just a few months ago), I visited with Cleon Skousen in his home in Salt Lake. It was a great visit. I fully expected him to quiz me about why I'm not a member. Instead, he shocked me by claiming that membership wasn't for just anyone. He said to me, "You can get into places we can't. You have credibility, precisely because you're not a member." This all came true just a few weeks later, when a member of the board of the Society of Christian Philosophers e-mailed me, telling me that they were preparing to vote on whether they should admit Mormons or not. One of their members presented a list of objections to Mormonism. Most of them were distortions, of course. I responded to all of them, fully documented. The motion to exclude Mormons failed.

I've also been invited to area churches to speak on the beliefs and practices of the Mormon Church. They've had the anti's; they won't invite a member. They're stuck with me. It's been an exciting time for me, defending a group of which I'm not even a member!

I know my involvement on the Mormon Internet, and with Mormonism in general, will continue to benefit me. There are riches beyond measure in the Mormon story, and I intend to mine it for a long time to come. But membership still eludes me (this was the subject of my last Sunstone presentation). Cleon Skousen said it best: don't join until the Spirit tells you it's time to join. I can still see him scowling at me: "That's the problem with the Church these days—too many lukewarm members."

Maybe he's right. In the meantime, I will continue to post and moderate, to meet more people.

To Strengthen Testimonies

Net users say their experience has had an overall positive effect on their testimonies of the gospel, helping them find answers to questions and draw strength from the insight of other members.

Sometimes that positive influence comes from unexpected sources. Brother Anderson from Seattle gives credit to his Internet contacts for helping to strengthen his testimony, "though I must admit that often it was spurred by the anti-Mormons who have pushed me to research our history and understand it better than I did before. In each case, I've come away stronger than before."

He offers advice to people just getting their toes wet in discussion groups. "For those who take things at face value and are offended or easily put off, I would say that the Net is a land mine waiting to annihilate you. For those who are strong to begin with, and patient enough to gather all the evidence and truth, the Net can be a fortifier of your testimony."

Oremite Thom Duncan says he found strength in meeting Saints who shared his "liberal" bent. "The Internet has had a positive effect on my testimony—and I mean this literally. When I first got on the Internet, my testimony was very shaky. It wasn't long before I found I was not the only Mormon liberal in the world and that many others had found a way to make their liberalism and their Mormonism work for them. I have learned from them and have actually implemented some of their suggestions. So I am still active today, possessed with an intellectual and a cultural testimony, but at least my temple recommend is current."

Robb Cundick, a Latter-day Saint living in Salt Lake City, has been strengthened by the "wonderful spiritual feelings" he's had while reading the personal experiences and testimonies he found on various Web pages and mailing lists, in particular a list called LDS-GEMS. "The LDS-GEMS mailing list has been tremendous! The stories of sacrifices made by early members of the Church have given me renewed motivation to emulate their example in facing life's challenges. I feel they've also blessed me with a stronger resolve to remain true to the faith."

To Expand Their Understanding of Gospel Topics

Another way Latter-day Saints use the resources of the World Wide Web is to study the gospel and expand their understanding.

When list discussions take an occasional turn toward the religious/philosophical side of things, says Brother Picht in Kyrgyzstan, they help him think about Gospel topics he'd given "short shrift" before. He says some of the ancient studies/ancient scripture sites he's run across have been extremely interesting and thought-provoking.

Brother Matteson, in Ann Arbor, has a fondness for historical sites, saying they give him access to information that's normally available only to Saints who live in Utah.

To Share the Gospel

Missionary work is a major motivation for Internet users who build Web pages, moderate newsgroups, and participate in various e-mail lists.

Latter-day Saints Kathryn and Clark Kidd, from the Warrenton-Virgina Stake, say the anonymity of the Internet lends courage to Saints who feel awkward approaching friends or strangers with the message of the Gospel. "Although some people feel comfortable about walking right up to a stranger and asking the 'golden questions,' that approach doesn't work for everyone," say Brother and Sister Kidd. "Computers appeal to the kind of person who would never think of striking up a Gospel conversation on an airplane, or in a grocery store. Even the most cowardly person can talk about the Gospel (or just about any subject) through the written word. Because the computer user can neither see nor hear the person on the other end of the modem, the online missionary will never have to worry about having a door closed in his face."

Arthur L. Wilde of Baytown, Texas, operates the LDS discussion forum on CompuServe. He says the online community was "instrumental" in bringing a Brother back into the Church who had been absent 26 years. "We'd never have had the opportunity to meet otherwise, as I was in Texas, he in Los Angeles."

Sister Parshall from Orem says she's had many opportunities to discuss the Gospel with people she's met on line. "In two cases, I have answered questions about touchy-churchy things (polygamy, Mountain Meadows); as part of that, I have offered my contacts a history of the Church to explain more. They have both accepted, so in addition to the textbook (the institute manual), I have sent copies of the Book of Mormon and *A Marvelous Work and a Wonder*." She's uncertain about the effect of her sharing. "It's too soon to know of any results from that, other than return messages that have been very favorable to the Church, our (my) candor about the touchy things, and a generally positive reaction. While I set out to be a helpful friend first, and a missionary second, these contacts would only have been possible through the Internet."

A member from Columbia, Missouri, Cindy Kilpack Potts, recalls a discussion where she spoke with a Muslim woman and a Catholic woman at the same time. "They more or less just asked questions about the godhead, and what doctrine supported our belief," she says.

Cathy Gileadi from Salem, Utah, approaches discussions in a different way. "I always mention BYU and Utah in context when I can, but it's pretty sideways missionary work."

Brother Cundick from Salt Lake City sees the missionary work being done on the Internet in more general terms. While not using the Internet for the specific purpose of proselytizing, he says, he has viewed it as a wonderful resource for spreading goodwill and a positive image of what members of the Church are really like. Because he's a member of the Tabernacle Choir, he's had even more opportunity to discuss "areas of common interest," he says.

Mike Downey, a Latter-day Saint living in Mesa, Arizona, writes that several years ago he had the unusual experience of participating in the conversion of an "anti-Mormon."

Brother Duncan says he's done his own brand of missionary work. "I helped reactivate a man through my participation on CompuServe. He found my liberal leanings quite refreshing and decided that not all Mormons were right-wing, anti-gay conservatives."

16

As a Resource for Work

When it comes to supporting a family, the Internet can be a valuable resource.

Chris Bigelow, a writer and editor in West Valley, Utah, invites members of his ward to submit material by e-mail for the ward newsletter he edits. As a Church employee at the *Ensign* magazine, he uses e-mail extensively to communicate with authors, Church leaders, and members worldwide.

Brother Downey from Mesa teaches Seminary, and finds useful material for his classes over the Internet. He corresponds with students by e-mail, as well. "I have been able to answer questions for students who didn't want to ask in class, as well as have makeup work sent to me," he says.

Another teacher, Thomas R. Valletta from central Utah, makes "extensive" use of the Net to aid his teaching. "I am constantly following specialty news and resource pages on the World Wide Web (e.g., *Jerusalem Post*, *Virtual Jerusalem*). The Web is now considered a basic aspect of my research methodology in preparing lessons and papers."

Writer Scott Parkin from Pleasant Grove says he has found e-mail discussion lists to be "absolutely wonderful" as a tool for interviewing people and getting a better sense of what they think and believe.

Another writer, Mark Cheney from Prescott, Arizona, is writing an LDS novel about ancient America, and does his research on line.

To Increase Knowledge

Many members report that the Internet has opened a whole new universe of information on Church history, scripture commentary, and other resources never before available to them.

Kevin Cundick, a Latter-day Saint from Ogden, Utah, says that because of his Internet experience, his knowledge of Jesus Christ has grown leaps and bounds. "Through the articles I have set up on my LDS site, I have learned much of Christ, and my love for Him has grown because of it."

Another Latter-day Saint, Jacob Proffitt from Vancouver, Washington, says that the Internet exposure has put his ideals to the test "in an arena where broad consideration and criticism are applied." As a result of the intellectual exercise, he has strengthened his own views, arguments, and historical knowledge "in order to stand up to the careful scrutiny occasionally applied."

Joe Laflin, a Bradenton, Florida, Saint, expresses amazement at how little he knows about the Church when he encounters the words and knowledge of other Netizens. "My strength and focus has always been on the spiritual part of the Church," he says. "The Net allows me to see a whole other side or view. I appreciate that."

Lynne Pike, from Nashville, Tennessee, appreciates the doctrinal material available on line. "There are a couple of scripture lists that I have found particularly beneficial: scripture-l and Kurt Neumiller's Isaiah Commentaries and LDS Seminar. I've also learned so much from a number of Web sites: an online scripture search utility, the various archives of different lists, the reference to the Davidic Chiasmus, and several other scripture sources from various religious organizations. Without the information I gleaned from those sources, my studies and understanding of the scriptures would be much more shallow than they are (not that I'm a 'scholar' in any sense of the word). I have been enriched, enlightened, and edified by these resources."

Brother Anderson from Seattle says he's found a wealth of information on the Internet, things he'd never seen before he went on line. "Through the Internet, I've learned tons of stuff about Church history that I had no inkling of before," he says. "Additionally, it has been wonderful to learn of archaeological evidence, linguistic evidence, etc., that favors the Book of Mormon and scriptures of the Church. Also, I've learned that for every situation in which there appeared to be something suspicious about a quote or criticism, there has always been a reasonable explanation, often exposing the critical stuff as being out of context, contrived, misrepresented, etc."

But it's more than just increasing the level of exposure to research materials. Robb Cundick from Salt Lake City also appreciates the opportunity the Internet gives him for learning from the experiences of other people.

According to Matt Grant from Walnut, California, the Net is a primary source for learning what other Saints think and believe. "It is interesting to hear different people's points of view, and see what others are thinking. Some things that I have read have made me curious and have prompted me to do some research, so I would say it has helped." He worries, though, that some users will falter at their first exposure to difficult issues or unfamiliar doctrine. He warns: "Do not change your opinion because of something you read on the Net without properly researching it first."

To Keep Up to Date

With quick electronic access to Utah newspapers, LDS Radio, the *Church News*, e-mail news lists, newsgroups, and virtually every LDS-oriented publication, members find themselves at the heart of every event.

Quint Randle, from East Lansing, Michigan, enjoys using the Internet to log into the *Deseret News* site. There he not only gets to read the news, but also can get the talks from Conference right away, rather than waiting for the *Ensign* to come out.

A Latter-day Saint from Ipswich, England, Hilary A. Croughton, finds the official LDS Web site particularly useful in keeping up to date. "The Church's Web site gives me a reference place for those who wish information about the Church, and at General Conference time provides me with the news, talks, etc., weeks before I would find out about them otherwise."

To Correct Misperceptions

Over and over, calm reasoned discussions and explanations are changing the hearts of even the most bitter critics of the Church.

The Kidds in Warrenton, Virginia, say they're heartened to see how much good one person can do by influencing just one other individual. "At one point, I was contacted by a stranger who had questions about the Church," says Brother Kidd. "It turned out that he was a student in a Protestant seminary, studying for the ministry. By the time we finished corresponding, he told me that he was going to use his pulpit to correct the misunderstandings that people of his denomination have about the LDS Church. He also wrote that he had shared our correspondence with other students at his seminary, and that every one of these future ministers had a new respect for Mormonism as a religion and for Latter-day Saints as followers of Christ."

To Conduct Ward Business

More and more, wards and branches of the Church are turning to the Internet to keep members updated, and to conduct the administrative work of the Church.

In Poway, California, says Internet user Toni Thomas, the local ward actually has a ward e-mail list that serves as a bulletin board for announcements—people looking for houses, jobs, and Elders Quorum service project pleas for able bodies. "I also use e-mail for my stake calling (Media Specialist, Public Affairs Committee) to obtain approval from the high councilman and then to send articles to the media. And I use the Net to research lessons and other Church-related presentations."

Shelly Johnson-Choong, a Latter-day Saint living in Western Washington, has used the Internet to send e-mail to the Young Women's president, who uses the Internet to get ideas and see what others in her position are doing.

Brother Randle says that in his ward in the Michigan State University area, the Elders Quorum secretary keeps in touch and follows up on home teaching via the Internet. Brother Randle's wife, who is the Relief Society president, keeps in touch with the bishop via e-mail.

To Conduct Genealogical Research

While genealogical resources can't yet give you an automated printout of your pedigree chart, the Internet is opening the way to vastly improved research. Sharing resources over the Internet is becoming a way of life for family history researchers.

My aunt, Internet user Judith Sullivan in Tacoma, Washington, says she has a very real sense of an Internet community, especially in the genealogical area.

Orem's Ardis Parshall has had some interesting experiences with genealogy and the Internet recently. "In the last few weeks, I have come into contact with three nonmembers who have just discovered that they have Mormon pioneer ancestry. Since genealogical and historical research is my 'thing,' I have helped find material on their families, visited and photographed family graves, and put them in touch with LDS cousins."

Brother Randle from Michigan has made genealogy contacts on Prodigy. He had a woman go to her local library in Illinois, while he was in California, to look up some information on his behalf. Similarly, Brother Parkinson from Ogden has researched a special family history lesson on the Net, using resources from family history publishers.

To Renew Friendships

Old college roommates, members of former wards, long-lost high-school buddies, former mission companions—all are keeping in touch now, better than they ever could before, with e-mail.

I'd long ago lost track of my favorite college journalism professor, Ed Eaton from Auburn, Washington. But one day I saw his name on an LDS mailing list, and we were back in contact. I wasn't the only one to get in touch with him. He writes: "I submitted a couple of things to LDS-GEMS [a widely distributed e-mail list], and had old friends and even new acquaintances contact me. My list of members with e-mail addresses is not long, but it is growing."

Bill James, a member of my ward in Pitman, New Jersey, had some success looking up the Web page from his mission in Finland www.neptune.net/~finnmish, where he was able to locate contact information for several old friends. (See chapter 6 for more mission pages and access to other missionary resources.) Brother Randle from Michigan was likewise able to locate old friends and mission companions through the Canada Montreal Mission Web site.

To Make New Friends

This is the heart of the Internet: Bringing together people with similar interests, people who would have been best friends in real life but for the geographic distance. The Internet removes that barrier, and in so doing, makes way for enduring friendships.

Brother Thomas R. Valletta of central Utah has made numerous new friendships through his Internet connections, particularly through his participation in the ZION mailing list.

Sister Julie A. Siler of Inkom, Idaho, has found new friends through her online chat channel (Chapter 9 contains more information on discussion groups.)

Writer Benson Parkinson from Ogden credits the Internet with having given him "more colleagues, critics, and fans during two years on our Mormon literature discussion list than the previous ten years at large."

Online friendships have been invaluable to Brother Matteson from Ann Arbor. He says the friends he's made through various online groups have been "good support" through some difficult times.

Florida's Brother Laflin treasures his online friendships, and laments only that he hasn't the time to build additional relationships. "We are a community of a sort and, if I had more time, I could add so many more Net friends."

To Discuss Ideas

Who hasn't lamented the lack of time to really discuss gospel issues in Sunday School? No more. With 24-hour access to members just as anxious as you are to explore their thoughts and share their experiences, you'll never run out of time again.

The Internet has helped Brother Bigelow from West Valley, Utah, to better appreciate other viewpoints and better explore and express his own ideas.

Brother Anderson from Seattle has had many opportunities over the years to hone his thoughts on numerous gospel-related ideas. He wonders, though, whether his writing has been entirely beneficial. "I'm not sure how helpful the things I've posted in CompuServe, alt.religion.mormon and soc.religion.mormon have been. They seem to have had a positive effect for some, no effect for others. A very few others seem to have taken offense," he says.

Latter-day Saints say their online discussions help them really think about what they believe. Nashville's Lynne Pike has discussed "many and varied gospel concepts with individuals from *all* walks of life! In the process, we've all gained something from one another. I know that I have personally learned from the Internet dialogues in which I have participated a great deal about my own personal values and about the divergent experiences and attitudes that exist within the culture of the Church."

Brother Burton from Murray, Utah, has a great interest in religious history, scriptural interpretation, and the interaction of science and religion, and has participated in several related e-mail groups. "Those interactions invariably influence my thoughts and comments on/in the Church," he says.

To Keep in Touch

When the Elders assigned to our ward discovered that I had e-mail access, they began making a habit of stopping by on their P-days to send off mass-mailings to extended family members. Thank goodness for transfers!

Brother Laflin from Florida is at the receiving end of similar exchanges. "We have a daughter on a Spanish-speaking mission in Texas," he says. "I contact local members from time to time and leave messages with them for her."

Brother Cheney in Prescott, Arizona, keeps in touch over the Net with an LDS student in Jerusalem, a friend of his daughter and member of their stake.

To Prepare for Church Callings

Imagine preparing your seminary or gospel doctrine lesson in half an hour—and doing a far better job of it than you ever did in two hours of preparation in the past. Members say they use the Internet all the time in preparing for Church callings.

Linda Adams, a Latter-day Saint from Kansas City, Missouri, says it is "wonderful" to find so many good LDS sites out there—"people who are striving to live the gospel, like me." It's like having "pen pals," she says. Most useful to her are the "interesting" mailing lists that can help with callings and provide a place for members of the Church to share their lesson ideas. "It's great."

Sister Siler from Inkom, Idaho, has taken things off of the Internet to share with others, particularly material for Primary.

Brother Eaton from Auburn, Washington, often speaks at firesides in his area, and saves ideas from the Internet for his talk file. "I use the material in high council talks in the hope that they won't be 'dry council' talks," he says.

Ardis Parshall from Orem has picked up and filed away some hints on "how I will do such-and-such if it is ever part of my calling."

The resources of the Internet have been useful to Brother Cheney from Arizona in his research on archaeology and the Book of Mormon for Gospel Doctrine class and firesides.

Brother Parkin from Utah used various cartographic references and some Scouting ideas pages when he was a Cubmaster for the ward Cub Scout pack.

Brother James from New Jersey finds the online edition of the *Church News*—especially conference issues—useful in obtaining quotes for talks. (See chapter 9 for more on reading the *Church News* and other LDS publications on line.)

Brother Cundick from Salt Lake City has occasionally used stories and experiences from the Internet in his Home Teaching messages.

Seattleite Craig Anderson has used online resources from CompuServe and the Web both in Young Men and in Scouts.

To Better Understand Other Members

Sunday contacts and monthly visits in a small geographic area give a narrow view of the membership of the Church. Meeting people with different experiences teaches tolerance.

Brother Burton from Murray, Utah, explains that because of his Internet exposure, he now has "a much broader vision" of the membership of the Church. "I have a better understanding of the differences between doctrine and culture/tradition/policy, and a much more tolerant feeling for those who have very different perceptions of the purpose of the Church," he says.

A Warning

It's not all positive, of course. As with anything good, the Internet can be used for bad, for distracting the members, for encouraging dissension, for enlarging misunderstandings.

Long-time users share their thoughts on the unsavory parts of the Internet, and offer advice for the unwary.

Ardis Parshall from Orem: "I've become aware of how many very vocal people there are out there who do not like the Church or its leaders at all, yet claim membership somehow. They seem to reinforce each other in a kind of negative community."

Kevin Cundick from Ogden, Utah: "The Internet is a prime example of how there is and always will be 'opposition in all things that righteousness might be brought to pass.'"

"There should be a note of caution sounded toward those who enter the Internet fray," says Brother Anderson from Seattle. "There's a ton of anti-LDS stuff out there. If you wade in unprotected, depending on the depth of your testimony, you could find yourself seriously doubting what you have accepted all your life. On the other hand, if you're willing to search a little deeper, there are usually some excellent responses to the junk dealt out by the antis, provided you're willing to withhold judgment on the matter until you've looked beyond the surface to find the larger truth about the situation in question."

Brother Grant from Walnut, California, wonders whether a lot of Latter-day Saints feel out of place or that they do not fit in. These are people who basically believe the Church is true, he says, but have some belief that is contrary to the teachings of the Church. "They use the Net to find people with similar beliefs, which I'm not sure is an entirely healthy thing."

Brother Cundick from Salt Lake City has similar concerns. "While the Cyberworld version of the Church has its benefits, there are certainly drawbacks as well. I learned on CompuServe that there are a vast range of opinions and outlooks. Most people seem to have questions they'd like to resolve. That means the controversial issues such as homosexuality, evolution, and polygamy seem to go round and round as new people come on and, not knowing what has been discussed to date, bring up these issues over and over again. I felt this caused a lot of divisiveness that was wearing and discouraging at times."

Michigan's Brother Randle says the pitfalls are sometimes of a more personal nature—specifically in the area of e-mail messages that don't permit facial expressions or humorous gestures. For example, he says, he was being "dry" (as in dry humor) in a response to the Elders quorum secretary about some home teaching problems, "and he actually thought I was all offended and serious. He then came back with this major apologetic reply."

Brother Parkinson says the Internet can cause relationship problems for people who get overly involved. "I get wind of people who end up spending too much time on e-mail and whose spouses get jealous. It works out around our house, since my wife's just as avid for the Internet as I am."

Brother Matteson from Ann Arbor is concerned that for some members, online activity will become the focus of their religious life. "While I have made some friends on the Internet," he says, "I still feel that the ward I attend is the central community of my Church involvement. In fact I have seen some who have tried to make the electronic forums a substitute for the normative Church involvement, and most of the forum leaders have noted that this is an inappropriate use of these forums. They are not the Church and should not substitute for regular Church activity."

Brother Burton has to remind himself sometimes that the LDS online community is a minority group, and that he must not get a distorted sense of the membership from his limited exposure.

For Brother Randle—and for many other LDS Internet users—the interaction with a broad cross section of the population can be problematic at best. "Most of the groups on AOL and stuff like that are so full of psycho anti-Mormons that they are no fun to participate in," he says.

Cathy Gileadi from Salem, Utah, is the mother of nine children, and has had to deal with the effects of the negative material available on the Internet in her family. "My next child to get ready to go on a mission has been looking, with a friend, at anti-Mormon Internet stuff and getting messed up and confused. Grrr. It's the standard kind of stuff and uncomely."

The Kidds believe that exposure is inevitable. "For good or evil," they write, "for better or worse, an electronic revolution is taking place that will permanently alter the way in which we live. There is much concern that this electronic medium, much like television, will become a new channel to let filth and worldliness into our homes. Indeed, computers should be used with prudence, just as television and other forms of entertainment should be used with discretion. There is no doubt that Satan will use computer communications to spread his message and bring misery into the lives of those who will listen."

The best advice: When it comes to conversing on line, remember always that all influence must be maintained "by persuasion, by long-suffering, by gentleness and meekness, and by love unfeigned; By kindness, and pure knowledge, which shall greatly enlarge the soul without hypocrisy, and without guile—Reproving betimes with sharpness, when moved upon by the Holy Ghost; and then showing forth afterwards an increase of love toward him whom thou has reproved, lest he esteem thee to be his enemy; That he may know that thy faithfulness is stronger than the cords of death. Let thy bowels also be full of charity towards all men, and to the household of faith, and let virtue garnish thy thoughts unceasingly" (D&C 121:41–45).

THE INTERNET RESOURCES RATING SYSTEM

I had a college roommate who recalled, with some distaste, a Seminary teacher who graded students on their testimonies. "You can't rate testimonies!" Jackie insisted. Her unwillingness to stand in front of her class, unprompted by the Spirit, ultimately had a rather negative effect on both her grade and her feelings about Seminary.

Jackie, if you're reading this, there'll be no repeating that mistake. Rating Web sites is a difficult exercise, particularly when the sites contain doctrinal material. There's always a risk that a rating might be misperceived as a commentary on the quality of the doctrine or testimonies on the site.

This rating problem is resolved, to some extent, by excluding from the outset sites that don't stand up to minimal standards. All the sites in this book have already passed the preliminary screening. Sites that contain no original material, that contain nothing more than links to other sites, or that are primarily "under construction" are not included. And sites that are overly silly, unfocused, irresponsible, or pointless do not appear on this list.

There was a bit of wrestling with the question of whether or not to include, in the name of being comprehensive, material openly hostile to the Church. Reviewing the actual sites, though, made the decision easy. They tended to be as silly, unfocused, and irresponsible as dozens of the friendly sites we excluded. For that reason, you won't find in this book links to sites that appear to exist solely to trash what Latter-day Saints hold sacred. At the same time, however, it's clear that one person's "honest" is another person's "hostile." These listings do include sites that contain well-researched scholarly materials on Church history and doctrine. Many of these scholarly materials are produced by active, believing Latter-day Saints; others are not. In any event, all contribute something valuable to the pool of knowledge.

So on to the ratings. Highest marks go to sites that are regularly updated, that contain original material, that are easy to use, and that are well edited. Organization, access speed, and readability also contribute to high scores. Low marks go to sites with outdated links, confusing structure, and unsubstantiated doctrine.

By any criteria, though, site evaluation is an inexact science. Your friendly author concedes all debates, acknowledging that her ratings are influenced primarily by how well-behaved her children were at the time she read the page. If you own a low-rated site, direct all hate mail at her kids, who probably poured grape juice on her carpet and roller-skated on her couch the morning she looked at your Web site.

THE RATING SYSTEM
The Internet site evaluations in this text employ a system of stars. Here's what the ratings mean:

★★★★★   Bookmark this site. It's worth visiting at least once a week.

★★★★   Stop by every month or so.

★★★   Information tends to be static, but it's good for background.

★★   Contains minimal information, but worth a visit if you're researching the subject.

★   Site contains at least some worthwhile material, but it may be out of date, of dubious authority, difficult to use, or commingled with ideology hostile to the Church.

📖   No rating. This site contains the text of conference talks, scripture, or doctrinal discourse where a rating simply doesn't apply.

$ Commercial site. Judge for yourself.

☑   A top twenty-five pick. The twenty-five best LDS sites on the World Wide Web. Chapter 14 contains an overview.

2

THE CHURCH'S OFFICIAL WEB SITE

In 1996 there appeared—almost out of the blue—a Web site at the Internet address www.lds.org. A few experimental souls had been checking that address regularly, so when the official page appeared, the news spread throughout the LDS online community within hours. To the disappointment of visitors, though, the page contained nothing more than a beautifully done piece of artwork and a promise that more information would follow.

Months passed. Then, one day, the page changed. The artwork disappeared, and in its place appeared real information from, and about, the Church. The official LDS Web site was born.

Much excitement ensued. Not only was the Church making an organizational dive into new technology, but it appeared to be giving an official blessing to the electronic communications revolution. Since that time, the official Web site of the Church of Jesus Christ of Latter-day Saints has grown, albeit at a careful and measured pace, to become one of the best LDS sites on the Web.

It's all part of an increasingly open way of interacting with the outside world. With an expanding missionary effort comes the need to find new tools for reaching out to that world. Leaders have been open and generous with their observations about the place of the official Web site in the Church's overall communication effort.

One in particular, Elder Jeffrey R. Holland of the Quorum of the Twelve Apostles, spent some time in conversation with the author of this book, explaining how the official Web site came into being, and what he hopes it will accomplish.

AN INTERVIEW WITH ELDER JEFFREY R. HOLLAND

I spoke with Elder Holland the day he returned from meeting with the Saints in South America. Although he was still feeling the effects of two weeks in Brazil, Elder Holland spoke candidly about taking the message of the gospel on line, and explained what he sees as the obligation of Latter-day Saints who participate in the online electronic community. These are his comments:

Q LAURAMAERY GOLD: *What were the circumstances surrounding the Church's original decision to create a Web site?*

A ELDER HOLLAND: Obviously there's been a lot of awareness of the Internet and of the increasing opportunity for communication it provides. I think the Church was appropriately cautious and measured, not rushing unduly to create a Web site. It was something we wanted to consider and review thoughtfully. I said once in another interview that we weren't "breathless" about using the Internet, but we also weren't unmindful of the potential that it had.

So we determined some basic things that would probably be of interest and at the appropriate time created the home page based on that.

Q *Content didn't appear on site until long after the page was established. What was the source of the apparent delay?*

A You noted that a page was held before we put much on it. That was done simply to let people know we were aware the Internet was available. While

28

we didn't feel any particular haste or overly urgent need to pursue it, we did want to hold the page, to put out the notification that more information would follow.

Q *How did you determine what material would appear on the site?*

A We decided early on that we would begin with materials in two general divisions, divisions that were actually not unrelated. One would be a media guide of sorts, directed at journalists and newsmakers, people who wanted to know about the Church and wanted an easy, convenient way to find that information. We put up resource materials that would be of general use to them—basic policy statements, basic facts about the Church.

The other somewhat-related general division was material to serve the nonmember, investigators who didn't know about us, people who were inquiring. We wanted them to have accurate information. We were aware that there was a lot of inaccurate information being put out by others. We wanted to share our own story with inquiring people not of our faith who were interested in the Church. Those were the two general guidelines that established what we did first.

What's related to that, and what may be obvious, is that we did not feel, and have not felt yet, that the Internet was necessarily the ultimate way to communicate with members of the Church. Members of the Church who have access to the Internet are such a small fraction of our total membership that it will be a very long time before we see it as a major vehicle to communicate with the Church at large. That day may come, but it surely is not upon us right now.

Q *Generally, how are Latter-day Saints to view technology—as a boon to missionary work, or as a tool for evil?*

A It is like most things in the world. First of all, there is a wonderful gift in this. God is blessing people in a manner consistent with the spirit of the restoration of the gospel. I love the passage from the Prophet Joel that Moroni quoted to Joseph Smith, in which he said that God would pour out His spirit on all the earth, on all people.

> "And it shall come to pass afterward, that I will pour out my spirit upon all flesh, and your sons, and your daughters shall prophesy, your old men shall dream dreams, your young men shall see visions."
>
> —Joel 2:28 (See Joseph Smith History 1:41)

I think we have to know that the wonderful world we live in is enhanced greatly by all kinds of technology and science and wonders. Those are blessings from God.

But, as with almost anything in life, there can be a negative application of those blessings. Automobiles are a wonderful blessing, but you can do a lot of damage with them. And that would be true with electronic technology. There are certainly a lot of unseemly things on the Internet, real filth. We would want our members to be guarded against that just as they would be guarded against inappropriate material anywhere—in television, movies, or any other medium. Use of the Internet will require judgment, maturity, and faithful responsiveness from Latter-day Saints, just as is required of us in every other aspect of our lives.

Q   *How can the Internet play a role in spreading the gospel?*

A   I mentioned that it's certainly one way we can tell our story widely—by widely, I mean globally. The numbers on line may not be overwhelming, but it gives us a certain global reach that allows us to tell an international audience about the restored gospel.

For those who are attuned to the technology and have Internet access to go along with their interest, we may be able to give facts and tell our story better than we could at any earlier time in history. These people may not have access to the missionaries. To those people, I'm sure the Internet will be a blessing, and there will be a certain kind of missionary effort going forth that way.

We're not overestimating it, but neither are we underestimating the potential missionary influence.

Q   *How aware is the leadership of the Church about the Internet and other technology?*

A   I think the leadership is very aware of it. But we are also very conscious that it reaches only a fraction, a very small group of the Church. So we are not putting much freight on that, (laughing) on that particular railroad car. It's just too small. But we're very aware of it. We have people who live all day, every day, with it. We have a large investment in technology.

Q   *Why isn't the Church's Web site bigger than it is?*

A   We're just taking that a step at a time. We've made a modest beginning—an appropriate beginning, but it's been modest. We have not been casual, but we've approached it with caution and a sort of measured step. We're putting on line what seems of interest. As that world unfolds, we'll be making comparable developments. We just haven't had much incentive to put a whole

PRESIDENT JAMES E. FAUST ON SOARING TO THE INFINITE
You must continue to function and live in this increasingly complex world. If you are to soar to the infinite, you will need to work very hard just to keep up with the changes in technology. You will need to be smart. You will need to learn wisdom.

President James E. Faust, BYU Commencement Exercises, August 1997, as quoted in the (Provo) *Daily Herald.*

host of things on line that wouldn't be of interest and wouldn't be of much help to people. But yes, you can expect to see more information in the future for the benefit of the members. If I use the word "research," that might be overstating it at present. But people will want to have more basic Church reference materials, and eventually they'll be able to find many of them there.

Q *What are the dangers for the Church in overemphasizing the Internet? Is there some perception among leadership that the Internet is ultimately more harmful than it is helpful to members?*

A One of the dangers I've already mentioned is to overestimate the number of people it reaches. We'd be foolish to think of the Internet as a mainline delivery system to a Church of 10 million members, only to find out we're reaching 30,000. Obviously that would be foolish and unwise.

There is always going to be a very special human relationship in the Church—missionaries talking face-to-face with people, families in family home evenings, exchanging experiences and laughter. I don't think the Internet is ever going to alter that very much. For example, we would not want fathers to substitute endless isolation watching television for endless isolation surfing the Internet.

We don't underestimate the ability to transmit a wonderful breadth of material. But we don't overestimate its role in substituting or replacing warm personal communication, the spirit-to-spirit contact we have in the Church. We need the goodwill and brotherhood and sisterhood found there. We won't ever expect the Internet to replace much of that.

Q *Members of the LDS online community regularly communicate with investigators about the Church, and there are already many, many instances of people joining the Church because of contacts that originated over the Internet. At the same time, there is a small number of people who say their perspective of the Church changed for the worse because of information they found on line. When you hear reports in Salt Lake regarding gospel contacts made over the Internet, what is their general tenor? Do they tend to be more positive than negative?*

A I don't know that we've had enough experience to know much about it. If it's happening, that's great. That's wonderful. We'd like to hear about it. On the other hand, we're always disappointed when people have a negative experience, and that's a risk whether it's the Internet, books, newspapers, or whatever. A lot of people publish a lot of things that really require a response. We would like the privilege—whether it's the Internet, television, or the printed page—we would like the privilege of telling the accurate true story of the Church. We would like our opportunity to tell the truth.

There are some who disagree with the Church, with its premises and purposes, and frankly are determined to do damage to it. That's a risk on the Internet, but it's a risk with other media as well.

Q What advice would you give to members who are considering getting on line?

A If that's an affordable way for people to communicate, wonderful. If they're wise and judicious about how they use it, knowing full well what exists out there, then that ought to be their privilege.

Q Have you any other advice regarding how people should conduct themselves on line?

A Be worthy and honorable Latter-day Saints. Defend the truth. Be clean. That is good advice for any time, and it is good advice for users of the Internet.

A TOUR OF THE OFFICIAL WEB SITE

In the next two chapters, you'll learn how to get on line, and how to navigate the Internet. For now, though, feel free to just sit back and watch the guided tour. If you want to follow along from your own computer, and are already connected to the Internet and can find your Web browser software, enter the address www.lds.org. (It was once necessary to enter the instruction "http://" before every address. Web browsers have gotten smarter over time, and no longer require this exercise.)

The Front Page

The first stop on any Web site begins with the front page. The official Web site of The Church of Jesus Christ of Latter-day Saints (see figure 2.1) features a simple page with tabs to various features. A banner across the top declares that this is the official Internet site of the Church. The major categories on the Web site are

FIG. 2.1

The front page: A list of links to additional pages

listed at the bottom of the page. Simply slide your mouse pointer over a category and click.

Click the **Languages** icon to go to the Choose a Language screen (see figure 2.2). Here you'll see a list of 19 additional languages to choose from. Read about Conferência Geral, Conférence générale, Generální konference, or Generalkonferenz in the language of your choice.

To leave the Languages section, go to the top bar of your browser and click the **Back** button. You'll return to the first screen.

Click the first tab, **Basic Beliefs**, to access a list of topics for investigators and new members of the Church (see figure 2.3). On this page you'll find links to The Articles of Faith, The Prophet Joseph Smith's Testimony, The Family: A Proclamation to the World, Family Guidebook, and an online version of the Gospel Principles manual outlining basic doctrines of the gospel of Jesus Christ. At the bottom of the page find a link to obtain a free Book of Mormon.

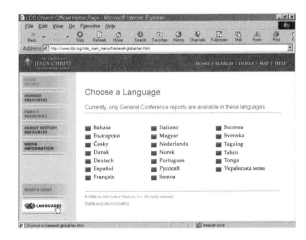

FIG. 2.2

Languages: Twenty versions of Conference.

FIG.2.3

The Basic Beliefs page works like
page two of a newspaper. You have to
open it to read.

No more backing out of each section, if you don't want to. From each section you'll be able to click a section name at the left to get to another section. And from anywhere on the site you can click one of the five buttons in the bar near the top (**Home, Search, Index, Map,** or **Help**) to move around the site. Here are the other major sections of the official Church Web site:

- **Member Resources.** Similar information, plus links to General Conference reports, the new Relief Society Declaration, Church magazine subscription info, and the Pioneer Story (see figure 2.4). You'll also find a new link to the Church Distribution Center at www.ldscatalog.com.
- **Family Resources.** Some of the same information found in other sections, plus *For the Strength of Youth*, *Building a Strong Family*, and *Family Activities*.

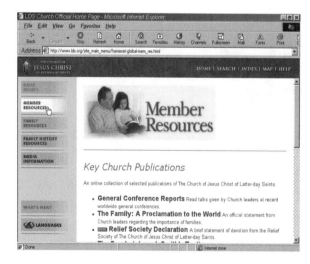

FIG. 2.4

Member Resources: General
Conference on line.

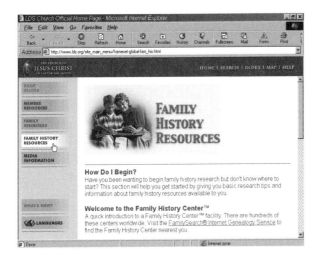

FIG. 2.5

Family History Resources. No more excuses!

- **Family History Resources.** Everything you need to get started on your genealogy (see figure 2.5). News, answers to frequently-asked questions, and more.
- **Media Information.** Everything your local reporter needs to report accurately (see figure 2.6). News, Global Media Guide, and transcripts of recent talks by leaders.

Confused? Relax. Chapter 3 will get you on line in no time, and chapter 4 provides additional navigational helps for the rest of the Internet. It's not the Liahona, exactly, but you will be able to use it to find your way through the electronic Deseret.

FIG. 2.6

Media Information: Official news of the Church is found here.

3

GET ON LINE

Getting on line is a simple four-step process. It boils down to this: Set up your equipment, get an Internet account, fire up the software, and go.

If you've yet to do any one of those things, read on. If you've done them all, feel free to skip this entire chapter, and move along to the good stuff in the rest of the book.

STEP ONE: SET UP THE EQUIPMENT

When purchasing a personal computer, you're faced with essentially two choices: a Macintosh, or an IBM-compatible PC (which, ironically, aren't always 100% compatible with IBM's personal computers. You're just as likely to purchase a machine that's Compaq, Dell, or Gateway compatible). In any event, all non-Macintosh home and business computers are classed together as PCs. (As always, there are some exceptions—but those are machines of the Star Trek class, called *workstations;* if you don't know what a workstation is, you don't need one.)

Approximately 80 percent of personal computers in use today are PCs. If you're not sure which to buy, here's a recommendation: You should buy whichever machine you use at your place of employment. The particular brand of PC is not significant, but do consider the benefits of being able to use the same computing conventions both at home and at the office. Efficiency outweighs any other consideration in the Mac/PC war.

If you're genuinely starting from scratch, here's the simple breakdown of considerations.

PC	Macintosh
More choices.	Easier to use.
More software choices.	Better software available.
Upgrades are cheaper.	Upgrades are easier.
Users have been known to curse their machines.	Product loyalty approaches cult status.

Computer writers can and do argue about each of these points, but for the most part, that's the way the arguments break out.

Whether you already own, or are looking to buy, this is the minimum configuration you'll need to make good use of your home PC. Any computer made after 1998 probably meets these recommended minimums.

Component	PC	Macintosh
Processor (Chip)	Pentium with MMX	PowerPC
Video adapter (card)	800 × 600	800 × 600 (built in)
Monitor	15" color, .28dp	15" color, .28dp
RAM	32M—"32 meg" for short	32M
CD-ROM drive	24x (pronounced 24-speed) or DVD	24x or DVD
Hard drive	1 gigabyte	1 gigabyte

If you're buying now, you'll find that most PCs being sold today are of the Pentium—think of it as a "586"—class. The non-Pentium PCs are powered by clones of equal or greater capability. Hard drives are generally 20 gigabytes and larger. DVD is fast becoming the standard replacement for CD-ROM drives. And video adapters are commonly 1,024 by 768. Rejoice while you can. In a few weeks, *whatever* you buy will be outdated.

The Modem

The modem connects your computer, through a telephone line, to the online world. Most computers sold today include modems as standard equipment.

If you have a notebook PC, or a machine purchased before 1997, you may have to purchase a modem. Virtually all desktop computers sold since then have a modem included as part of the standard equipment. The standard transmission rate for prepackaged modems is 56,000 baud, or 56 kilobits per second. (*Baud* describes the data speed of the modem. Loosely translated, it means bits of data per second—although purists will dispute that definition. Nod and smile when they do; a more technically precise definition won't change how quickly, or slowly, your modem functions.) For World Wide Web access, don't consider anything slower than a 33.6-kilobit modem. As a general rule: The higher the speed, the better. For users serious about their Internet access cable, satellite, ISDN, and DSL high-speed connections are also available in many areas. Contact your local telephone company and cable operators for details.

Another consideration is whether to buy an internal or external modem. An internal modem is the simpler of the two. It consists of a printed circuit board that you plug into an expansion slot in your computer. A telephone cable plugs into a standard jack on the end of the board. If you're reluctant to open your computer, most retailers will be happy to do it for you—for a modest fee.

Slightly more expensive, an external modem has its own power supply, plastic casing, and blinking lights to tell you when it's communicating. It also has extra cables for connecting to your computer, usually through the serial port. The phone line plugs into a jack on the modem. The advantages of the external modem are that it is easily portable—meaning it can be used on more then one personal computer; that you

Why It's Worth the Cost

Kimmel Norwood, Laconia Ward, New Hampshire <*kimmellee@yahoo.com*> writes: "Well, personally, we don't have to pay the fees. My uncle owns his own Internet company so we get our sign up for free. If by chance we don't receive this service anymore we would look for something cheaper than $25 a month with unlimited hours. If we could not find that, then we would not be on the Internet any longer. It is addictive and you get in a habit of using it. It's great for research and to meet people. I feel closer to the Church because of all the information that I have read on the Internet. If I had just investigated with the books I read, instead of talking to people and reading their sites with their testimony, I think it would have taken longer for me to be baptised."

Eric and Brenda Brower, Marysville, Washington, Sixth Ward, Marysville Stake <*brower@gte.net*> write: "First of all, we started with our provider when it first started three years ago at a reduced rate. Because we have stayed with them through their trials and growing pains, we continue to pay the reduced rate even though their rates have increased. I feel that the benefits we receive are worth the cost. I could easily spend $15 to $20 a month in gas—running around to the library for my children's school work and shopping for household items. I have also used the Internet to check on investments needs. I especially enjoy having access to the conference talks, woman's conference and other Church things that are on line. They are so uplifting."

have a visual indicator of the modem status; and that when your connection hangs up, you can shut down the modem without shutting down the entire computer.

If you're ready to invest in a modem of your own, spend the extra money on speed rather than the external box. Reduce the clutter in your work area, and buy a 56K internal modem.

Notebook computer users have other concerns. You could use an external modem, or you could use a PC Card internal modem. The PC Card is a credit-card-sized unit designed to plug into a PC Card (formerly *PCMCIA*) slot. Most laptop computers sold since 1998 have at least two of these slots.

STEP TWO: GET AN INTERNET ACCOUNT

PRESIDENT SPENCER W. KIMBALL ON SPREADING THE GOSPEL

Technology will help spread the gospel. We need to enlarge our field of operation. We will need to make a full, prayerful study of the nations of the world which do not have the gospel at this time, and then bring into play our strongest and most able men to assist the Twelve to move out into the world and to open the doors of every nation as fast as it is ready. I believe we have many men in the Church who can be helpful to us, who are naturally gifted diplomats. I believe we should bring them to our aid and . . . I have faith that the Lord will open doors when we have done everything in our power.

I believe that the Lord is anxious to put into our hands inventions of which we laymen have hardly had a glimpse.

A significant revelation states: "For, verily, the sound must go forth from this place into all the world, and unto the uttermost parts of the earth—the gospel must be preached unto every creature." (D&C 58:64.)

The Teachings of Spencer W. Kimball, *Seminar for New Mission Presidents and Regional Representatives* (June 27, 1974), p.587.

To get to the Internet and World Wide Web sites, you need an account through a commercial online service, such as America Online or CompuServe, or through a dial-up Internet service provider, called an *ISP*.

Commercial Online Services

The major commercial services provide excellent Internet access and have adjusted their prices to be competitive with the ISPs. In addition, the commercial services offer something that the ISPs do not—content. Each service provides its own discussion forums, databases, and other features that are available only to its members.

Even if you already have an ISP, a commercial online service may be a worthwhile investment. Besides the additional content, commercial online services organize and categorize the most useful functions of the Internet into easily navigated menus and icons. The amount of time you save searching for data may be enough to offset the extra cost. In addition, commercial services are portable—you can access them toll-free from most large towns and cities around the world.

Connection software is provided by the commercial services free of charge. In many cases, it comes pre-bundled with the operating system. (Bundling is the practice of including additional software packages with the PC at no extra charge. The vendors hope you will use the service provided—and begin paying for the subscription, which usually is necessary.) Get your software by calling the toll-free number listed in the following sections, or from the disks that fall out of any number of computer magazines and junk mailings. In addition, most personal computers sold today include the connection software for at least one of the commercial online services.

America Online and AT&T Worldnet are the two most popular services available today. Together they boast a user base of more than 20 million subscribers. (The World Wide Web addresses, called URLs *[Uniform Resource Locators]*, that are listed with each of the following descriptions are explained later in this chapter.)

America Online   America Online features an easy-to-use graphically oriented interface. Its reputation is as a fun, family-oriented service, although the LDS-oriented pickin's are slim. Users interested in getting together for private, invitation only discussions may appreciate the convenience of AOL's private chat rooms. Contact AOL at (800) 827-6364, www.aol.com.

> ## ON THE ATTRACTION OF AOL
> I've never found anything uniquely AOL very useful. There are supposedly Mormon chat rooms that are haunted by the usual bashers, and genealogy forums which are ho-hum. There are much better genealogical resources elsewhere, obviously frequented by LDS. I've corresponded with a few AOL users who have posted genealogical materials on AOL, but they always include instructions on how non-AOLers can access their material, so I guess that's not a peculiarly AOL resource either. I did find a Deseret Alphabet font for my Mac in the AOL software library. I doubt if that is available too many places. I used to visit Scott Card's Hatrack River when it was on AOL, and that was good. But it hasn't been the same since he moved it to his own Web site.
>
> Ardis Parshall, Orem, Utah
> *<AEParshall@aol.com>*

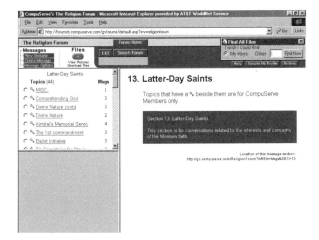

FIG. 3.1

CompuServe: Strong sense of community.

CompuServe CompuServe (see figure 3.1) was a pioneer in providing online services and had a significant impact on the online LDS community through the Latter-Day Saints section of the Religion Forum. (The section name is another example of long-time moderator Keith Irwin's policies of inclusiveness: The hyphen is for the LDS members, the capital D is for the RLDS members.) Current section leader Arthur Wilde continues Brother Irwin's policies of civilized, inclusive discussion, barring ad hominem attacks and welcoming diverse points of view. Contact CompuServe at (800) 848-8990, www.compuserve.com.

Other Commercial Services

The definition of what a commercial service is and how it is accessed is constantly changing. Competition has caused some services to readjust their focus. The following services exist in a new, not-yet-fully-developed zone between a simple ISP and a full-service commercial online service:

AT&T Worldnet.   (800) 967-5363 www.att.com
Concentric.   (800) 939-4262 www.concentric.com
Earthlink.   (800) 395-8425 www.earthlink.com
IBM Internet Connection.   (800) 722-1425 www.ibm.net
MayberryUSA.   (800) 383-5854 www.mbusa.net
Microsoft Network.   (800) 373-3676 www.msn.com
Mindspring.   (800) 677-7464 www.mindspring.com
Prodigy.   (800) 776-3449 www.prodigy.com

Internet Service Providers

Cheaper (sometimes), more flexible (usually), faster (at least potentially), and more accessible (unless you travel), Internet service providers are gradually putting the commercial services out of business. ISPs differ from commercial online services in lots of little ways. They tend to be local—except when, like RCN (servicing much of the northeast United States), they're huge. ISPs tend to be less expensive because they do not provide the additional information resources found on commercial online services. What an ISP does give you is a direct gateway to the Internet. At a minimum, your ISP should furnish:

- toll-free telephone access
- rate discounts for long-term service contracts
- unlimited access
- free telephone support

- a high ratio of access lines to users (You don't want to reach a busy signal when you call in.)
- a software bundle customized for your computer operating system (See the following section on Internet Software Tools for a list of what you'll need.)

To find a provider, check the local yellow pages under Internet Services or Computers—Internet. Read a few local newspapers, watch a few TV ads, make a few phone calls. Every ISP charges about twenty dollars a month for access, and the smaller providers may be willing to negotiate.

Having trouble getting started with your new software? Good ISPs will hold your hand through the set-up process, doing all that they can to ensure that your online experience is trouble free. Take advantage of the support line to get yourself properly set up.

Internet Software Tools

These Internet tools let you do something after you get on line. If you're using a commercial online service, most of these tools will be included on a disk with your access software. Check back regularly, though, to be sure you're using a current edition of every piece of software.

Web Browser. You've heard about the great war between Netscape Navigator and Internet Explorer. Start with the package you receive from your Internet service provider. Then download the other from either the Navigator www.netscape.com or the Explorer www.microsoft.com/ie/default.asp Web sites to make your own comparison.

Electronic Mail Reader. Your Web browser has built-in e-mail capabilities, but there are better choices. Your Internet service provider will supply you with an e-mail reader to get you started. After you're on line, try a couple of different readers to see which best suits your needs. All readers can read, create, and send mail. The better ones give you advanced features and improved screens. Two popular and often praised mail readers are Eudora www.eudora.com and Pronto 96 www.commtouch.com. Microsoft Office users will generally find that Outlook or Outlook Express is

> ### ON THE INTERNET AS A RESOURCE
> Overall, I see the Internet as a resource, rather than a building tool. It is like asking if the library is a building tool. Many individuals go there, but they don't bond. They each go to the library to obtain the information they need.
>
> I suppose I differentiate between two aspects of the Internet: e-mail versus the Web. One involves communication and that in itself may be considered a building tool. The other is basically a resource and unless communication, via e-mail, occurs, it is basically a library.
>
> Tonia Izu, Berryessa Ward, San Jose, California, East Stake
> <Tonialzu@ix.netcom.com>
> Web master, LDS Members' Home Pages
> www.netcom.com/~toniaizu/cmembers.html

already installed on their systems. Some online services such as AOL and CompuServe come with their own proprietary e-mail software. You'll find that most commercially available e-mail software will not function with AOL or CompuServe mail.

News Reader. Both Navigator and Explorer contain built-in newsgroup readers. However, you may find that a dedicated newsgroup reader, such as Forte's Free Agent www.forteinc.com, offers easier-to-use features and greater flexibility. Free Agent has the ability to work offline, saving you toll charges if you're being metered.

Chat Software. In chapter 9, you'll learn about an Internet feature called Internet Relay Chat (IRC). If your service provider doesn't include chat software in your start-up package, you'll want to pick up a package of your own. One recommended software package that can get you started is mIRC. The latest version requires that after you try it, you register and pay a fee. Older versions are completely free of charge. A fast, clean front-end for IRC, with useful options and tools, can be found at www.mirc.co.uk/get.html. Download is free.

STEP THREE: START BROWSING

Among the pieces of software included with your start-up software will be a thing called a *Web browser*. It's very likely that your Web browser will be called either *Netscape Navigator* or *Microsoft Internet Explorer*. (Actually, it's a virtual certainty that you'll receive one if the aforementioned Web browsers. There are alternative browsers but those are generally the domains of hackers and other mavericks.)

Your first online adventure will be to browse (you've heard it called *surf*) the Web. Install the browser as your provider directs, open it, and in the Address or Location box—the only space on the page where you're allowed to type something—type this:

www.lds.org

Press the Enter key, and you'll be transported to the home page for the Church of Jesus Christ of Latter-day Saints (see figure 3.2). Click anywhere on the page, and you'll find the inside front page for the site (see figure 3.3).

You'll notice that a home page, also called a *Web site* or simply a *page*, looks something like a magazine

---

Duke of URL

Throughout this text, we designate Internet addresses, or URLs, in this manner:

Page Name   address.domain/
 filename   description rating

You can manually copy the names from the text to your Web browser, or you can go directly to the pages from hyperlinks on the Mormons on the Internet Web site at www.writerspost.com/mormonnet. When you copy URLs from this book, remember that URLs and e-mail addresses contain no spaces. If you're browsing from the Web site, you'll be required to register the first time you use the Web site.

FIG. 3.2

The Address box in Explorer. In Navigator, the same box is called the Location box.

cover. The line you typed is called an *address* or an *URL*—pronounced Earl and short for Uniform Resource Locator. URLs are key to finding every page on the World Wide Web.

Surfin' Safari—Entering URLs

Entering URLs looks a little tricky, but it's actually quite simple. Ninety-five percent of the Internet addresses you run across in your life will begin with the designation http://. Another 4.5 percent will begin with ftp://. If you run across the other half percent, you'll probably be looking at things so obscure they don't really bear learning about.

As a rule of thumb, the HTTP designations, short for hypertext transfer protocol, indicate an address for a graphically enhanced, magazine-cover-like World

FIG. 3.3

Using a browser to surf.

Wide Web page. The FTP (file transfer protocol) designations, on the other hand, indicate ugly, non-graph-
ical, non-viewable files that you download to your own
computer, at which point they might get installed and
become quite pretty after all. FTP is the method by
which you will do virtually all of your Net file transfers. When you need a file or a piece of software,
chances are good that you will use FTP to get it.

A Faster Surf: Hyperlinks

As you slide your mouse pointer around the Church
Web page, you'll notice that it changes shape when it
points at certain elements on the page called *hyperlinks* (see the hand-shaped pointer in figure 3.3, for
example). A hyperlink is a quicker way to get to
another page. Click a hyperlink, and it will automatically enter the URL for you,
saving you the trouble of typing. Most hyperlinks appear as underlined text, but
they can also take the form of pictures, clickable buttons, logos, and menu bars.

To see a menu of other things you can do with a hyperlink, position your
mouse cursor over the hyperlink and click the right mouse button.

Back and Forth on the Web

To navigate your Web pages, you have three additional tools:

Toolbar buttons.   The toolbar buttons appear in a row across the top of your
browser (see figure 3.4). The left and right arrow keys move you back and forth

Toolbar buttons

FIG. 3.4

Toolbar buttons.

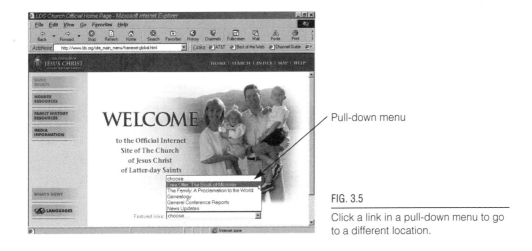

FIG. 3.5

Click a link in a pull-down menu to go to a different location.

through pages you've already viewed. The Stop button prevents a page from loading. The Refresh option reloads a page.

Pull-down menu. Select recently used addresses from the pull-down Address box (Location box in Navigator) list (see figure 3.5). Click the down arrow at the right of the box. Alternatively, go to the Go menu and select a different recently viewed page.

Scroll bars. Pages larger than your screen can be navigated horizontally and vertically from the scroll bars across the bottom and along the right side of your screen (see figure 3.6). If pages are consistently wider than your screen, consider decreasing your display size. (Go to the Control Panel, select the Display tool, then the Settings tab. Change the Desktop Area.)

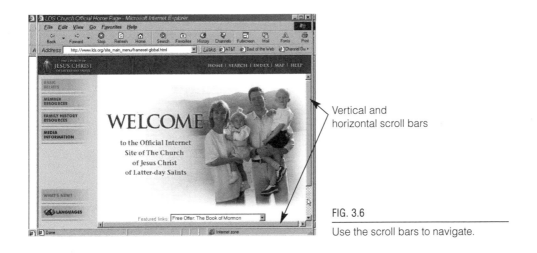

FIG. 3.6

Use the scroll bars to navigate.

Beyond the World Wide Web

Once you're comfortable with the whole Internet thing—or at least the World Wide Web portion of it—you're ready to graduate to something more complicated.

E-Mail. The most basic of services provided by ISPs and commercial online services is e-mail. *E-mail* is simply electronic mail sent and received over the Internet. Until recently, e-mail was strictly text based. Now it's possible to format e-mail and attach audio, graphics, and additional files.

Mailing Lists. These are discussion and information exchanges conducted via e-mail. Discussions are limited to a particular subject, carried on among a group of subscribers. Subscribers e-mail their responses to the mailing list, and the list is then automatically mailed to all subscribers. Some mailing lists are *read-only*, meaning that the discussion is more of a lecture.

UseNet Newsgroups. *UseNet newsgroups* are open forums for public discussion. Newsgroups can be an effective way to engage a wide variety of people in ongoing correspondence concerning virtually any subject.

FTP Sites. Files (data, graphics, audio, and software) can be transmitted over the Internet. The method used to *upload*, or send, and *download*, or receive, files is called *FTP*, short for *File Transfer Protocol*. When we direct you to an FTP site, you'll be downloading a file. Files are stored on a remote site. When you want the file, you enter the URL, which begins with the designation ftp://, in the Address or Location box of your browser. Your browser will automatically download the file to your computer.

STEP FOUR: GO!

And that's why you've got the remainder of this book. In chapter 4: "Getting Around," you'll begin your online adventure by learning about a thing called "Netiquette," and visiting the Web sites of other Latter-day Saints.

4

GETTING AROUND

Once you're set up on the Internet, you'll need to find your way around. The bulk of this chapter is dedicated to a thing called a search engine—the tool you'll use to find things on the Internet long, long after this book goes out of date.

First, though, a brief introduction to a special feature for buyers of this book: the *Mormons on the Internet* Web site. Then comes a brief section on Netiquette for Latter-day Saints, followed by some People Finders—Internet sites that will help you locate other Latter-day Saints online. The remainder of the chapter consists of a lengthy introduction to Search Engines, information that you'll want to keep handy for all your Internet research.

LINKS TO LINKS

Throughout this text you'll find the addresses, or URLs, of hundreds of LDS-oriented Internet sites. While you could enter each of them manually, you're invited to use a simpler Internet tool created just for buyers of this book.

Open your Web browser and enter the URL for the *Mormons on the Internet* Registry at www.writerspost.com/mormonnet (see figure 4.1). Bookmark the Registry page (see page 54) so that you can return to the site with the click of a button.

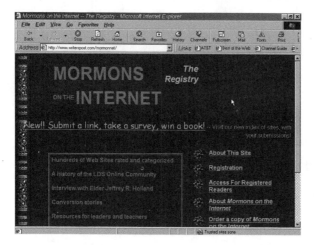

FIG. 4.1

The *Mormons on the Internet* Registry: Most complete listing of LDS sites on the Net.

HOTLINKS

All About Mormons
www.mormons.org

GospeLibrary.Com.
www.gospelibrary.com

Jeff Lindsay's Cracked Planet.
www.jefflindsay.com

LDS Historical Information.
www.math.byu.edu/~smithw/Lds

LDS Info Resources.
www.deseretbook.com/map.html

Mormon Town.
www.mormontown.org

MormonLinks.
www.mormonlinks.com

Mormons on the Internet Registry.
www.writerspost.com/mormonnet

Nauvoo at BYU.
nauvoo.byu.edu

The first time you visit the Registry site, you'll need to complete a brief registration form. On subsequent visits from the same computer, you'll be able to go directly to the Web site without any intermediate steps. (If you visit from a different machine, you can enter your password to access the site without re-registering.)

Once in the Registry, you'll be able to click on chapter names, section names, and Web sites to get to any site in this book. You can also conduct word searches on the text to find the information you're looking for. Site locations and content change over time, so as LDS sites move or disappear, and new sites appear, the Registry will be updated. The site will be maintained as long as this book, or subsequent editions of this book, remain in print.

The following sites provide some great links to LDS sites around the Net. See page 26 for an explanation of the ratings.

All About Mormons www.mormons.org John Walsh's very large site containing texts on virtually anything anyone has ever wanted to know about Mormonism. It's, ahem, encyclopedic in its coverage. In fact, it makes extensive use of the Encyclopedia of Mormonism and a few other classic Mormon texts. Good information. I'd be happy to see it stay around. ★★★★★ ☑

Broadbent Family   members.xoom.com/tlbroadbent A place where the authors share their beliefs, testimony, ideas, and opinions. ★★★

Cybersaints   www.iperform.net/jwr/email.html John Redelf's guide to LDS mailing lists. Extensive, but not complete. ★★★

Deseret Best   www.deseretbook.com/ldsinfo/home.x.html A list of top LDS Web sites, as chosen by the Deseret Book. ★★★★

DJ's best LDS links directory   www.davejennings.freeserve.co.uk/linkmenu.html Submit your favorite LDS links here. ★★★

e.mormon.community   www.emormon.com A bare-naked site when we went to press, but the owners claim it'll soon be "one of the largest of all LDS Web site communities in existence." We'll keep watching. ★

Favorite Links to LDS related sites   www.geocities.com/Athens/Styx/5581/Link.html A brief list of links. ★★

Gordon Banks' Mormonism Page   www.pitt.edu/~gebanks/pers/Mormonism.html Good history of and introduction to the Church with lots of links. ★★★

GospeLibrary.Com   www.gospelibrary.com Search the scriptures on line, along with the Topical Guide and the Inspired Version of the Bible. The Topical Guide makes this site a treasure, as do the Gospel Classics and the seven-volume history of the Church. ★★★★★ ☑

Harv's LDS Church Links   barney.usu.edu/~slarv/church.html A handful of LDS links. ★★

Jeff Lindsay's Cracked Planet   www.jefflindsay.com Scores of articles responding to critics of the Church, examining science and the gospel, and more. This is a phenomenal effort. ★★★★★ ☑

KC's LDS Links and Info Page   www.konnections.com/kcundick/church.html LDS links with information about the Church of Jesus Christ of Latter-day Saints. Brief and a bit outdated. ★★

Latter-day Saint Web Resource Page members.xoom.com/lhunter An ambitious attempt to link Internet resources regarding the Church of Jesus Christ of Latter-day Saints. At present, though, there aren't all that many links. ★★★

Latter-day Saints' Resources on the Internet www.erols.com/jdstone One big long list of links. Big. Long. And a list. Without much commentary. But it's long! ★★★★

LDS (Mormon) Related Sites www.ipa.net/~ozarks/lds-info.html Opinions and testimonies in support of the LDS Church. Getting a bit dated, and the site is somewhat cluttered, but there's some vital information there. ★★

LDS Historical Information www.math.byu.edu/~smithw/Lds William Smith's excellent collection of papers and original diaries and texts. Includes Teachings of the Prophet Joseph Smith, History of the Church, all the versions of the First Vision, and much, much more. Unfortunately, there isn't a search engine, but it is a very good—albeit unattractive—site. ★★★★★ ☑

LDS Info Resources www.deseretbook.com/map.html Deseret Book's listing of LDS information, alongside the Deseret's Best LDS Web Sites compilation. ★★★★

LDS Links www.lds-info.com/links.html Very attractive, well-organized sites with links to sites of particular interest to women and children. ★★★★

LDS Resource Archives www.wnetc.com/resource/lds By Gregory Woodhouse. Short and sweet—the Web site, that is. Brother Woodhouse may or may not be short, but he does maintain a great scripture mailing list, and his Web site's worth a look. ★★★

LDS Resources www.lds.npl.com The Bengali Project presents the original LDS Internet resource. A good place to find stuff, but it's a bit counterintuitive. ★★★

Why I Love the Internet

Annette Nay, Bremerton, Washington, Silverdale Fourth Ward <*annettenay@ aol.com*> writes: It is my virtual office to the world. I have Multiple Sclerosis (MS) and cannot keep regular office hours because I do not know when I will have a bad hour/day/week etc. With the Net I don't have to even put on a face if I can't do it that day. Helping takes my mind off my problems and helps others. Another reason is I love to have information at my fingertips. Running to the University or the library is not an option for me. Traveling gives me vertigo, a MS-related problem.

Carol and Steve Andersen, Thousand Oaks, California, Second Ward <*afamserv@ix.netcom.com*> write: It's the best quick resource for just about anything if you use it judiciously.

Dave Wolverton, Orem, Utah, Canyon View Stake, writes: It's a business/research tool. I get letters to my editor and agent quickly, can respond to business deals promptly, and can talk to people all over the world. And it's cheaper than phone calls for staying in touch.

LDS Women on the Internet www.geocities.com/Heartland/Hills/6811/ring.html A Web ring of sites by and about LDS women, operated by Kellie Stanger. ★★★

LDS World www.ldsworld.com Great looking site, but it often fails to live up to its promise. Includes links to Gospel Study, News & Events, Missionary Work, LDS Family History Network, Arts & Culture, Mormon Marketplace, and LDS Web links. Tends to be quite commercial—not surprising, given that Infobases is, after all, a successful commercial enterprise. A complicated search engine affiliated with Infobases. Extensive, but somewhat inaccessible. ★★★★

LDS-1 www.lds1.com Tremendous resource for investigators, and lots of other interesting links. But it's dark and hard to look at. ★★★★

LDSCN Directory www.ldsdirectory.com Mailing lists and a searchable submit-it-yourself directory of listings. But you've got to scrounge through a lot of ads to get to the links. ★★

LDSWeb www.ldsweb.org Yahoo-like organization with plenty of room to grow. ★★★

Mormon Town www.mormontown.org It takes a village . . . to justify spending hours on the Internet. Here's your village. Larry Barkdull's site is a must-mark. The commercial bits are a disappointment, but if they fund the rest of the site, they're worth putting up with. ★★★★★ ☑

Mormon.com www.mormon.com Eclectic mix of links, articles, and features. ★★★

MormonLinks www.mormonlinks.com Tremendous site operated by a group of students. Updates are spotty, but the basics are amazing. If this site is still around in a year, it'll be a top 20 site. ★★★★★

Why I Love the Internet

Debbie Gates, Miami, Florida, Kendall Lakes Ward, <gates@gates.net or dgates@cccpp.com> writes: Where else can you go to find information on ANYTHING you need to know? Where else can you stay in touch with family and friends instantly? Where else do you have worldwide access to do genealogy research? And for less than $20 a month! That's a bargain in my book!

Greg A. Anderson, Modesto, California, Stake, Modesto Fourth Ward <webmaster@byondf1.com> writes: I love the people I have the chance to meet. It is truly an online ward.

Philip L. Musgrave , Kailua, Hawaii, Third Ward, Kaneohe Stake <musgrave@ email.com> writes: With the Internet I can actually reach out and communicate with someone in Sydney, Australia, or Tokyo, Japan, or anywhere else on this planet, just as easy as walking into the next room. It brings us all together.

Richard C. Russell, Taylorsville, Utah <lderlore@xmission.com> writes: Resources. Information. Research. E-mail. It has become a necessity. When my daughter and her husband went to Moscow five years ago I got on line and have never looked back. I spend at least one hour a day with it.

Mormons on the Internet Registry   www.writerspost.com/mormonnet Absolutely the best site for locating information on LDS Web sites. ★★★★★ ☑

Nauvoo at BYU   nauvoo.byu.edu Welcome to Nauvoo, a family-friendly cyber-community designed by faculty and students from Brigham Young University's Communications Department as a safe gathering place for people reflecting values associated with The Church of Jesus Christ of Latter-day Saints. Nauvoo also serves as a laboratory for BYU faculty and student use of Internet technology, and provides a topical gateway to high-quality BYU and Latter-day Saint resources. Visitors are welcome! Links to Church, Kids, The Academy, The Arts, News, Friends, Neighbors, Family, and Sports. Includes a search tool and a public bulletin board. ★★★★★

Mark the Spot

A Web browser's Bookmark feature makes it easy to return to a favorite site. Whenever you find a great search tool, add it to your list of bookmarks. Here's how: Go to the Web page you want to bookmark.

In Internet Explorer: GO to the Favorites menu and click the Add to Favorites command. Use the Organize Favorites command to set up the folders for grouping bookmarks by category.

In *Netscape Navigator:* Use the Ctrl+D key combination command to add the command to your bookmark list. Alternatively, go to the Bookmarks menu, and click the Add to Bookmarks command. The Go To Bookmarks command lets you organize your bookmarks by category.

To return to the bookmarked page at a later time, simply click the Favorites (or Bookmarks) menu and select the site from the drop-down list.

Pearls   www.ldscn.com/pearls A well-considered list of good LDS links. ★★★★

Samuel Brown's LDS Resources   web.med.harvard.edu/~sabrown/lds.htm Lots of interesting goodies, including essays and translations found nowhere else. You'll particularly enjoy the infuriating and thought-provoking essay on God and fat people. ★★★★

Top 10 LDS Web sites   www.iperform.net/jwr/top10.html Cybersaint's excellent guide to eight, not 10, top LDS sites. ★★★★

Top Ten Mormon Sites   www.geocities.com/Heartland/1830 Several top 10 lists of best LDS sites in various categories. Sites were specifically chosen for those who may be new to the Church. ★★★★

Uplifting LDS Links   www.geocities.com/Heartland/4034/content.html Compiled by Jennifer Morgan with links added by visitors. ★★★

NETIQUETTE FOR LATTER-DAY SAINTS

A few years ago I received—completely out of the blue—an e-mail note from a stranger who was hoping, I suppose, to "save" me from my faith. His note to me came complete with the usual invectives and vituperations. It read, in part: "Also according to the Smithsonian as well as your own BYU, there is no historical data to backup the book of Mormon. The above is the TRUTH and I have checked it against Mr. Joseph's Smith's own writing while I was in Utah. You can yell 'FALSE' but it is not. I have not shown you hatred. If I did hate you I would have destroyed your web site. . . . If your are truly willing to look at your own religions teachings seriously, please write back. If not, I hope you like the path you've chosen and that your heaven will be here on earth because once Jesus comes again, this earth will end (2 Peter 3:11–13; Revelations 21:1). I will pray for you." (Spelling and grammar unchanged.) My correspondent signed his full name, appended by "A Christian."

I considered putting some energy into responding to my correspondent's concerns, but in the end, I simply wished him the best, reminded him that destroying Web sites is a bad thing to do, and sent him off to visit Arden Eby's Web site www.teleport.com/~arden/nccj.htm censuring anti-Mormon bigotry.

I didn't say this to my new friend, but my heaven really is here on earth. I have a happy life, a wonderful husband, great kids, and a pretty solid relationship with God. And it's for those reasons that I no longer bother trying to bash with the insincere. Bashing throws life out of balance. It requires turning away from God and facing darkness. It saps energy that rightfully belongs to my family and to the twelve-year-olds I teach in Sunday school. And above all, it's not polite.

Over time the Internet has developed a code of conduct, a set of behavioral standards for participants that is known, collectively, as "Netiquette." While there will always be a percentage of participants bent on breaking the "code," most people really do try to be civilized. In the Latter-day Saint online community, in particular, people have managed collectively to adhere to a high standard of conduct.

If you want to be welcome there, here's what you need to know about Internet etiquette—the "rules of the road" for the Information Superhighway.

First, do no harm. Be sure that every place you go is better because you were there.

ON LIVING YOUR FAITH

When it comes to netiquette, there are two things to remember:

One: Live the thirteenth Article of Faith in what you do, say, and make available on the Internet. I think that's the basis for most etiquette/netiquette rules. If we all remembered to be honest, virtuous, and of good report, a lot of the other rules wouldn't be needed.

Two: In the frame of mind, don't argue with the "anti-Mormons." That's what they want to do, and it doesn't do any edifying for them, you, or other listeners.

Curtis (Jewell) Whalen, Poplar Bluff, Missouri
<curtis_jewell@bigfoot.com>

ON AVOIDING CONFRONTATION

I personally try to avoid getting into debates with anyone who is confrontational. In many discussion forums online, you'll meet mainline Christians who feel their call is to go save the misled Mormons from damnation, and they do this not by talking about ours. I avoid getting into conversations and debates that have no potential to go anywhere or bear any good fruit.

Ronald Conrad Schoedel, III, Ontonagon, Michigan
<schoedel@up.net>

Second, don't spam. Spamming once referred strictly to mass mailings issued to lots of newsgroups. Now it includes the practice of sending irrelevant messages to newsgroups, mailing lists, and even individuals. (Newsgroups are explained in more detail in chapter 9 on page 220.) People gather on the Internet for a purpose. Do not waste "bandwidth" (the finite space on the Internet's "airwaves") by sending information—especially commercial information—to people who didn't ask for it.

Third, remember that the person who reads your words is not a computer, but is a child of God, someone who will make decisions about his or her future in the Church based on your behavior.

Fourth, remember that members of the Church are often just as fragile as nonmembers. Sometimes Latter-day Saints have tended to treat other Saints with a degree of contempt in the impersonal arena of the Internet—and have caused no end of hurt feelings by doing so. Assume that everyone you speak to is feeling vulnerable, and needs your loving words to get through the day. And remember that any disagreement you have with another Latter-day Saint is, ultimately, pretty insignificant.

The following Web sites provide some excellent background information on what you need to do to avoid offending—and being offended by—other members of the community.

HOTLINKS

FAQ About Lists
www.whitestag.org/lds/
faq_faq.html

LDS Hoaxes and Mormon
Urban Legends
www.ldsworld.com/gems/ul

Acronyms, Abbreviations, and Buzzwords FAQ
www.netins.net/showcase/gershom/acronym.html Some of it's amusing, some is just educational. Worth knowing, though, if you plan to be a Mormon on the Internet. ★★★

Charter: soc.religion.mormon www.lds.npl.com/special/usenet/srm A brief outline of policies for the soc.religion.mormon newsgroup (covered in chapter 9 on page 219). Standards by which all participants must abide. ★★

FAQ About Lists www.whitestag.org/lds/faq_faq.html An excellent introduction to mailing lists, particularly to lists of an LDS bent. Explains their advantages and disadvantages, along with some basic netiquette for Latter-day Saints using the lists. Also includes links to a number of mailing lists of interest to Latter-day Saints. ★★★★

LDS Hoaxes and Mormon Urban Legends www.ldsworld.com/gems/ul Before passing along any Internet rumors, check them first against this site. Affiliated with LDS-GEMS. ★★★★

LDS Sisters www.geocities.com/Heartland/Meadows/ 2528/LDS_Sisters.html Everything you need to know if you're going to participate in mailing lists. Oh, and it's also the home page for a good mailing list. ★★★★

Links to Netiquette and HTML Web Sites www.netcom. com/~toniaizu/ehtml.html A good collection of information on Internet etiquette, using the Internet, building Web sites, and more. Includes links to other LDS Web sites. ★★★

Manners www.columbia.edu/~ycl6/a.r.m.manners. microfaq Alt-Religion-Mormon's guidelines. All about the etiquette of posting to newsgroups. Read it and you'll learn much about the rules of the road for mailing lists and chat rooms, as well. If you're still unsure, read the corollary at www.columbia.edu/~ycl6/ a.r.m.microfaq. ★★★

PEOPLE FINDERS

One of the first things you'll want to do, once you get on line, is look around for other Latter-day Saints.

You'll find us everywhere: building our own Web sites, debating in newsgroups, chatting in chat rooms, engaged in discussions on e-mail lists, offering advice in genealogy forums, and sharing stories in online testimony meetings.

The following Web sites are a good place to get started. Here you'll find the BYU Alumni Association, several organized meeting spots, and collections of personal Web pages. If you're looking for information on a particular ward, branch, or stake of the Church, you'll find them listed under "Online Units of the Church," page 197. Single Adult Saints may be interested in browsing chapter 11's dating and courtship sites, beginning on page 248.

Alumni Association alumni.byu.edu Helpful links to Brigham Young University's Aspen Grove family

ON REMBERING YOUR PRIORITIES

When I first began researching and writing responses to criticisms from the anti-Mormons, I was quite abrasive. I felt by dashing to bits the arguments of the critics I was somehow doing a great service for the Lord. One day, as I sat listening to the First Counselor in the First Presidency Gordon B. Hinckley speaking in General Conference, he made some comments that completely changed my outlook on responding to critics.

I realized that we are in this as a battle with Satan for souls, not war with critics. I began removing much of the acrimony from my responses, realizing that if I offend someone badly, they won't even listen to the LDS message, [and] I might bear responsibility for their failure to ever join the Lord's kingdom, realizing ultimately that they bear responsibility also. I began to tailor my writings more to helping Latter-day Saints as well as honest investigators with these issues.

Generally, now I try to stay away from direct conversations with the critics and spend my time more in dealing with the issues. Of course, having a Web page where critics can write to me creates a situation where I must occasionally respond directly to them. I generally try to be patient even when ad hominem is lobbed at me and insulting remarks are made about the faith I espouse. Of course, sometimes nothing gets through to them and one has to part company or forever spend time in trivial communications. Once in a while feelings can be hurt, but I believe it is best to part company as friends.

While I have made enemies in the past, I have also made friends. Some time ago, for example, I was asked to rebaptise a former Mormon who had left the Church and become an anti-Mormon. It was a wonderful experience.

Steve Barker, Denver/metro, Colorado
<sbarker@mmt.com>
SHIELDS Webmaster
www.shields-research.org

camp, Cougar Club, Varsity Club, reunions, and much more. If you've ever had any affiliation with the Y, you'll want to return to this site. ★★★★★

Famous Mormons www.vitrex.net/~ronj/fam.htm Ron Johnston's amusing page of prominent Latter-day Saints. ★★★

LDS Friends Worldwide www.ldsfriends.com A great place to find old friends and meet new ones. Half a million visitors can't be wrong! ★★★★★

LDS Members on the Internet—ICQ List ldsicq.byondf1.com The LDS Members on the Internet—ICQ List has chosen ICQ as the preferred method of communication between its members. Members can chat whenever they like, and share ideas, discuss similar interests, or anything else. Recently added a Members Resource Links List. ★★★★

HOTLINKS

LDS Friends Worldwide
www.ldsfriends.com

Mormon Town
www.mormontown.org

Nauvoo
www.nauvoo.com

World Wide Web First Ward
www.uvol.com/www1st

LDS Members' Home Pages www.netcom.com/~toniaizu/cmembers.html A list of more than 200 pages, sorted by last name. ★★★

LDS Net www.geocities.com/Eureka/Park/7029 Internet LDS community with plenty to choose from. Annoying pop-up screens. ★★

LDS Web Ring www.ldscn.com The LDS Web Ring is a system for allowing Web surfers to jump easily from one site to the next. Sites that carry the LDS Web Ring logo have links to the next site in the Ring. This Ring is limited to sites that have faithful information. The Ring's Requirement: "Anything on your page regarding the Church, its operation, leaders, and teachings must be as true as the gospel." ★★★★

LDS-Webmasters www.egroups.com/list/lds-webmasters Discussion list and e-mail forum for LDS Web masters. Pose questions, collaborate on content, share secrets, and more. ★★★

Locating Members of the Church www.netins.net/showcase/gershom/location.html Here's the procedure for contacting long-lost mission companions or roommates through the Church. ★★

Mormon Ring www.california.com/~rpcman/LDS.HTM Another Ring that works on the same principle. This Ring allows any page with Mormon content to join. Many—

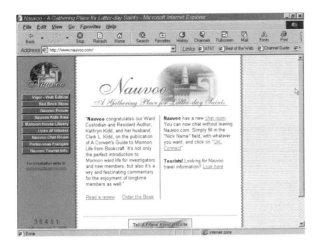

FIG. 4.2

Nauvoo: Best Hangout on the Web.

perhaps most—of the sites are tremendously antagonistic toward the Church. The criteria for joining the Mormon Ring is: "Sites in which the Webmaster indicates whether or not they believe in Mormonism are certainly welcome. In other words, both pro and con sites can join. Sites with significant new LDS-related content that may be rejected are those with blatantly false information." ★

Mormon Town   www.mormontown.org It takes a village . . . to justify spending hours on the Internet. Here's your village. Larry Barkdull's site is a must-mark. The commercial bits are a disappointment, but if they fund the rest of the site, they're worth putting up with. It's the Church Lessons that propel this into the top 10. ★★★★★ ☑

Nauvoo   www.nauvoo.com Once upon a time, Nauvoo was a forum on AOL. Now everyone can participate—and should. This is easily the best discussion place on the World Wide Web (see figure 4.2). Orson Scott Card's sponsorship gives it cachet; his Vigor newsletter gives it substance. Follow the links to the kids' forum, the Red Brick Store, the Mansion House library, and more. It's the Vigor publication, along with the great bulletin board, that make this an especially memorable site. ★★★★★ ☑

World Wide Web First Ward   www.uvol.com/www1st Virtual ward complete with auxiliaries, gospel, doctrine, and homemaking. Includes columns, testimonials, letters from readers, and more. A top-notch site. ★★★★★

WWW LDS Visitor's Center   www.mich.com/~romulans/lds.html Lots of links if you're interested in finding LDS Institutes of Religion; online LDS family history center resources; LDS news, people, and cultures; LDS education institutes of religion and organizations; and LDS shopping mall. ★★★

SEARCH THE INTERNET

Every time a bell rings, the Internet gets new things—or so we're told. There are thousands of LDS-oriented Internet sites out there; new locations appear every day. Sites we describe in this book will disappear, they'll move to new locations, they'll get new and better information. Whatever the case, you'll want to have the skills to go out and search on your own for whatever you need on the Internet. Search engines will be helpful in finding not only LDS-oriented sites, but also for searching out Internet sites on virtually any topic that interests you.

How Search Engines Work

Simply put, search engines are akin to a phone book for the Internet. They're free, and they're invaluable for their flexibility and their power to light the darkest corners in order to find the information you're seeking. Use a search engine much as you'd use the index of a book or the yellow pages of a telephone directory. Bookmark them (see instructions on page 54) so that they're easily available.

The search engines discussed in this chapter are much grander in scope than the search vehicles you might find on the individual Web sites featured throughout this book. For the most part, on-site search engines don't reach beyond the archives of their particular site.

Search engines in this chapter index more sites—in some cases the entire Internet—to accumulate information for vast databases. From these search engines, you'll get better, more varied tools for querying data and interpreting results.

Although many of the search engines featured here may seem similar, significant differences lie just below the surface. Their primary focuses differ, and the information you generate will likewise be different. Several different types of user interfaces are featured. Some are extremely user-friendly, and others are extremely powerful and better left to the seasoned user.

ON CREATING A COMMUNITY OF SAINTS

One day [Roger Brown and I] were searching the Net in search of a pen-pal service for Latter-day Saints. We were disappointed to find nothing. I suggested that we start one of our own. . . .

In December of 1995, we finally brought the first "Mormon" pen-pal site to the Internet. . . . So far it has been a great success. I estimate that about 30 people have married or gotten engaged as a result of meeting on the site; the number may be much higher.

We are trying to create a unique environment of community. I think this is a "brave, new world," and the possibilities for good are endless.

Christian Adams, Provo, Utah
<orad@ldsfriends.com> or
<friends@ldsfriends.com>
Webmaster and Associate, LDS Friends
Worldwide Page
www.ldsfriends.com

A Few Words About Boolean Algebra

Boolean algebra is the backbone of all search engines. It sounds French but isn't. And it's certainly worth knowing about before beginning what could be a lifetime of sweeping Internet searches.

Boolean algebra was developed by the English mathematician George Boole in 1847. It brings together logical concepts and mathematical representations. A special set of mathematical *operators,* each having specific characteristics, is used to define Boolean logic. The basic operators, those used in most search engines, are AND, OR, and NOT.

This section explains the operators; the next section will show you how to use them for searching.

The AND Function

The AND function requires that all elements with the search term be present. If you type in a list of words, the search engine will return only the links that include *all* the search words. The AND function is usually represented by placing a plus (+) sign or the word "AND" directly in front of a word (mormon +utah) or (mormon AND utah).

The OR Function

The OR function requires only one of the elements in the search term to be present for the search to produce a positive result. In other words, if you entered (mormons OR utah), the search engine would return links to all sites that contained the terms "mormon" or "utah." The OR function is the presumed default funtion in most search engines.

The NOT function

The NOT function produces a positive result only if the designated element is not present. Many search engines allow you to designate a NOT by placing a minus sign (−) or the word "NOT" directly in front of the search term.

The GOOD News: Fortunately, the more sophisticated search engines relieve you of the necessity of creating Boolean equations—a simple English sentence is all you'll need to know in many cases.

How to Conduct a Search

All search engines feature an input box where you can enter what are known as *keywords.* The keyword is the beginning of your search. You begin your search when you enter your keyword, click the Search or equivalent button, and wait for the search engine to produce results.

It's not feasible to cover every method of conducting a search in the space allotted here. But it will be possible to touch on the basics—the features common to all search engines.

Unique Word Searches

You can begin your search by entering a single word in the keyword box and clicking the Search button. This is a wonderfully simple way to conduct a search if the keyword you're using is so unique that it is unlikely to produce many results. Searching for the keyword `Zoramite` produces no more than a handful of results. But a less specific term, `religion`, for instance, can easily produce better than a million matches.

Don't despair. A million places to look isn't really as hopeless as it sounds. Search engines don't return results in a random order. Using complicated algorithms, the best search engines rank the matches, and list the most relevant sites first.

Combined Word Searches:
Using the AND, OR, and NOT Operators

A better method of conducting a search is to combine words. In this way you can easily narrow the field from tens of millions of matches to a much more manageable number. Multiple word searches take advantage of the Boolean operators.

The OR operator is the default condition for most search engines. Type in the keywords without any symbols in front or in between to invoke the OR operation. As an example, the search string `LDS Mormon` will produce results if either, or both, of the keywords are present.

On the surface this doubling up would seem counterintuitive to your efforts to minimize irrelevant items when you search. If one word produces tens of millions of results, shouldn't two words produce more? They should and do. However, once again, the ranking algorithms come into play. The ranking of sites depends on several factors including, but not limited to, the number of times your word combination appears in a document, at what point—nearest to the beginning—the words appear in the document, how closely the two words appear in a document, and others.

The criteria used for ranking may vary from search engine to search engine. The more words you give the algorithm to work with, the more accurate the resulting rankings will be. Again, the highest-ranked sites are listed first. What this means is that, although you'll likely get millions of matches for multi-word searches, the most relevant matches will be the relatively few that appear at the top of the list.

To further define your search, invoke the AND operator. Although the method for invoking the AND function varies among search engines, the characteristics of the function do not. Currently, the most common way of searching with AND is to place a + sign directly in front of the keyword.

The AND function in the search string `+Mormon +Saints` produces results only when both keywords, Mormon and Saints, are present. (By the way, search engines also tend to be case sensitive. Uppercase letters search only for proper nouns. Lowercase letters return everything, proper or not.)

The NOT function provides an excellent means of eliminating items that may often be present with your keywords, but are of absolutely no interest to you. The NOT function can generally be invoked by placing a minus (–) sign in front of the keyword. The search `+Mormon +Zion –Moab` will return documents containing the keywords Mormon and Zion, but only if those documents do not contain the word Moab.

Grouping Words

Placing your words in groups can further narrow your search. Use this method when looking for "Mormon Zion" but not "Zion Mormon." The method for placing words in groups varies among the search engines. The two most common methods are placing them within quotes (`"Mormon Zion"`), or joining them with a colon (`Mormon:Zion`).

Spelling Counts—Somewhat

Not sure whether it's Rameumton or Rameumptom? Sometimes you're not sure of the exact spelling of a word. Other times, you're looking for several similar words (Mormon, Mormons, Mormonism). In either case a wild card character allows you to enter the part of the word you know and ignore the rest. For instance, try entering `Mormo*` if you're looking for anything on Mormonism. In this case the asterisk (`*`) is the wild card character that tells the search engine to look for all words beginning with the letters M o r m o.

Filters

All search engines employ some sort of "search only" filtering mechanism. As the name implies, you can use a filtering mechanism to force the search engine to consider only pages in a defined category. All other pages are filtered out. Selecting the category Religion, for example, restricts your search to religion-oriented sites. Methods for applying filters vary among search engines, but basically they all involve selecting a primary subject category from a list.

The Best Search Engines

In this section, we list a few of the growing number of search engines on the Internet. With a few exceptions, the search engine home pages consist of a list of topics—to help focus your search—and an input box for your keyword.

Searches on different engines yield different results. There are reasons for this variation, including the frequency with which the search engine database is updated, the algorithms used to determine the most relevant matches, and the different restrictions the search engines place on themselves when listing sites.

The search engines are listed here alphabetically. Each offers unique features, advantages, and disadvantages. Ratings are based on the author's personal likes and dislikes. Because the search engines don't compare with the LDS sites in the rest of this book, the rating system used here is entirely different. Not to worry. You'll pick it up pretty easily.

AltaVista

AltaVista (see figure 4.3) claims to be the largest Web index. The 31 million pages on 627,000 servers, plus 4 million articles from 14,000 Usenet groups, go a long way in supporting that claim. AltaVista is the primary search engine powering many of the subject-oriented search engines on the Internet.

The primary user interface consists of a simple keyword box and a Submit button. AltaVista uses Boolean searches. Detailed search instructions are available by clicking the Help or Advanced Help buttons.

Perhaps because yours truly is an old Luddite who enjoys doing things manually, AltaVista is my favorite search engine. Although it could really use an intuitive user interface, recently added "screen tips" make it a bit easier to navigate.

FIG. 4.3

Alta Vista: A simple concept. Type in the keyword and click Submit. The new Refine feature narrows the search.

A search on the term `Mormon*` (the * is the wild card that causes the search to return words like Mormonism and Mormonania), returned 50,160 hits. Plus Alta Vista suggested additional search categories such as "Famous Mormons," "Mormons in Utah," "Jack Mormon," "the mormons," and others. AltaVista gets a rating of **A**. View the site at www.altavista.com.

Ask Jeeves

If Boolean algebra is not your thing, and you would prefer to conduct your web searches in the same manner in which you conduct your everyday life—in a perfectly civilized manner—then Jeeves, the butler, just may be your cup of herbal tea. Jeeves understands, and even requests, that you ask him questions in the same manner you would of anyone. "Where do snowflakes come from?" or "Which way is it to the post office?" Jeeves will have a pretty good idea of what you want to know and he will offer several helpful suggestions to get you started in the right direction.

The question "tell me about mormons" produced several categories of responses from which to seek an answer. Categories returned included "Where can I learn about religious beliefs of the Church of Jesus Christ of Latter-day Saints?" and "Where can I find information on the history of Mormons?" Each subcategory links the user to what Jeeves believes is the best answer—in this case the official LDS Web pages. Additional links to other search engines produced thousands of relevant results. For ease of use and the relevance of the returned data Ask Jeeves earns an **A+**. Jeeves can be found, presumably polishing the silver at www.ask.com.

America Online Mailing List Resources

America Online Mailing List is an easy-to-use directory featuring over 3,200 mailing lists. The search function includes filtered keyword searches. When the Directory locates a mailing list, it provides a synopsis and detailed information on how to subscribe. The home page features links to useful items, including Working with Mailing Lists, Glossary of Terms, and a weekly Top 20 list. Search instructions are found at the bottom of the opening screen.

This is a nice site, more useful than most. A recent search on the term `Mormon*` returned six mailing lists, including the Overland Trails discussion list with references to the Mormon trail. This site earns a **B+**. The America Online Mailing List Directory is online at www.webcom.com/btsadmin/links/maillist.htm.

Deja.com

Deja.com is a place of ideas. Here you'll find discussions (a.k.a. Usenet groups and forums), user ratings of products ranging from toasters to movie stars and community groups. (You'll find more information about newsgroups in chapter 9 on page 219.) Deja.com employs a Boolean-style search mechanism along with radio buttons to weed through ratings, the thousands of online communities, and over 60,000 current discussions.

A recent search on the word `Mormon*` turned up 5,501 newsgroup messages. Search features include pattern matching (the use of partial words with wild cards), filtered searches, and time-sensitivity ranking.

For depth and scope this site, which is still re-inventing itself, gets a **C** rating. Visit Deja News again and again at www.deja.com.

Dogpile

Dogpile is a metasearch engine. A metasearch engine is one that searches other databases as well as its own database in order to produce your result. Many of the search engines are actually metasearch engines of varying degrees. It is the filtering mechanisms used that provide the real distinction. What Dogpile does so well is to take your query, run it through other search engines, and return everything—in a dogpile, so to speak. Sorting through the pile is largely your job. Still, if thoroughness is what you're after then you're definitely not barking up the wrong tree with Dogpile. For depth and scope and a real ability to pile it on Dogpile gets a **B+** rating. Watch your step when visiting the Dogpile at www.dogpile.com.

Excite

Excite features Boolean Web searches. Filtering selections help to redirect your search from the entire Web to Usenet groups, NewsTracker, or Web Reviews. The home page (see figure 4.4) also includes links to yellow pages, e-mail directories, shareware, maps, and more.

FIG. 4.4

Excite: The Excite page features the standard keyword input box, Search button, and links to other useful locations.

It's worth noting that Excite's search engine has the ability to build relationships between sets of words and concepts. In other words, Excite can equate the term "peace officer" with the word "policeman" when conducting a search.

A search on the term `Mormon*` brought up 15,548 hits, a top 10 list, nine Excite selected web pages, 18 community Web sites, and a list of alternative subjects. Additionally, Excite suggested other terms to search for such as Mormonism, Lehi, Nephi, LDS, and, er, humorless, polygamy, and watchtower. Harumph.

For its ability to offer suggestions and alternative search words, and its ease of use, this site earns an **A+**. You'll find all this excitement at www.excite.com.

Google

Google is an easy-to-use, basic Boolean search engine. It features a no-frills approach that is neat and clean and produced 2,416 matches for "mormon." Because it picks a job and does it well, Google rates a **B**. Set your goggles on Google at www.google.com.

HotBot

HotBot would be just another web site vying to be everybody's everything if not for a unique feature of its search engine: it has an easy-to-use drop-down box that allows you to narrow down your search based on time. Easily weed out the old material from the new by selecting only those links that are less than a week old, or two weeks old, or four months old. You get the idea; you decide.

A search on the word "mormon" produced the usual tens of thousands of sights to browse, but by narrowing it down to data posted in the last week, well nothing there, but change it to two weeks and, voila, 25 sights that had been updated in the last 14 days! In addition to the time-frame feature, HotBot features all the bells and whistles that are becoming mandatory in a popular search engine these days. A click of the mouse will make it your browser's home page if you wish.

For general usefulness and especially for the ease with which it lets you search for new Web content HotBot rates a **B**. Burn up the Web on HotBot's Web site at www.hotbot.com.

InfoSpace

InfoSpace is a comprehensive directory tailored to locating people, businesses, government offices, toll-free numbers, fax numbers, e-mail addresses, road maps, and URLs. You'll be able to locate organizations by city, by address, or by name. Get door-to-door directions, obtain local city guides, access apartment locators, and even check weather and ski conditions.

Directory information is also available for federal, state, and local government offices. The downside? It's awfully slow. But because it appears to do everything it's advertised to do—and that's a lot—this site rates a **B+**. Make space at www.infospace.com.

Liszt

Liszt is another directory of mailing lists. Currently there are over 90,000 entries compiled from servers around the world. Searches can be conducted using Boolean search methods, or you can choose from a smaller assortment by selecting specific topics. Perhaps even more important is the fact the Liszt is updated each week, ensuring against wasting your time with expired mailing lists.

A search on "Mormon" located seven LDS mailing lists. For its ease of use, depth, scope, and the general uniqueness of its service, Liszt rates an **A**. You'll find Liszt at www.liszt.com.

Lycos

Lycos is an especially user-friendly indexed Internet search engine. It features excellent instructional pages for its point-and-click-driven search protocol. Lycos employs a fuzzy search mechanism, finding like words and concepts. If you're looking for a lost roommate, Lycos's People Find feature is among the best on the Internet.

Searching on the term `Mormon*` turned up over 100 categories where Mormon sights could be found. For basic ease and convenience, this is a **B** rated site. Lycos lies at www.lycos.com.

Mining Company

Faster than you can create an alphabetical listing for the much-hyped Mining Company along comes About.com to rename the day.

The name may change, but the service is still there. The new About.com wants to be your friend. Expert guides, including an LDS guide, hold your hand through the World Wide Web pointing out the highlights and warning you to be careful if it appears you may fall. If Mr. Rogers ran his own search engine, this would be it; it's friendly, it's helpful, and, in spite of its lack of excitement, you'll always find yourself stopping back once more. For ease of use and that additional helping hand, About.com rates a **B**. Learn about the Web at either lds.miningco.com or www.about.com.

Magellan Internet Guide

Magellan would be just another entry in the user-friendly, category-oriented search engines if not for the unique filtering options offered on the home page. Searching the entire Web is one option. Selecting Reviewed Sites Only limits your search to the 60,000 plus Web sites reviewed by Magellan's editorial staff. Select the Green Light option to avoid those sites intended for mature audiences.

Magellan was able to generate 180 hits from the search term `Mormon*`. Because full access is always a plus and its options are good too, we rate this a **C+** site. Explore Magellan at magellan.excite.com.

MormonSearch

Submit your own links, and search a well-indexed engine for LDS sites at the *Mormons on the Internet* search engine. MormonSearch categorizes LDS sites topically and is available to all readers of *Mormons on the Internet* (see figure 4.5).

Because it's got everything, and it's got it categorized, and, quite frankly, because I wrote it, MormonSearch gets an **A+** rating. Find what you're looking for at www.writerspost.com/mormonsearch.

Search.Com

C|NET's tool Search.Com is designed to be a user-friendly search vehicle. Features include links to telephone and e-mail directories. Search topics include Arts, Business, Computers, Employment, UseNet, and Web. Search.Com is one of several sites powered by the AltaVista search engine. Searching on the term `Mormon*` generated 53,047 hits. Search.Com also found related search terms "Church of Jesus Christ of Latter-day Saints," "Parks & Wilderness Areas," and "Museums & Parks in Utah." Sure beats "Watchtower"!

As a high point in a long list of excellent search engines, this site gets an **A** rating. Start your search at www.search.com.

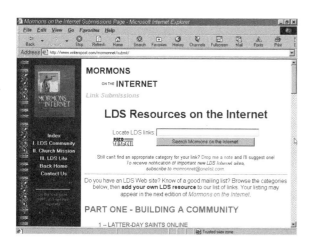

FIG. 4.5

MormonSearch: Links to 7,000+ LDS sites, categorized and reviewed.

WebCrawler

WebCrawler features a comprehensive index of the World Wide Web. The primary user interface supports Boolean search operators. Searches can be aided by selecting one of the 18 categories listed. A help section offers detailed instructions for conducting advanced searches. Click Special to find the Top 100 list and other items of interest.

A search on the term `Mormon*` returned 822 easy-to-read links. If you like what you find, click on the "Similar Pages" link after the detailed description. Just clicking on a few of these produced additional thousands of links. WebCrawler rates an **A** for its ease of use and comprehensiveness. Crawl over to the site at www.webcrawler.com.

Yahoo

Yahoo (see figure 4.6) is an indexed search engine, capable of comprehensive searches. Yahoo prioritizes matches and returns the highest-rated 100 matches. Searches can be better focused by choosing from e-mail listings, Usenet groups, or the seemingly endless hierarchy of categories and subcategories. Yahoo offers links to Religion, Genealogy, and other helpful categories. Searches can be as simple or as complicated as you choose.

A search on `Mormon*` generated only 126 hits, an unhealthy number of which are mean-spirited in nature.

The editorial decisions that go into adding a site to Yahoo make it a tremendously out-of-date and biased collection of sites. Add to that the fact that it fails to index the content of the pages it lists, and Yahoo is an all-around nonstarter. The hierarchical structure gives it some value, though, so Yahoo rates a grudging **B**. Do your own whooping and hollering at Yahoo's Web site, at www.yahoo.com.

FIG. 4.6

Yahoo: The Religion category is waaaay down there at the end.

Zion Search

Zion Search, like Yahoo and several others, is an indexed search engine capable of comprehensive searches. Unlike other search engines, however, all of the links found on Zion Search must uphold the standards of the Church. Links that are deemed inappropriate are removed from Zion Search's database. Zion Search features a plain-vanilla, user-friendly design. Searches generally produced only 6 to 10 links but Zion's database is growing. You can find Zion Search, a **C** site, at www.zionsearch.com.

5

CREATING A
SAFE PLACE
ON THE NET

The many sites in this book demonstrate that there is a wealth of information specifically for Latter-day Saints available on the Internet. Throughout this book, you'll find information for teaching your family, fulfilling your callings, studying the gospel, researching your family history, and talking with other Latter-day Saints.

But that's only the beginning of uplifting sites available to you and your family on the Internet. General interest sites include some of the world's greatest museums, such as the Louvre in Paris mistral.culture.fr/louvre/louvrea.htm or The New York Metropolitan Museum of Art www.metmuseum.org/htmlfile/opening/enter.html The Internet is full of good literature—see the Shakespeare site at daphne.palomar.edu/shakespeare or Books Online at www.cs.cmu.edu/books.html—and scientific data—see the NASA site at www.nasa.gov or Sky and Telescope at www.skypub.com—that can enrich minds.

The Internet has become the world's largest shopping mall. There are books www.amazon.com, music www.musicboulevard.com, flowers www.ftpflowers.com, and more www.internet.net. The World Wide Web is where the world's largest organizations compete to display their goods and services alongside Aunt Harriet's favorite family recipes.

For better and worse this book can only represent the tiniest fraction of what exists on the Internet. Most of what is out there can be classified under good, better, best, or totally inane. There is, however, an underbelly to the Internet. There are sites and resources that most parents would prefer never entered the home. It's this dark side of the Internet that has kept many from even considering Internet access. It is the world of stalkers, pornographers, and other purveyors of tawdry information.

Fortunately the World Wide Web does not have to be a place to be avoided. It *can* be made safe for, ahem, women and children. This chapter will explore a few methods for assuring that—at least the portion of the information superhighway you and *your* family roam—is well lit, safe, and clean.

> ## PRESIDENT KIMBALL ON PURITY
>
> Each person must keep himself clean and free from lusts. He must shun ugly, polluted thoughts and acts as he would an enemy. Pornography and erotic stories and pictures are worse than polluted food. Shun them. The body has power to rid itself of sickening food. That person who entertains filthy stories or pornographic pictures and literature records them in his marvelous human computer, the brain, which can't forget this filth. Once recorded, it will always remain there, subject to recall.
>
> —Spencer W. Kimball

RULES OF THE ROAD

Most of the rules for Internet safety are just common sense and good parenting. If you need help getting started, though, here are a few rules that should be mandatory for any Web browsers in your family. Have a talk with the kids. Make them sign a contract, if you must. The peace of mind you'll experience when these rules are followed is worth the inconvenience.

1. Never give out personal information over the Internet. This rule especially holds true in chat rooms and with e-mail to somebody you met in a chat room.
2. Do not respond to anything that makes you feel uncomfortable. You are under no obligation to respond to unsolicited e-mail or online messages. In most cases, it is best to simply delete the e-mail, or ignore the instant message. Notify a parent when you discover inappropriate messages, so they can deal with the offender properly. Some online services, such as America Online, have special forwarding addresses to handle inappropriate communications. If a child receives offensive or inappropriate e-mail, parents can report the offense to the CyberTipline at www.missingkids.com/cybertip.
3. Do not accept or open e-mails, attached files, or links from people you don't know or trust.

4. Do not give your password out to anyone. Providers that require passwords don't ask for them except when you log on. Report any instances of someone attempting to get your password.

5. Never arrange to get together with anyone you meet online alone. It's natural that after communicating with someone online over a long period of time you may wish to meet face to face. Many great friendships have started online. But caution is the keyword in these types of situations. People are not always who they say they are. Never arrange for a meeting in anything but a public place, never in a place where you could be followed or become vulnerable in any way, and never without parental knowledge and consent. There are no exceptions to this rule.

6. Parents should consider placing the computer in a family room or other accessible area to make it less likely that children will engage in undesirable explorations of the Web. Additionally, it will help assure your immediate availability should a family member accidentally come across objectionable material.

A Short Plug for CyberTipline

CyberTipline is a federally funded initiative for reporting child sexual exploitation. It is administered by the National Center for Missing and Exploited Children (NCMEC), in cooperation with the Federal Bureau of Investigation, the U.S. Customs Service, and the U.S. Postal Inspection Service.

> ON TAKING RESPONSIBILITY
> No one in America has the inalienable right to turn left on a red light.
> When they do, innocent people often suffer.
> And no one has the inalienable right to be reckless on the "Information Highway" either.
> Those who are should suffer consequences.
> There's no God-given liberty to play fast and loose with the lives of others.
> Irresponsibility on the freeway leads to twisted metal and bodies.
> Irresponsibility on the information highway can lead to twisted minds.
>
> —Jerry Johnston, *Deseret News*, May 8, 1999

As the nation's resource center for child protection, the NCMEC spearheads national efforts to locate and recover missing children, and raises public awareness about ways to prevent child abduction, molestation, and sexual exploitation.

CyberTipline and the Child Pornography Tipline can be contacted at 1(800) 843-5678.

FILTERED INTERNET SERVICE PROVIDERS

One of the better methods of assuring that children don't accidentally come across objectionable material on the Internet—short of discontinuing your Internet service or duct-taping the keyboard—is to make sure the objectionable materials are not even available to be seen. Filtered Internet Service Providers provide a family-safe Internet by filtering out the objectionable portions of the World Wide Web, usually violence and pornography, and letting through the rest.

Using a filtered Internet Provider has several advantages over other methods of regulating Web content on your home PC. By necessity, software solutions require disk space. How much space is required can vary depending on your usage and how often you attempt to access objectionable sites. Most filtered ISP packages require no more space then a normal ISP would require. Another advantage that filtered ISPs have over their software-solution counterparts is that clever and curious kids sometimes find it relatively easy to circumnavigate the software package's security. (In all fairness this is often, inadvertently, the parents' fault. Hands up if you've ever used baby's name as a password.) A filtered Internet service provider's blocking mechanism is virtually 100-percent tamper proof. (Hackers be still. We're talking about normal, otherwise-good kids on home computers.)

> ### PRESIDENT KIMBALL ON PORNOGRAPHY
> We abhor pornography that seems to be flooding the land. Legislation makes an effort to curb it, but the best way to stop it is to have men and women, with their families, build barriers against it.
>
> —Spencer W. Kimball

The downside of a filtered ISP is, for lack of a better phrase, Big-Brother syndrome. Much of the filtering that takes place with filtered ISPs is automatic: a computer program searches for objectionable phrases and blocks the site. However, much of the filtering is manual: real people browse the Web and make decisions about what shouldn't be seen. The possibility exists that these censors-for-hire may not share your sensibilities.

This option isn't entirely Orwellian; filtering ISPs will provide, in writing, the guidelines they use to determine what is inappropriate. In general, you'll find that the sites blocked out are those specifically advertised as being adult-only, that contain excessive violence, sites that promote hate against any race, religion, or other group, and sites that promote illegal activities. Within these general guidelines, there will be variations on what each provider will block. Some will block all offensive content, while others allow subscriber latitude in determining what type of sites will be filtered out.

> ### PRESIDENT BENSON ON CHOICE
> The greatest right humans possess is the right of free choice, free will, free agency. This above all is what today's true conservative strives to preserve for his fellowmen and for himself.
>
> —Ezra Taft Benson

It is important to remember that not even the filtered ISPs claim 100 percent efficacy. Just as fast as they are working on methods to automatically filter out objectionable materials, the purveyors of such materials are working to evade the automatic filtering. One of the filtered ISPs covered in this chapter, Family Based Internet, claims that 275 new pornographic sites go on line every day. Against such numbers, maybe a little assistance from a filtered ISP isn't such a bad idea.

76

ClearViewNet www.clearviewnet.net ClearViewNet (see figure 5.1) uses a combination of automated-computer sweep and manual reviews to generate its log of offensive sites. ClearViewNet creates an alternative Internet community—a common feature among filtered ISPs. While all filtered ISPs deny access to objectionable Web sites, it is still possible for objectionable site information to get through the barriers whenever you conduct a search. ClearViewNet boasts of a proprietary search engine that even filters the objectionable sites from hits during your Web searches. You can contact ClearViewNet at (800) 250-5757.

CTR Online www.ctronline.com This Murray, Utah-based filtered Internet Service Provider is excellent for anyone who doesn't want to deal with Netly grime and filth. The server-based filter uses the same filter as the DOL site. The $17.95 monthly fee provides access to dial up numbers in 600 to 800 locations nationwide. The company can be reached toll-free at (877) 368-2872.

DeseretOnline www.deseretonline.com Deseret Book's filtered ISP service. DOL is based in Salt Lake City, and has dial-up numbers nationwide. The service uses a customized version of CyberSnoop to filter offending materials. The monthly fee is $19.95, which includes a bonus software package. Dial toll free at 1-877-DOL-link (1-877-365-5465) or sign up via the Web site. Large calling area. ★★★

Family Based Internet (FBI) www.safeplace.net/home Family Based Internet (see figure 5.2) is another company that takes the task of filtering Web content very seriously. Like ClearViewNet, they maintain a database of objectionable (mostly pornographic) sites and do not allow access to those sites. Contact Family Based Internet by phone: (219) 881-2701 or e-mail *<sales@safeplace.com>*.

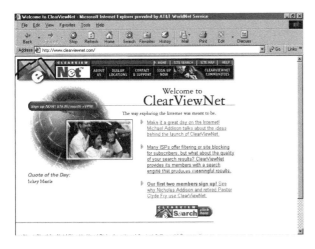

FIG. 5.1

ClearViewNet.

FIG. 5.2

safeplace.net.

LDS.NET   www.lds.net LDS.NET's filtered dial-up service pre-screens the pages you search so that no unwanted pages will display. The company offers subscribers free scripture videos with prepaid subscriptions. Limited calling areas.

MayberryUSA   www.mbusa.net There was no sign of Sheriff Andy but the implication is obvious. MayberryUSA (see figure 5.3) has created an Internet zone that is a wholesome place where you don't feel the need to worry about the safety of your family. This doesn't mean that MayberryUSA is all saccharine or free from strife and discussion. In addition to the family-oriented fun sites, there are Web sites dedicated to politics, business, and current events. The only controversies

FIG. 5.3

MayberryUSA Gazette.

you'll find missing from MayberryUSA are the X-rated variety (fans of the X-Files excepted). Visit MayberryUSA at (800) 833-5854.

America Online   www.aol.com   America Online is at the end of this list instead of in its usual alphabetic placement because, technically, America Online is not a filtered Internet provider. America Online's normal default configuration allows full access to all areas of the Internet. However, its "Parental Controls" feature (see figure 5.4) gives parents the capability to restrict AOL and Internet access to designated sub-accounts. America Online allows up to five of these accounts, each with its own login password. The categories assignable to these accounts are as follows:

- **Kids Only.** This option restricts users to the "Kids Only Channel" on AOL. It also places restrictions on e-mail attachments and chat room access.
- **Young Teen.** This option places restrictions on chat room access, as well as blocking Web sites deemed inappropriate for the selected age group. Restrictions are also placed on Internet newsgroups that allow file attachments. Young teens cannot access premium services.
- **Mature Teen.** Similar to Young Teen except slightly less restrictive.
- **18+.** The user has full access to all America Online and Internet content.

America Online also allows some additional customization of access rights making it possible to block specific Web addresses and e-mail. Contact America Online at (800) 827-6364.

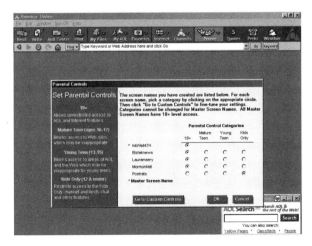

FIG. 5.4

Parental Controls.

Internet Safety

What are Latter-day Saints doing to keep their families safe on the Internet? Here's what they say:

Ben Moon, Joplin, Missouri, Stake <*webmaster@ldsonline.org*> writes: "Teach correct principles."

Annette Nay, Bremerton, Washington, Silverdale Fourth Ward <*annettenay@ aol.com*> writes: "We are with AOL. They have different ratings of access for the Net. It is very restrictive. They can't get into things they shouldn't."

Barbara Barney, Federal Way, Washington, Second Ward <*MamaBarney@ aol.com*> writes: "Our children have been told that we can monitor their Web visits and know where they have been. They've been really good about avoiding the bad that is out there. My children delete any messages that might even hint at being pornographic in nature. We also do not open any e-mail unless we know who the sender is or the subject line is specific. The delete key is our best friend."

Melissa Amy C. Johnson, Surrey 3d Ward, Surrey BC Stake <*go_canada_go@ hotmail.com*> writes: "I'm 16 and what keeps me away from bad sites is my standards, the standards I have learned from the Church. I know that I don't have to degrade myself with those pages. There are plenty of good ones!"

George Galletly, Mississauga Ward <*g_galletly@hotmail.com*> writes: "With great difficulty. In fact, I'm not altogether certain that they don't occasionally look at 'stuff' out there too readily available."

A Go Between

It is possible that none of the Internet providers identified as filtered providers has a local access number in your area. Rather than support your local telephone company by paying long-distance charges every time you log on to the Internet you can sign up for a service that provides filtered Internet protection while letting you continue to use your local ISP.

GuardiaNet   www.guardianet.net GuardiaNet is server-based Internet filtering software. Server based just means that most of the filtering software sits on GuardiaNet's computers. Theoretically, this frees up the disk space that would be required on your PC to store the URLs of all of the restricted or no-access Web sites. Additionally, somewhat like America Online, GuardiaNet allows you to set up different levels of access for different users. Contact GuardiaNet at (888) 638-7007.

FREEDOM OF SPEECH

While many people are opposed to the objectionable materials on the Internet, others remain equally opposed to the prospect of government intervention. They feel that the primary problem with government censorship is not determining where it will begin but determining where it will end. For that reason, several corporations and citizens groups have come together to find a viable alternative to censorship, while ensuring that freedom of speech will continue to be protected for all. One such alternative to government intervention is the voluntary rating of Web sites. In the same manner that voluntary ratings saved the movie industry from official censorship, key players in the online community have moved to implement a system whereby adults can control the content of what is allowed to reach their homes. This system of voluntary regulation and the software designed to implement it is sometimes known as the RSACi system.

What's a RSACi?

RSAC is the Recreational Software Advisory Council, an independent, nonprofit organization that makes its home in Washington, D.C. The small "i" stands for Internet. RSAC attempts to provide consumers with information about the level of sex, nudity, violence, and other objectionable content in computer games and on Web sites.

THE RATINGS STANDARD

In order to set your browser correctly you'll need to understand how RSACi ratings are applied.

Webmasters complying with the RSACi standards are required to fill out a standard questionnaire. How they respond determines what rating code they receive. The code is then inserted on their Web page. Unlike movie ratings, RSACi are not meant to be read by humans, only your computer needs to understand the code. When you access the Web site your RSACi-enabled browser (more on that a little later on) treats the Web page as determined by your control settings.

If you have a Web site of your own, you'll want to strongly consider rating your site according to the RSACi standards. Compliant Web browsers have only two settings for nonrated sites: blocked or unblocked. Many prudent parents, who could possibly benefit form the information on your site, will choose safety (blocked) first.

The following ratings correspond to both the questionnaire to be filled out in rating the Web sites and the settings that parents can select for access rights on their home computers.

Internet Safety

William Steele, Rossford, Ohio, Perrysburg Ward <bsteele@lds.net> writes: "We use LDS.NET. It screens sites and topics at the server to LDS standards."

Jordan D. Jones, New Haven, Connecticut Stake <jordan@ldscn.com> writes: "In our family, the younger children are monitored. Parents will frequently check on the child's activity. 'Who are you talking to? What are you doing? What kind of chat room is that? Should you really be there?' Also, children need to be taught what information should NEVER be released in profiles or during chats. Full names, addresses, telephone numbers, sports teams, etc."

Sheryl Bagwell <melody@aros.net>, Salt Lake City, Manhattan Ward, Granger South Stake: "I have a filter on my browser that controls what types of pages can be accessed."

Eric & Brenda Brower, Marysville, Washington, Sixth Ward, Marysville Stake <brower@gte.net> write: "We monitor closely where they go on the Internet. They are only allowed to go on line while we are at home. We check the "history" often to see where we all have gone during the previous days. For the most part, we haven't had many problems with the Internet."

Scott Jensen, Hooper Utah <jensens@vitrex.net> writes: "I don't give them my Internet access account password. They have to ask to get on the Internet, and I monitor what sites they access. We also have a policy never to divulge phone numbers, addresses, or last names."

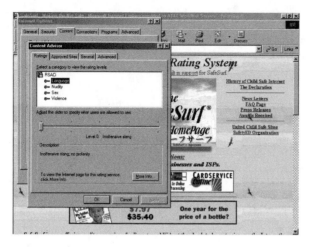

FIG. 5.5

Content Advisor.

	Violence Rating Descriptor	Nudity Rating Descriptor	Sex Rating Descriptor	Language Rating Descriptor
Level 4	Rape or wanton, gratuitous violence	Frontal nudity (qualifying as provocative display)	Explicit sexual acts or sex crimes	Crude, vulgar language or extreme hate speech
Level 3	Aggressive violence or death to humans	Frontal nudity	Non-explicit sexual acts	Strong language or hate speech
Level 2	Destruction of realistic objects	Partial nudity	Clothed sexual touching	Moderate expletives or profanity
Level 1	Injury to human beings	Revealing attire	Passionate kissing	Mild expletives
Level 0	None of the above or sports related	None of the above	None of the above or innocent kissing; romance	None of the above

The SafeSurf System

SafeSurf is not another filtering mechanism, but as employed today, represents an implementation of the RSACi rating system.

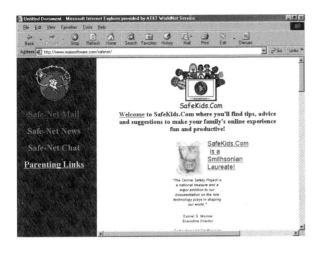

FIG. 5.6

Safe-Net Mail.

The SafeSurf system provides parents with a means of filtering Web page accessibility based on the voluntary RSACi system. The most current version of this system employs slide controls (see figure 5.5) for all of the key categories. Once the controls are set, a password protects them from being modified or allows them to be temporarily bypassed.

As mentioned before, there are only two options available for unrated sites, blocked or unblocked. Since new, objectionable sites may be unrated, it may be better practice to block unrated sites. However, if Aunt Harriet is unaware of the RSACi rating system, her site of most-loved cookie recipes will also be blocked. In those instances, it is best to use the password to temporarily bypass the filter and send Aunt Harriet an e-mail note asking her to rate her site. It'll only take her five minutes.

Get the Software

If you're using Netscape Navigator 4.0 or Internet Explorer 3.0 or higher, you already have the SafeSurf system, which uses the RSACi rating system, installed on your computer.

It's not very likely, but if the version of the browser you have is too old to support the SafeSurf system version, there really is no excuse for not updating—it's free! Netscape Communicator can be found at home.netscape.com/communicator/v4.5 and the latest version of Internet Explorer is located at www.microsoft.com.

SAFE MAIL

As mentioned previously, there are some commonsense precautions you can take concerning e-mail. Don't open mail or files from strangers. The reality is, however, that there are many times when a finger click to the mouse travels three times the speed of a thought through the brain.

Safe-Net Mail (see figure 5.6) is an easy to use POP3 e-mail filtering system. (A POP3 system will not work with America Online, CompuServe, or most free-e-mail accounts.) Safe-Net Mail is capable of filtering out language, violence, and spam.

To get a copy of Safe-Net Mail, and other family-oriented, Internet-safety software and news, visit Safe-Net Suite at www.maiasoftware.com/safenet.

OTHER SITES WORTH BOOKMARKING

Cyber Patrol   www.cyberpatrol.com This is an excellent resource for keeping up to date on the most recent Internet filtering software solutions.

Internet Parental Control FAQ Page   www.vtw.org/pubs/ipcfaq Internet Parental Control features the answers to your most frequently asked questions, as well as additional information on filtering software.

The Learning Company   www.learningco.com/parents/resource/cprefer.htm The Learning Company features links on Internet safety, as well as educational links for parents and teachers.

PART TWO

THE MISSION
OF THE CHURCH

6

PROCLAIM
THE GOSPEL

The Church of Jesus Christ of Latter-day Saints is a church on a mission—a three-part mission to be specific. Our task? To proclaim the gospel, to perfect the Saints, and to redeem the dead.

In this chapter, you'll find reviews, histories, and commentaries that address the first part of that mission: proclaiming the gospel. We begin with testimony—the conversion stories and spiritual experiences of Latter-day Saints throughout the world. Following that is an introduction to the Church. You'll find there information about contacting the Church, as well as background, doctrine, and an introduction to the Book of Mormon, the keystone of our religion. Finally, you'll find sections on responding to critics of the Church and doing missionary work.

TESTIMONY PAGES

As noted in the introduction to this book, I'm more than a little fond of the Internet. I perceive it as one giant week-long testimony meeting, albeit one where there are altogether too many distractions.

Over the past several years, I have become a collector of conversion stories. The stories I was reading at various Web sites were moving—so much so that I eventually was motivated to gather them in a single place in order to share my discovery with the world.

Grant Johnson, webmaster at the New Jerusalem site, did an even better thing, setting up a site where people could submit their conversion stories, and publishing not just links, but actual stories that would never otherwise have been available for public view.

A handful of other Latter-day Saints have built their own testimony and conversion story sites, giving Net surfers a fine selection of testimony sites worth visiting. If you do nothing else on the Internet, if you study no other LDS-oriented pages, you must at least take a look at these great sites.

HOTLINKS

Classic True LDS
www.xmission.com/~dkenison/lds/
ch_hist

My Beliefs
www.osmond.net/donny/beliefs

My LDS Faith Explained.
www.geocities.com/TimesSquare/
Alley/8329/church.html

Testify!
www.writerspost.com/testify

Testimonies
www.geocities.com/Heartland/
Plains/7717/sacred/testimonies.
html

Caelum Fides members.visi.net/~atom/ totally A very nice collection of testimonies and conversion stories. ★★★★

Classic True LDS www.xmission.com/ ~dkenison/lds/ch_hist More than 500 stories from LDS history and personal experiences. This site fascinates. ★★★★★

Conversion Stories www.geocities.com/ Heartland/Flats/5623/conversion/conversion. html A thoughtful collection of modern conversion stories. ★★★★

Dodsons' Latter-day Saints Page www.geocities.com/Heartland/Plains/6612 Links to the authors' conversion story and a tribute to a sweet soul that blessed lives. ★★★

Get to Know the Mormons www.geocities. com/paris/6923/LDS.html Short testimony and the Articles of Faith. ★★

In Search of the Spiritual home.sol.no/~lbennett/Spiritual.htm Testimony and the author's effort to help members feel the Spirit. ★★

LDS References members.aol.com/ssh81675/ldsrefer/ldsrefer.htm The testimonies of the Hoyt family, talks by the First Presidency, and other information about the LDS Church. ★★

Links to the Author's Web Site and Testimony   www.TheLordJesusChrist.net Link to the author's Home-page and Testimony. A lot of work went into this page. ★★

My Beliefs   www.osmond.net/donny/beliefs/ Donny Osmond explains his beliefs. Actually, a very thoughtful page. Worth a read. ★★★★★ ☑

My Conversion   www.geocities.com/Heartland/Prairie/4775/conversion.htm Beautifully told story of one sister's conversion. ★★★

My Family's Testimony   www.geocities.com/Athens/Styx/5581/Family.html A testimony of the Book of Mormon and of the Gospel of Jesus Christ from a member family in England. ★★★

My LDS Faith Explained   www.geocities.com/TimesSquare/Alley/8329/church.html Dan Birch's in-depth explanation of why he's a Latter-day Saint. Very well done. ★★★

My Testimony   www.geocities.com/Heartland/Hills/8652/testimony.htm Bonnie Howell's conversion story. ★★★

New Jerusalem Testimony Stories   new-jerusalem.com/testimony/stories.html New Jerusalem's conversion stories from Latter-day Saints around the world (see figure 6.1). In just over a year, this site received more than 100 conversion story submissions, all of which testify to miracles worked in the lives of investigators, new members, and long-time members. Unfortunately, it hasn't been updated since. ★★★★★

FIG. 6.1

New Jerusalem: Absolutely the best, most uplifting site on the Internet.

Paul Guymon a.k.a. Gramps www.freeyellow.com/members2/pguymon A brief testimony along with miscellaneous family information. ★★

Personal Conversion Account www.sandycentre.com/conversion Sander J. Rabinowitz's story of his conversion from Judaism. ★★★

Personal Testimonies and Conversion www.triax.com/fannocreekward/personal.htm A new and growing site for sharing of conversions and testimonies. ★★★★

Share Your Testimony 204.201.132.101/cgi-bin/gb/gbview.cgi?file=mormon A guest book page looking for entries. ★★

Should We Pray About the Truthfulness of the Book of Mormon? members.visi.net/~atom/totally/Mike.html And why not? A tremendous response to those who would say no. ★★★

Subscriber Submissions www.xmission.com/~dkenison/lds/gems/arc_subs.html Personal experiences and essays submitted by subscribers to the popular LDS-GEMS mailing list. Organized in order of submission. ★★★★★

Testify! www.writerspost.com/testify Conversion stories. Arranged by contemporary individuals, historical individuals, contemporary collections, and historical collections. It's my own page, but I'm tremendously fond of it, and give it a correspondingly high rating. ★★★★★ ☑

Testimonials www.uvol.com/www1st/testimonies A small collection of conversion stories and testimonies. ★★★★

Testimonies www.geocities.com/Heartland/Plains/7717/sacred/testimonies.html Several pages of conversion stories collected by Sheri Green. ★★★★★

Testimonies www.mormons.org/testimonies A collection of testimonies borne by general authorities. ★★★★

Testimony www.davejennings.freeserve.co.uk/testmny.html Testimony and feelings about the church from a member in England. Includes "40 reasons for people going less active." ★★★

Testimony and Knowledge www.jefflindsay.com/LDSFAQ/FQ_Testimony.shtml Answers to questions about the nature of testimonies. What do Latter-day Saints mean when they speak of their "testimonies"? Isn't it just based on emotion? What role does intellect play? What is the gift of the Holy Ghost? How does one "follow the Spirit"? ★★★

The Church of Jesus Christ of Latter-day Saints www.geocities.com/Yosemite/Trails /8092/LDS.HTM Despite the title, this is only a small page with the testimony of a young LDS woman. ★★

The Prophet Joseph Smith's Testimony www.lds.org/library/the_pro_jos/ the_pro_jos.html From the official Web site. First vision, visit of Moroni, testimonies of witnesses, more. ★★★★★

INTRODUCTION TO THE CHURCH

As you make your way around the Internet, and begin telling people in various chat rooms and mailing lists about your affiliation with Mormonism, you'll often be asked questions about the Church by people who are completely unfamiliar with it. In this section, we present a collection of sites that make a good starting point for introducing the Church.

At these sites you'll find information about contacting the Church, information that includes toll-free telephone numbers, meeting house locations, and other helpful resources. The section on Background information describes the history and teachings of the Church. In the Gospel Principles section, you'll discover a large number of Internet sites dedicated to explaining the fundamental principles of the gospel, most of which tend to be thoroughly documented from scriptural sources. After that comes a section introducing the Book of Mormon, followed by a section on other resources for investigators.

Contacting the Church

I was raised in an unenthusiastically LDS family—one where my contact with the Church consisted primarily of Wednesday afternoon Primary, where my busy mom would occasionally drop us off so that she could run errands. But when I was young teenager, a great bishop (probably at the urging of my vastly more enthusiastic grandmother) persuaded me to participate in a temple trip that changed my life. On that temple trip, I discovered the gospel, and returned home with a profound desire to be actively involved in Church.

The very next week, I convinced my parents to take me to Church on Sunday morning. We pulled up just as the building was emptying out. I'd gotten the time all wrong. Someone I recognized from my Primary days straightened me out. A couple of weeks later, I talked my parents into taking me back. It wasn't good. The doors were locked and the building was dark. Later I found out about a thing called Stake Conference.

A short time later, I gave it another shot. They drove me all the way back to the meeting house. The doors were locked. The building was dark. Later I found out about General Conference.

A few weeks passed. They took me back and let me off at the door. This time the building was open, full of people even, but I didn't recognize any of them. It was a different ward. The meeting schedule had changed.

Eventually, I figured out the system, found a regular ride to Church, and got so involved that I became the one other people called to find out what was going on. It certainly would have made life easier back then if I'd have had access to these great Internet resources.

Atlas of North American LDS Temples, Missions, and Stakes   members.theglobe.com/mschind Web master Marc A. Schindler is working to develop a site that covers all units of the Church. ★★★

LDS Meeting House Locator   www.deseretbook.com/locate Whether you're planning a trip or moving to a new location, Deseret Book's listing of meeting houses is a worthwhile resource (see figure 6.2). The most complete listings on the Internet. ★★★

Other Resources   The Internet isn't the only electronic resource for contacting the Church. For a free copy of the Book of Mormon in the United States call (800) 528-2225. For a free copy of the Holy Bible (King James Version), call (800) 408-4343. *Together Forever,* a free video, explains Heavenly Father's plan of happiness. Get a free copy by calling (888) 917-5858. *Family First,* a free video, teaches practical ways to build stronger and more loving families for real home improvement. Order a free copy from (800) 832-2900. The main operator at Church headquarters can be reached at (800) 453-3860. The Church may also be contacted at Public Programs, Salt Lake City, Utah 84150.

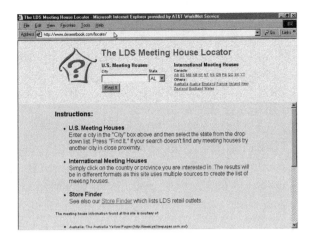

FIG. 6.2

LDS Meeting Houses: Travel anywhere, and still get to the Church on time.

Background on the Church

For me, conversion to the gospel was the easy part. The thrill that went through me as I stood on the temple grounds early one evening at the close of a testimony meeting, and quietly joined in singing "I Know that My Redeemer Lives"—that was the moment I knew it was all true.

The harder part was—and still is, really—learning what it meant to be a practicing Latter-day Saint. When I figured out the joke about the plastic grapes, I knew I was making progress.

Here, online, is the New and Prospective Members class I've always wanted to organize, the one where investigators find out that being Mormon means not only a change of heart, but also a change of life.

Part Three of this text, Living a Latter-day Saint Life, is devoted to an in-depth discussion of all the facets of the Mormon experience. This section you're reading now just skims the surface, a bit like the dust on the decorative bowl of plastic grapes my gramma—and everyone else's gramma—made at homemaking meeting one afternoon in 1967. Please pass the Jello!

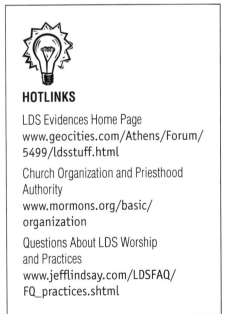

HOTLINKS

LDS Evidences Home Page
www.geocities.com/Athens/Forum/
5499/ldsstuff.html

Church Organization and Priesthood
Authority
www.mormons.org/basic/
organization

Questions About LDS Worship
and Practices
www.jefflindsay.com/LDSFAQ/
FQ_practices.shtml

Brief Introduction www.math.byu.edu/~smithw/Lds/LDS/Intro_to_LDS_Church.html A Brief Introduction to the Origin, Organization, and Doctrines of The Church of Jesus Christ of Latter-day Saints, taken from various teachings of Joseph Smith. Much of the content is expanded in the book *A Marvelous Work and a Wonder*, by the late Elder LeGrand Richards. ★★★

ON GOD AND TECHNOLOGY

It is my firm belief that Heavenly Father has brought forward the technology necessary for the Internet in order to help us communicate better with one another and learn more about each other.

Hilary A. Croughton, Ipswich, England
<hathi@enterprise.net>

Church Organization and Priesthood Authority www.mormons.org/basic/organization Articles on the administration of the Church. Includes information on the Contemporary Church Organization, Branch, Districts, Lay Participation and Leadership, Common Consent, Following the Prophets, Priesthood Organization, Auxiliary Organizations, Relief Society, Young Women, Primary, Correlation of the Church, Administration, Church Education System (CES), Church Publications, Record Keeping, Disciplinary Procedures, Organizational and Administrative Church History, Organization of the Church in New Testament Times, and The Worldwide Church. Very thorough. A Mormons.Org page. ★★★★★

Daily Living www.mormons.org/daily A collection of articles and links to other sites describing life as a Latter-day Saint. Includes information on Activity in the Church, Agriculture, Attitudes Toward the Arts, Attitudes Toward Health and Medicine, Attitudes Toward Business and Wealth, Callings, Church Organization and Priesthood Authority, Dating and Courtship, Education, Family History or Genealogy, Family Home Evening, Church History, Holidays and Celebrations, Interfaith Relationships, Teachings About Law, Lay Participation and Leadership, Meetings and Conferences, Military and the Church, Missionary Work, Parenting, Politics, Teachings About Prayer, Reverence, Sabbath Day, Teachings About Sexuality, Tithing, Welfare and Humanitarian Assistance, and the Word of Wisdom. ★★★★★

Dan Forward's LDS Information Page www.geocities.com/Athens/Acropolis/1890/LDS_Pamphlet_Library.htm A library of pamphlets published by the Church on various topics. ★★★

DJ's LDS tips www.davejennings.freeserve.co.uk/ldstips.html Tips for teaching, for washing white shirts, or any other general tips for solving mishaps around the LDS home, garden, chapel, etc. The author invites you to contribute great organizational tools, activities that prove popular with the youth, tricks for getting children to actually sit still in sacrament, or a fun activity for all the family on Family Home Evening. ★★★★

Gospel Basics Homepage   www.geocities.com/Heartland/Ranch/9159 Author John Hesch has been a member of the church for 18 years, and testifies that the Gospel of Jesus Christ will bring happiness into your life if you ponder, study, act, and endure by doing the basics. It is the simple things that bring joy. ★★★★

Gospel Essentials   www.new-jerusalem.com/gospel/essentials.html   Basic information on the mission of the Church from New Jerusalem. Heavy scripture. ★★★

History   www.geocities.com/Heartland/Plains/1796/ldshome/history.html A basic history of the Church. Lots of interesting articles here. ★★★

LDS Evidences   www.geocities.com/Athens/Forum/5499/bom/ldsstuff.html An impressive collection of proofs for the historicity of the Book of Mormon and the Church in general. Author Gary Smith addresses, generally quite persuasively, such issues as Yale Pres Ezra Stiles Predicted Church's Restoration; Did Joseph Smith Copy the Names Moroni and Cumorah? The Ruin of the House of Lehi; Trans Oceanic Travel; Book of Mormon's Bountiful Found in Oman; There's No Such Thing as Proof; Breaking the Maya Code and Mormonism; The Peruvian Heart—An Egyptian Connection; Are Mormons Christian? Jimmy Carter Responds; Critique of Anti-LDS Web Sites; The Great Apostasy; The Bible Is Inspired, but Is It Complete? Egyptian Hieratics and Reformed Egyptian; Samaipata: Pre-Incan Religious Fortress; Finding Evidence in Mesoamerica; King David; Minimalists and the Book of Mormon; Comparison Between a Hymn in the Dead Sea Scrolls and Nephi's Hymn; and much, much more. Somewhat difficult to read, but the content is very well done. ★★★★

Overview   www.mormons.org/overview_eom.htm An illustrated overview of the history, name, and organization of the Church. Top-quality information, well documented. 📖

Pencil/God Dilemma   members.visi.net/~atom/totally/Pncl_god.html A parable about the gospel. ★

Press Kit www.scsv.nevada.edu/~blake/presskit.html Rawlin Blake's brief introductory information about the Church of Jesus Christ of Latter-day Saints. See a similar site, Selections from the LDS Press Book, at www.jefflindsay.com/press.html. 📖

Questions About LDS Worship and Practices   www.jefflindsay.com/LDSFAQ/ FQ_practices.shtml Well-written responses to basic questions about LDS beliefs and practices. Includes information on fasting, the Word of Wisdom, genealogy, more. ★★★★

The Church of Jesus Christ of Latter-day Saints www.erols.com/jdstone/lds.html A brief overview, history, and list of beliefs and practices. ★★★

Unofficial Introduction to The Church of Jesus Christ of Latter-day Saints www.jefflindsay.com/LDS_Intro.shtml Answers to common questions about the Church. Are we Christians? Why do we call ourselves "Latter-day Saints"? Why the term "Mormons"? What is the Book of Mormon? Not bad stuff. ★★★

Gospel Principles

Theology, anyone? Set down that glue gun. It's time now to get some real doctrine. In this section, you'll find links to material that describes fundamental Mormon doctrine, the teachings and background that everyone needs to be able to teach a class of rowdy twelve-year-olds.

Chapter 7, "Perfect the Saints," page 123, moves into more advanced material. Here, though, are all the basics for new and prospective members wanting to understand fundamental Church doctrine:

Articles of Faith www.geocities.com/Athens/Styx/5581/Articles.html The 13 Articles of Latter-day Saint Belief, as given to the world by Joseph Smith. Pretty basic. ★★

Basic Beliefs www.mormons.org/basic Good collection of information on fundamental teachings of the Church (see figure 6.3). Contains the text of articles on Articles of Faith, The Purpose of Life, The Gospel of Jesus Christ, Teachings About Jesus Christ, The Book of Mormon, The Holy Bible, Teachings About the Godhead, Teachings About the Family, Teachings About Temples, Church Organization and Priesthood Authority, Teachings About the Afterlife, Teachings About Our Premortal Existence, and Doctrines of the Gospel. Good background material. ★★★★

HOTLINKS

Basic Beliefs
www.mormons.org/basic

Gospel Essentials
www.new-jerusalem.com/gospel/essentials.html

Gospel Principles
www.lds.org/en/3_Gospel_Principles/00_Contents.html

Questions About Baptism
www.jefflindsay.com/LDSFAQ/FQ_Baptism.shtml

The Plan of Salvation
www.geocities.com/Heartland/Ranch/2065/theplan.html

Word of Wisdom
www.jefflindsay.com/WWisdom.shtml

Does the Father Have a Tangible Body? members.visi.net/~atom/totally/Tng_body.html Edited extract from the site owner's book *One Lord, One Faith: Writings of the Early Christian Fathers As Evidences of the Restoration.* Heavy. ★★

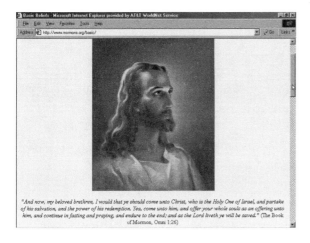

FIG. 6.3

Basic Beliefs: Yep, that about covers it.

Faith, Grace, and Works www.jefflindsay.com/faith_works.html An insightful theological discourse on the LDS view of the relationship between faith and works. Includes a link to a separate page listing key scriptures for study on this topic. ★★★

Falling Away and Restoration Foretold www.xmission.com/~health/mormon/apostasy.html Quotations, illustrations, explanations of the apostasy and restoration. ★★★★

Godhead www.danvillestake.org/s/danville/beliefs2.html Beliefs and teachings of general interest. Good links. ★★★

Gospel Essentials www.new-jerusalem.com/gospel/essentials.html New Jerusalem's explanation of the three-fold mission of the Church. ★★★

Gospel of Jesus Christ www.mormons.org/basic/gospel A collection of some 25 topics on basic gospel-centered themes. Includes articles on The Gospel of Jesus Christ, Joining the Church, The First Principles of the Gospel, The Plan of Salvation, The Plan of Our Heavenly Father (First Missionary Discussion), The Gospel of Jesus Christ (Second Missionary Discussion), The Restoration of the Gospel of Jesus Christ, Faith in Christ, Repentance, Baptism, Baptism of Fire and the Holy Ghost, Born of God, Conversion, Discipleship, Enduring to the End, Abrahamic Covenant, Gospel of Abraham, Latter-day Covenant Israel, Elect of God, Fall of Adam, Last Days, Dispensations of the Gospel, Fullness of the Gospel, and Missionary Work. ★★★★

Gospel Principles Course www.nettally.com/LDS/gospel.html A description of each element of the Sunday School course for new members. ★★★

Gospel Principles www.lds.org/library/gos_pri/gos_pri.html Text from the Gospel Principles study guide. It's not yet indexed, though, so it's less valuable than it could be. ★★

Immortality & Eternal Life of Man www.xmission.com/~pengar/allen/book.html A discussion of the basic principles of the Gospel. ★★★

Joseph Smith's Testimony www.lds.org/library/the_pro_jos/the_pro_jos.html Joseph Smith's Testimony from the official LDS Web site. ★★

Our Search for Happiness www.deseretbook.com/oursearch "Answers To Some Of The Most Important Questions Ever Asked" by Elder M. Russell Ballard. DeseretBook's answers to some of the most important questions ever asked. Responses to Who am I? Where did I come from? What is life all about? Does God have a plan for me? What is my relationship to Jesus Christ? Is there a purpose in what I am doing in my life? How can I find peace and happiness? In Spanish and English. Perfect place to refer investigators who want to know about LDS beliefs in Christ, how to find peace when bad things happen, and more. ★★★★

Premortal Existence www.shire.net/mormon/pre.html Accurate representation of the LDS belief in antemortality. Documented and readable. Quite brief. ★★★

Purpose of Life www.mormons.org/basic/purpose_life.htm Article on the Purpose of Life. ★★

Questions About Baptism www.jefflindsay.com/LDSFAQ/FQ_Baptism.shtml Baptism by Immersion by Authorized Ministers of God: Nice Idea or Essential Ordinance? The page describes why baptism is essential to salvation. ★★★

Teachings About Prayer www.mormons.org/daily/prayer A brief collection of articles on LDS beliefs about prayer. ★★

Teachings About the Afterlife www.mormons.org/basic/afterlife A large collection of articles related to LDS beliefs about the afterlife. Includes information on Death and Dying, The Afterlife, The Spirit World, Salvation for the Dead, Final Judgment, Judgment, Resurrection, Exaltation, The Church of the Firstborn, Degrees of Glory, Celestial Kingdom, Terrestrial Kingdom, Telestial Kingdom, Hell, Heaven, Spirit Prison, Eternal Progression, Everlasting Burnings, Book of Life, Buffetings of Satan, and Damnation. A Mormons.Org page. ★★★★★

Teachings About the Godhead www.mormons.org/basic/godhead Articles relating to LDS beliefs about the Godhead. Includes articles on God, The Godhead, God the Father, Jesus Christ the Son of God, The Holy Ghost, Condescension of God, Godhood, and Early Christian Deification. A Mormons.Org page. ★★★★

Teachings About the Premortal Existence www.mormons.org/basic/premortal Brief collection of articles on antemortality. A Mormons.Org page. ★★★

The Family: A Proclamation to the Church and the World www.lds.org/library/ pro_of_the_fam/pro_of_the_fam.html Text of the 1995 official proclamation from the First Presidency. 📖

The Mormon God and the Problem of Evil www.teleport.com/~arden/evilfaq.htm Mormonism's most important contribution to theology. ★★

The Plan of Our Father in Heaven www.new-jerusalem.com/plan/plan.html Excellent explanation of the plan of salvation. Illustrated, documented, thorough. An equally well-done page by another writer is available at www.xmission.com/ ~health/mormon/plan.html ★★★★

The Plan of Salvation www.geocities.com/Heartland/Ranch/2065/theplan.html Linked map of man's origin, purpose on earth, and destiny. A visual representation of Heavenly Father's Plan of Salvation. Beautifully done. ★★★★★

Word of Wisdom www.jefflindsay.com/WWisdom.shtml The LDS Code of Health. Text of the 1833 revelation to Joseph Smith forbidding the use of tobacco, alcohol, tea, and coffee, and providing nutritional guidelines with an emphasis on grains. A bit of commentary at the end. ★★★

Word of Wisdom www.nettally.com/LDS/WofW.html Origin and history with links to medical commentary. ★★★

The Role of the Book of Mormon

I admit with some chagrin that when I entered the Missionary Training Center, I still hadn't read the entire Book of Mormon. Many chapters, many sections, but I had never read it through cover to cover. The MTC cured that problem in short order.

One afternoon, while the elders were building strong bones and muscles in the MTC gym, my companion and I sat out on the front lawn reading scriptures. I

HOTLINKS

23 Questions Answered by The Book of Mormon
www.xmission.com/~health/mormon

How can the Book of Mormon help me be a better Christian?
www.deseretbook.com/oursearch/set4q1.html

The Book of Mormon: An Overview
www.mormons.org/basic/bom/overview

wasn't but a few verses into King Benjamin's address (Mosiah 2–5) when I suddenly realized that my mind was absolutely and completely clear, and that I was being given a perfect understanding of the material I was reading. That sensation continued throughout my reading that day. I was receiving inspiration and guidance from on high, and I knew it without any doubt. That sublime, inspired sensation filled me with awe, and let me know that the Book of Mormon was precisely what Joseph Smith claimed it to be. The experience has never been forgotten, and has only rarely been repeated.

In this section, you will find introductory material for the Book of Mormon, suitable for aiding the understanding of the first-time reader.

Sites containing the complete Book of Mormon text are found in chapter 7 on page 143. And responses to critics of the Book of Mormon, as well as additional study materials, are listed in chapter 12, "Pursuit of Excellence"—Personal Scripture Study, in the Book of Mormon section, page 280.

23 Questions Answered by The Book of Mormon www.xmission.com/~health/mormon Poses questions about theology and life, and lists Book of Mormon scriptural responses to those questions. Includes good links to pages on the apostasy, Christ in America, and an explanation of the Book of Mormon. ★★★★

Biblical References to the Book of Mormon www.xmission.com/~health/mormon/bomref.html A somewhat better list of references with brief commentary. ★★★

BOMSTDY www.geocities.com/Heartland/Ranch/9159/bomstudy.html An e-mail list devoted to helping members of the Church of Jesus Christ of Latter-day Saints and investigators study and learn the Book of Mormon. ★★

Brief Introduction to The Book of Mormon: Another Testament of Jesus Christ www.jefflindsay.com/BOMIntro.shtml Jeff Lindsay's very well-documented responses to basic questions about the Book of Mormon. Answers What is the Book of Mormon? What is its purpose? Who wrote it? Who was Mormon? How did we get it? How was it translated? Who else saw the gold plates? How does the Book of Mormon relate to the Bible? Does the Bible say anything about the Book of

Mormon—for or against? Who were the Book of Mormon people? What did the Book of Mormon people know of Christ? Why should I read the Book of Mormon? How can I know if it is true? Wait a minute—the Bible says there can be no more scripture! We've already got a Bible! and other objections to the Book of Mormon. Includes a link to Evidences for the Book of Mormon. ★★★★

How Can the Book of Mormon Help Me Be a Better Christian? www.deseretbook.com/oursearch/set4q1.html Elder M. Russell Ballard addresses some of the unique contributions of the Book of Mormon to the understanding of Christ and the gospel. Read or listen to Elder Ballard's address. ★★★★

My Favorite Scripture from the Book of Mormon www.nettally.com/LDS/favpray.html A discourse on poverty from Alma 32. ★★

Take the Book of Mormon Challenge www.erols.com/jdstone/Challeng.html I'm a professional. Don't try this at home. ★★★

The Book of Mormon: An Overview www.mormons.org/basic/bom/overview Chapter-by-chapter descriptions of the content of the Book of Mormon. A Mormons.Org page. ★★★★★

Items of Interest to Investigators and New Members

Here it is, the inevitable miscellaneous section, a list of basic information that doesn't quite belong anywhere else. You'll find here answers to questions, information lists, and a few other items worth a look.

1 Minute Guide to the Church www.geocities.com/Athens/Olympus/5234/1minute.htm A collection of lists for readers who are completely new to the Bible, Jesus Christ, the Church, or the Book of Mormon. Quick and simple, for complete beginners. Refer all questioners to this site. ★★★★★ ☑

All About Mormons www.mormons.org John Walsh's very large site containing texts on virtually anything anyone has ever wanted to know about Mormonism (see figure 6.4). It's, ahem, encyclopedic in its

HOTLINKS

1 Minute Guide to the Church
www.geocities.com/Athens/Olympus/5234/1minute.htm

All About Mormons
www.mormons.org

Ask The Elder
www.webb.net/sites/Ask-The-Elder

Answers to Frequently Asked Questions
www.mormons.org/faq

Quest For Truth
www.geocities.com/Athens/Parthenon/2848

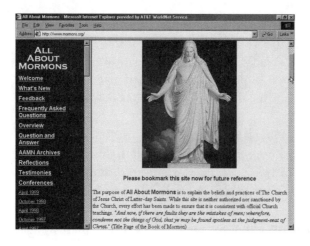

FIG. 6.4

All About Mormons! The name doesn't mislead.

coverage. In fact, it makes extensive use of the *Encyclopedia of Mormonism* and a few other classic Mormon texts. Good information. I'd be happy to see it stay around. ★★★★★ ☑

Answers to Frequently Asked Questions www.mormons.org/faq From All About Mormons. What does LDS stand for? Are Mormons Christian? Do Mormons Believe in the Bible? Who Was Joseph Smith? and other questions about distinctive LDS theology, the restoration, plural marriage, the role of women, LDS holidays, crosses, and more. Very thorough responses. A good reference for nonmembers who express curiosity. ★★★★

Ask The Elder www.webb.net/sites/Ask-The-Elder Questions About Our History And Doctrine. Answers about the doctrines, practices, and beliefs of the Church of Jesus Christ of Latter-day Saints. Very kindly responses to tough questions. ★★★★★

Biblical Evidences for LDS Beliefs www.vt.edu:10021/B/bbickmor/Evidences.html Author Barry Bickmore asks: "Do the '17 Points of the True Church' make you want to hurl? Same here. Anyway, with the help of a couple other people I made up this list which is hopefully not as pathetically infantile as the other one. (Can you tell I don't like the '17 Points'?) We tried to use only references that support LDS positions fairly solidly." It IS a better list. ★★★

Daily Living www.mormons.org/daily How Latter-day Saints apply Gospel principles in their everyday lives. ★★★★★

Evidences of the True Church www.nettally.com/LDS/evidence.html Contains the old legend about a group of nonmembers compiling the list of 17 points. If someone ever substantiates that story, I'll eat the list. ★★

Evidences of the True Church www.nettally.com/LDS/43.html Forty-three of 'em! I distrust these "True Church" lists for the same reason I distrust people who try to appropriate the word "Christian" exclusively for themselves. If I can create a list to define myself as the "True" Church, other people can just as easily create their own opposing lists using their own definitions. The *only* valid evidence of truth, as far as I'm concerned, is the witness of the Spirit. That being said, this list is the most thorough I've seen. Very well documented. ★★

Evidences of the True Church ourworld.compuserve.com/homepages/MGriffith_2/points.htm This time, it's just 41 Points of the True Church. List compiled by Michael T. Griffith. ★★

Frequently Asked Questions about Latter-day Saint Beliefs www.jefflindsay.com/LDSFAQ/FQ_index.shtml Jeff Lindsay's common questions and answers about LDS beliefs and practices. Contains links to entire pages that respond to: Are Latter-day Saints a Cult? Are Latter-day Saints Christians? Did Joseph Smith Make Any Accurate Prophecies? Is Baptism Essential? Are We Christians? Why Do We Call Ourselves "Latter-day Saints"? Why the Term "Mormons"? What Is the Book of Mormon? Also, Questions About the Restoration (and the Apostasy), Joseph Smith and Modern Prophets, Joseph's First Vision Accounts, Baptism for the Dead, Testimony and Knowledge, the Divine Potential of Man, Relationships Between God and Man, Salvation and Exaltation, Science Fiction, Race, LDS Temples, LDS Worship and Practices, the Book of Mormon, and the Book of

---

ON RESPONDING TO CRITICS

A year ago, I got the shock of my life when I received a letter from a person who claimed to be an ex-Mormon and pestered several of us in the WW-LDS list. The first letter I got was kind of [odd] and I thought it was a sacrilege to what we hold sacred. I even wrote a complaint to the list-owner about not screening such posts, not realizing that there were people who would find pleasure doing such an evil thing, and not just leave the Church quietly when they became disaffected. The message was a parody of a popular song of long time ago about our temple activity. I was kind of shocked and I felt angry that a thing that I had come to consider as very sacred was being desecrated. [This behavior is not practiced in Japan.] What I did was I tried to get to the people who were leading the group and report that one of their members was being obnoxious. I made threat also to report the matter to the police, even the Interpol, as I live in Japan and the person was in the USA. Then all of us in the list that were bothered by the ex-Mormon wrote to the ISP provider and complained. The ISP provider apparently made the investigation, even warning an ex-Mormon group to stop such activity. Also, the "culprit" did the same sort of spamming with members of the ex-Mormon list and was asked to stop. If you encounter such spam, you should do the same thing as we did to stop the spammer, and if you are sure that the person sending you such mail is an ex-Mormon and a member of the ex-Mormon group, you may send your complaint to their ISP. And most of all, fast about it. In fact, I asked for a brother to give me a blessing to protect me from such person, and I fasted and prayed that I would not be bothered by that person again.

Yuko Takei, Tokyo, Japan
<ystakei@gol.com>

Abraham. An excellent site. Many of these pages show up individually throughout this text. ★★★★★

Got Questions? List of questions and answers: members.aol.com/cumorahhil/qa.htm Question submission form: members.aol.com/cumorahhil/got_questions.htm A brief listing of questions from visitors to the Cumorah's Hill Web site. A submission form lets visitors ask more questions about the Church. It's tremendously short, but the potential is there for growth. ★★

Have You Ever Wondered? members.tripod.com/Aarius/eternity.html Responses to questions such as Where Did I Come From? What Is My Purpose on Earth? Where Do I Go When I Die? Why Are There So Many Churches, Yet One God? A bit cumbersome. ★★

MormonForum www.homestead.com/mormons A fine place for asking questions about the Church, doctrine, policies, or history. Anonymous questions are allowed on the bulletin-board style page. ★★★★

Mormons-reactivated www.egroups.com/list/mormons-reactivated A Latter-day Saint oriented E-group, for those who feel a little lost on the pathway back. Help others by sharing your own experiences. Much needed. ★★★★★

My LDS Page millennium.fortunecity.com/lavender/655 Answers to questions about the Church. Post questions via e-mail or to the message board. Hard to read, but the idea's a good one. ★★★

New Member Discussions www.nettally.com/LDS/lesson.html The seven discussions for new members, along with commentary from a relatively new convert to the Church. ★★★

Quest For Truth www.geocities.com/Athens/Parthenon/2848 An interesting attempt to prove logically that the Church and the gospel are the source of truth. ★★★

Questions about LDS Worship and Practices www.jefflindsay.com/FQ_practices.shtml Answers to questions about the Cross, fasting, the Word of Wisdom, welfare, the sacrament, ordination of deacons, and more. ★★★

Seventeen Points of the True Church tdholder.com/seminary/17points.htm Presented by Tim and Dolores Holder. Part of the Seminary Files site. ★★

RESPONSES TO CRITICISM

I lived in Taiwan at the time of the open house and dedication of the temple there. Throughout those events, the members were disturbed by the presence of a handful of vocal protesters who did their disruptive best to interrupt the proceedings. At one point, I spent a bit of time talking with a couple of them. After I accepted their literature, the two became quite forthcoming about their presence. Both admitted they were absolutely unfamiliar with the Church, not even knowing, in fact, which church it was they were objecting to. They said they'd actually been through a quick indoctrination session prior to arriving in Taiwan, where they'd been assured that the Church was a cesspool of iniquity, and that they'd be doing a fine service to raise a ruckus. Their real incentive, they told me, was a free vacation to Asia.

The problem with responding to critics is that it's an unwinnable task. Even if it were possible to win all the big battles, there'd always be a critic arguing that the Book of Mormon is an obvious fraud because the name Sam is too short, and the name Coriantumr is missing a vowel. Respond to these fights, and within moments you find yourself swatting at gnats instead of sharing the gospel. Nevertheless, failing to respond implies inability to respond. So the Natural Man rises to the fore and takes on all comers.

Reponses to critics range from the scholarly and thoughtful to the reactionary and insupportable. Because many of the page authors arrange their responses as a sort of "to do" list, these pages sometimes raise more questions than they answer.

The responses listed in this section are general in nature, and apply to the whole range of LDS doctrine, history, and policy. Specific responses to critics of the Book of Mormon are listed in chapter 12, "Pursuit of Excellence," in the Personal Scripture Study section, page 285.

Accusatory Questions   www.mormons.org/response/qa Responses to 45 questions raised regularly by critics. A Mormons.Org page. ★★★★

HOTLINKS

Barry's Early Christianity and Mormonism Page
www.vt.edu:10021/B/bbickmor/EC.html/

Book of Mormon Answerman
www.new-jerusalem.com/bom-answerman

Christian and Jewish Leaders Condemn Anti-Mormonism
www.teleport.com/~arden/nccj.htm

FAIR
www.fair-lds.org

FARMS
www.farmsresearch.com

Mormonism Researched
www.cyberhighway.net/~shirtail/mormonis.htm

Response to Criticism
www.mormons.org/response

SHIELDS
www.shields-research.org

STUMPUS
www.new-jerusalem.com/stumpus

Anti-Mormon Witnessing Techniques   www.mormons.org/response/general/walsh_tactics.htm Caveat prayer. ★★★

Archive   www.homestead.com/thearchive A collection of research on The Book of Mormon, early Christianity, the Book of Abraham, Hugh Nibley and his works, answers to criticism, and the Doctrine Library. ★★★★

Are Latter-day Saints a Cult?   www.jefflindsay.com/LDSFAQ/FQ_cult.shtml Detailed discussion on many popular topics used to condemn the Church as a cult. ★★★

Are Latter-day Saints Christians?   www.jefflindsay.com/LDSFAQ/FQ_Christian.shtml Another good Jeff Lindsay page. ★★★

Are Mormons Christians?   199.227.118.92/response/general/christians Dr. Stephen E. Robinson discusses the specious arguments used to exclude Latter-day Saints from the Christian community. Thoroughly reasoned. ★★★

Baptism for the Dead FAQ   www.jefflindsay.com/LDSFAQ/FQ_BaptDead.shtml Very lengthy treatment of the historicity of vicarious baptism. ★★★

Barry's Early Christianity and Mormonism Page   www.vt.edu:10021/B/bbickmor/EC.html Barry Bickmore has put together an amazing collection of quotes and documents on the relationship between LDS and early Christian doctrines. ★★★★★ ☑

Bible Code and Biblical Inerrancy   www.fair-lds.org/Research/Scripture/Bible/bib01002.html By FARMS' John A. Tvedtnes. Interesting. ★★

Book of Mormon Answerman   www.new-jerusalem.com/bom-answerman Intelligent responses to questions about the Book of Mormon. The submission form at this site allows you to ask questions of your own. The Book of Mormon Answerman has responded to some 1,000 questions. The Book of Mormon Answerman is a fun read; what it lacks in authority, it makes up for in enthusiasm. Unfortunately, it now is littered with references to the John Birch society, making it an unlikely missionary tool. ★★★★★

Changes in Early Texts of the Book of Mormon   www.flash.net/~mdparker/BofMChanges.htm An Ensign article concerning this worn-out claim by those that oppose the Church. Read Jeff Lindsay's approach to the same topic, Changes in the Book of Mormon, at www.jefflindsay.com/LDSFAQ/FQ_changes.shtml. ★★★

Chattanooga Cheapshot, or The Gall of Bitterness www.farmsresearch.com/frob/ frobv5/dcp.htm Review of the anti-Mormon tract "Everything You Ever Wanted to Know About Mormonism." Edges over to cynical, but probably not without cause. 📖

Christian and Jewish Leaders Condemn Anti-Mormonism www.teleport.com/~arden/ nccj.htm Christian and Jewish leaders speak out against the religious bigotry directed at Latter-day Saints. ★★★

Church History Criticism www.mormons.org/response/history Intelligent responses to issues raised by critics of the Church and its history. Responds to *Mormonism— Shadow or Reality,* and incendiary claims related to divine Adam, the occult, freemasonry, blood sacrifice, prophecies, Danites, and Mountain Meadows. ★★★★

Clean Thoughts on a Dirty Wall: Essays on the Restoration www.geocities.com/ Athens/Styx/5581/Essays.html Articles, essays, and short stories dealing with the Restoration of the Gospel of Jesus Christ. Includes very intelligent responses to critics of the Church. ★★★★★

Constancy amid Change www.farmsresearch.com/frob/frobv8_2/dcp.htm FARMS Editor Daniel C. Peterson is nothing if not enthusiastic. He's the Captain Moroni of respondents to critics of the Church, and this review of Ankerberg and Weldon's *Behind the Mask of Mormonism* is in keeping with his generally combative approach. If you disagree with his point of view, you'll find him obnoxious. People who agree will consider him, well, delightful. 📖

DCP's Gospel Research InfoNet www.linkline.com/personal/dcpyle/gri Very strongly worded material, and not yet a lot of it. This site is largely under construction. Addresses specific tracts from critics of the Church. ★★

Defending The Faith—LDS Apologetics Conference shields-research.org/DTFC A meeting for defenders of Mormonism. 📖

FAIR www.fair-lds.org The Foundation for Apologetic Information and Research. FAIR is a nonprofit, apologetic organization formed in late 1997 by a group of LDS defenders of the faith who frequented the America Online Mormonism message boards. The group is dedicated to providing solid, well-documented answers to critics of LDS doctrine, faith, and practice. The "About Us" section at www.fair-lds.org/AboutUs/AboutUs.html alone is worth memorializing. ★★★★★ ☑

Faith, Grace and Works www.vt.edu:10021/B/bbickmor/ECFGW.html Barry Bickmore's commentary from his Early Christianity pages. Considers issues such as whether all are sinners, whether only the grace of Jesus Christ can save, faith in Jesus Christ, whether true faith produces good works, and eternal security. ★★★

FAQ Alt.Religion.Mormon www.cc.utah.edu/~nahaj Disturbed by the misinformation he saw being promulgated on the newsgroup alt.religion.mormon, participant John Halleck—who was not a member of the Church—put together a FAQ (frequently asked questions) document to respond to the accusations. Very accurate presentation of material. Interesting footnote: John has since joined the church. ★★★★

FARMS Criticism Papers www.farmsresearch.com/critic/reviews.htm Book reviews—or more precisely, responses to critical publications. I get a letter every couple of days from Internet users who are either investigating the Church, or bent on saving my soul from evangelical hell. In both cases, these letter writers are posing questions derived from anti-Mormon tracts. What a relief it is to have the Foundation for Ancient Research and Mormon Studies standing out there, waving its arms, so that I can direct my correspondents to a safe landing. If FARMS wrote nothing more than what it posts on this page, it would be a worthwhile institution. Each of the current items is reviewed in this text. Check back for new additions from time to time. FARMS' front page is a top-25 site, largely because of this page. ★★★★★ ☑

Frequently Asked Questions About LDS Beliefs www.jefflindsay.com/LDSFAQ/ FQ_index.shtml By Jeff Lindsay. A lot of thought went into these pages. Politely and thoroughly covers questions that repeatedly arise from readers of cult classics such as *The GodMakers*. Covers the perennial favorites: Are Mormons Christian? Was Joseph a Fallen Prophet? (and related allegations), Why Baptism for the Dead? Do Mormons Really Think They Will Become Gods? Was Satan a Brother to Christ? Do Mormons Worship Adam? and Are LDS Temples Derived from Masonry? Also covers Book of Mormon questions, questions on the role of Christ in the Church, the Book of Abraham, and faith vs. works. Not to be missed. ★★★★★

Fulfilled Prophecies of Joseph Smith www.jefflindsay.com/LDSFAQ/FQ_prophecies.shtml Describes prophecies made by Joseph Smith and their fulfillment. Several examples covering a variety of topics. Ultimately, it's proof of nothing, but if the question even arises, here it is. ★★

General Criticism www.mormons.org/response/general Articles addressing Anti-Mormon Publications, Are Mormons Christians? Are Prophets Infallible? Dealing with

Difficult Questions, Anti-Mormon Tactics, Apostates, Blacks and the Priesthood, *The GodMakers*; A Better House, the RLDS Church, and Mormon Fundamentalists. A Mormons.Org page. ★★★

Hearsay and Gossip www.mormons.org/response/general/hearsay.htm Responding to silly stuff. ★★

I was wondering . . . www.osmond.net/donny/beliefs/faith.htm#quest14 Brother Osmond responds, beautifully, to someone who asks, "I am a part of a 'recovery from Mormonism' group. I . . . was wondering what your thoughts are about those who leave the Church." Part of "Donny's Beliefs Page," www.osmond.net/donny/beliefs, a substantial body of answers to questions about the Church. ★★★★★

Ignoratio Elenchi www.farmsresearch.com/frob/frobv5/norwood.htm The Dialogue That Never Was. A review of White's *Letters to a Mormon Elder,* by L. Ara Norwood, who says, "Crafting only his own letters, he controls the content and thereby easily escapes the cross-examinations which would surely be forthcoming from a true dialogue." 📖

Joseph's First Vision Accounts www.jefflindsay.com/LDSFAQ/FQ_first_vision.shtml Responses to questions about varying accounts of the First Vision. Responds to inquiries about timing, contradictions, historical errors, and multiple accounts. ★★★

Kevin Graham's LDS Q&A Site www.angelfire.com/ga/kevgram Kevin Graham, a former Baptist, attempts to reply to anti-Mormon questions. And does a mighty fine job of it. Responds to all the standard accusations apparently making the evangelical rounds this year. These answers would have saved me hours of responding over the past 12 months. ★★★★★

LDS Teachings on the Divine Potential of Human Beings www.jefflindsay.com/LDSFAQ/FQ_theosis.shtml Discussion of the ancient Christian concept of "theosis" and its presence in LDS theology. Author Jeff Lindsay answers questions about whether Mormons think they will become gods, whether LDS doctrine teaches that there are multiple gods, the LDS doctrine of deification, early Christian beliefs about the divine potential of humans, and whether LDS people believe God was once a man. ★★★

Mormon Fortress www.xmission.com/~mash Previously listed in Mormons on the Internet as MASH—Criticism Studies. Author Mike Ash responds to attacks on the doctrines/beliefs/prophets of the LDS Church. New and improved. More articles, along with links to related sites, but altogether too many graphics. It's a very slow load. ★★★

Mormon Mom's Apologetics Pages www.geocities.com/Heartland/Oaks/9401/critics/replydir.htm A handful of well-considered responses to critics. ★★★

Mormonism Researched www.cyberhighway.net/~shirtail/mormonis.htm Kerry Shirts' apologetics site. It ain't pretty, but it's smart. ★★★★★ ☑

Mormons and Militias? www.jefflindsay.com/militias.shtml Jeff Lindsay's response to misinformation linking the Church to militia groups. ★★★

Mormons and Other Christians FAQ www.netins.net/showcase/gershom/mocfaq.html How the Saints are Christian; how they differ from other Christian faiths. A good response to the question of LDS Christianity. ★★★

National Conference of Christians and Jews www.mormons.org/response/general/godmakers/Independent_Reviews.htm Review of that abysmal *GodMakers* film. ★★★★

No Man Shall Add to or Take Away members.aol.com/ssh81675/ldsrefer/documents/hunter.htm Text of a discussion by Howard W. Hunter (president of the Church) on the assertion that the Bible says there will be no additional scripture. Lawyerly. 📖

Prophets in Latter-day Saint Religion www.jefflindsay.com/LDSFAQ/FQ_prophets.shtml Answers to common questions about prophets and about Joseph Smith in particular. Responds to questions about what prophets are, the "heresy" of modern prophets, infallibility, imperfections, the role of the prophet, continuing revelation and changes, the character of Joseph Smith, document forgeries, and others. Very well done. ★★★

Relationship Between Brace, Works, and Eternal Life www.jefflindsay.com/faith_works.html Author Jeff Lindsay discusses the relationship between faith, works and salvation. Are Biblical and LDS views compatible? A related List of key scriptures on faith and works is found at www.jefflindsay.com/faith_works_list.html, categorized by subject, in case anyone ever asks. ★★★

Pulling the Lies from the Anti-Mormons millennium.fortunecity.com/bertisevil/375/braithwt.htm Two people talking back and forth. A discussion with John Braithwaite, proprietor of "The Ministry for the True Jesus." S'awrite. ★★

Q&A: Are Anti-Mormons "Christians"? www.fair-lds.org/Pubs/Apologia/July/ page4.html By Russell McGregor. A well-considered discussion. ★★★

Quest for Eternity www.shire.net/mormon/book.html Author Allen Leigh spent several years in online discussions with nonmembers of the Church. In response to the questions of critics, Brother Leigh conducted a great deal of research. Many of his responses to those critics have been compiled into an electronic document that explains the basic teachings of the Church and answers many of the criticisms of Mormonism. Commentary is fairly well documented, and thoroughly scriptural, without being argumentative. ★★★★

Questions About LDS Views on Salvation and Exaltation www.jefflindsay.com/LDSFAQ/FQ_Salvation.shtml Responses to questions about grace and works, the status of nonmembers, and the potential for godhood. ★★

Questions About Relationships Between God and Man www.jefflindsay.com/LDSFAQ/ FQ_Relationships.shtml Jeff Lindsay responds to questioners who ask if Jesus is our elder brother, whether we believe that Christ and Satan are brothers, whether God was once a man who had a heavenly father, whether God the Father and Christ are different beings, and whether Christ "progressed" and Mormons believe they can become like God. Answers questions about polytheism, whether Joseph Smith ever said that he was greater than Jesus, an anthropomorphic God, worshipping Adam, and denying the miraculous birth of Christ. ★★★★

Questions About the Book of Abraham www.jefflindsay.com/LDSFAQ/FQ_Abraham. shtml and part 2 at www.jefflindsay.com/LDSFAQ/FQ_Abraham2.shtml An LDS FAQ from Jeff Lindsay. Very extensive response to questions about the Book of Abraham, its source, its content, and the Prophet's comments about the facsimiles. Massive. Covers a multitude of questions. ★★★★★

Response to Criticism www.mormons.org/response A discussion about criticism and links to pages of response to critics of the Church and its doctrine. Includes responses to accusatory questions, general criticism, Book of Mormon criticism, Church history criticism, and Book of Abraham criticism. Very thorough. ★★★★★

Response to the Mormon Critics   www.digitalpla.net/~russ/response.htm   Russell Anderson's very well done responses to polemical attacks on the Church (see figure 6.5). He writes: "This site is not provided to answer the critics. They don't believe there is an answer. This information is for those who have faith in the Gospel of Jesus Christ but don't know how to answer some of the critic's questions." The site includes responses to Decker's insufferable *GodMakers*, as well as his *To Moroni with Love* and *Complete Handbook on Mormonism*, the Tanners' *Mormonism: Shadow or Reality*, Martin's *Maze of Mormonism*, Brodie's *No Man Knows My History*, Marquart and Walters' *Inventing Mormonism*, and Bodine's CRI Paper "Book of Mormon vs. the Bible (or Common Sense)." It also includes a comparison of early Christianity and Mormonism, and addresses frequently repeated allegations regarding Joseph Smith, the First Vision, the Book of Mormon, the Book of Abraham, Changes to Scriptures or History, Temples, and Brigham Young. The Internet is a better place for this site. ★★★★★

Review: Ask Your Mormon Friend   www.farmsresearch.com/frob/frobv7_1/lij.htm   LeIsle Jacobson reviews McKeever Johnson's *Questions to Ask Your Mormon Friend: Effective Ways to Challenge a Mormon's Arguments Without Being Offensive*. Is it any surprise that the reviewer finds the text both ineffective *and* offensive? 📖

Sci-Fi Connection in LDS Theology   www.jefflindsay.com/LDSFAQ/FQ_SciFi.shtml   Good responses to a couple of actual questions relating science fiction and Church doctrine. Ooo-oooo. ★★

SHIELDS   www.shields-research.org   Scholarly and Historical Information Exchange for Latter-day Saints. Responses to issues raised by critics of the Church. I had

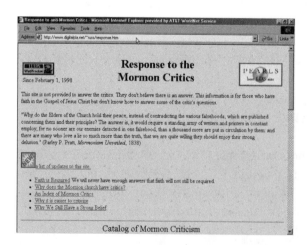

FIG. 6.5

Response to the Mormon Critics: Help for the faithful.

much hope for this site, but there's just not enough content yet to make it worth-while. The gem here is in a buried page responding to an organization called CARM www.shields-research.org/CARM.htm. For those responses alone, this page gets a rating of ★★★★

Students of the Gospel   millennium.fortunecity.com/bertisevil/375/scholars.htm Brother Barker is a lifelong member and 30+ year defender of the church. How-ever, he has not been trained for the ministry. A listing of significant gospel apol-ogists from scholars and professors to independent Web proprietors. A bit of chestpounding goes a long way. ★★

STUMPUS   www.new-jerusalem.com/stumpus Questions answered by the New Jerusalem team. Are they stumped yet? ★★★★★

Stumpus Team of Missionaries   www.new-jerusalem.com/stumpus/questions.html Take the challenge. ★★★★

The Chapman LDS Resource   www.2s2.com/chapmanresearch/side1.html A collection of thirty-some research papers responding to questions raised by critics, as well as other topics from all over the map. Some of the documents are excellent. ★★

The Gainsayers   199.227.118.92/response/general/gainsayers Darrick T. Evenson was converted, then apostatized, and became affiliated with the anti-Mormon group Ex-Mormons for Jesus. This page documents his eventual return to the fold of Christ. In it, he describes the techniques used by dishonest critics to dis-credit the Church. 📖

They Lie in Wait to Deceive   shields-research.org/Brown Well-documented series by Robert and Rosemary Brown that exposes deception of critics of the Church. ★★★★

What Certain Baptists Think They Know About the Restored Gospel   farmsresearch. com/frob/frobv10_1/dcp.htm A thoughtful review by Daniel C. Peterson. ★★

Triptych   www.farmsresearch.com/frob/frobv8_1/intro.htm See more of Peterson's Editor's Introductions on related themes: Daniel C. Peterson's 1996 Editor's Introduction wherein he describes the anti-Mormon technique of creating, then destroying, straw man arguments. Now there's more here than last time it was reviewed, but FARMS *still* needs to build a front page listing all these docu-ments: An Embarras de Richesses www.farmsresearch.com/frob/frobv3/intro.htm, By

What Measure Shall We Mete? www.farmsresearch.com/frob/frobv2/intro.htm, Doubting the Doubters www.farmsresearch.com/frob/frobv8_2/intro.htm, History of the Signature/FARMS Conflict www.farmsresearch.com/frob/frobv6_1/intro.htm, Human Fallibility www.farmsresearch.com/frob/frobv7_2/intro.htm, Of Implications www.farmsresearch.com/frob/frobv7_1/intro.htm, Of Paying Attention to the Book of Mormon www.farmsresearch.com/frob/frobv1/intro.htm, Of Polemics www.farmsresearch.com/frob/frobv6_2/intro.htm, Questions to Legal Answers www.farmsresearch.com/frob/frobv4/intro.htm, Traditions of the Fathers www.farmsresearch.com/frob/frobv9_1/intro.htm. A word of advice to FARMS, and any other Webmaster needing a free, GOOD search tool for their Web sites: picosearch.com. 📖

HOTLINKS

LDSMissions.com
www.ldsmissions.com

LDSMissions.net
www.ldsmissions.net

LDSMissions.org
multiplexer.ldsmissions.org

Mission Funnies
www.ysite.com/mission/funnies.htm

Mission.Net
www.mission.net

Six Discussions
www.nettally.com/LDS/diss.html

MISSIONARY PAGES

My high school class reunion took place recently. What is it, I wonder, that compels people to reunite with faintly remembered faces they've not seen for more than half a lifetime?

Part of it was curiosity. So many years spent so far from "home" meant that I'd missed seeing what my former classmates had done with their lives. Some of us have kept in touch via e-mail, but we hadn't really spent any time together. What, I wondered, do the people who grew up around me look like, work like, live like after twenty years?

Another part was a sociology experiment. I want to know how many high school romances turned into long-term marriages. Did popularity serve the cheerleaders well in real life? Did the athletes grow up healthier than the chess players? Did the science clubbers end up wealthier than the rod-and-gun clubbers?

For me, though, the biggest motivation may have been my need to be the missionary I never was in high school. I grew up in the wilds of the "mission field," not among nonbelievers, but among people who believed differently, and much more publicly, than I did. It was a place where my loudly religious classmates reminded me of nothing so much as the exuberant 1820s revivalists portrayed in *The First Vision*. The Prophet's young confusion there was in proportion to my own teenage awkwardness in the face of my vehemently non-LDS classmates. Their evangelical zeal, their oft-proffered "Praise the Lord" buttons, and their invitations to youth rallies and prayer meetings came to me at every turn.

At one point in my junior year, as I sat in study hall memorizing verses for an upcoming seminary class, an otherwise good friend noticed my reading and began plying me with evangelical tracts she'd collected from her minister. I protested to her their exclusionary definition of "Christian," written not to include all who worship Christ, but to exclude all who come to Him as Latter-day Saints do. I described to her the vast gulf between what the pamphlets proclaimed about LDS belief and what Mormons really believe. My arguments served only to create divisiveness—as arguments always do—so I quietly withdrew from the debate.

Hers was one of several offensives being made on Latter-day Saints by members of our community at the time. Being then relatively unacquainted with theology and religious history and various points of doctrine, I became rather reticent about publicizing my own religious beliefs. I wish I could say that I finally took courage, stood up in a school assembly, and proclaimed my faith. I have to admit, though, that when I graduated, there were probably no more than a dozen people in my entire school who knew I was a Latter-day Saint.

I take no pride in this past, especially when I compare my behavior to the courage shown by another teenager, Priscilla Mogridge Staines,[1] who joined the Church in England in the 1840s—coincidentally at about the same time and place as my earliest LDS ancestors joined the Church. Priscilla had become dissatisfied with the Anglicanism she'd been raised with, and prayed earnestly to be shown "the true religion." At the age of nineteen, she heard the restored gospel preached and was converted. Over the objections of her family, she resolved to be baptized. She said of that experience:

> It is proper to here state that baptism was a trial to the converts in England in those days. They had to steal away, even unknown to their friends oftentimes, and scarcely daring to tell the saints themselves that they were about to take up the cross; and not until the ordinance had been administered, and the Holy Ghost gave them boldness, could they bring themselves to proclaim openly that they had cast in their lot with the despised Mormons. Nor was this all, for generally the elders had to administer baptism when the village was wrapt in sleep, lest persecutors should gather a mob to disturb the solemn scene with gibes or curses, accompanied

[1]The Priscilla Mogridge Staines story appeared in 1877 in Edward Tullidge's book *The Women of Mormondom*, reprinted by Truth in the 1970s. Both editions are difficult to find. To obtain a copy, call Benchmark Books (800-486-3112) or Sam Wellers Zion Bookstore (800-333-7269), and ask to be put on the waiting list. Sam Wellers can be contacted via e-mail at <*wellers@xmission.com*>. Readers with an interest in old LDS books will want to participate in the LDS-Bookshelf mailing list. (See chapter 12 for more on LDS-Bookshelf.)

AN ONLINE BAPTISM

One of my first electronic missionary experiences involved Beth.

Beth was one of the members of the Hatrack River area on America Online. Her screen name was "Dorcas Bee." One night, when we were both online together, I asked Beth if her screen name referred to Dorcas in the Bible. This led to a religious discussion, where Beth told me she was quite interested in finding out what Mormons believed. I told her I would be glad to answer any questions or let her know more about my religion.

After that, Beth and I exchanged electronic mail on a regular basis.

One day, I asked if Beth would be interested in reading the Book of Mormon. After receiving an affirmative reply, I mailed a copy to her and waited for her reaction.

I did not receive any e-mail from Beth for over a week after she received the book. Needless to say, this was a cause for concern. I wondered if she was offended by something she had read, or if her minister had persuaded her not to read it. There is always a risk in sharing the gospel with others. I hoped that Beth hadn't decided to break off our electronic friendship.

When Beth finally renewed our discussion, she sent good news. She had been staying away from the computer because she had been reading the Book of Mormon. After the excitement of our discussions, she had been worried that she would find something in the book too strange to accept. Yet she had found no such doctrine.

About this time, my husband became involved in the correspondence with Beth, and we both exchanged e-mail with her on a regular basis to answer her questions and encourage her gospel study. We suggested that

---

with stones or clods of earth torn from the river bank and hurled at the disciple and minister during the performance of the ceremony.

On the evening of a bitterly cold day in mid-winter, as before stated, I walked four miles to the house of a local elder for baptism. Arriving at his house, we waited until midnight, in order that the neighbors might not disturb us, and then repaired to a stream of water a quarter of a mile away. Here we found the water, as we anticipated, frozen over, and the elder had to chop a hole in the ice large enough for the purpose of baptism. It was a scene and an occasion I shall never forget. Memory today brings back the emotions and sweet awe of that moment. None but God and his angels, and the few witnesses who stood on the bank with us, heard my covenant; but in the solemnity of that midnight hour it seemed as though all nature were listening, and the recording angel writing our words in the book of the Lord. Is it strange that such a scene, occurring in the life of a Latter-day Saint, should make an everlasting impression, as this did on mine?

Having been thus baptized, I returned to the house in my wet and freezing garments.[2]

---

[2]The above excerpt from *The Women of Mormondom* was distributed by David Kenison via LDS-Gems mailing list. LDS-Gems distributes stories from LDS Church history to subscribers by e-mail. Subscriptions are free. You'll find subscription information at www.lds-gems.com.

it was time for her to search out her local ward and attend services there. She looked in the phone book, called the bishop of her ward in Grand Rapids, Michigan, and obtained the meeting times and directions to the chapel.

It is an unsettling experience to send someone off on her own to attend her first LDS service. Would she have a good experience? Would she be ignored or welcomed? Would she enjoy the meetings? We glued ourselves to our computers on that first Sunday, waiting for any word from Beth. Fortunately, the Saints in Grand Rapids came through with flying colors. Beth was immediately met by the full-time missionaries, as well as several members of the ward who were serving as greeters that day. One greeter had formerly attended the same church as Beth was then attending, and he took Beth under his wing.

Just a few months after our chance meeting in an electronic chat room, Beth took the missionary lessons and accepted the challenge to be baptized. She wrote us a lovely e-mail that same evening, and I think we felt the spirit of the experience through her words. My husband and I found it ironic that we shared great joy with a good friend that day—yet we had never seen her face, had never heard her voice, and had never been in the same room with her.

After Beth's baptism, we continued our communication and friendship. Her husband Jeff fully supported Beth's decision to be baptized, and finally became a member of the Church in April of 1996.

Kathryn H. Kidd
<custodian@nauvoo.com>
Moderator, Nauvoo www.nauvoo.com
as told to Clark L. Kidd, Algonkian Ward, Warrenton, Virginia Stake

Priscilla's family was unhappy over her decision to be baptized, and she was forced to leave them. She prepared to "gather to Zion," leaving England on December 27, 1843. She recorded:

I was alone. It was a dreary winter day on which I went to Liverpool. The company with which I was to sail were all strangers to me. When I arrived at Liverpool and saw the ocean that would soon roll between me and all I loved, my heart almost failed me. But I had laid my idols all upon the altar. There was no turning back. I remembered the words of the Saviour: "He that leaveth not father and mother, brother and sister, for my sake, is not worthy of me," and I believed his promise to those who forsook all for his sake; so I thus alone set out for the reward of everlasting life, trusting in God.

Priscilla married William C. Staines and emigrated to Utah. I, on the other hand, spent a short time at a local college, then packed my bags and went away to BYU, and from there to many other places. And through all the years I've wondered if I'd been a stronger, more courageous Latter-day Saint in high school—if I'd had the courage of my ancestors, and of people like Priscilla Mogridge Staines—would I have given others the strength to listen to the missionaries when they came, to hear the messages of the gospel, and to find the same joy in serving the Lord that I've had?

Perhaps nothing would have changed. Perhaps I even did the right thing by refusing to enter the fray. But I'll always wonder. And that's why my class reunion was spent finding out not how people changed after our little high school community disbanded, but how they chose to live.

For readers who originally read this tale when it was still in the future tense, here's what I learned. As it turns out, most people were much the same folks they'd been in high school. Happy people continued to be happy; cranky people didn't show up. That was testimony to me that, first, externals have really very little to do with how we end up in life. It was also a pretty good piece of evidence that we really will take our personalities, tendencies, and knowledge with us beyond death. If people who were exuberant in their gelatinous, unformed teens are still laughing and happy through sour marriages, misbehaved offspring, obesity, death, and disease, they're just plain making good choices. It'll be a delight to meet with them again at our 150th reunion.

Book of Mormon Languages www.new-jerusalem.com/bom-answerman/bomlanguages.html A list of every language that The Book of Mormon is translated into plus information on how to get a free Book of Mormon. ★★

Cartoons members.aol.com/pgrundberg/cartoon.html Cartoon excerpts from the journal of a returned missionary. ★★★

Go Ye Into All the World www.indirect.com/www/crockett/membmiss.txt Dave Crockett's page of discussions used by stake missionaries to teach member families how to do member missionary work. Presented in a familiar discussion format. ★★★

INmission members.tripod.com/INmission The INmission Project was designed to help support missionaries currently serving in the mission field. Write a missionary or if you will be soon going on a mission, register yourself. A wonderful idea! ★★★★★

LDS Mission Alumni Pages www.et.byu.edu/~harmanc/missions/shortlist.html Links to 270 mission pages and counting. ★★★

LDS Missionary Help members.xoom.com/missionary Devoted to helping those who support LDS missionaries, are planning to go on a mission, or who have just returned. Gives information on costs, supplies, and more. ★★★★

LDS Missionary Moms www.larsonfamily.org/lds_missionary_mom.html A place where Missionary Moms can share ideas of what they are doing to sustain their missionaries while in the field. ★★★

LDSMissions.com www.ldsmissions.com A very cool mission resource site with featured missions, featured missionaries, and more. A very well done site. Your future missionary should have this one marked. ★★★★★

LDSMissions.net www.ldsmissions.net A complete, up-to-date listing of LDS mission home pages. Get the feeling there are a bunch of underutilized return missionaries out there? ★★★★★

LDSMissions.org multiplexer.ldsmissions.org And that just about covers all the LDSMissions domains, right? This one is an LDS Missions multiplexing service. Easy link to your mission home page. There're dozens of dozens of 'em. ★★★★★

List of Missionary Necessities www.uvol.com/www1st/ missionary.html Mr. Mac is ready to tell you what you ought to buy. Compare it to the list you get in the mail. ⑀

Mission Central php.indiana.edu/~dostlund/mission.htm A collection of Mormon Missionary folklore. Urban legends, a few first-person stories, lots of pranks, funny stories, and more. Funny stuff and none of it edifying. ★★★

Mission Funnies www.ysite.com/mission/funnies.htm Funny stuff. Great photos. Seeking mail. (Remember that feeling?) ★★★★

Mission Home Pages www.desnews.com/missionmaps/home.htm A graphical world map showing the locations of missions and areas. Pretty cool. ★★★

Mission.Net www.mission.net Find your mission on the Internet (see figure 6.6). The Mission.Net site lists mission home pages, information about many countries, and help for new missionaries. For alumni of various missions of the Church of Jesus Christ of Latter-day Saints. This site facilitates e-mail, reunions, and snail-mail contacts. Also, young men and women who are called on missions may find the information on these pages useful as they prepare to enter the mission field. How do you chose from amongst so many fine sites? ★★★★★ ☑

Missionary Girlfriends Website www.azstarnet.com/~maile Dedicated to creating a community for missionary girlfriends to turn to for advice, ideas, and emotional

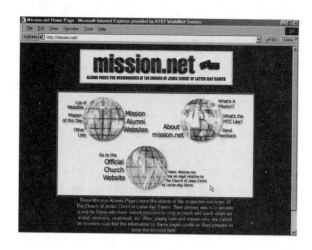

FIG. 6.6

Mission.Net: The meeting place for prospective and return missionaries.

support. Apparently, time flies faster than those left-behind girlfriends anticipated, because there's not much action on this page. ★★

Missionary Work   www.mormons.org/daily/missionary A collection of articles on topics related to missionary work, mission prep, the MTC, and more. ★★★

Missionary Work of the Church   www.orst.edu/~nedinr/Keith.htm Answers to prospective missionary questions: Why missionary work? Who can go on a mission? Where do missionaries go? How are missionaries expected to act? What do missionaries teach? ★★★ 📖

Missionary World   www.ysite.com/mission Part of the "Y" site at BYU. Includes links to missionary pages, scriptures, stories, shopping, and more. ★★★★

Missions   www.deseretbook.com/ldsinfo Find an extensive list of missions, alphabetized, at this Deseret Book-sponsored site. Needs a front page. ★★

Mormon Missions   www.emulateme.com/lds Mormon Missions is a resource for outgoing missionaries. Discover information about your mission, including political environment, weather, and national anthem. Lots of work here. ★★★★

President Gordon B. Hinckley   www.lds.org/General_Conference/97_Oct/Priesthood/ Hinckley-Some_Thoughts_on_.html President Hinckley gives "Some Thoughts on Temples, Retention of Converts, and Missionary Service." 📖

Proclaim the Gospel   www.uvol.com/www1st/proclaim/homepage.html Ward mission projects, mission preparation, other links of interest to member missionaries and full-time missionaries. ★★

Proclaiming the Gospel of Light and Truth   www.geocities.com/Athens/Aegean/1410 Proclaiming the Gospel of Light and Truth to the World! Information about the restored gospel by Elder Keith J. Wilson. Conversion story, doctrinal discussions, chat site, and a link to the Mormon Elder's Web page. A little dark and broody. ★★

Six Discussions   www.nettally.com/LDS/diss.html An expanded summary of new member discussions. The commentary is enlightening. ★★★

Six Lessons   www.nettally.com/LDS/lesson.html A brief summary of the formal missionary discussions. ★★

7

PERFECT
THE SAINTS

The second—and probably the most significant—aspect of the Church's three-fold mission is perfecting the Saints. And because the Church *is* its members, that means members need to work together to perfect themselves.

It seems an overwhelming task—learning to follow the Savior, to heed the counsel of prophets and apostles, to serve other people, and at the same time build an eternal family, study the scriptures, and continually increase in knowledge and wisdom.

Fortunately, because there's a community of Latter-day Saints out there prepared to help, nobody's on his or her own. So after prayer, after contemplation, after making wise use of all the usual resources available through the associations in your family and your ward, consider turning to the electronic library that is the Internet for further inspiration. The Internet sites listed in this chapter focus on following Christ, seeking inspiration, finding service opportunities, building families, studying the scriptures, and obtaining an education.

COME FOLLOW ME

I have a lot of favorite Primary songs. Very near the top of my personal Mormon Primary Hit Parade, though, is "I'm Trying to Be Like Jesus." It runs through my mind as I drag myself out of bed on Sundays at 5 a.m. I hear the refrain as I drive through the rain to go visiting teaching. It's the song I sing in my head whenever I'm tempted to tie a couple of my contentious children to the roof of the station wagon.

Like every Latter-day Saint, I really am trying to be like Jesus. And so I was startled the other day to realize, for the first time, that the person I'm trying to emulate was several years younger than I am now when He *finished* His mortal mission.

And then it occurred to me that it's now too late even to be like the Prophet Joseph. He'd already done more by the age of twenty than I will be able to accomplish in twice that time. Somehow, I thought, I still had some time to get my life straightened out. Guess I'd better move a little faster.

The Life and Mission of Jesus Christ

Knowing the Savior is the foundation of becoming like Him. Here you'll find a selection of Web sites that describe the life and the mission of Jesus Christ.

A Physician Testifies About the Crucifixion   www.konnections.com/kcundick/crucifix.html A doctor's insights on the Crucifixion of Jesus Christ. Valuable medical insight into what was happening to Christ on the cross. ★★

Atonement of Jesus Christ   www.mormons.org/basic/christ/atonement A collection of authoritative articles on the subject of the atonement. ★★★

Developing Faith in Christ   www.vii.com/~nicksl/bateman.html Text of an address delivered by Merrill J. Bateman to all Stake Presidents in the Utah North Area. Describes steps in the process of developing faith.

Encircled in the Arms of His Love   coned.byu.edu/cw/cwwomens/kapp99.htm Ardeth Greene Kapp's 1999 Women's Conference address. 📖

From Jesus to Christ   www.pbs.org/wgbh/pages/frontline/shows/religion Companion site for the PBS special on the first Christians. Dozens of key issues, disagreements, and critical problems relating to Jesus' life and the evolution of Christianity. Throughout the site, maps, charts (for example, the fortress of Masada), ancient texts (including Perpetua's diary), pictures of the archaeological discoveries, ancient imagery, and audio excerpts from the television program complement and illuminate the scholars' commentary. Fascinating information helpful in understanding the foundation of Christ's earthly ministry. ★★★★

How Well Do You Know the Saviour? A parable
www.konnections.com/kcundick/knowing.html ★★

Is Jesus Historical?
webm8101.ntx.net/rh/emma/teach1.htm As the Church expands internationally, missionaries and other members will deal more and more with investigators who are entirely unfamiliar with Christianity in any form. Here's an interesting non-LDS site about the historicity of Jesus Christ. ★★★

HOTLINKS

Jesus Christ
www.mormon.com/html/jesus_christ.html

Experiences with Leaders
www.ldsworld.com/gems/leaders

Teachings About Jesus Christ
www.mormons.org/basic/christ

Teachings of Gordon B. Hinckley
www.indirect.com/www/crockett/hinckley.html

The Prophet Joseph Smith
www.mormons.org/daily/history/people/joseph_smith

Jesus Christ
www.mormon.com/html/jesus_christ.html Background, table of parables, and more. Very readable; an excellent site. ★★★★★

Peaceable Followers of Christ
www.lds.org/med_inf/chu_lea_spe/19980201_Packer.html An address given by President Boyd K. Packer, Acting President of the Quorum of the Twelve Apostles, at Brigham Young University on February 1, 1998. 📖

Pictorial Mission of Jesus Christ
www.new-jerusalem.com/jesus/jesus.html The picture and scripture of the day. ★★★★★

Resurrection of Jesus Christ
www.mormons.org/basic/christ/resurrection Articles relating to LDS teachings about the resurrection. ★★★

Second Coming of Jesus Christ
www.mormons.org/ basic/christ/second Very small collection of articles on the second coming. ★★

Teachings About Jesus Christ
www.mormons.org/basic/christ A collection of some thirty Christ-centered topics (see figure 7.1). Includes articles on Jesus Christ Our Redeemer, An Apostle's Testimony of Jesus Christ, Come Unto Christ, Christians in Belief and Action, Teachings About Christ, Atonement of Jesus

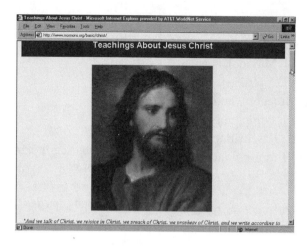

FIG. 7.1

Teachings About Jesus Christ: A vast assortment of authoritative material.

Christ, Head of the Church, Faith in Christ, Testimony of Jesus Christ, An Overview of the LDS View of Jesus Christ, Christology, Jehovah, Prophesies About Jesus Christ, Firstborn in the Spirit, Only Begotten Son of God, Birth of Jesus Christ, Baptism of Jesus Christ, Ministry of Jesus Christ, Crucifixion of Jesus Christ, Resurrection of Jesus Christ, The Forty-Day Ministry of Jesus Christ, Appearances of Jesus Christ, Second Coming of Jesus Christ, Fatherhood and Sonship of Jesus Christ, Taking the Name of Jesus Christ upon Oneself, Names and Titles of Jesus Christ, Types and Shadows of Jesus Christ, Second Comforter, and Sources for Words of Jesus Christ. Most of the material comes from doctrinal sources, and in particular, the *Encyclopedia of Mormonism*. ★★★★★

The Easter Story www.geocities.com/Heartland/4034/easter.html Jennifer Morgan's beautiful site describing the reason for Easter. ★★★

Prophets and General Authorities

In this section you'll find a great deal of information about past presidents of the Church, along with biographical information about the prophet, apostles, and other general authorities of the Church.

Chart of LDS Apostles: Part 1 www.cc.utah.edu/~joseph/Apostles1.gif An increadible graph showing every apostle of the modern Church along with information about their callings. See part 2 at www.cc.utah.edu/~joseph/Apostles2.gif. ★★★

Chronology of the Development of Apostolic Succession of the First Presidency www.marshall.edu/~brown/suc-pres.html A well-documented chronology of the development of the apostolic succession from 1831 to 1848. ★★★

Church Leaders www.desnews.com/confer/leaders/leaders.htm Photos and short biographies of Church leaders. Features each of the General Authorities and General Auxiliary presidencies. ★★★

Comprehensive Time-Line www.deseretbook.com/hinckley/hbio_tline.html An interactive time-line about the life of Gordon B. Hinckley. This site is affiliated with the Deseret Book biography of President Hinckley. Includes a compilation of hundreds of dates in chronological order that represent his activities throughout life. ★★★

Experiences with Leaders www.ldsworld.com/gems/leaders See also the former site at www.xmission.com/~dkenison/lds/gems/arc_gena.html. A compilation of fond memories of Church leaders from Heber J. Grant to Gordon B. Hinckley, as well as numerous general authorities, submitted by the subscribers of LDS World-Gems. ★★★★

Following the Prophets www.mormons.org/basic/organization/priesthood/prophets A short collection of articles on prophets and prophetic infallibility. A Mormons.Org page. ★★★★

Gems from the Teachings of the Prophets www.xmission.com/~dkenison/lds/gtp Collection of quotations arranged by subject. Includes a useful search tool. ★★★★

General Authorities of the Church members.aol.com/cumorahhil/ga/general_authorities.htm Scanned-in photo chart from, apparently, the *Ensign.* ★

General Authorities of the Church www.xmission.com/~dkenison/lds/genauth.html Statistical information about ages and dates various people have served in various leadership positions. Fun. ★★★

> And while we meditated upon these things, the Lord touched the eyes of our understandings and they were opened, and the glory of the Lord shone round about.
>
> And we beheld the glory of the Son, on the right hand of the Father, and received of his fullness; And saw the holy angels, and them who are sanctified before his throne, worshiping God, and the Lamb, who worship him forever and ever.
>
> And now, after the many testimonies which have been given of him, this is the testimony, last of all which we give of him: That he lives! For we saw him, even on the right hand of God; and we heard the voice bearing record that he is the Only Begotten of the Father—that by him, and through him, and of him, the worlds are and were created, and the inhabitants thereof are begotten sons and daughters unto God.
>
> D&C 76:19-24

Gospel Doctrine www.math.byu.edu/~smithw/Lds/LDS/Doctrine/Gospel-Doctrine Sermons and Writings of Joseph F. Smith, 6th President of the Church of Jesus Christ of Latter-day Saints. ★★★

Hinckley, President Gordon B. www.indirect.com/www/crockett/gbhlife.html Stories and lessons from the life of President Hinckley. ★★★

In Search of Joseph home.fuse.net/stracy Really, really cool site based on one person's search for an accurate image of the Prophet and Hyrum Smith. Must see. ★★★★

LDSWorld General Authorities Information www.ldsworld.com/leaders/1,2194,,00.html Pictures and biographies of current leaders of various auxiliaries, from Deseret News Almanac. ★★

Living Oracles www.geocities.com/Athens/Oracle/6504 Quotes and articles from Apostles and Prophets that give guidance and inspiration about Jesus Christ and everyday topics. Includes links to other LDS Web sites and other edifying material. Includes information about prophets and apostles, talks, sermons, and 42 pages of quotes. ★★★★

Living Voice: Continuous Revelation members.visi.net/~atom/totally/Rev.html A chapter from the book by Michael T. Griffith. 📖

Photo Album www.geocities.com/Athens/Academy/1581 Nice portraits of current and past leaders. Includes pictures of Jesus Christ and modern-day prophets and apostles. ★★

Photograph of The Prophet Joseph Smith, Jr. www.comevisit.com/lds/js3photo.htm A daguerreotype claimed to be of the Prophet Joseph Smith, along with biographical information. ★★★★

Presidents of the Church Trivia www.marshall.edu/~brown/trivia.htm A brief trivia quiz concerning the Presidents of the Church. Cute. ★

Teachings of Gordon B. Hinckley www.indirect.com/www/crockett/hinckley.html Quotes from a collection of over 200 talks, organized by subject. ★★★★

Teachings of Howard W. Hunter www.indirect.com/www/crockett/hunter.html (HTML) or www.indirect.com/www/crockett/hunter.txt (text) Quotations organized by subject matter. ★★★

The Prophet Joseph Smith   www.mormons.org/daily/history/people/joseph_smith A nice collection of articles on the history, martyrdom, and prophecies of the Prophet Joseph. A Mormons.Org page. ★★★★

Messages of Inspiration

I once attended a meeting at BYU where the speaker casually misquoted a scripture, and then proceeded to expound on the errant quote to prove her point.

Being young and stupid, it never occurred to me to actually look up the scripture and try to understand it for myself. Instead, I kept the popular—though inaccurate—misquote in the back of my mind, turning it over and over for—well, let's be honest here—a couple of years.

At about this time, the spring of 1985, the international press began to have a field day with a thing it called the "salamander letter," a troubling document that seemed to cast doubt on the origins of the Church. I was by then living overseas, and my only source of information was the wild exaggeration of the local eight-page English-language newspaper.

With both these difficulties weighing on my mind, late one night I found myself reading the Book of Mormon and wavering back and forth on the edge of sleep. As I was drifting, I'd struggle to read one more verse, then another, while sinking ever deeper into my pillows. As I came to the last verse, I suddenly shot bolt upright in bed, wide awake. For there it was. The answer to the question I'd been puzzling over for two years, the accurate Book of Mormon interpretation of the misquoted Biblical scripture. I'd wrestled all those months over nothing.

And then came to my mind the response to my other "struggle," the clear, ringing words: "There's an answer to everything." I was made to understand that I needed to have patience, and that sometime, somewhere, I'd find all my answers.

I resigned myself to the probability that I'd never in this lifetime understand that document called the salamander letter. Instead, I decided to simply trust in the Lord, and get on with life.

So you'll understand the depth of my interest when, a few months later, the events surrounding the Mark Hofmann document forgeries began to unfold. The discovery of Hofmann's forgeries is a complicated drama that, among other things, uncovered the fact that the so-called salamander letter was just one in a series of bogus, completely fabricated documents without any historical basis.[1]

It seems I got my answer.

---

[1]Additional information on Hofmann and his murder/forgery scam is available on the Internet from the Utah Collections Multimedia Encyclopedia at www.uen.org/cgi-bin/websql/ucme/media_display.hts? file_name=ta000522.txt&media_type=text&media_item_id=222, or at www.mormons.org/response/history/forgeries_eom.htm.

It's not often that inspiration is quite so dramatic. God saves the drama for stubborn, obstinate people like me—and like the apostle Paul, whom he had to knock down in the middle of the road in order to be heard.

For better people—those who are teachable and humble—inspiration tends to be a quiet understanding, a peaceful assurance. The following sites provide a vast store of inspirational materials—quotes, stories, counsel, and direction. Some are delivered straight to your e-mail box; others require you to do some Web browsing.

HOTLINKS

Aspiring to Greatness
www.osmond.com/chill/aspiring

LDS Daily WOOL
www.ldscn.com/wool

LDS-GEMS
lds-gems.com

Aspiring to Greatness www.osmond.com/chill/aspiring Poems, quotations, and stories collected by a Latter-day Saint. Ever growing. ★★★★

Classics in LDS Doctrine www.xmission.com/~dkenison/lds/lds_quo Collection of quotes and excerpts on religious themes. Loosely arranged. ★★

Daily Picture Scripture www.new-jerusalem.com/jesus/daily.html A scripture a day. ★★★★

Daily Words of Wisdom www.dailywow.com Another mailing list of inspirational quotes. Offers information in several different languages. Sometimes includes advertising and promotions for commercial ventures. ★★★

Faith and Values members.aol.com/kgrant100/faith.html Good personal thoughts about faith by a member of the Church. ★★

Hope Gallery www.hopegallery.com A very nice site with touching images. Commercial, but some images are free. ★★

Inspirational Stories www.inquo.net/~smudge/stories.html Collected by Darrell F. Davis. Lots of material here. ★★★

JOSEPH <majordomo@Mailing-List.net> Just Ordinary Saints Endeavoring to Promote Harmony. A mailing list for faithful members. To subscribe, send an e-mail request to <joseph-owner@bolis.com>. Digest available. ★★★

LDS Daily WOOL www.ldscn.com/wool Words of Our Leaders, delivered daily. Each day's mailing adheres to the theme of the week. Archive available at Web site. ★★★★

LDS Spiritual Thoughts www.geocities.com/SunsetStrip/3880 Small collection of uplifting stories on LDS themes. Most of these stories will be familiar. ★★

LDS-GEMS www.lds-gems.com The best mailing list on the Web. If you have e-mail access, you need to sign up. Daily traffic is about five messages, which includes 150 Years Ago Today, LDS news, stories from Church history, messages from general authorities, and inspiring subscriber submissions. Recently introduced commercial bits make it slightly less valuable, but the content is excellent nonetheless. ★★★★★ ☑

LDS-SOTD www.onelist.com/community/LDS-SOTD Receive a scripture a day from the LDS standard works. Scriptures are usually short (1–3 verses) and follow a "theme" to go along with the monthly message from the First Presidency. This is not a discussion list. The list sends out one scripture each day. ★★★

LDS_THOUGHTS www.onelist.com/community/LDS_thoughts Religious thoughts from the scriptures and General Authorities. List members can submit quotes and scriptures for consideration. Seems to have lost steam. ★

PEP Puente's Electronic Periodical. An inspiring and spiritual electronic newsletter. To subscribe send an e-mail message to: *<intense@acadia.net>*, and in the subject write: `Subscribe PEP`. 📖

Quotes www.inquo.net/~smudge/quotes.html Richard L. Evans-style inspirational quotes arranged by subject matter. ★★★

Scriptures to Ponder www.danvillestake.org/s/danville/ponder.html Select passages with peaceful graphics. A very small collection. ★★

Shining moments www.desnews.com/cgi-bin/libheads_reg?search=%22Shining+moment%22&limit=999 A collection of inspirational stories from the *Church News.* ★★★★

Service Opportunities

The Internet came in handy in developing a united effort in the Church's Sesquicentennial Pioneer Heritage Day service project.

After the First Presidency invited every ward and branch to contribute 150 hours of community service, and about nine days before the scheduled day of service, the LDS-GEMS mailing list asked its more than 9,000 subscribers to report from their home wards on the service activities being planned.

Within a day, GEMS had received nearly 200 reports. Replies came from subscribers around the world. The Hansen Military Servicemen's Branch in Okinawa, Japan, planned work at two local nursing facilities. Costa Rica's Barrio La Loma planned to clean up and paint an elementary school. In the Austria Vienna Stake, Wien 3 said it expected to build a fence around a piece of land in a public park. The Capalaba Ward in Brisbane, Australia, had made plans to door-knock to raise money for Children's Hospital Ronald McDonald House. In Perth, the Mundaring Branch of the Dianella Stake arranged a multitude of projects, including tree planting, sewing for a nursing home, and quilting for charity. From the Brighton Ward of the Crawley, England, stake came plans to feed and entertain the elderly, clear rubbish, and collect items for charity. A ward in Birmingham, England, announced plans to clean up a local nature park. From Heidelberg, Germany's Military Ward came a report of renewing a public park in North Heidelberg.

In a service project of his own, Brother Crockett posted plans for the day of service to his Web site, www.indirect.com/www/crockett/service/service.html, helping to make the day of service a truly united, Church-wide effort.

It should be no surprise that there's not much—short of building your own uplifting Web site—that you can do on the Internet to serve others. Service necessarily, and properly, is best done in your own geographical community.

Nevertheless, if you're looking for a place to serve, there a few things you can do to help.

HOTLINKS

Angels in Our Midst
www.geocities.com/Heartland/
Plains/6358/angelsin.htm

Genealogy Helplist
www.posom.com/hl

SaintlySaints
www.homestead.com/SaintlySaints

Somebody's Mother
www.itstessie.com/mother

Angels in Our Midst www.geocities.com/Heartland/Plains/6358/angelsin.htm Sweet stories of kind acts of service and charity. Many links. ★★★★

FHUnion FHUnion is an organization established to bring all Family History Center personal holdings on line (in the form of catalog listings with detailed descriptions) in a single, searchable database. Family History Centers of the Church of Jesus Christ of Latter-day Saints have assembled regionally significant genealogical information that is unique to each FHC. FHUnion needs people to assist in cataloging and submitting FHC regionally unique holdings. The organization needs a Web page construction team, and those who can assist in organizing from national and multistake territories to enter FHC data to the FHUnion

Web site. Later, local FHC volunteers will be needed to perform look-ups per their schedule. To sign up to assist FHUnion, send a message to *<FHUnion-L-Request@emcee.com>* with the subject `subscribe fhunion`. 📖

Genealogy Helplist www.posom.com/hl Volunteers who are willing to help others by looking up specific family history items at institutions near them, or help supply other information easily accessible to them. ★★★★

Hearts and Minds www.heartsandminds.org Nonprofit organization that provides information on making volunteering and self help more fulfilling and effective. Not specifically LDS. ★★★

Impact Online www.impactonline.org Also available at www.volunteermatch.org. A nonprofit organization that matches volunteers with service opportunities. Includes a virtual volunteer project that looks for volunteer service projects that can be done over the Internet. Not specifically LDS. ★★★

National Center for Missing and Exploited Children www.missingkids.com/html/index_howhelp.html The volunteering portion of the main NCMEC site. Many ways you can assist with locating missing children and protecting kids from sex offenders. Not specifically LDS. ★★★

Newborns in Need www.townsquareusa.com/nin/help.html A charity for babies. All about newborn and premature sick and needy babies and how you can help them when they can't help themselves. Not specifically LDS. ★★★

SaintlySaints www.homestead.com/SaintlySaints Finding service opportunities for Latter-day Saints. Register here as a volunteer, post links to your own projects and service sites, and suggest sites for posting. Formed in 1999 to locate and link both LDS and non-LDS service organizations and opportunities from a single site. ★★★★★

Somebody's Mother www.itstessie.com/mother Latter-day Saint Teresa Holladay's true story of a mother's return from the street. Dedicated to homelessness prevention. ★★★★★

Welfare and Humanitarian Assistance www.mormons.org/daily/welfare Extensive collection of articles on LDS humanitarian service and the calling of Latter-day Saints to serve others. ★★★★

Welfare and Humanitarian Services www.lds.org/med_inf/glo_med_gui/08-Welfare_and_Humanitar.html Learn about the welfare program of the Church, organized in 1936 to supplement the efforts of individual members and ecclesiastical leaders in helping the needy to help themselves. ★★★

BUILDING FAMILIES

It's a tough job, keeping a family together in a busy world where everyone has more commitments than time.

The Internet can help, with tools for improving your parenting, loads of recreational and educational material for families with children, and resources that can help build marriages. You'll find some of them listed here.

Parenting Resources

My husband and I are raising a very nontraditional mix-n-match family of seven children, only some of whom I've lived with since their birth. The brood consists of adopted children, stepchildren, and various kinds of biological children. This is what life's like in our house:

A few weeks ago, David, the oldest, decided it was time to pack up and move to Florida. His daddy is pretending not to worry. But Sunday I found Dan still wide awake at three in the morning, waiting for a promised phone call that still hasn't come.

David was about to become a senior in high school when I met him. Because David didn't grow up in my house, because David has never called me Mom, Dan thinks I can't know, that I can't understand who David really is.

In his quiet panic over David's choices, he doesn't see that we're waiting together.

David sits square in the middle of his dad's heart. Fortunately, his soul is kind—like his father's—and he doesn't take advantage of his power. He has a tough exterior, a sulky put-out-teenager mien, a way of walking and dressing and ignoring adults that challenges anyone to like him. Despite his best attempts to prevent it, though, I like David.

And because my view of David isn't overlaid with memories of David-as-a-child, I think I see things in him that his daddy doesn't. Here are the parts of David I find so likeable.

Once on an overnight cross-country trip, in a van packed with sleeping family, David sat up front to help me stay awake while driving. Keep talking, I told him. In my coffee-free world, chatter is the only thing that keeps me on the road. So David talked. From central Ohio to west Indiana, David talked. Told me what he writes, why he likes to write, how to play the dungeons and dragons games I abhor and he loves. (Imagine my surprise when—in building my LDS Authors Web page www.writerspost.com/mormonj/mjauthor.htm—I discovered that one of David's favorite fantasy writers, Tracy Hickman, is an LDS writer from Arizona. Our worlds aren't so far apart as I'd imagined.) Perhaps riding through well-forested roads in the dark of night gave him an alternative to the black clothing he hides in by day, but in any event, I found him mature and intelligent and entertaining. Rush and Dr. Laura and all the other voices that populate the airwaves at night have nothing on David.

HOTLINKS

FatherWork
fatherwork.byu.edu

Love@Home
www.loveathome.com

Parent's Guide
www.mormons.org/daily/parenting

Teachings About the Family
www.mormons.org/basic/family

Why Families Are Important
www.konnections.com/kcundick/
SearchInstitute.html

I gained respect for David as an adult during another conversation, this one between him and his dad. The summer after high school, David was unclear about his future. Dan was worried about David's nondirection, and was gingerly trying to goad him into making some plans. (It's a fun thing to watch, Dan's parenting. It's sometimes quiet, sometimes teasing, but always interesting. He doesn't lecture; he doesn't berate. He just teases and jollies his offspring into acquiescence.) Dan's concern was well-founded. There are members of his own family who, nearing their forties, have yet to leave home and make lives for themselves. As often happens between David and Dad, the conversation turned into a bit of a spar. It came to this: "So, David, you're going to college? Or are you planning to sleep forever on this couch?" David looked at him with adult-sized disdain, and proclaimed "I'm *not* going to turn into my uncle, if that's what you're thinking."

Life's been hard for David these past few years. For a while, it looked as if he actually *might* turn into his uncle. Finally, though, he took his life back, and decided to move to Florida, get a clean start. So now, despite his pride, Dad is worried. David's got no place to live. He's staying with friends. He's sleeping on park benches. He'll be eaten by alligators. His only nutrition is the greasy hamburgers he eats during shift breaks at work.

I hear all of it, and think "David's doing well." He's independent, he's making do, he's struggling, he's making a life. He's working his way to Daytona, looking for college and meaning and friendship. . . all the things he should be doing. And it's hard for him. As it should be. There's no phone, no permanent address yet, so we can't call. We talk about setting up an Internet account for him so that we can exchange e-mail, but he's living without regular access to a telephone. So instead, we wait for those collect calls to come through, progress reports meant to ease Dad's concern. But they seldom do.

So when David called Saturday afternoon and reported that he didn't know where he'd be sleeping that night, Dad panicked. "As soon as you find something, call and tell me where you are." But the call hasn't come.

So we wait.

When parenting feels tougher than it should, the following Web sites can help:

Before, Now and Forever—A Christ-created Family www.vitrex.net/~chenille/ BNFWEB/LoganFamily.html The author and her husband are parents to 10 children. This site contains the complete text of her book on raising children in an active LDS home. ★★★

Being a Righteous Husband & Father www.inquo.net/~smudge/fathers.html Text of a talk given in the priesthood session of General Conference by President Howard W. Hunter. 📖

Faithful Fathering faithful-fathering.byu.edu To assist fathers of all faiths to bless their children's lives. BYU's College of Family Home and Social Sciences encourages any and all fathers who see this site to contribute their ideas and experiences. The authors especially invite religious leaders of all faiths to contribute to the development of this site. ★★★★

Family Guidebook www.lds.org/library/fam_gui/fam_gui.html Family Guide Book from the Church's official site. ★★★

FatherWork fatherwork.byu.edu Helping fathers to strengthen family relationships (see figure 7.2). Stories, Ideas, and Activities to Encourage Generative Fathering. ★★★★★

LDS_SAHMS www.onelist.com/community/lds_sahms A list for stay-at-home moms who are members of the Church. Participants discuss parenting, doctrine, breastfeeding, and world affairs. Or subscribe with an e-mail request to <*karlp@ slcolubs.com*>. Daily traffic is about 30 messages. Very active. ★★★

LDS-MOTHERHOOD www.onelist.com/community/lds-motherhood A collection of thoughts on Motherhood from an LDS viewpoint. Each week, receive a quote, poem, article, or story. More information is available from <*Anita14501@aol.com*>. 📖

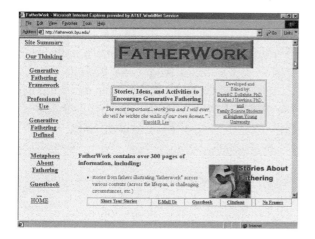

FIG. 7.2

FatherWork: A BYU-affiliated site
encouraging good fathering.

Living through Loss members.aol.com/Ethesis/sloss.htm Materials on surviving the loss of a child. Good help for survivors and those who love them. ★★★★★

Love@Home www.loveathome.com An Internet Resource for Large Families. A family of nine authors this page that discusses learning from each other, and sharing ideas and solutions to the problems faced by larger families and families of any size in today's world. Not specifically LDS. ★★★★

Parent's Guide www.mormons.org/daily/parenting The booklet that discusses LDS parenting. 📖

Parenting, the Lord's Way www.xmission.com/~pengar/allen/parent.html A long, well-documented discourse on parenting by Allen Leigh. ★★★

PARENTS www.ldscn.com/twintales/subscribe.shtml LDS parenting list is for the general discussion of parenting issues from an LDS perspective. 📖

PARENTS LDS e-mail group for parents. To subscribe, send an e-mail request to <karlp@ slcolubs.com>. 📖

PRODIGAL www.homestead.com/prodigalkids A support list for good Latter-day Saints raising a problem child. ★★★★

Teachings About Fatherhood and the Role of Men www.mormons.org/basic/family/fathers Being a Righteous Husband and Father, and other addresses and commentaries on fatherhood. ★★★

Teachings About the Family www.mormons.org/basic/family A collection of articles on the Church's strong positions about the importance of family. Includes articles on The Family: A Proclamation to the World, The Family, The Eternal Family, The Joy of Living the Great Plan of Happiness, Teachings About the Family, Teachings About Marriage, Teachings About Motherhood and the Role of Women, Teachings About Fatherhood and the Role of Men, Teachings About Children, Teachings About Sexuality, Brotherhood, and Abuse of Spouse and Child. A Mormons.Org page. ★★★★★

TwinTales www.ldscn.com/twintales How an LDS family with adopted twins manages life. ★★★

Values Parenting parenting.netpub.com A page from Richard and Linda Eyre dedicated to teaching basic values to kids. Includes a discussion page, weekly parenting tip, more. ★★★★

Why Families Are Important www.konnections.com/kcundick/SearchInstitute.html A refutation of recent well-publicized research indicating families have no bearing on the way kids grow up. A study showing how families help youth to grow up to be healthy, caring, and responsible. ★★★

HOTLINKS

101+ LDS Sunday Activities
www.mormon.com/gunthers/
sabbath.html

Family Forum
www.ysite.com/forum

Family Home Evening
www.mormons.org/daily/
FHE_EOM.htm

IMDB
www.imdb.com

Family Resources—Recreation, Activities, Family Home Evening Resources

Perhaps mine is the only family on the planet where the kids pout and sulk if we *miss* Family Home Evening. I suspect they're only in it for the treats, but hey, whatever works.

If it takes more than a bowl of ice cream to get your family enthusiastic about spending time together, here's help:

101+ LDS Sunday Activities www.mormon.com/gunthers/sabbath.html Guidelines one LDS family uses for its Sabbath days. By Jay and Victoria Gunther, who list plenty of ideas and activities to help keep the Sabbath day holy. ★★★★

Ask Jeeves www.askjeeves.com Gives you smart answers fast. Fun for kids, useful for adults. Investigate it for your next family home evening. ★★★

Brigham Young University Sports   sports.byu.edu Next time you're in Provo, here's something to do. If you're a nonstop sports fan, you'll also want to subscribe to Cougar-Net at www.cougar-net.com. ★★★

Comic Zone   www.unitedmedia.com/comics Web site for major, nationally syndicated cartoons. Not specifically LDS. ★★★

Crosswalk.com   www.crosswalk.com A site for rating movie content for pornography, violence, and other objectionable content. Check out the movie BEFORE you check out the movie. ★★★★

Donna's Day   www.ktca.org/donnasday Fun, creative activities for the whole family. ★★★★

Family Forum   www.ysite.com/forum Exchange useful ideas with other LDS families in this new family-friendly discussion forum at Y-site (see figure 7.3). ★★★★★

Family Home Evening   www.mormons.org/daily/FHE_EOM.htm An excerpt from the Encyclopedia of Mormonism. 📖

Family.Com   www.family.com Disney's page of family activities. Great fun. ★★★★★

Family-tested Web Sites   www.geocities.com/Heartland/9530/family.html A new site reviewing Web sites for the whole family. Not specifically LDS. ★★

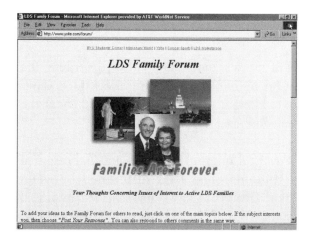

FIG. 7.3

Family Forum: A discussion area for LDS families.

How Stuff Works www.howstuffworks.com Learn about how things work. Great fun. ★★★★

Idea Box www.theideabox.com An add-your-own-ice-cream Family Home Evening activity. Great suggestions for parents. ★★★★

IMDB www.imdb.com Internet Movie Database. One of the top entertainment sites on the Internet. Read descriptions and reviews of virtually any movie ever made. Screen for appropriateness before you rent that video. Our family sometimes prints out reviews and histories of movies before we view them, and discusses themes and issues of what we're about to see, so we know what we're looking for. A great teaching tool. ★★★★★

Kids www.yelmtel.com/~mrwizard/kids.htm Safe sites for kids and teens. Includes links to Yahooligans, Your Own Newspaper, Teen Net Magazine, Hieroglyphs, Kid-Safe Internet, and more. Not specifically LDS. ★★★★

Library of Congress lcweb.loc.gov/z3950/gateway.html Gateway access to its catalog and other institutions. Given the state of the Web these days, this site is a disappointment. But it's probably worth visiting nevertheless, if only so you can say that you have. ★★

Microsoft TerraServer terraserver.microsoft.com What does your neighborhood look like from space? And when you get bored with that, spy on someone in China. Turnabout's fair play. Unfortunately, this information isn't in real time. In fact, it's sadly dated. ★★

MyFamily.com www.myfamily.com Free, private place to share family news, calendars, albums, and more, on the Web. Includes content for families such as a family-safe search engine. ★★★

Screen It www.screenit.com Reviews of movies, music, and videos describing the content and every conceivable (ahem) point of objection. Gives away the endings for too many movies, but worth bookmarking if you're at all concerned about the content of the media you see and hear. ★★★★

Searchopolis www.searchopolis.com Powerful Internet search engine and resource site for primary and secondary students. The BIG difference between Searchopolis and other search engines: Every site has been reviewed by a real person and is appropriate for youngsters. Word of the day, site of the day. ★★★★

Building Marriages

My husband is perfect. Really. He's absolutely the finest human being I've ever known, and I adore him.

One of his many fine qualities is that he doesn't fight. Oh, he can fight. But he tends not to. It's a good thing, because we're both opinionated, obstinate, and confident of the obvious truth of our own positions—a combination of characteristics that could prove fatal to an otherwise healthy marriage.

Believe it or not, this has something to do with the Internet.

We've finally worked out a system, it seems. When a subject arises on which we can find no agreement, we don't do battle. It's too fraught with emotion, too easy to let loose a volley of careless words.

Instead, we send e-mail. We follow the rules, of course. We try to be kind. But somehow, dancing around a sensitive issue in writing seems to bring out the best in both of us.

Here are some other ways the Internet can help:

HOTLINKS

LDSWeddings.com
www.ldsweddings.com

Making Marriage Work
www.danvillestake.org/s/danville/
advice.html

Marriage Builders
www.marriagebuilders.com

Being a Righteous Husband and Father www.inquo.net/~smudge/fathers.html By President Howard W. Hunter. Comments on a husband's role in and obligations to his family. 📖

Cornerstones for Building Homes www.lds.net/ldslife/families/cornerstones.html President Gordon B. Hinckley's fireside message to young couples. Deals with advice for strengthening and preserving marriage. 📖

LDSWeddings.com www.ldsweddings.com Everything you need to plan an LDS wedding. Find help for honeymoons, bridal showers, temples, and more! Very thorough, amazingly well done. ★★★★★

Making Marriage Work www.danvillestake.org/s/danville/advice.html Great collection of family articles, helps, and resources by general authorities and other Church members. ★★★★

Marriage Builders www.marriagebuilders.com Building marriages to last a lifetime. In this Marriage Builders site, you will be introduced to some of the best ways to overcome marital conflicts and some of the quickest ways to restore love. Eternity would be better, but a lifetime's still good. The principles taught here are worth knowing in any event. ★★★★

Married Mormon Women www.geocities.com/Heartland/Ranch/4828 For young married LDS women seeking strength from one another. Growing. ★★★

SANCTIFY www.ldscn.org/sanctify A mailing list to support part-member families. Often bitter, although many members work overtime to be inclusive. ★★★

Teachings About Marriage www.mormons.org/basic/family/marriage Quotes from various authoritative sources on questions of marriage, eternal marriage, divorce, celibacy, and more. Fairly static; more theory than practice. ★★★

You Believe What?! www.marriagebuilders.com/graphic/mbi5040_qa.html How to resolve conflicts of faith. Part of the excellent Marriage Builders Web site at www.marriagebuilders.com. Sound advice for part-member families. ★★★★

GOSPEL DOCTRINE STUDY TOOLS

Studying the words of the prophets and the apostles—whether written in the form of scripture, or spoken in testimony before the Saints—is fundamental to attaining perfection.

In this section you'll find sites for reading the scriptures online, along with transcripts from conferences and other addresses, and doctrinal texts available online.

Scriptures Online

One of the best things about the Internet is its capacity for making texts—particularly scriptural texts—available online.

This section contains only the online text of each book of scripture. You'll find personal study tools for each of these books in chapter 12: "Pursuit of Excellence."

The scriptures you'll find here take several forms: Web pages where you can read the text straight through, downloadable text files, searchable databases, and more.

The section is organized by individual texts, followed by a list of sites containing multiple books of scripture.

Book of Mormon

The Book of Mormon was introduced in chapter 6: "Proclaim the Gospel." In this section, you'll find the actual text online in a variety of formats.

Book of Mormon members.aol.com/cumorahhil/bom_search.htm Multiple search tools, in an easy-to-understand format. The search hits come up in context. Click on the hyperlinks to read additional surrounding text. ★★★★

Book of Mormon www.math.byu.edu/~smithw/Lds/LDS/LDS-scriptures/Book_of_ Mormon Straight text, chapter by chapter. Use the Find/Search command on your browser to search any chapter. ★★

Free Book of Mormon www.lds.org/fre_boo_of/ fre_boo_of.html From the official site. Includes a toll-free number as backup. ★★★

Free Book of Mormon www.mich.com/~romulans/ freebom.html Another site for obtaining a free personal copy of the Book of Mormon. See chapter 6 for similar resources. ★★

Mormon's Story www.enoch.com/voicesfromdust/ mormonstory/mormonstory.html The text of the Book of Mormon in a simpler English. While I'm a great fan of reading scriptures in their original form, I'm an even greater fan of understanding the scriptures—in whatever form generates understanding. Timothy Wilson's rewrite of the Book of Mormon is beautifully done, and it's all available online at this Web site. If this is the kind of simplification it takes to get a child or a new reader through the Book of Mormon, it's a worthwhile venture. ★★★★★ ☑

HOTLINKS

Free Book of Mormon
www.lds.org/en/1_Free_BOM/
FreeBOM.html

Mormon's Story
www.enoch.com/voicesfromdust/m
ormonstory/mormonstory.html

Audio Bible
www.audio-bible.com/bible/
bible.html

DOCTRINE
www.onelist.com/subscribe/
Doctrine

The Pearl of Great Price
www.deseretbook.com/scriptures/
pgp_home.html

Search the Book of Mormon www.hti.umich.edu/relig/mormon Use the Web to search the Book of Mormon by word or phrase. Great search tools. A Project Gutenberg text, housed at the University of Michigan. ★★★★

The Book of Mormon www.deseretbook.com/scriptures/bom_home.html Deseret Book's online text of the Book of Mormon. Very readable. Lacks a search tool. ★★★

Bible

The large online community of Christians does a good job of presenting the Bible in electronic form. Most of the following sites contain several versions of the entire biblical text.

Audio Bible www.audio-bible.com/bible/bible.html Listen to the Bible via Real-Audio. ★★★★★

Bible Browser Advanced goon.stg.brown.edu/bible_browser/pbform.shtml Simple but powerful interface designed to help you browse the Bible actively, in a way that is not possible with traditional printed books. Using the Bible Browser, you can look up biblical passages directly, by keyword, substring, or word pattern. You can also perform phrase searches, execute logical operations on groups of passages, retrieve passages from different versions, and limit in various ways the quantity and range of material retrieved. By the Scholarly Technology Group. ★★★★

Bible Gateway bible.gospelcom.net Full text of six English-language versions of the Bible, plus six non-English translations. Includes a very good search engine and a topical guide. ★★★★★

Bible Text www.math.byu.edu/~smithw/Lds/LDS/Ancient-history-items/Bible Includes information on canon dates and Vulgate texts. Great content, absolutely no design, and no search engine. ★★

Bible ccel.wheaton.edu/bible_study_txt The text from about 20 Bible translations. Files must be downloaded to your computer to be read. ★★★

Bible www.math.byu.edu/~smithw/Lds/LDS/LDS-scriptures/Bible Text only. Alphabetized list of chapters of the King James version of the Bible, ready for download. ★★

Blue Letter Project Bible www.khouse.org/blueletter With Concordance/Search and Hebrew/Greek. Interesting. ★★★

Free Copy of the Bible (King James Version) www.mich.com/~romulans/freebible.html Request a copy online. ★★

Online Bible for Windows www.onlinebible.simplenet.com Available for download. ★★

Project Gutenberg   www.thalasson.com/gtn/gtnanon.htm Scroll to the Bible listings. Choose between the King James and Douay Rheims versions, or the Apocrypha. Download a text file for online reading or a zip file for downloading and offline reading. ★★

Smiley Scriptures   www.smileyscriptures.friendpages.com A silly Web site. The KJV of the Bible with smiley faces. An interesting twist to reading scriptures. ★★★

Worldwide Study Bible   www.ccel.org/wwsb The text from about 20 Bible translations, along with commentaries. ★★★

The Doctrine and Covenants
You'll find here both text and hypertext (Web language) editions of the Doctrine and Covenants.

Doctrine and Covenants   www.deseretbook.com/scriptures/dc_home.html A Deseret Book scripture search site. ★★★★

Doctrine and Covenants   gopher://wiretap.spies.com/11/Library/Religion/Mormon/ Doctrine Available online, the text of the Doctrine and Covenants divided in 14 sections. ★★★

DOCTRINE   www.onelist.com/community/doctrine A chapter of the Doctrine and Covenants and Pearl of Great Price every week day. Open discussion of the chapters being studied and of Church history is strongly encouraged. 📖

Index of Scriptures   www.math.byu.edu/~smithw/Lds/LDS/LDS-scriptures/Doc_and_Cov The text of the Doctrine and Covenants. Fixed line lengths. ★★

The Pearl of Great Price
The following sites contain both the entire text of The Pearl of Great Price, as well as shorter excerpts—primarily the Articles of Faith—from the full text.

Articles of Faith   www.jefflindsay.com/art_faith.html. Other well-presented pages for the Articles of Faith are located at www.deseretbook.com/scriptures/pgp/aof/aof1.html and www.danvillestake.org/s/danville/aof.html. The basic doctrines of the Church. Graphically appealing, but contains no explanation or insight beyond the text itself. ★★

Articles of Faith www.mormons.org/basic/articles_faith.htm The text followed by documented commentary and history. ★★★

Book of Abraham www.math.byu.edu/~smithw/Lds/LDS/Ancient-history-items/Book-of-Abraham Similar site is available at wiretap.spies.com/11/Library/Religion/Mormon/Pearl. Original texts as found in Times and Seasons. Great content, terrible design. ★★

The Pearl of Great Price www.deseretbook.com/scriptures/pgp_home.html A good Deseret Book site for reading and searching The Pearl of Great Price. ★★★

HOTLINKS

GospeLibrary.Com
www.gospelibrary.com/
scrip-query.html

LDS Scripture Search
www.mormon.com/html/
scriptures.html

Standard Works
208.201.207.12/scriptures

Standard Works
www.deseretbook.com/scriptures

Standard Works
The complete set of scriptures online.

Gospel Library www.ldsworld.com/library/freecontent/1,2670,,00.html The commercial site is located at infobase.ldsworld.com/sdbin/sdext.dll?f=file[fbrowse-h.htm]. Infobases' collection of scriptures, including the Inspired Version of the scriptures, and several hundred other texts. Searching the scriptures and a couple of other books is free, but other searches require a paid subscription. ★★

GospeLibrary.Com www.gospelibrary.com/scrip-query.html Search the scriptures online, along with the Topical Guide and the Inspired Version of the Bible. The Topical Guide makes this site a treasure. ★★★★★ ☑

GospelLink www.gospellink.com Deseret Book's Master Reference Library. A commercial site for buyers of GospeLink software. ⑤

LDS Scripture Search www.mormon.com/html/scriptures.html All the scriptures, searchable, along with a searchable edition of *Das Buch Mormon*. ★★★★

Mormon Gopher wiretap.spies.com/11/Library/Religion/Mormon Includes The Book of Mormon, Doctrine and Covenants, and the Pearl of Great Price. Perhaps the first version of LDS scripture on the Net. ★★★

Religious and Sacred Texts webpages.marshall.edu/~wiley6/rast.htmlx Something from everyone. In addition to links to LDS scriptures, you'll find here links to

Apocryphal, Islamic, Hindu, Confucian, Taoist, Bahai, Sikh, Egyptian Book of the Dead, Gnostic, Zen, Early Christian, Zoroastrian, Divrei, Torah, Urantian, Ethiopian, and Medieval texts. Leave a trail of bread crumbs. The page is compiled by Dave Wiley, a Latter-day Saint. ★★★★

Scriptures of the LDS Church www.math.byu.edu/~smithw/Lds/LDS/LDS-scriptures Full standard works in text form are available for downloading directly to your own computer to be read offline. ★★

Scriptures.Org hollender.org/scriptures Separate search sites for each book of scripture. The index feature is nice, but the overall site is very slow loading. ★★★

Standard Works 208.201.207.12/scriptures Gregor McHardy's very nicely done site for reading the scriptures online. You can also download the entire collection for free so that you can read the scriptures on your own computer offline. No search tool, but the indexed tabs are familiar and easy to use. ★★★★★ ☑

Standard Works www.deseretbook.com/scriptures Scripture search site from Deseret Book. Beautifully done. ★★★★★ ☑

Messages/Proclamations Online

The following Web sites contain the text of messages and proclamations from the First Presidency:

HOTLINKS

The Family: A Proclamation to the World www.lds.org/en/4_Official_Church_Policy/Proclamation.html

Continuing Revelation members.aol.com/ssh81675/ldsrefer/documents/reveal.htm The First Presidency Message for the August 1996 edition of the *Ensign,* given by President James E. Faust. 📖

Doorway of Love members.aol.com/cumorahhil/fpm1096.htm The First Presidency Message for October 1996, given by President Thomas S. Monson. 📖

First Presidency Messages members.aol.com/cumorahhil/first_presidency_message.htm Small collection of monthly messages from the First Presidency. ★★★

Strength Through Obedience members.aol.com/ssh81675/ldsrefer/documents/obey.htm The First Presidency Message for July 1996, given by President Thomas S. Monson. 📖

The Family: A Proclamation to the World www.lds.org/library/pro_of_the_fam/ pro_of_the_fam.html Official Church Proclamation, issued September 23, 1995. The First Presidency and the Council of the Twelve Apostles issued the proclamation that clearly states the role of the family and the Church, and the importance of marriage, children and families. Also found online at members.aol.com/ cumorahhil/proclmtn.htm and at www.jefflindsay.com/LDSFamDecl.shtml. Text of the 1995 official proclamation on families. 📖

General Conference

It's been just a couple of years now that General Conference has been available online almost as it happens. In this section, you'll find various Conference reports, as well as information about where to go to get the next session of Conference.

Conferences www.mormons.org/conferences Transcripts of General Conferences from October 1996 to the present, including Priesthood, Relief Society, and Young Women's sessions. No search tool. ★★★

HOTLINKS

LDS General Conference
www.desnews.com/cn/confer

General Conference Live
www.generalconference.com

General Conference www.lds.org/conference/General_ Conference_en.html Transcripts from General Conference since April, 1997. No search engine, no supplemental materials, but it's official. ★★★

General Conference Live www.generalconference.com A brand new site with lots of capacity, so everyone can tune in. Listen to General Conference via the Internet. Fourteen languages and growing. ★★★★★

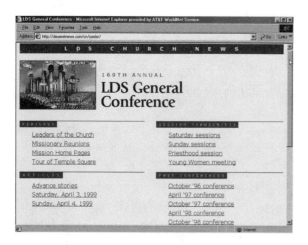

FIG. 7.4

Deseret New Web Edition: This popular site is inundated with visits during General Conference.

LDS General Conference www.desnews.com/cn/confer (See figure 7.4.) Conference transcripts since October 1996, along with supplemental materials published in the Church News. Very heavily used during General Conference. No search tool. ★★★★

Talks, Speeches

In this section you'll find the texts of talks and speeches delivered by prominent members of the Church in settings other than General Conference.

60 Minutes LDS Segment www.xmission.com/~dkenison/lds/gems/60min.txt Transcript of a 1996 television interview with President Gordon B. Hinckley. 📖

BYU Devotional and Fireside Speeches advance.byu.edu/devo.html A listing of the devotional and fireside speeches available at this Web site (see figure 7.5). Includes talks by President Hinckley, Elder Packer, LeGrand Richards, Elder Holland, Hugh Nibley, Elaine Jack, and many more. ★★★★★ ☑

BYU Speeches of the Year www.math.byu.edu/~smithw/Lds/LDS/BYU-speeches Collection from 1984 to 1991. ★★★

HOTLINKS

BYU Devotional and Fireside Speeches
advance.byu.edu/devo.html

King Follett Discourse
www.geocities.com/
CapitolHill/3500/kfd1.html

Music and the Spoken Word
www.ksl.com/TV/word.htm

Talks
www.desnews.com/cn/talks.htm

Women's Conference
coned.byu.edu/cw/cwwomens/
talks.htm

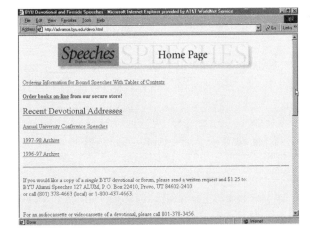

FIG. 7.5

BYU Devotional and Fireside Speeches: Access the best thinking of speakers at BYU.

Fourteen Fundamentals mach.cs.cmu.edu/afs/cs/usr/dba/www/ETBenson-14-Fundamentals Downloadable text of address by Ezra Taft Benson. 📖

King Follett Discourse www.geocities.com/Athens/Styx/5581/king.html President Joseph Smith delivered this funeral sermon before about 20,000 Saints in 1844. The last major public address—just a few weeks before his martyrdom—wherein he boldly and clearly explicates many of the doctrines unique to the Church of Jesus Christ of Latter-day Saints. 📖

King Follett Discourse www.geocities.com/CapitolHill/3500/kfd1.html Full text and Chiasmus. Fascinating site. ★★★★★

Larry King Live www.lds.org/en/4_News_Update/19980908_CNN_Transcript.html Transcript of Larry King's interview with Gordon B. Hinckley on September 8, 1998. 📖

Messages from Our Church Leaders www.geocities.com/Athens/Styx/5581/Messages.html Statements, sermons, or declarations of faith from the presiding leadership of the Church of Jesus Christ of Latter-day Saints. Rarely updated. ★★

Music and the Spoken Word www.ksl.com/TV/word.htm Transcripts from Sunday broadcasts. Wonderful. ★★★★

Previous BYU Devotionals www.kbyu.byu.edu/tv/devos Schedule of devotionals to be rebroadcast on KBYU. Probably not of much use outside of the Utah Valley. ★★

Seven Deadly Heresies ftp.sims.net/pub/organizations/zion/documents/heresies Transcript of well-known address by Elder Bruce R. McConkie. 📖

Talks www.desnews.com/cn/talks.htm Selected transcripts of recent talks given by LDS general authorities and officials. Great resource frequently updated. ★★★★★

Women's Conference coned.byu.edu/cw/womens.htm Transcripts from recent BYU Women's Conferences. Addresses by prominent women in the Church. Very nicely done. ★★★★★

Other LDS Texts Online

In this section, you'll find a selection of doctrinal texts written by apostles, other general authorities, and other prominent members of the Church.

All About Mormons www.mormons.org John Walsh's very large site containing texts on virtually anything anyone has ever wanted to know about Mormonism. It's, ahem, encyclopedic in its coverage. In fact, it makes extensive use of the Encyclopedia of Mormonism and a few other classic Mormon texts. Good information. I'd be happy to see it stay around. ★★★★★ ☑

As A Man Thinketh www.coolcontent.com/TheToolOfThought Treatise on the power of thought by James Allen. 📖

Book of John Whitmer erdos.math.byu.edu/~smithw/Lds/LDS/Early-Saints/whitmer,j Kept by Commandment. Typescript of John Whitmer's history of the Church. 📖

Encyclopedia of Mormonism www.infobases.com Order a free copy of the Encyclopedia, along with the Standard Works, on CD-ROM. Pay $4.95 for shipping. 💲

Gospel Classics www.gospelibrary.com/clas-query.html Search the text of Talmage's *A Study of the Articles of Faith, The Autobiography of Parley P. Pratt,* Widtsoe's *Discourses of Brigham Young,* Smith and Sjodahl's *Doctrine and Covenants Commentary,* Joseph F. Smith's *Gospel Doctrine,* Heber J. Grant's *Gospel Standards,* George Q. Cannon's *Gospel Truth,* all seven volumes of the *History of the Church,* Talmage's *Jesus the Christ,* Joseph Smith's *Lectures on Faith,* and Joseph Fielding Smith's compilation of *Teachings of the Prophet Joseph Smith.* ★★★★★

HOTLINKS

All About Mormons
www.mormons.org

Gospel Classics
www.gospelibrary.com/
clas-query.html

History of the Church
www.gospelibrary.com/
hc-query.html

Into the Wardrobe of C.S. Lewis
cslewis.drzeus.net

Gospel Doctrine www.math.byu.edu/~smithw/Lds/LDS/Doctrine/Gospel-Doctrine The sermons and writings of President Joseph F. Smith (text appears in sections). 📖

History of Joseph Smith www.uvol.com/www1st/tsquare/story.html His own words. All five chapters. 📖

History of the Church www.gospelibrary.com/hc-query.html Search all seven volumes of the history compiled, edited and annotated by B. H. Roberts. ★★★★★

History of the Church   www.math.byu.edu/~smithw/Lds/LDS/History/History_of_
the_Church From a 1935 edition of the seven-volume set (text divided into sections). Another copy is available at www.byu.edu/Academic-Info/rel1/books/
jsteach/jshead.htm, and a plain text version is maintained at www.math.byu.edu/
~smithw/Lds/LDS/Joseph-Smith/Teachings 📖

Into the Wardrobe of C.S. Lewis   cslewis.drzeus.net OK, so he's not LDS. But given the number of times he's been quoted in General Conference, you've gotta give him some extra credit. ★★★★★

Introductory Library   mall.infobases.com/infobases/enofmor.html The Encyclopedia of Mormonism and Standard Works on CD for free—nearly. You pay the shipping. $

LDS Archive Publishers   www.spectre.com/ldsarchive Reprints 40 of the all-time favorite classics of LDS literature. Commercial site for books that have been out of print for a number of years but give the biographies, experiences, and doctrinal vantage of the early prophets and those who were close to them. $

LDS-related Infobases   www.enol.com/~infobase/lds_stuff.html For owners of the Infobases Folio reader, the documents on this site can be downloaded and added to your collection. Very useful. ★★★★★

Teachings of the Prophet Joseph Smith   www.math.byu.edu/~smithw/Lds/LDS/
Joseph-Smith Compiled by Joseph Fielding Smith. Teachings is divided into six sections. 📖

EDUCATIONAL RESOURCES: LDS-AFFILIATED COLLEGES, UNIVERSITIES, INSTITUTES

I've been a student at more colleges and universities than I have children—and I have a lot of children. So when I engaged in an online discussion sometime back about the nature of academic freedom at Brigham Young University, I spoke with some authority.

My correspondent had been a BYU student in the 70s, and still took umbrage at the dress codes and honor codes that he considered stifling. There is, he said, no freedom of thought at BYU.

I was the wrong person to pick an argument with that day. I'd had an ugly morning at the University of Missouri. There a journalism professor made the outlandish and contradictory suggestion that all "censorship" should be outlawed. And the entire class of students obediently nodded heads in agreement.

I couldn't stay quiet. "*All* censorship?" I asked. The instructor looked surprised. It was, after all, a graduate journalism course. How dare I think otherwise? "Do you mean to say that nobody, anywhere, should have the right to restrict what any other person reads or views?"

The entire class jumped to his defense. I was a pariah for questioning his judgment.

By the end of the hour, I was standing up to argue. Alone, among all the students, I continued to do battle. Nope, they said, nobody should be able to restrict anything. Not communities, not governments dealing with national security, and for that matter, not even parents choosing books for their own children. It was a bloody war, and I was alone. My thinking was incorrect, my speaking out was an affront, and my attitude was unacceptable.

As I left class that day, feeling completely discouraged, I thought longingly of my time at BYU, when I had participated in amazingly intelligent discussions with people who were open-minded, open with their disagreements, and openly loving when they engaged in debate. Is it any wonder, then, that I couldn't agree with my online correspondent that BYU was the school that lacked academic freedom?

I learned at BYU to see the world in all new ways. Sure there's the rare administrator who makes bad, even embarrassing, decisions. But that wasn't the case in the classroom. There I gained perspective, a broader view of man and society that has continued to serve me well through the years. I learned about world religions from James Moss. I gained a macro view of economics and society from Clayne Pope advance.byu.edu/devo/PopeW97.html. I learned to write; I learned to really read; I learned to connect all the dots from some of the most free-thinking, broad-minded people in the world.

And I did it all wearing a dress.

Latter-day Saints are regularly admonished to improve their education, to seek wisdom, learning, and understanding. In this section, you'll find a large number of resources to aid in education. The section begins with information on continuing education, then introduces you to institutes of religion, colleges and universities, and additional educational resources.

Continuing Education

If full-time college isn't for you, consider expanding your knowledge with continuing education courses.

BYU Continuing Education   coned.byu.edu Home study, travel study, education week, bachelor's degrees, conferences and workshops, more. An excellent resource. ★★★★★

HOTLINKS

BYU Continuing Education
coned.byu.edu

BYU Independent Study
coned.byu.edu/is/indstudy.htm

Education Week
coned.byu.edu/ed/edweek.htm

Know Your Religion Schedules
coned.byu.edu/ed/kyr_desc.htm

BYU Independent Study   coned.byu.edu/is Attend BYU on the Internet and earn high school or university credit from home. I've investigated independent study programs at most universities in the United States and abroad and BYU's is world class. Maybe even better than world class. ★★★★★ ☑

BYU Religious Education   reled.byu.edu Courses offered by Religious Education. Good information. ★★★

BYU Travel Study   coned.byu.edu/ts/homepage.htm Study in the Holy Land, Central/South America, Europe, Asia, or Nauvoo. Informative page. ★★★

Church Education System   www.lds.org/med_inf/ glo_med_gui/09-Church_Educational_Sy.html CES operates religious studies programs in the United States and in over a hundred other countries and territories. Text from the official Church Web site. 📖

Education Week   coned.byu.edu/ed/edweek.htm BYU's annual Education Week program may be the largest educational event in the world. Some 1000 classes are conducted on campus. The site includes everything you could want to know about education week, including travel and housing information. Includes links to similar programs at Ricks College and BYU-Hawaii. ★★★★★

Know Your Religion Schedules   coned.byu.edu/ed/kyr_desc.htm Searchable schedules and locations from the Church Educational System. If there's a listing for New Jersey, they've got a great site. And they do. ★★★★

Institutes

A partial listing of institutes of religion and LDS student associations. You'll find more listings for college-age single adults in chapter 10: "Auxiliaries," the Single Adult section.

California (Riverside) Institute   members.aol.com/cumorahhil/riversd.htm Class schedules, activities, more. ★★★

California (Stanford) LDSSA   www.stanford.edu/group/ldssa The LDS student association at Stanford. ★★★★★

Clemson University LDSSA   hubcap.clemson.edu/ldssa Excellent page for this South Carolina LDSSA. Very informative. ★★★★★

LDS Student Associations   www.mich.com/~romulans/ldssa.html A good list of links. ★★

LDS-GRADS   E-mail discussion list for single LDS graduate students. Send a subscription request to *<tnrands@princeton.edu>* Daily traffic: About 8 messages. 📖

LDSSA   members.tripod.com/~moroni Louisiana (Baton Rouge) Latter-day Saint Student Association. Includes an intro to LDSSAs. ★★★

Missouri (Columbia) Institute   students.missouri.edu/~ldssa Activities, courses, more. (But I'm a former student, so ratings may be overstated.) ★★★★

Missouri (Rolla) LDSSA   www.umr.edu/~ldssa Students at the University of Missouri at Rolla. Nice information source. ★★★

MIT LDSSA   web.mit.edu/afs/athena.mit.edu/activity/l/ldssa/www Very thorough site, with schedules, information about the Church, and much more. ★★★★★

North Carolina State University LDSSA   www2.ncsu.edu/ncsu/stud_orgs/latter_day Wonderfully designed page. Lots of helpful information. ★★★★★

Ogden, Utah, LDS Institute   www.relia.net/~ldssa The Ogden LDS Institute's home page at Weber State University. ★★★★

Sigma Gamma Chi   www.cs.utah.edu/~ruefenac/sigma_gamma_chi The national college fraternity for LDS single men. Good background information. ★★★

U.S. Air Force Academy LDSSA Home   www.geocities.com/CollegePark/1097/Institute.html Brief information site with only a few links, no schedules. Very nicely laid out. ★★★

West Virginia (Huntington/Marshall University) LDS-SA   webpages.marshall.edu/ ~brown/ldssa.html A short compilation of information. ★★

Teach ye diligently and my grace shall attend you, that you may be instructed more perfectly in theory, in principle, in doctrine, in the law of the gospel, in all things that pertain unto the kingdom of God, that are expedient for you to understand; Of things both in heaven and in the earth, and under the earth; things which have been, things which are, things which must shortly come to pass; things which are at home, things which are abroad; the wars and the perplexities of the nations, and the judgments which are on the land; and a knowledge also of countries and of kingdoms—

That ye may be prepared in all things when I shall send you again to magnify the calling whereunto I have called you, and the mission with which I have commissioned you.

The Doctrine and Covenants 88:78–80

Yahoo! www.altavista.digital.com/cgi-bin/query?pg=q&what=web&kl=XX&q=ldssa&
search.x=38&search.y=3 List of LDS Student Associations. Some 250 links. ★★

Colleges and Universities

This section lists the Web sites of Church-affiliated colleges and universities, along with a handful of Utah schools that no longer have any direct Church affiliation—although they do have significant LDS student populations.

Admissions—Brigham Young University adm5.byu.edu/ar/proj/app_intro.html
Applications, forms, and instructions for admission. 📖

Brigham Young University www.byu.edu Main site. 📖

BYU-Hawaii www.byuh.edu Church-owned, four-year undergraduate university located in Hawaii. 📖

Dixie College www.dixie.edu Two-year college in St. George, Utah. 📖

LDS Business College www.ldsbc.edu Church-owned, two-year trade school in Salt Lake City. 📖

Ricks College www.ricks.edu Church-owned, two-year college in Rexburg, Idaho (see figure 7.6). 📖

Snow College www.snow.edu Two-year college in Ephraim, Utah. 📖

FIG. 7.6

Ricks College: Typical of most college pages, the Ricks Web site provides academic and admissions information to prospective students.

Southern Utah University   www.suu.edu Four-year university in Cedar City, Utah. 📖

Southern Virginia College   www.southernvirginia.edu New two-year college in Buena Vista, Virginia, at the foot of the Blue Ridge mountains. The school is operated by members of the Church, and requires students to maintain academic and behavioral standards comparable to those at BYU. 📖

University of Utah   www.utah.edu The Salt-Lake-City-based university. 📖

Utah State University   www.usu.edu Four-year university in Logan, Utah. 📖

Utah Valley State College   www.uvsc.edu Two-year college in Orem, Utah, with a very large LDS student population and an excellent institute program adjoining campus. 📖

Weber State University   www.weber.edu Four-year university in Ogden, Utah. 📖

Other Education-oriented Resources

You'll find here a list of miscellaneous educational resources oriented toward adult education. Home schooling resources are listed beginning on page 268 in chapter 11.

BYU & Other LDS Educational Institution Sites   benson.byu.edu The Ezra Taft Benson Agricultural and Food Institute has long been focused on helping overcome malnutrition in underdeveloped countries. It works hand-in-hand with local universities and colleges in countries such as Guatemala, Ecuador, and Bolivia.

BYU Alumni Association   www.byu.edu/alumni Sponsoring numerous educational events and programs. ★★★★★

BYU Jerusalem Center   coned.byu.edu/jc BYU's Jerusalem-based center for Near Eastern Studies. ★★★★

BYU Library   www.lib.byu.edu Online searchable card catalog, library info, Web search, course reserve, and more. Everything, in fact, but the books. ★★★★

Deseret Academy   www.deseretacademy.com An LDS-operated private school that offers a well-rounded education for all children, grades K–12. Includes programs for home-school families. $

Education for Eternity   www.byu.edu/tmcbucs/fc/ee/ee.htm   A compilation of material on the subject of the eternal nature of education. Notable is the collection under the Education and the Gospel link, where the works of apostles and various LDS scholars are found. Lacks a search tool. ★★★

Education   www.mormons.org/daily/education   A collection of articles on LDS teachings about education, and educational resources. Includes the history of LDS education and much more. A Mormons.Org site. ★★★★

8

REDEEM
THE DEAD

In the previous chapters, you were introduced to the first two elements of the Church's three-fold mission. This chapter looks at part three of that mission: redeeming the dead.

Uniquely among Christian churches, the Church of Jesus Christ of Latter-day Saints holds to the belief that every member of the entire human family will—whether in this life or the next—have the opportunity to hear the gospel of Christ, and to make individual decisions about how to accept that gospel.

Part of accepting the gospel is taking on the name of Christ and being baptized into the body of the Church. It also involves other necessary ordinances, including the sealing of marriages for eternity, and sealing together family units. All of these ordinances are performed by faithful Latter-day Saints on behalf of deceased ancestors in temples around the world, thus literally fulfilling Malachi's prophecy of Elijah, turning the heart of the fathers to the children, and the heart of the children to their fathers (Mal. 4:6).

In order to perform those services, Latter-day Saints maintain extensive family histories and search out the genealogical records of their ancestors.

This chapter considers Internet resources for researching genealogy and maintaining family histories, takes a brief look at pioneer histories and diaries, and introduces the temples of the Latter-day Saints.

GENEALOGY/FAMILY HISTORY PAGES

Living overseas can sometimes be a struggle. It's not the unfamiliar surroundings or the unusual food or the unaccustomed language. More than anything, it's missing the family that was left behind. And so it happened that while I was living in Hong Kong, and missing my parents and cousins and sibs, I decided to get to work on my genealogy. I hauled a laptop computer and a couple of boxes of pedigree charts into town for a visit to the family history center.

The first order of business was to enter existing names into my computerized family history database. I cracked open the first book and began inputting records, but was dismayed to discover that the books of pedigree charts weren't in very good shape. Fortunately, the computers in the FHC stood ready and waiting. I randomly entered the name of my great-great-grandmother and pressed the enter key.

There she was. Grandma. And Grandpa. And all their kids. Too cool. I was so excited, I decided I'd print out a descendants chart.

The list was four or five pages long. What fun! As I walked back to my seat, I scanned the list. Aunts, uncles, cousins. . . .

And then, whoa! There was a name I recognized. I looked, and looked again.

Yep. No doubt about it.

I was related to someone I knew. It seems I had a not-so-distant cousin I'd already met . . . a counselor in the bishopric—of my ward in Hong Kong.

Guess I wasn't so far from home as I'd imagined.

You won't need to travel overseas or even to your local library to get started with a family history. When you're hunting for your own long-losts, turn to the resources of the Internet.

There are, literally, thousands of genealogy pages on the Internet. They fall into several categories: pages from individual families, pages from family organizations, information from genealogy organizations, research databases, commercial products, LDS-oriented links, and more. Most pages contain links to LDS resources, but few give more than a passing reference to the wealth of information available online.

But there's one site that does more: the new FamilySearch page from the Church of Jesus Christ of Latter-day Saints at www.familysearch.org. Is it possible to say enough good things about this page? When it went on line at the end of May 1999, it was so immediately successful that user overload caused a system

THE MISSION OF THE CHURCH

crash the very first day. The Church was forced to implement a waiting list system as more than 500 people a second tried to access the site. Five weeks later, when the Church began distributing a free copy of its Personal Ancestral File software from FamilySearch, the system again went into overload—but this time, without the six-hour crash.

FamilySearch is as good as the Internet gets. Records on more than 400 million people were available when the system went on line, and the Church planned to add another 200 million individuals by the end of the first year. Expect to see those numbers grow over time, as the rest of the 2 billion individuals on record are added, and their billions of brothers and sisters join the list.

This section contains a compilation of some of the best starting points for genealogical research.

alt.genealogy   news:alt.genealogy A newsgroup discussing genealogy in very general terms. Low traffic, useful information. See chapter 9, page 219, for instructions on accessing newsgroups. ★★★★

Ancestors   www2.kbyu.byu.edu/ancestors The family history and genealogy television series, presented by KBYU-TV and PBS. The site contains tips, a resource guide, downloadable charts, software, and more. ★★★★

Ancestry Home Town   www.ancestry.com An entire community dedicated to helping you discover your ancestors. Includes a genealogy library with 108 databases, a community family tree, answers to genealogy questions, genealogy lessons, and commercial links. The genealogy lessons are a tremendous help to beginners. ★★★★

HOTLINKS

Cyndi's List of Genealogy Links
www.CyndisList.com

FamilySearch
www.familysearch.org

Genealogy Lady
www.new-jerusalem.com/
genladynew

Chart for Figuring Relationships   www.rootsweb.com/~genepool/cousins.htm Can't tell your grandniece from a first cousin once removed? Here's how to figure it all out. ★★★

CompuServe Roots   ourworld.compuserve.com/homepages/roots The genealogy forum on CompuServe. Worth visiting if you're a member. Very helpful. ★★★★

Cyndi's List of Genealogy Links   www.CyndisList.com Perhaps the best-planned, most thorough noncommercial site on the entire Internet. More than 22,000 genealogy sites categorized into seventy-some categories, including adoption, biographies, books, microfilm and microfiche, cemeteries, funeral homes and obituaries, census-related sites worldwide, events and activities, family bibles, handy online starting points, heraldry, historical events and people, hit a brick wall?, how to, LDS and family history centers, medieval, genealogy home page construction kit, photographs and memories, preserving your family's treasures, stories and genealogical research, professional researchers, volunteers and other research services, software and computers, terms, phrases, dictionaries and glossaries, and sites for every region, country, and U.S. state. ★★★★★ ☑

Deciphering Old Handwriting www.firstct.com/fv/oldhand.html An article full of examples and explanations of old handwriting. Very useful. ★★★

Elijah-L genealogy.emcee.com/~holdiman/elijah-l An LDS Genealogy mailing list. To subscribe, send an e-mail request to *<elijah-l-request@genealogy.emcee.com>*. Daily traffic is about 10 messages. The Web site is an additional source of information. ★★

Everton's Genealogical Helper www.everton.com A commercial site with a few free databases. Research helps and other tools are tremendously helpful. ★★★★

Family History Centers of the Church www.deseretbook.com/famhis Organized by state. Addresses and phone numbers only. The same information is available over the phone at (U.S.) 1-800-346-6044. ★★

Family History www.lds.org/en/2_How_Do_I_Begin/0-How_Do_I_Begin.html How Do I Begin? Information from the Church's Web site on Why family history?, Why do members of The Church of Jesus Christ of Latter-day Saints do family history research?, What can I do first?, What is a Family History Center?, and Where is the nearest Family History Center? ★★★★

Family History www.mormons.org/daily/family_history A collection of background information on why Latter-day Saints do genealogy. Includes articles on Family History or Genealogy, Family History Library, Family History Centers, Ancestral File, Family Registry, FamilySearch, Family Organizations, Genealogical Society, Granite Mountain Record Vault, and Book of Remembrance. A Mormons.Org site. ★★★

FamilySearch www.familysearch.org Who ever thought this day would come? The site is incredible, and it is, I suspect, the real reason we humans have made any technological progress in recent years. Nah, I don't just suspect it. You can quote me! Go here (see figure 8.1), find your ancestors, learn what your third cousin

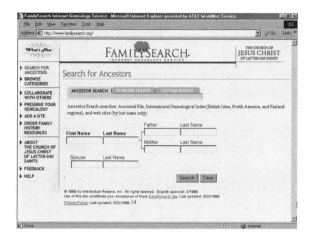

FIG. 8.1

FamilySearch: Internet Genealogy
Service.

Beulah discovered about your Grandpa Wild Bill. Now you know how to contact Cousin Beulah and you know where to get started finding Grandpa Bill's wild father. Did I mention that this is now the best site on the Internet? The numbers back me up. FamilySearch is the new Only-Site-On-The-Web-To-Receive-This-Rating site: ★★★★★★

FHL—Brigham Young University To contact the BYU Family History Library, send an e-mail message to *<FHL@byu.edu>*. 📖

FHL—Salt Lake City To contact the SLC Family History Library, send an e-mail message to *<famhistlib@aol.com>*. 📖

Gendex www.gendex.com/gendex Indexes hundreds of World Wide Web databases containing genealogical data for over two million individuals. Incredibly helpful site with an altogether unattractive format. ★★★★

Genealogy Lady www.new-jerusalem.com/genladynew See also the older files at www.new-jerusalem.com/genealogy/questions.html. The Genealogy Lady—part of the fantastic New Jerusalem suite of LDS Web sites—answers questions put to her by amateur genealogists. Visit this page to read her responses. ★★★★★

Genealogy Online genealogy.emcee.com This site is for discussion of genealogy. Includes links to the Genealogy Chat site, events database, the 1880 census, and much more. Quite helpful. Little original content. ★★★

Genealogy Online's Events Database events.genealogy.org Add your own "events" (birth, marriage, death, other) to contribute to the site's 4,000 existing entries. ★★

Genealogy Resources on the Internet members.aol.com/johnf14246/internet.html An "obsessive" list of mailing lists, UseNet newsgroups, FTP sites, Gophers, Web, Telnet, and e-mail resources. Ugly but thorough. ★★★★★

Genealogy World www.enoch.com/genealogy/homepage.html This site contains access to both free genealogy information, and a commercial genealogy service (see figure 8.2). The free links include Surname Forums (a search and submission tool for people doing work on any given family name), Genealogy Lady Answers (answers to questions about genealogy research roadblocks), Genealogy Bookstore (books categorized by state, country, and surname, along with books on CD-ROM), monthly genealogy newsletter (good hints and information sources, also available via e-mail), and more. If you want additional help, Plan A, at $36 a year, and Plan B, at $24 a year, offer professional genealogical assistance. ★★★★

GEN-ROOTERS A mailing list for Latter-day Saints to share ideas and helpful hints on the "how-to's" of genealogy. Send your subscription request to Dianne Morris at <*azdee@aol.com*>, with a brief description of your Church affiliation and a request that you be added to the list. 📖

HANDCART <*maiser@rmgate.pop.indiana.edu*> Genealogy of Mormon handcart peoneers. Discussion area for anyone with interest in the genealogy, journals, and stories of the pioneers who settled in the Salt Lake Valley from 1847 to 1860. Subscribe with an e-mail request to <*MAISER@rmgate.pop.indiana.edu*>, with the message `subscribe handcart`. 📖

How to Gather 1001 Names an Hour from a Family History Center www.firstct.com/fv/lds1.html Robert Ragan, operator of the Treasure Maps site, has written a

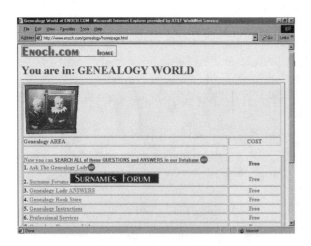

FIG. 8.2

Genealogy World: Worth a subscription.

guidebook for using Family History Centers. Read part of his tutorial—and order the book—at this site. ★★★

LDS-GENEALOGY   members.tripod.com/~Genealogy_Infocenter/ldsgen-list.html Mailing list for genealogists, particularly those interested in the software and databases maintained by the LDS Church. These databases include the IGI, the Ancestral File, the entire FamilySearch system, and Personal Ancestral File software. Also, any questions about the LDS Church's role in genealogy and family history are welcome. 📖

Military USA   www.militaryusa.com/enhance/enhance.html-ssi Locating Veterans Worldwide. 📖

Treasure Maps   www.firstct.com/fv/tmapmenu.html Good how-to information (see figure 8.3) compiled by a member of the Church. Numerous Family History Center links and a free monthly genealogy newsletter. ★★★★

US GenWeb   www.usgenweb.com Gateway to the huge U.S. GenWeb project. Volunteers across the United States maintain links to information for their states and counties. This page contains information about the project and links to state-level GenWeb sites. ★★★★★

Family Histories

Every faithful member of the Church is a pioneer in his or her own right. At some point, you made the choice to be part of the body of the Saints. So whether you can count Mormon Trail walkers, Nauvoo dwellers, and Mormon Under-

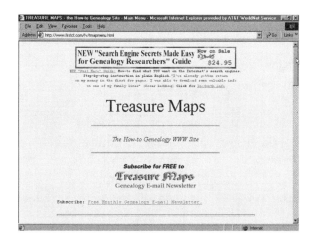

FIG. 8.3

Treasure Maps: Learn how to locate your own ancestors.

grounders among your ancestors, or you're the descendent of recent immigrants, school teachers, farmers, or college students, you've got a story worth telling the kids. No matter where your roots originate, your family has a story to match all that genealogy. Here's where you can go on the Internet if you want to write some family history.

Book Binding www.sil.org/lingualinks/library/literacy/vao144/krz1832/krz414/index.htm Learn how to bind journals and family history books by hand. Great stuff! ★★★

Coats of Arms www.baronage.co.uk/nl/nl-01-04.htm An Online Newsletter from The Baronage Press. User Dave Birley writes: "If any of your genealogical research includes leads into Great Britain, and if you have ancestors who were assigned coats of arms, you will find this newsletter and Web site helpful. There are many companies who set up in shopping malls offering to provide you with a copy of 'your family's coat of arms.' In fact, there is no such thing: a coat of arms (or blazon) is given to an individual, not a family. The crest, on the other hand, may be assigned to a family. This newsletter tells more about all of this, and offers a way to subscribe. The newsletter appears to be issued about quarterly." ★★★

HOTLINKS

Family History
www.mormon.com/html/family_
history.html

Oral History Questions
www.rootsweb.com/~genepool/
oralhist.htm

Tracing Mormon Pioneers
www.vii.com/~nelsonb/pioneer.
htm

Personal Ancestral File
familysearch.org/OtherResources/
paf4

Early-Saints www.math.byu.edu/~smithw/Lds/LDS/Early-Saints Large collection of biographies of early Latter-day Saints. Really unattractive site, but the information is invaluable. ★★★

Family History Moments www.desnews.com/cgi-bin/libheads?search=family+history+moments&limit=50 Archived stories from the Church News. ★★★★

Family History www.mormon.com/html/family_history.html Great activity for teaching youth about the promise of Malachi. ★★★

Family Letter webols.everton.com/familyletter/fl_welcome.html A service for building a family Web site, newsletter, and history accessible to family members around the world. Great idea. Implementation is a bit rough. ★★★

Family Tree Maker www.familytreemaker.com This commercial site includes some excellent noncommercial resources: an online genealogy class, an Internet family name search tool, a how-to guide, a biography writing assistant, and much more. ★★★★★

Genealogy Software www-personal.umich.edu/~cgaunt/ software.html Reviews of software, links to developers, utilities and add-ons, and archives. Very useful if you're looking for a new genealogy package. ★★★

Light Impressions www.lightimpressionsdirect.com Fine archival storage, display, and preservation supplies. Commercial. $

List of Occupations cpcug.org/user/jlacombe/terms.html A very interesting list of the old names of ancient occupations. Sure to be of some use if you can trace your family history back several generations. ★★★

ON TECHNOLOGY

Modern technology has played a significant role in the advance of family history in the second half of the twentieth century. . . . As a result, doing family history research has never been easier than it now is. . . . As name extraction programs convert information from paper records (such as the 1880 U.S. Federal Census and the 1881 British Census) and as people from around the world contribute information to the Ancestral File, the computer resources associated with FamilySearch will make identifying one's ancestors a much simpler task.

Encyclopedia of Mormonism, Vol. 2, Family History, Genealogy

Oral History Questions www.rootsweb.com/~genepool/oralhist.htm A good list of questions for evoking detailed memories during an oral history interview. ★★★

Personal Ancestral File familysearch.org/OtherResources/paf4 Download your own copy of this Windows-based genealogy program from the Church. What's long been the best deal in software has now become history's best deal in software: It's free. ★★★★★

Tracing Mormon Pioneers www.vii.com/~nelsonb/pioneer.htm Tips for those tracing their Mormon pioneer ancestry from Europe to Salt Lake City, Utah. Information regarding online and conventional resources of Mormon pioneer ancestry. Phenomenal page. Well worth reading through if you had ancestors arriving in the Salt Lake Valley from 1847 to 1869. ★★★

What was the Cause? www.bgsu.edu/colleges/library/cac/ac0892.html#diseases Historic Names of Diseases. Now I know what dropsy is. ★★★

You Can Publish Your Own Family Keepsakes www.rootsweb.com/~genepool/ keepsakes.htm Tips for publishing family records. Excellent. ★★★★

TEMPLES

Latter-day Saints are a temple-building people. The temple is the center of our worship, the place we go to find answers, revelation, and peace.

The temple is also the place we go to perform service on behalf of those who have gone before, reaping the blessings not only of serving others, but also, in so doing, of being edified and taught ourselves.

Here you'll find some of the most sacred and important doctrines and experiences being shared among faithful Saints by various means over the Internet. This section includes personal accounts of temple experiences, temple dedicatory prayers, and research on ancient temple building and ceremonies. Also listed here are sites that provide temple schedules and events, as well as information about the history of individual temples.

Temple Experiences

The Latter-day Saint experience is, at its root, the story of the temple. Here is the place where man communes with God. All the work we do in our families, in our communities, and in the world at large has at its root the work of the temple.

It's no surprise that the temple is so elemental to our communication with God. The testimonies and stories associated with the temple are among the most powerful events that Latter day Saints experience.

In this section you'll find a collection of personal stories about experiences in the temple.

HOTLINKS

Temple Dedications
www.lds-gems.com/archive/temple

Temple Moments
www.desnews.com/cgi-bin/
libheads_reg?search=temple+
moment&limit=50

Testify!
www.writerspost.com/testify

A Heavenly Manifestation www.homestead.com/manifestation A vision received by Heber Quincy Hale in 1920. A testimony of the importance of temples. 📖

A Temple Experience www.homestead.com/zclan/temple.html Stan Zielinski describes an experience he and his wife had during their marriage ceremony in the Seattle Temple. 📖

Materials On Heavenly Visitations www.vii.com/~nicksl/visits.html About angels, visitations, and other manifestations related to temple work. ★★★

Temple Dedications www.lds-gems.com/archive/temple From the LDS-GEMS Archive Index, a compilation of personal experiences associated with the temple, as related by subscribers to the LDS-GEMS mailing list. ★★★★

Temple Moments www.desnews.com/cgi-bin/libheads_reg?search=temple+moment& limit=50 Stories of temple experiences submitted by readers of the Deseret News. ★★★★

Testimonies www.mormons.org/testimonies/walsh_wj.htm The conversion story, along with an account of a compelling temple experience, of W. John Walsh, Webmaster of Mormons.Org. 📖

Testify! www.writerspost.com/testify Search on "temple" to read various accounts of temple-related experiences. ★★★★★ ☑

The Story of . . . www.new-jerusalem.com/testimony/grant.html and www.new-jerusalem.com/testimony/deanmacy.html Just a few of the many conversion stories located at the Testimony Stories Web site. These relate specifically to temple experiences. 📖

About Temples

This list is a collection of educational information on temple ordinances, dedicatory prayers, ancient temples, and more. Stop and study for awhile.

Chronology of LDS Ritual, 1829–1842 www.vii.com/~nicksl/chrono.html Gives an overview on key events in LDS ritual history. 📖

David O. McKay Temple Address www.vii.com/~nicksl/domlect.html An address on the Temple ceremony by President David O. McKay given Thursday, September 25, 1941, at 8:30 A.M., Salt Lake Temple Annex. Prophetic perspective on Temple symbolism. 📖

HOTLINKS

Nick Literski's Latter-day Saint Temple Home Page
www.vii.com/~nicksl

Richard Satterfield's LDS Temple Pages
www.ldschurchtemples.com

Teachings About Temples
www.mormons.org/basic/temples

Mormon Heritage: The Temple Collection webusers.anet-stl.com/~sharon A commercial site for purchasing resin replicas of various temples, including Nauvoo and Kirtland. Photos appear on site. $

Mormon Temple Ceremony www.teleport.com/~arden/temple.htm Describes the temple endowment as a beautiful Christianization of the ancient Hebrew temple rite. Well documented, useful links. ★★★★

Nick Literski's Latter-day Saint Temple Home Page   www.vii.com/~nicksl (See figure 8.4.) From the opening hymn ("The Spirit of God Like a Fire Is Burning") to the closing links, there's not a better place *in the world* for understanding the temple. The site includes temple dedicatory prayers, photos, plans for new temples, and talks and documents related to LDS temples. Be sure to read Nick's newest link: Letters from Visitors to the Home Page. ★★★★★ ☑

Passing by the Angels   www.vcaa.com/epistles/angels.htm Cordell Vail's discussion of Brigham Young's explanation of the endowment: "Let me give you a definition in brief. Your endowment is, to receive all those ordinances in the house of the Lord, which are necessary for you, after you have departed this life, to enable you to walk back to the presence of the Father, passing the angels who stand as sentinels, being enabled to give them the key words, the signs and tokens, pertaining to the holy Priesthood, and gain your eternal exaltation in spite of earth and hell." Well documented, worth considering. ★★★

Questions About Baptism for the Dead   www.jefflindsay.com/LDSFAQ/FQ_BaptDead. shtml Part of Jeff Lindsay's frequently asked questions suite. Provides answers to several questions: Why do Mormons believe in baptism for the dead? Did early Christians practice baptism for the dead? Where does the Bible advocate baptism for the dead? Well reasoned. ★★

Richard Satterfield's LDS Temple Pages   www.ldschurchtemples.com Statistical information and more on LDS temples. ★★★★★

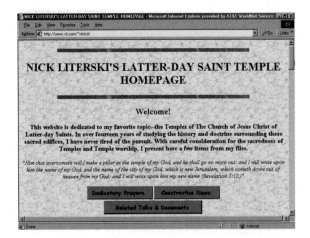

FIG. 8.4

Nick Literski's Page: Marvelous collection of temple-related background.

Teachings About Temples www.mormons.org/basic/temples A fantastic collection of articles relating to temple worship (see figure 8.5). Includes information on Why these Temples?, Latter-day Saint Temple Worship and Activity, Salvation for the Dead, The Temple and the Atonement, Temple Ordinances, Baptism for the Dead, Washings and Anointings, The Endowment, Temple Sealings, Temple Recommends, Garments, Altars, and Early Christian Temple Rites. A Mormons.Org page. ★★★★★

Temple Dedications www.vii.com/~nicksl/temdeds.html Extremely well-done collection of dedicatory prayers. Site owner Nick Literski describes the prayers given in the dedication of temples as "some of the most valuable doctrinal and historical writings in the LDS Church." Includes prayers in chronological order from the Temple of Solomon to the Temple at St. Louis. ★★★★

Temple Endowment webpages.marshall.edu/~wiley6/40_days.html Dave Wiley's research on the circumstances that indicate Jesus Christ taught the apostles about the temple after his resurrection. Heavily footnoted. Consider shutting off the dark background before attempting to read. ★★★

Temples www.lds.org/med_inf/glo_med_gui/06-Temples_and_Families.html Basic temple information from the Global Media Guide of the Church of Jesus Christ of Latter-day Saints. Names, locations, and dedicatory dates for all the latter-day temples. ★★

Temples www.xmission.com/~dkenison/lds/templist.html The same content, slightly expanded, is available here. ★★★

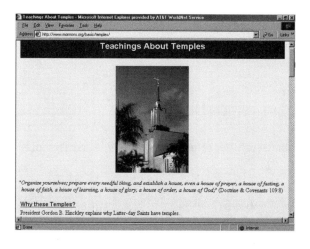

FIG. 8.5

Teachings About Temples: Helpful articles on temple ordinances.

To Him That Overcometh webpages.marshall.edu/~brown/overcome.htm Lisle Brown's writings on the ancient precedent of temple ordinances. Brother Brown is the director of special collections at Marshall University. 📖

General Temple Information

This list includes schedules, maps, and basic temple information.

Atlas of LDS Temples, Missions, and Stakes members.theglobe.com/mschind Atlas of LDS temples, missions, and stakes for North America. New and growing. ★★★

LDS Temple Web Ring www.webring.org/cgi-bin/webring?ring=ldstemplering;index See all the best Temple-related Web sites linked together through this Web ring. ★★★★★

HOTLINKS

LDS Temple Web Ring
www.webring.org/
cgi-bin/webring?ring=
ldstemplering;index

Links to Temple Web Sites
www.ldschurchtemples.com/
links.html

Temples
www.deseretbook.com/temple

Links to Temple Web Sites www.ldschurchtemples.com/links.html Just what it says. A good source with intelligent reviews of sites. See also Webmaster Richard Satterfield's main temple page at www.ldschurchtemples.com, with links to his other useful temple statistical information and graphics. ★★★★★

Temples www.lds.net/churchnews/buildings/temples.html Postcard-like fact pages for most of the temples. Needs an update. ★★★

Temples www.deseretbook.com/temple Schedules, maps, and photos. Each map includes an address and driving directions, along with links to bookstores in various temple districts. A very nicely organized page by Deseret Book. ★★★★★

Individual Temples

This list contains the histories of various individual temples.

Anchorage, Alaska, Temple www.mission.net/alaska/anchorage/AlaskaTemple/Temple.html About the Alaska temple. 📖

Anchorage, Alaska, Temple www.dowl.com/users/mnichols This is an unofficial site for the Anchorage, Alaska, Temple. It has a lot of information on schedules and procedures as well as a history of the site and its construction. It is updated regularly. 📖

Albuquerque, New Mexico, Temple www.geocities.com/Heartland/Bluffs/6216/abq.htm Pictures of the construction on the Albuquerque Temple, updated at least every two weeks. A little tough to read. ★★★

Boston, Massachusetts, Temple Page acs.bu.edu:8001/~baird/templehome.html; Temple history: acs.bu.edu:8001/~baird/TempleStory.html; an artist's rendering: www.deseretbook.com/temple/SCHBSTN.html. Absolutely not to be missed is the history of the temple written by a member who grew up in the region. Altogether an excellent site built with an obvious love for both the temple and the New England region as the birthplace of the Church. ★★★★

HOTLINKS

Construction News
www.vii.com/~nicksl/newtemps.html

Omaha, Nebraska, Temple
www.discoveromaha.com/community/groups/LDS/local/Temple

Rebuilding of the Nauvoo Temple
www.vii.com/~nicksl/newnauvoo.html

Construction News www.vii.com/~nicksl/newtemps.html What you want to know about the current state of temples under construction. ★★★★

Frieberg, Germany, Temple members.aol.com/ranenb/chris.htm A visitor testifies to the miracle of the temple in the former Eastern Bloc. 📖

Hong Kong Mission Alumni Home Page www.1source.com/~hop/mission.html See schedule and photo at www.deseretbook.com/temple/SCHHK.html. Includes photos and the dedicatory prayer for Hong Kong Temple. ★★

Las Vegas, Nevada, Temple www.nevada.edu/home/16/blake/www/LV.temple.html See schedule, photo, and more at www.deseretbook.com/temple/SCHLV.html. Background information on the temple in Las Vegas, Nevada. Very thorough. ★★★

Logan, Utah, Temple cyberfair.gsn.org/usdblhs/ldstemple.html History and early photos of the Logan, Utah, temple. ★★★

Monticello, Utah, Temple nauvoo.byu.edu/Church/Temples/Monticello/underside2.cfm The Monticello Temple was dedicated on July 25th and 26th. Learn about one of the new "small" temples. 📖

Nauvoo Temple History www.ldsworld.com/gems/nauvoo Detailed History of the Nauvoo Temple by David R. Crockett. ★★★★

Nauvoo, Illinois, Temple Tour www.indirect.com/www/crockett/nauvoo.html Photos, history, diagrams, and a descriptive tour of the original temple. Completely fascinating. A valuable document worth revisiting. ★★★★

Omaha, Nebraska, Temple www.discoveromaha.com/community/groups/LDS/local/ Temple One of the newest temples announced. This site went up immediately after the announcement. ★★★

Orlando, Florida, Temple Page www2.gdi.net/~lemuel Schedules, photo, map, and more are at www.deseretbook.com/temple/SCHOR.html. The Building of the Orlando Temple. Someone should have this much love for every temple. ★★★

Preston, England, Temple nauvoo.byu.edu/Church/Temples/Preston_Temple/ underside2.cfm The Preston Temple, the 52d operating temple of The Church of Jesus Christ of Latter-day Saints, opened on June 7, 1998. See pictures, view video clips, and read about the new temple in Northern England. ★★★★

Rebuilding of the Nauvoo Temple www.vii.com/~nicksl/newnauvoo.html Nick Literski's favorite project. ★★★★★

Saint George, Utah, Temple www.infowest.com/Utah/colorcountry/History/Temple/ temple.html Great history site. Very well done. ★★★

Saint Louis, Missouri, Temple www.ezl.com/~eggbtr Building the St. Louis Temple. From the Hammond home page, there are links to information related to the St. Louis temple. ★★★

Salt Lake Temple www.uvol.com/www1st/tsquare Max Berlota provides a nice tour of Temple Square and nearby historical sites. ★★★★

Salt Lake Temple, History www.nettally.com/lds/hist.html Great page, chock full of explanations and a photographic history (see figure 8.6). An excellent site, and the quality of the historic photographs makes it well worth visiting. It would be nice to be able to click on the pictures and have them expand to fill the entire screen. ★★★

Salt Lake Temple, Tour of Temple Square www.desnews.com/confer/sqtour/tour.htm Online photo tour of Temple Square, with descriptions and histories of the buildings and monuments located there. ★★★

FIG. 8.6

Tour of Temple Square.

Sweden Temple   www.elfi.adbkons.se/~richard/sdh.html In Swedish. Try reading aloud, just for fun. ★★★

Temple Square   www.uvol.com/www1st/tsquare/square.html Great page, with tons of photos and links to historical sites (see figure 8.6). An excellent site. ★★★

Vernal, Utah, Temple   nauvoo.byu.edu/Church/Temples/Vernal_Temple/underside2.cfm Find out all of the facts, see pictures, and read local members' feelings about Utah's 10th temple and the 51st operating temple worldwide of The Church of Jesus Christ of Latter-day Saints. ★★★

LIVING A LATTER-DAY SAINT LIFE

9

THE LIVING CHURCH

The threefold mission of the Church describes in a very inclusive way what the Church is all about: reaching out to the world, reaching out to the members, and strengthening family ties.

Part 3 of this book, called "Living a Latter-day Saint Life," is much more narrowly focused. This first chapter in Part 3, "The Living Church," looks at news of the Church in all its forms. The subsequent chapters consider the auxiliaries of the Church, interest groups, the pursuit of excellence, the glory of God, and finally, a roundup of the LDS Internet experience.

Being a member of a living Church can be a bit like catching fish with bare hands. It takes constant vigilance, sensitivity, keen perceptions, a measure of intelligence, and a willingness to act quickly. The reward, of course, is a feast for the soul.

The Church today is a vital force, one that changes— albeit at a marked pace—to accommodate the changing needs of its membership. In the 1970s, an expanded international missionary effort lead to a great deal of prayer over the issue of expanding the priesthood base. In the 1980s, changes in the demographics of member families resulted in a block meeting

> **THE LIVING CHURCH**
> It is very nettling to be reminded by the living God, through living prophets, the living scriptures, and the living Church, of one's unfinished work and of one's remaining possibilities. The living God reinforces his promptings by our consciences; the living prophets particularize painfully; the living Church lays heavy duties and responsibilities upon us; the living scriptures add to the stimuli, for the word of God can scarcely be opened without giving us a start, suggesting something that needs to be done or undone. So much livingness does not seem to leave much room for repose.
>
> Neal A. Maxwell, *Things as They Really Are,* p. 35

My Story

Jean Borde, Port of Spain Trinidad District <*jabb@trinidad.net*> writes: One of the best ways to get info and to find concern groups is to join a Web ring . . . . I have found that they can sometimes be more effective than search engines. Stick with those that are "good" and form your own little community.

Jordan D. Jones, New Haven, Connecticut, Stake <*jordan@LDScn.com*> writes: The Internet is truly a wonderful way to reach out to those in need. In maintaining several Church-related Internet sites, I have had the opportunity to hear from several people whose lives have been changed by what I have done. People who were touched by the words I put on a site, or people who felt the spirit while reviewing my sites. I have received letters from the less active who have since returned to Church, after seeing something on my site. I'm happy to report that two people went on to e-mail me and tell me of the progress in their family. How they returned to Church, were sealed in the Temple, and the example they are setting for more less active family. The Internet has many wonderful opportunities.

Tom Nedreberg, Eureka, Utah <*tned@cut.net*> writes: My grandfather came to the U.S. from Norway in 1925. By doing a people search, I have found and begun regular correspondence with two second cousins from the same home town as my grandfather. It's been great to meet them and learn about the homeland.

schedule. In the 1990s, rapid growth led to an expansion in the number and makeup of general authorities. In recent years, the number of temples has gone from an easily memorized dozen to more than 50. From a membership of 5 million in the 80s, the Church has more than doubled to its present size of over 11 million. In our march to the millennium, we as a Church have continued to find new ways to meet one another's needs. And the Internet will play an ever-increasing part in that outreach.

This chapter lists resources that allow Latter-day Saints—no matter where they live—to keep pace with the change. The first section, the International Church, contains information for members living outside of North America. It's followed by a listing of major events and activities; a large section on news about the Church; a sampling of online wards, branches, and stakes of the Church; and a section on electronic discussion areas that invite member participation.

THE INTERNATIONAL CHURCH

Now that more than half the membership of the Church lies outside the borders of the United States, redirecting the focus internationally is more important than ever before.

Members throughout the world are building Web sites that reflect their own cultures and communities. Together, their sites constitute a diverse, multicultural perspective that fulfills scriptural prophesies of the gospel going to "every kindred, and tongue, and people, and nation" (Revelation 5:9).

ArabLDS/al-malaak aT-Ta'ir   arabLDS.cjb.net The first Arabic LDS Web site, this one aims to present an accurate image of the Church in the Arab world. 📖

AsiaCyberWard   www.onelist.com/subscribe/AsiaCyberWard A list for current and former members of any English-speaking Asian unit of the Church. Slow. ★★★

Australia: Australian LDS Home Page www.iinet.net.au/ ~soneil/LDS.html Information about The Church of Jesus Christ of Latter-day Saints in Australia. Includes local contacts, Sydney temple information, and more. ★★★★

Austria: LDS Resources www.ettl.co.at/mormon A bilingual German/English site. Lots of links. ★★★★

Basque-speaking: Ongi Etorri Mormoi Euskaldunen Etxeko Orrialdera www.cyberhighway.net/~goodies/basque An introduction to the LDS Church in Basque (see figure 9.1). Includes a history of the Church, the Articles of Faith, and the Proclamation on the Family. No English. ★★★

Book of Mormon Languages www.new-jerusalem. com/bom-answerman/bomlanguages.html A partial list of the languages of the Book of Mormon, plus information on how to get a free Book of Mormon. ★★

HOTLINKS

ArabLDS/al-malaak aT-Ta'ir
arabLDS.cjb.net

Chinese LDS Resources
www.erols.com/eepeter/LDS.html

Eastern Europe Mission Center
members.tripod.com/~kyiv

Grant's Legacy
www.egroups.com/list/j-LDS

Mission.Net
www.mission.net

Worldwide Saints
www.LDSworld.com/gems/wws

Brasil-SUD www.xmission.com/~dkenison/brasil/sud Discussions in Portuguese for LDS members. Subscribe with a message to *<majordomo@xmission.com>* or contact list administrator David Kenison *<dkenison@xmission.com>*. The companion Web site **Brazil: Página Das Missões Brasileiras** at www.xmission.com/ ~dkenison/brasil describes the Church in Brazil, including information on the São Paulo temple. Includes an English translation. ★★★★

FIG. 9.1

Ongi Etorri Mormoi: Basquing on the Internet.

BYU Multicultural Student Services www.netcom.com/~toniaizu/gmss.html Privately collected information regarding the Multicultural Student Services department at BYU. ★★

Cambodia: The Church in Cambodia www.orst.edu/~charlesb/sasana.html News, photos, and information about the branches of the Church in Cambodia. Very timely. ★★★★

Centro Hispanico www.chitrenet.net/santos An LDS resource page in Spanish to help Spanish speakers learn more about the Church. Contains links to great Spanish-language resources. ★★★★

Chinese LDS Resources www.erols.com/eepeter/LDS.html Various Chinese-related LDS Resources, including a searchable English-Chinese Church term dictionary, selections from The Book of Mormon in Chinese, and links to other Chinese LDS sites. A site for people interested in the Church in Taiwan and Hong Kong. Includes links to different Chinese LDS sites, a searchable glossary of Chinese translations of English LDS terms, and some chapters from the Chinese Book of Mormon. Lots of links, but the site itself is in English. ★★★

Eastern Europe Mission Center members.tripod.com/~kyiv English- and native-language information for missions in the Ukraine, Russia, Lithuania, Hungary, Poland, Romania, and Yugoslavia. ★★★★★

> **PRACTICAL RELIGION**
> In other words the world needs practical religion—it needs applied Christianity. It needs not only to pray, "Thy kingdom come. Thy will be done in earth, as it is in heaven," (Matt. 6:10) but also to work for the "establishment of divine government among human beings."
>
> David O. McKay, *Gospel Ideals*, p. 294

Free Book of Mormon www.xmission.com/~health/mormon/bom.html Numbers to call to get a free Book of Mormon in over 80 different languages. 📖

German-speaking: Das Buch Mormon www.geocities.com/Heartland/Hills/1037/inhalt.htm The Book of Mormon in German. ★★★

German-speaking: Proclamation on the Family in German www.ettl.co.at/mormon/deutsch/familie.htm Read Webmaster Michael Stanek's account of how the proclamation influenced one nonmember. 📖

Germany: The Germany Munich Mission Unofficial Homepage www.mission.net/germany/munich/gmm.html In English. History of the Germany Munich Mission and its predecessors: the South German/Germany South Mission, the Bavarian Mission, and the West German Mission. Includes an alumni list. ★★

Grant's Legacy   www.egroups.com/list/j-LDS   In 1901, Elder Heber J. Grant was the first LDS missionary to open Japan to the restored gospel. Since that time, membership of the Church in Japan has grown to over 100,000. This English-language list discusses the special blessings (and challenges) of being LDS in Japan. Open to everyone who has any connection with Japan, or even those who are only interested in Japan. Japanese and gaijin, residents and nonresidents, members and nonmembers, return missionaries, military personnel who are serving or have served in Japan, and parents of missionaries serving in Japan, are all invited to share stories, news, insights, and questions. Subscribe at the Web site, or by sending an e-mail request to *<j-LDS-subscribe@egroups.com>*. Moderated by Bill Lewis *<billewis@rnac.ne.jp>* of Mizusawa, Japan. ★★★★

Holland: De Kerk van Jezus Christus van de Heiligen der Laatste Dagen   www.worldaccess.nl/~collinst An unofficial Church site in Dutch. Includes English-language information about the Dutch missions. ★★★★

Hong Kong: HK Saints   home.netvigator.com/~bonken Bilingual site (but mostly Cantonese) with information about the Church in Hong Kong. ★★★★

> **THE INTERNATIONAL CHURCH**
> We are one in our testimonies of the gospel. . . . We are one in faith, hope, and charity. We are one in our conviction that the Book of Mormon is the inspired word of God. We are one in supporting President Hinckley and the other General Authorities. We are one in loving each other. . . . [it is essential that Church members around the world know one thing about each other—] that we are all His children.
>
> *Church News*, April 13, 1996, p. 9, quoting Chieko N. Okazaki in General Conference

International   www.wnetc.com/resource/LDS/international.html Brief list of links to sites related to the international Church. ★★

Japan: Bountiful   Chat/communication list in Japanese. Uncontroversial. Subscribe with an e-mail request to *<majordomo@iijnet.or.jp>*. Requires Japanese-language computer capability. Daily traffic: 10 messages. 📖

Japan: Irreantum   Japanese-language discussion of LDS matters for those who have not been satisfied by formal answers. Subscribe by sending an e-mail request to *<owner-irre@iijnet.or.jp>*. Requires Japanese-language computer capability. 📖

Japan: LDS-J   Mailing list for a general discussion of LDS topics. To subscribe, send your request to *<owner-LDS-j@iijnet.or.jp>*. Requires Japanese-language computer capability. 📖

Japan: Plates   Discussion and information list about PC and data application to gospel study in Japanese. Mainly for those working with data input, translation,

Braille materials, etc., or Church materials in Japanese. Send a subscription request to *<plates-ml-request@yk.rim.or.jp>*. 📖

LDS/Korea Page   www.geocities.com/Heartland/Ranch/2065 Information about the LDS Church and Korean culture. Useful resources for study of Korean language and culture, including online language study, books, software, and Korean search. ★★★★

Mexico: Benemèrito de las Amèricas   www.geocities.com/Athens/Acropolis/1789 Web site for the LDS-operated school in Colona Juarez, Mexico. Spanish only. ★★★

Mission.Net   www.mission.net Find your mission on the Internet. The Mission.Net site lists mission home pages, information about many coutries, and help for new missionaries. For alumni of various missions of the Church of Jesus Christ of Latter-day Saints. This site facilitates e-mail, reunions, and snail-mail contacts. Also, young men and women who are called on missions may find the information on these pages useful as they prepare to enter the mission field. ★★★★★ ☑

Our International LDS   www.mich.com/~romulans/Intl_LDS_Online.html Community online LDS Web sites around the world. Links only; no original content. ★★

Portugal SUD   www.geocities.com/Athens/Acropolis/2532 No English. History of the Church in Portugal, translations of English-language documents, and more. ★★★

Portugal: Queluz-Portugal Branch   www.geocities.com/Athens/Acropolis/7595 All English with good general background information on the Church. Very little of specifically Portuguese interest. ★★★

Russia: The Church in Russia   LDSmissions.net/rspm Russia St. Petersburg mission homepage. Information in English and Russian. ★

Scandinavia: EP Friend   A mailing list for Latter-day Saints with an interest in Scandinavia. The list operates in Swedish. To subscribe, send an e-mail request to *<Richard.Bruvik@adbkons.se>*. 📖

Spanish-speaking: Creencias de la Iglesia de Jesucristo de los Santos de los Ultimos Días   cc.usu.edu/~slc9d/nicaragua/doctrina.html Teachings of the Church in Spanish. Quite brief. ★★

Spanish-speaking: Historia de la Iglesia SUD cc.usu.edu/~slc9d/nicaragua/historia.html A history of the Church in Spanish. Includes links to Nicaragua mission. ★★★

Spanish-speaking: Light at the Top of the Mountain A monthly e-mail magazine (bimonthly in Spanish) of LDS messages and doctrine. Subscribe by e-mailing a request to <*marda@burgoyne.com*>. 📖

Sweden: LDS Resources 130.244.7.117/~richard/sdh.html A list of resources for Latter-day Saints in Sweden. Non-English. ★★★

Worldwide Church www.mormons.org/basic/organization/world Articles related to the international Church. Topics include: Community, The Church in Africa, The Church in Asia, The Church in Australia, The Church in the British Isles, The Church in Canada, and Gathering and Colonization. A Mormons.Org page. ★★★

Worldwide Saints www.LDSworld.com/gems/wws See also the Worldwide Church History Archives www.xmission.com/~dkenison/ lds/gems/arc_wrld.html. Share the history of the Church as it rolls forth among the nations of the Earth. This LDS-GEMS project documents history and stories from Church members in various countries around the world. You will find experiences submitted by many people who have participated and witnessed these miraculous events. ★★★★

WW-LDS mdavies.for.ilstu.edu/ww-lds International resources on the Church of Jesus Christ of Latter-day Saints outside of the United States and Canada Arranged and organized by Mark Davies, Illinois State University. This old site in a new home includes country information, Worldwide LDS Directory Church Areas (Administrative Units), and the WW-LDS email discussion group. It's great to see someone looking outward in this way. ★★★★★

EVENTS AND ACTIVITIES

There's no end of events and activities available to Latter-day Saints. In this section, you'll find the home pages for activities ranging from the Polynesian Cultural Center in Hawaii to the Hill Cumorah Pageant in New York.

America's Witness for Christ www.ldscn.com/hcp Well-done page full of information about the Hill Cumorah pageant, as well as some Historical Church sites in the Palmyra area of New York. Includes links to the Hill, the Pageant, the Sacred Grove, the Smith Home, the Martin Harris Home, the Grandin Printing Shop,

HOTLINKS

America's Witness for Christ
www.ldscn.com/hcp

Church Pageant Schedules
www.deseretbook.com/pageant.
html

Mormon Arts Foundation
www.thewatchmen.com/ma

Polynesian Cultural Center
www.polynesia.com

the Peter Whitmer Home, and the Fayette Chapel, as well as a map of the area. ★★★★

BYU Sports   sports.byu.edu Stats, coaches, players, and more, for every BYU sport. ★★★★★

Calendar of Events   www.deseretbook.com/events Deseret Book's listing of concerts, speakers, and just about anything else you can think of. Readers are invited to submit information about public events for inclusion on the calendar. ★★★★

Church Pageant Schedules   www.deseretbook.com/pageant.html Schedules and information for Church-sponsored pageants. A schedule for next year would make this a tremendously useful site. ★★★

Church Trivia   members.aol.com/cumorahhil/church_trivia A fun page. Test yourself. Questions change from time to time. ★★★★

City of Joseph Pageant   www.nauvoo.com/vacation/dates.html Information on this summertime Nauvoo, Illinois, pageant. ★★★

Cougar Sports Network   www.ysite.com/csn Headline news for BYU Cougar sports fans (see figure 9.2). ★★★★★

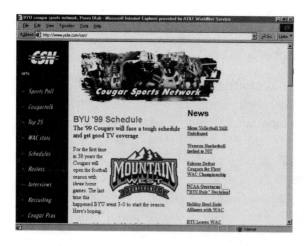

FIG. 9.2

Cougar Sports Network: The next best thing to being there.

Cougar-Net www.cougar-net.com Information via e-mail about Brigham Young University athletics. Links to the Cougar-Net and Cougar-Best e-mail lists, plus archives of earlier discussions. ★★★

Goin' to Zion www.gointozion.com A musical journey of the heart . . . or the heat, given the location. Summer musical sponsored by the Georgia Atlanta Mission and the Jonesboro Georgia Stake uses multimedia and special effects to update the acclaimed 1997 production. This moving musical uses a cast of over 150 to bring to life the epic story of the exodus of the Mormon pioneers. ★★★★

Holidays and Celebrations www.mormons.org/daily/holidays Articles on LDS-celebrated holidays and events. Includes commentary on Halloween, Easter, the Hill Cumorah Pageant, more. ★★★

Jesus the Christ Pageant www.tcsaz.com/mesapageant/pictures.html Information on the Mesa, Arizona, Church pageant. ★★★

LDS Calendar www.desnews.com/cgi-bin/libheads_reg?search=%22LDS+calendar%22& limit=999&x=47&y=9 LDS events running in the *Church News*. A new entry each Friday. ★★★★★

Lilacs of the Valley www.igoshopping.com/lilacsplay Home page for the pioneer pageant Lilacs in the Valley. Includes music from the presentation. ★★★

Mesa Temple Easter Pageant www.tcsaz.com/mesapageant.html Information about the Pageant held each year at Easter in Mesa, Arizona. ★★★

Mormon Arts Foundation www.thewatchmen.com/ma Information on the art gallery and the festival at Tuacahn. ★★★

Mormon Miracle Pageant www.manti.com/pageant.htm The Mormon Miracle Pageant performed in June on the grounds of the Manti Temple. Free admission. Site hadn't been updated for the next pageant, so the rating looks worse than it deserves to be. ★★

Palmyra Ward's "Hotel Palmyra" The Palmyra Ward sometimes sponsors a bed-and-breakfast service for visitors to the area each year. Families and groups are welcome to stay in the homes of members of the Palmyra Ward. Sponsored by the Palmyra Youth, donations are accepted, and breakfast can be provided. Respond by e-mail to another of my distant cousins, Owen Allen, at *<oallen@ix.netcom.com>*. 📖

Polynesian Cultural Center   www.polynesia.com Delightful site full of valuable information for visitors to the Center in Hawaii (see figure 9.3). Contacts and everything you need to know to make your visit enjoyable. ★★★★★

Question of the Week   www.desnews.com/cgi-bin/libheads_reg?search=%22Question+of+the+week%22&limit=999&x=92&y=13 Another trivia test with questions running each week in the *Church News*. ★★★

The Spirit of Nauvoo   www.nauvoo.com/vacation Lodge at the Nauvoo House one day or longer. Available in July and August at $17.50 per day. $

Tuacahn   www.showutah.com An excellent site describing events at Tuacahn, the Mormon art center. Links to information on Tuacahn Events, Ticket Info, About Utah!, and Photos. A very nice page. ★★★★

NEWS OF THE CHURCH

The only real difference between living among the main body of the Saints and living out in what used to be called the "mission field," is access.

During my years living overseas, I found lack of access to be something of a burden. Mail delivery overseas was generally unreliable, and always slow. At one point, I was living on a small island outlying Hong Kong, far away from the other Latter-day Saints in my ward, which meant that even secondhand news was hard to come by.

Going on line opened up the world for me. The newsgroup I participated in became my primary—in fact, my only—source of Church news. It was still a form of secondhand information, but Utah-dwelling Saints were quick to announce every bit of Church-related news they came across.

It was, in effect, the very first LDS Wire Service in existence. I was the first in the ward to know about deaths, callings, policy changes, and every other scrap of information that fascinates those who can't get it without some effort.

Now, as you'll see from the resources listed in this section, news about the Church is easy to find. The following resources are divided into three groups: broadcasters, traditional print publishers, and new electronic publishers.

Broadcast

My grandparents had to walk miles to school in the snow—yeah, yeah, yeah, Grandpa, and it was uphill both directions, right? My parents remember when they didn't have television at all—I know, I know . . . and that was before color was invented, right Dad? So the other day, when my husband told our 12-year-old that when we were young, we actually had to walk all the way across the room to . . . , our son interrupted and finished his sentence for him—"to push the buttons. I know, Dad."

"No," my husband said. "We didn't have buttons. We had to turn a dial." Our son looked surprised and then burst into laughter.

Now our son's already got the next round for his children. "When we were young," he'll tell his babies, "we used to stand around the computer and listen to radio broadcasts."

It's Internet radio, and that's what we really do. Whenever I listen, the kids gather 'round and ask, in wonderment, "Where's that coming from?" Ha! I've one-upped them.

To me, this is incomparably the most fascinating part of the Internet: listening to online broadcasts of LDS radio programming.

The following sites offer some great listening through the speakers and sound card on your PC. You'll need a copy of the software that plays the broadcast. It's available for free by clicking on the download icon at each site.

HOTLINKS

LDS Radio Network
www.ldsradio.com

KSL Radio/TV
www.ksl.com

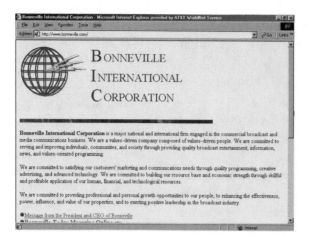

FIG. 9.4

LDS Radio Network: Listen to live LDS programming through the sound card and speakers on your PC.

Bonneville International www.bonneville.com Links to all the Bonneville media properties (see figure 9.4). ★★

KBYU Radio/TV kbyuwww.byu.edu Information-heavy page from KBYU, the BYU media affiliates. Listen to KBYU-FM over the Internet. ★★★★★

KSL Radio/TV www.ksl.com Watch KSL TV, and listen to KSL Radio live over your Internet connection. ★★★★

LDS Radio Network www.LDSradio.com Twenty-four-hour programming from Bonneville International. Listen to conference talks, uplifting music, Church news, and BYU sports from your desktop. One of the most helpful sites on the Internet. ★★★★★

Print

The sites below are associated with traditional print publications, including magazines, journals, and newspapers.

A few of the publications listed here have no direct LDS affiliation, but do carry a larger-than-average quantity of information either about the Church or about subjects of specific interest to Latter-day Saints.

Alumni Publications ucs.byu.edu/alumni/alum-pub.htm A collection of publications from the Alumni Association at Brigham Young University. Includes links to *Brigham Young Magazine*, Alumni Today, Emeritydings (a newsletter for emeritus BYU-ers), and Passages (the alumni tours newsletter). ★★★★★

AML-List cc.weber.edu/~byparkinson/aml-list.html List of LDS and LDS-affiliated publications. View a list of newspapers at cc.weber.edu/~byparkinson/aml-list.html#newspapers. A list of LDS journals is maintained at cc.weber.edu/~byparkinson/aml-list.html#journals. Webmaster Benson Parkinson does a great job of keeping these lists up to date. ★★★★★ ☑

Ancient American Archaeology ancientamerican.com No known LDS affiliation, but certainly of interest to members of the Church. Ancient American is a bimonthly, color, popular science magazine, describing with photographs and reports the accounts of overseas visitors to America hundreds . . . even thousands of years before Columbus. ★★★★

Brigham Young Magazine www.byu.edu/bym The BYU alumni publication, which is distributed quarterly (see figure 9.5). This site contains the current issue and archives of several back issues. Great reading. ★★★★★

BYU Public Communications www.byu.edu/news A great site listing BYU news and events, along with links to the text of selected devotionals; calendars for fine arts productions, conferences, and workshops; BYU sports; construction updates; and much more. Maintained by BYU Public Communications. ★★★★★

HOTLINKS

AML-List
cc.weber.edu/~byparkinson/
aml-list.html

Brigham Young Magazine
www.byu.edu/bym

BYU Publications
advance.byu.edu/pdf.html

Church News
www.desnews.com/cn

Newsnet @BYU
newsline.byu.edu

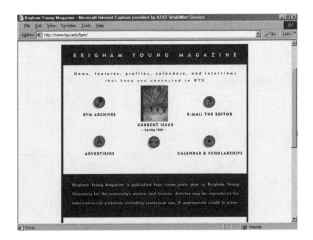

FIG. 9.5

Brigham Young Magazine: The alumni publication is filled with well-written articles on a variety of topics.

How I Net

Tonia Izu, San Jose, California, San Jose, California, East Stake, Berryessa Ward *<Tonialzu@ix.netcom.com>* writes: Family gatherings. We have a family e-mail list. We can now share information with our extended family and receive the latest news on weddings, birth announcements, and other family information with cousins that live around the nation. We just began this list, but I am hoping it will bring generations closer together.

Robert F Patterson, San Leandro, California, Stake *<bobpatt@home.com>* writes: We're just getting familiar with the LDS resources on the Internet. Have been participating in Pioneer Cooking on LDSCN for some time. Just accessed Mormon News and LDS-Gems. Currently checking out many of the preparedness links. Some of the lesson-related materials look really interesting. Nothing so far regarding my calling (Stake mission president), but still looking around. In our Stake, we're setting up a number of e-mail distribution lists. Within the Stake mission, we've set up one for the presidency and one for Ward mission leaders. Also preparing lists for bishops and Stake missionaries.

BYU Publications   advance.byu.edu/pdf.html Includes *BYU Magazine, Clark Memorandum* (law school), *Exchange* magazine, course catalogs, and more. Documents must be downloaded to an Adobe Acrobat reader available from a link at the site. ★★★★

BYU Studies   humanities.byu.edu/BYUStudies/homepage. htm BYU's scholarly journal. Dedicated to the correlation of revealed and discovered truth and to the conviction that the spiritual and the intellectual may be complementary and fundamentally harmonious avenues of knowledge. This multidisciplinary journal has been published continuously since 1959. Its objective is to publish the best possible LDS scholarly journal, along with one or two major books a year, and occasional smaller monographs or special issues. The Web site contains a subscription form, on index to content, and information about events. While the journal itself is fantastic, the site lacks real content. ★★

Church News   www.desnews.com/cn Deseret News's semiofficial *Church News.* The site used to be publicly accessible. Then it wasn't. Now they've found a happy medium and it seems to work. Full access requires a subscription, but there's enough public access material on the site to make it worth visiting. ★★★★

Church Publications   www.mormons.org/basic/organization/ publications A collection of articles describing publications of the Church. Includes information on *Church News,* Conference Reports, Curriculum, General Handbook of Instructions, Bulletin, Distribution Centers, Doctrinal Works, *The Children's Friend,* Comprehensive History of the Church, and *The Contributor.* A Mormons.Org page. ★★

Deseret News   www.desnews.com Salt Lake City's number two paper, owned and indirectly operated by the Church. Good site for staying current on Utah politics or issues. ★★★★★

FARMS Review of Books   farmsresearch.com/frob/main.htm Reviews of books on LDS topics. Of particular note is the presence of refutations of critical works. Includes ROB's predecessor, *Review of Books on The Book of Mormon.* ★★★★

Hartmut Weissman's Betrachtungen ("Reflections") A Euro-*Sunstone/BYU Studies.* Write Weissman at Gartner Platz 10, 61130, Nidderau, Germany, or e-mail him at <*74371.174@compuserve.com*>. 📖

Insights: An Ancient Window farmsresearch.com/insight/main.htm The newsletter of the Foundation for Ancient Research and Mormon Studies (FARMS). ★★★

Journal of Book of Mormon Studies farmsresearch.com/jbms/main.htm Scholarly journal for Book of Mormon research, published semiannually by FARMS. ★★★★

KeAlaka'i websider.byuh.edu/kealakai BYU Hawaii's campus bulletin. Not regularly updated, but if you're a BYU-H alum, you'll want to stop by. ★★★

Latter-day Herald www.LDHerald.com Washington's LDS Newspaper. Minimal online content, but this home page for the monthly, independent LDS newspaper for the Washington, DC, area and the mid-Atlantic states has potential. Subscribe from the Web site. 💲

Latter-day Messenger www.jps.net/ldm Stories, news, and more about Northern California Saints, newly expanded to cover Wasatch Front LDS news, as well. ★★

LDS Periodicals www.writerspost.com/mormonj/mags A list maintained at Mormon-J: The LDS Journal-List. ★★★

(Logan) Herald Journal www.hjnews.com No archive, no search engine. Sometimes you'll stumble across Church news for Cache County, though. ★★

How I Net

Linda Adams, Raytown Ward, Kansas City, Missouri <*adamszoo@sprintmail.com*> writes: As a writer, I have enjoyed participating in AML-List and in LDSF-List. I've met other writers, people with the same dreams I have, where before I went "on line" I felt fairly isolated. I have also learned a lot about the business end of writing and many "how-to's" this way. I have not used it extensively in my callings so far, other than posting our Ward Newsletter to my Web page.

Barbara Barney, Federal Way, Washington, Second Ward <*MamaBarney@aol.com*> writes: I use the Internet to keep in touch with family and friends, keep current for my home-based business, communicate with others who do the same thing I do. Owning a home-based business is wonderful yet challenging. Being able to communicate with others keeps me current with company trends and gives me great advice in how to juggle family obligations and work. It's fun exchanging hints, tips, and ideas with others in the same situation as me. I use the Internet in my calling as Relief Society compassionate service leader to keep me focused on the eternities. It's great to receive e-mail from the different e-mail lists that I'm on. I learn so much from other LDS people and get great ideas on how to help those I serve.

Newsnet @BYU newsline.byu.edu The KBYU/*Daily Universe* (BYU student newspaper) page. Campus events, live cam coverage of construction at the Lee Library, sports, Utah news, more. ★★★★

(Ogden) Standard-Examiner www.standard.net Good religion coverage. An excellent newspaper. ★★★★★

(Provo) Daily Herald www.daily-herald.com Utah Valley's best daily. (Take my recommendation with a grain of salt. This was the paper that trained me up in the way I should go; now that I'm old, I will not depart far from it.) The *Herald* operates a fine religion section that tries too hard to be diverse. ★★★★

Salt Lake Tribune utahonline.sltrib.com The Not-The-*Deseret-News* Salt Lake daily. Articles about the Church are frequent. A very well-done site. ★★★★★

Scroll On-Line www.ricks.edu/Ricks/News/Scroll/scrollonline.html This is the online version of the Scroll, the student newspaper for Ricks College. Lots of good information. ★★★★

Submitting an Article to the Church News www.mich.com/~romulans/desnews.html For budding writers. ★★

Sunstone The publication is not yet on line. There is, however, an e-mail contact at <*SunstoneUT@aol.com*> 📖

Utah Historical Quarterly www.xmission.com/~drudy/ushs/uhq.html A 60-year index, which stops in 1995. No other content. ★

Electronic

I'm an old-school journalist, trained from youth to love printer's ink, racks of type, and loud presses. So it's with mixed emotion that I acknowledge the progress that has taken over my profession and made the future of publishing into something composed of electronic bits and bytes.

As happens with all progress, my excitement about the future is tempered by nostalgia over losing the past. That's not to say that progress in publishing is all, or even mostly, bad. It's not. It's mostly good. Electronic publishing has a number of advantages over traditional publishing, advantages that affect both the publisher and the reader. Not only is it less expensive—it eliminates two of the three costs of publishing: paper and postage—but it's also more timely and better focused.

For readers, electronic publications enable research. No more newspaper morgues, clipping services, or tattered library copies on microfilm when you need to search for information. Everything published electronically remains available for as long as the publisher maintains an archive. Readers get their information faster and at a lower cost than they've ever had from traditional media.

As you'll see from the following list of electronic periodicals, online publishing also enables anybody—absolutely anybody—to jump into the fray. The quality of information available from "small-press" online periodicals varies with the skill and resources of the publisher, but overall, the world is a better place because of their contribution.

HOTLINKS

Gazette
www.mormontown.org/gazette

The Wasp
www.xmission.com/~estep

Vigor
www.nauvoo.com/vigor

Gazette www.mormontown.org/gazette Very professionally done worldwide electronic newspaper for LDS people. ★★★★★

James Talmage Society Newsletter cpms.byu.edu/cpms/talmage The Latter-day Saint Association of the Mathematical and Physical Scientists (LAMPS). A group publishing information about LDS scientists and issues related to science and religion. Chatty. Science Departmental. Sometimes valuable. ★★★★

Ketav lal.cs.byu.edu/ketav/standard/homepage.html BYU's Department of Computer Science's online magazine. Essays on computer science, religion, and more. Great content. Unfortunately, it's not been updated for months. ★★

Leading Edge humanities.byu.edu/tle/theleadingedge.html Science fiction and fantasy magazine produced by an all-volunteer staff at Brigham Young University, featuring fiction, poetry, and art. It's actually quite good. ★★★★

Light at the Top of the Mountain Free gospel topic magazine only published on the Internet. E-mail: *<marda@burgoyne.com>*. No Web site. 📖

Mormontown Digest www.mormontown.org/digest A showcase for literary submissions from readers. Unexpectedly well done. ★★★★★

The Wasp www.xmission.com/~estep LDS journal of news, reviews, and commentary published by Christopher and Deanna Estep. Humor, opinion . . . not nearly so biting as its Nauvoo-period namesake. ★★★★★ ☑

Vigor www.nauvoo.com/vigor A thoughtful publication of essays edited and sometimes written by Orson Scott Card. Published irregularly, but well worth the read. ★★★★

Women's Magazine www.mormontown.org/women A professionally written, well-designed electronic magazine for LDS women from Mormontown.org. Impressive. ★★★★★

Worldwide LDS FriendsZine www.LDSfriends.com/ezine/marchapril98 A small collection of stories and poetry infrequently updated. ★★

Youth Magazine www.mormontown.org/youth Another great online publication from Mormontown by and for youth of the Church. Regularly updated. ★★★★★

Zion's Fiction www.zfiction.com Writer Thom Duncan's fascinating new publishing venture. Works of LDS-themed speculative fiction are available electronically. It's all quite forward-looking. ★★★★

Recent Articles About the Church

As the Church grows, so does news coverage about the Church. These Internet resources gather together breaking news about the Church. Stay up to date with these great sites.

Latter-day Saint News Source www.ldsnews.lds.net Get up-to-date news and headlines for the LDS Church. This site makes a great home page. ★★★★★

MORMON-NEWS www.panix.com/~klarsen/mormon-news A mailing list for news of the Church. Average daily volume: 8 messages. Digest version available. Subscribe by sending an e-mail request to *<majordomo@mailing-list.net>* containing the message `subscribe mormon-news`. ★★★★★ ☑

News www.byu.edu/news News from Brigham Young University. An excellent site. ★★★★

News Archives www.LDS-gems.com/archive/news An archive of news items posted to the LDS-GEMS mailing list. Items are culled from articles in newspapers and other publications. Makes a great clipping service. ★★★★

ONLINE UNITS OF THE CHURCH

Ready to move beyond news from downtown Salt Lake City? If your ward or stake has developed a Web site, you already know where to go for a local calendar of events.

Many units of the Church have created home pages as part of their public communications effort. The following Internet sites will be of interest whether you're building a Web page for your own ward, or just want to keep in touch with friends from a former ward.

Here you'll find links to both branch/ward sites and stake home pages, along with other information about the organization of the Church.

Contemporary Church Organization www.mormons.org/basic/organization/ Contemporary_Organization_EOM.htm An *Encyclopedia of Mormonism* article describing how the Church is organized. 📖

Stakes www.geocities.com/Heartland/4034/content.html#stakes The stake listings are buried deep in this long list of good links. ★★

Wards-Branches LDS-online.com/Wards-Branches.htm Short list, but it's being updated often. ★

Stakes and Wards with Home Pages www.danvillestake.org/s/danville/LDS_pgs.html Stake and ward home pages worldwide. 📖

Units of the Church www.deseretbook.com/LDSinfo/units.html A nice listing of wards, stakes, districts, and branches with their own Web pages. ★★★

Wards www.geocities.com/Heartland/4034/content.html#ward Links to various wards and branches. ★★

DISCUSSION GROUPS

Though you might not know it from the information presented earlier in this book, the Internet is much, much more than a collection of Web pages! In fact, Web browsing consumes only a little bit of the average Internet user's online time.

Far more significant, for most people, is the two-way communication that comes out of discussing the gospel with other members of the Church. Discussions take many forms: private electronic mail, e-mail lists, real-time chats, newsgroups, and discussion forums. The nature of these discussions ranges from the positive and uplifting, to the scholarly and academic, to the negative and critical, to the downright nasty and loathsome.

No matter what your own inclination, you'll find like-minded Latter-day Saints in various discussion areas eager to hear your point of view—and even more eager to tell you theirs.

Mailing Lists

A mailing list is, quite simply, a small group of people who send e-mail to one another. Mailing lists generally have a theme, some reason for being, which defines the subject matter up for discussion.

Lists create communities—small groups of people who have in common not only their basic religious affiliation, but also some additional interest that binds them together.

To participate in an e-mail list, you must first subscribe. To subscribe to a list, send an e-mail request to the moderator or sponsor named in the listings below. The sponsor may write back to you personally acknowledging your request, but more often, you'll be signed up automatically, just because you asked.

Some lists are closely moderated, meaning that off-topic submissions are returned to the sender. Others are barely moderated, and some aren't moderated at all. A caution: Even among otherwise good Latter-day Saints, unmoderated lists sometimes become a bit hot, creating animosity and hurt feelings. Participation requires a thick skin, a sense of humor, a deeply rooted faith, and an ability not to take things personally.

Moderated lists, on the other hand, can degenerate into a sort of sing-song pedantry, unless the moderator has a gift for steering with both patience and faith. The best lists have a very specific purpose, and a light-handed moderator who discourages tangents and encourages discussion.

Lists of Lists
The following sites describe LDS e-mail lists, and are regularly updated.

LDS Internet Resources cc.weber.edu/~byparkinson/goble.faq Content is mirrored at www.whitestag.org/LDS and ftp://ftp.wnetc.com/LDS/LDS-resource-faq. Clark Goble's very well-maintained list of LDS mailing lists. Clark's compilation is a primary resource for the listings that appear in the next section. ★★★★

LDS Mailing Lists www.wnetc.com/resource/LDS.lists.html A somewhat less complete list of mailing lists. ★★★

The LDS E-mail Lists

The following listing of sites is only a sampling of the many LDS e-mail lists available. Additional lists are found in other chapters, where their focus is directly related to a specific topic addressed elsewhere in this book. The lists are unrated here, but may appear with ratings when they're addressed topically in other chapters.

2NDSPOUSE www.egroups.com/list/2ndspouse/info.html LDS Second Spouses and Step-Parents. 15 members.

AML-LIST cc.weber.edu/~byparkinson/aml-list.html A discussion list for members of the Association for Mormon Letters. Welcomes all scholars and fans of Mormon literature. Maximum volume is 30 posts per day. Send subscription request to *<aml-request@cc.weber.edu>* with the message `subscribe aml-list "Your Name in Quotes" <your@ address.in.brackets>`. Digest and low-volume magazine versions are also available. Benson Parkinson *<byparkinson@cc.weber.edu>* moderates the list.

BML www.egroups.com/list/bml/info.html Book of Mormon Linguistics. Ninety-six members.

BOM www.onelist.com/community/bom A chapter of the Book of Mormon each week day (but probably not during holidays). The list is also open for discussion. Discussion of the current chapters is actively encouraged. Think of this as Sunday School in e-mail.

BOMSTDY www.egroups.com/list/bomstdy/info.html Book of Mormon Study. Thirty-three members.

CLEAN-LDS members.tripod.com/~RexGoode/Clean.html Support list for members of the Church who struggle with pornography addiction. Membership in the list is not restricted to members, but topics will be consistent with LDS teachings. Use of clean language is madatory. All subscription requests must be sent directly to *<rexg@coil.com>*, after reading the requirements at the Web site. A sister list,

HOTLINKS

AML-LIST
cc.weber.edu/~byparkinson/
aml-list.html

ELIJAH-L
www.genealogy.org/~holdiman/
elijah-l

LDSFORUM
www.onelist.com/subscribe/
LDSForum

LDS-GEMS
www.lds-gems.com

LDS-HIST
www.kingsleymc.com/clark/Lists/
lds-hist.htm

LDS-NET
<listproc@mainstream.net>

LDS-POLL
www.egroups.com/list/LDS-poll/
info.html

LDSPROPHECY
www.egroups.com/list/
LDSprophecy/info.html

LDS-SEMINAR
<majordomo@LDSchurch.net>

CLEAN-SUPPORT, helps family members of Saints trying to overcome the practice. Subscribe to either list with a request to <*rexg@coil.com*> after reading the requirements at the Web site. Very well moderated, appears to be a tremendous strength to its members.

COUGAR-BEST   Selected messages from COUGAR-NET. Subscribe with an e-mail request to <*listserv@byu.edu*> with the message: `subscribe COUGAR-BEST FirstName LastName`. Operated by David Kenison <*dkenison@xmission.com*> and my distant cousin, Newell Wright <*nwright@wcu.edu*>.

COUGAR-NET   High-volume list for discussions of BYU sports. Topics include games, recruiting, BYU alumni in the pros, and other WAC teams. Subscribe with an e-mail request to <*listserv@byu.edu*> containing the message `subscribe cougar-net`. Archives available at the Web site.

DAILYE-MAIL   www.egroups.com/list/dailye-mail/info.html Usually a thought and a couple of "clean" jokes, with an occasional FYI. Older samples archived at: www.accesscom.com/~newitts/DailyEmailArchive/DailyEmail.txt.

DISCIPLES   users.aol.com/disciples2 For those who struggle with issues of same-sex attraction but are committed to obedience to the gospel of Jesus Christ and the teachings of modern apostles and prophets. Anonymous participation is permitted. Charter is strictly enforced, as is confidentiality. The list welcomes parents, spouses, priesthood leaders, and counselors. Subscribe with a request to <*subscribe-disciples2@discuss.dundee.net*>. Subject line should read `Subscribe Disciples`. The body of the e-mail should include your name, address, and phone. Charter is at the Web site.

DNABOM   www.onelist.com/community/dnabom Searching for genetic evidence that Book of Mormon people originated from the Middle East. Microbiologists, geneticists, anthropologists, or any other "serious" pursuers of scientific evidence post here. Contact the moderator for permission to subscribe. For more information, see www.latterdaylampoon.com/gazelem/dnabom.htm.

DOCTRINE   www.onelist.com/community/doctrine This list will mail out a chapter of The Doctrine and Covenants and Pearl of Great Price each weekday. Open discussion of the chapters being studied and of Church history is strongly encouraged.

ELIJAH-L   www.genealogy.org/~holdiman/elijah-l Genealogy discussion from an LDS perspective. Moderator Byron Holdiman <*ByronDH@aol.com*> started the list in 1994 after seeing a member get bashed on a non-LDS forum for mentioning temple work. Members needed a safe place to discuss this mission of the Church, he says. There are presently about 300 people subscribed to the list, including several that are not members of the Church. Discussions range from topics about Family History Centers, official announcements of temples, genealogy helps, and PAF, to teaching genealogy, submitting names to the temple, and testimonies. Traffic is about five messages a day. Subscribe with an e-mail message to <*Elijah-L-Request@genealogy.org*> with the subject line `subscribe`. Archives are maintained at www.escribe.com/genealogy/elijah.

EMMBP   www.onelist.com/community/emmbp Quality stories and jokes for nearly anyone. Send stories to the moderator at <*emmbp@uwyo.edu*> for consideration. All in all, it is a good, uplifting, low-volume list.

EP-LIST   www.netman.se/adbkons/sdh.html Scandinavian Saints and those interested in talking about Scandinavia. The list is limited to LDS members, preferably those with some connection to Scandinavia. Subscribe with an e-mail to <*Richard.Bruvik@adbkons.se*> with your name and a little information about yourself. Archives at the Web site.

EYRING-L   www.kingsleymc.com/Clark/Lists/eyring-l.html The Mormonism and Science list. Includes discussions on evolution, the ethics of various scientific techniques, and the interplay that scientists have between their disciplines and their religion. FAQ: www.frii.com/~allsop/eyring-l/faq. Subscribe at <*eyring-l-request@mail.kingleymc.com*>. Operated by Clark Goble and Colin Robertson.

FAMILIES   members.aol.com/disciples2/families.htm A discussion list for families of LDS members dealing with same-sex orientation. Not negative toward the Church. Subscribe with an e-mail request to <*d2moderate@aol.com*>. More information is available at the Web site.

FAMILYFELLOWSHIP www.onelist.com/community/familyfellowship Volunteer service organization, a diverse collection of Mormon families engaged in the cause of strengthening families with homosexual members. The moderator says: "We share our witness that gay and lesbian Mormons can be great blessings in the lives of their families, and that families can be great blessings in the lives of their gay and lesbian members. We strive to become more understanding and appreciative of each other while staying out of society's debate over homosexuality. We seek to put behind us all attitudes which are anti-family, which threaten loving relationships, and which drive family members apart. All who can support these goals are welcome to contribute." For more information, see www.arcticmen.com/familyfellowship.

FREE-SAINTS www.graceweb.org/FreeSaints Nonmembers and Latter-day Saints debate the truthfulness of the Church. The list is designed for rigorous discussions, and people who engage in personal attacks are removed. And it's not nearly so nice as it sounds. The bashing runs rampant, and gets very personal. Subscribe with an e-mail request to *<free-saints-request@graceweb.org>* with the body `subscribe`.

GAYMORMON www.onelist.com/community/gaymormon For all Latter-day Saints with same-sex attraction. The moderator says: "This is a positive place: a place of tolerance, of acceptance, and of holiness. We do not condemn same-sex attraction (neither the attraction nor the sex) nor do we condemn The Church of Jesus Christ of Latter-day Saints. We are a community of faithful Latter-day Saints who happen to have same-sex attraction, and are willing to live a moral and acceptable life (a monogomous relationship, no porno, no anonymous sex, no other "immoral" activity, maintaining a sense of decency, etc.). Nonmembers are allowed, as long as they do not trash the Church and as long they uphold our morals." Members who wish to maintain confidentiality will have their privacy guaranteed. For more information, see www.geocities.com/Athens/Academy/ 6261/.

HANDCART Genealogy of Mormon handcart pioneers. Discussion area for anyone with interest in the genealogy, journals, and stories of the pioneers who settled in the Salt Lake Valley from 1847 to 1860. Subscribe with an e-mail request to *<MAISER@rmgate.pop.indiana.edu>*, with the message `subscribe handcart`.

JEWISHBOM www.egroups.com/list/jewishbom/info.html Jewishness of Book of Mormon. One-hundred forty-four members.

JOEMILLER www.egroups.com/list/joemiller/info.html Moderator writes: "The Joe Miller Joke List is named for the oldest joke book known to exist. (Must be awfully rare, since the Joker tried to steal it in every fifth Batman story in the 1950s.) Clean humour only. The list started in Mormon country, so it's a good idea to imagine these stories and gags going to your old maiden aunt. My bishop is on this list, and he'll whop me upside the head if I get outta line. All seriousness aside, we're here for good clean fun."

JOSEPH   Moderate mailing group to discuss topics related to the gospel. Political or social issues are not allowed here. The emphasis is on learning to live the gospel and is an attempt to have discussions without the bickering and arguments that are on many other lists. It is moderated to ensure that all posts fit the theme and charter of the list. JOSEPH is now at *<joseph@mailing-list.net>*.

JOYFULNOISE   www.onelist.com/community/joyfulnoise For those interested in hearing when a new single is released on Mark Hansen's "A Joyful Noise" Web site. Mark makes spiritual, uplifting, LDS-oriented rock music. For more information, see www.g-web.net/mrkh.

JRCLS   An Internet e-mail list for members of the J. Reuben Clark Society, an association of LDS legal professionals. To subscribe, send an e-mail request to *<listserv@lawgate.byu.edu>* with the message `subscribe jrcls-l <your name>`.

LAMPS Latter-day Saint Association of Mathematical and Physical Scientists (James E. Talmage Society). Send a subscription request to *<carrie@csoffice.cs. byu.edu>*.

LATTERDAYLAMPOON   www.onelist.com/community/latterdaylampoon Mormon Culture Parody and Inside Humor Including Headline News, Spiritual Roulette Interactive Games, Gossip, Science and Religion Updates, Top Ten Lists, Virtual Patriarchal Blessings, and Testimony Contests. Subscribe and receive a bi-weekly e-mail magazine containing all the posts, news, and nonsense from the site. This way you never have to surf the site again because you automatically receive all the new stuff twice a month. For more information, see www.latterdaylampoon.com.

LDISABLED   For members of the Church who are disabled or chronically ill in any way and their families and friends. To subscribe, send an e-mail request to *<listserv@home.ease.lsoft.com>* with the message `subscribe LDISABLED <your name>`.

LDS Scripture of the Day   www.geocities.com/Heartland/Garden/5213/SOTD.html Brief, memorable. To subscribe, visit www.onelist.com/subscribe/LDS-SOTD.

LDS www.onelist.com/community/lds Discussion of issues related to Mormonism.

LDS_BOOKCLUB www.onelist.com/community/lds_bookclub The group reads several different books each month. Choose the book of the month you would like to read, comment on, and make submissions for books. Members vote on books that have been submitted by club members. Selected books are sent out to all members.

LDS_CHAT www.onelist.com/community/lds_chat For members of the Church and those interested in the Church to post questions, comments, concerns, and get to know other people.

LDS_GENEALOGY www.onelist.com/community/lds_genealogy Particularly for those interested in the software and databases maintained by the LDS Church that are genealogically significant. These databases include the IGI, the Ancestral File, and also include the entire FamilySearch system and Personal Ancestral File. Also, any questions about the LDS Church's role in genealogy and family history are welcome. For more information, see members.tripod.com/~Genealogy_Infocenter/ LDSgen-list.html.

LDS_HOMESCHOOL www.onelist.com/community/lds_homeschool List for LDS families who are thinking about or are currently homeschooling their children. Share ideas, uplift, and support each other in the education of children. If you are not LDS, this list is not for you. No advertising, no anti-Mormon sentiments allowed.

LDS_OR_SIS www.onelist.com/community/lds_or_sis For sisters that live in the Portland, Oregon, area to get to know other LDS women.

LDS_SAHMS www.onelist.com/community/lds_sahms A list for LDS stay-at-home moms to discuss parenting, doctrine, breastfeeding, world affairs, you name it.

LDS_SISTERS_BOOKCLUB www.egroups.com/list/LDS_sisters_bookclub/info.html LDS Sister's Book Club. Twenty-six members.

LDS_TOURETTES www.onelist.com/community/lds_tourettes For Saints who have the neurological disorder Tourettes or family members who have Tourettes that would like to exchange ideas about this problem.

LDS-AP www.egroups.com/list/LDS-ap/info.html LDS Attachment Parenting. Thirty-five members.

LDS-BOOKSHELF www.wenet.net/~kirwin/bshelf.html A mailing list designed for those who collect or have a serious interest in collectible books related to Mormon Americana. Subscribe with an e-mail request to *<majordomo@xmission.com>* with the body `subscribe LDS-bookshelf`. List operators are Keith Irwin and Hugh McKell. Archives are maintained at the Web site.

LDS-CMERS www.onelist.com/community/lds-cmers For Latter-day Saint home-schoolers who are using or studying the Charlotte Mason method of education.

LDS-DIABETICS www.egroups.com/list/LDS-diabetics/info.html A support list for LDS people dealing with diabetes.

LDS-DIVORCE-SUPPORT www.egroups.com/list/LDS-divorce-support/info.html Another support list, this for people who are working through the fallout from divorce. Very supportive.

LDS-DOCTRINE www.onelist.com/community/lds-doctrine This list will be used to discuss the doctrines of the LDS church compared to the teachings of the Bible.

LDSF www.zfiction.com/LDSf Mailing list for writers and readers of Mormon specu-lative fiction, which includes all forms of science fiction and fantasy by and for Mor-mons. Some subscribers are published writers in the LDS market; others are LDS writers published in the national science fiction market; others want to be published writers; and still others are LDS folk who just love to read science fiction. List owner Thom Duncan says participants discuss market issues, science fiction in gen-eral, scientific principles—"just about everything that a bunch of literary enthusiasts might talk about around the dinner table. Overarching all our conversations is a love and enthusiasm for the Church of Jesus Christ of Latter-day Saints in general and science fiction in particular." Subscribe from the web page or by sending an e-mail message to *<LDSf@zfiction.com>* with the word `subscribe` in the subject line.

LDSFORUM www.onelist.com/community/ldsforum A wide-ranging discussion list founded by former members of the Compuserve LDS Religion Forum. New members are moderated. Quite active.

LDS-FUNNIES www.egroups.com/list/LDS-funnies/info.html LDS funny stuff.

LDS-GEMS www.lds-gems.com A low-volume, heavily moderated list that includes Church news, excerpts from talks, and more. It also includes the distribution of

Dave Kenison's "Church History Stories" and Dave Crockett's "150 Years Ago in Church History." To subscribe, send an e-mail request to *<majordomo@ xmission.com>* with the body `subscribe LDS-gems.` The list is operated by Dave Kenison and Dave Crockett. Archives are available at the LDS-GEMS Web site.

LDS-GRADS   A chat group for single LDS graduate students or those who are like-minded. The list is primarily for social support and open-minded discussions. While discussions about dating and social concerns are found here, much more is intended. To subscribe, e-mail a request to *<LDS-grads-request@cs.umd.edu>* with your name and a little information about yourself.

LDS-HIST   www.kingsleymc.com/clark/Lists/lds-hist.htm A high-traffic list for the discussion of LDS history. Subscribe at www.egroups.com/list/LDS-hist/info.html, or send an e-mail request to *<lds-hist-request@mail.kingsleymc.com>*. Contact the list operator at *<Clark@mail.kingsleymc.com>*.

LDSHOMEED   www.onelist.com/community/ldshomeed For those members of The Church of Jesus Christ of Latter-day Saints (Mormon) who have chosen to educate their children at home and need support from other LDS Home Educators. Registration can only be done through www.utw.com/~kpearson/LDShomeed. Any registrations that come from this site, unless pre-approved, will be denied. For more information, see www.utw.com/kpearson/LDShomeed.

LDS-INFERTILITY   www.egroups.com/list/LDS-infertility/info.html Waiting in Faith. Thirty-seven members.

LDS-IRCD [DIGEST]   The Latter-day Saints' Mormon-IRC Mailing list. Subscribe with an e-mail request to *<majordomo@wizards.net>*, with the message `subscribe LDS-ircd.`

LDS-L   www.onelist.com/community/lds-l LDS Lesbians was created for lesbian women who are current or former members of the Church, as well as other interested parties. List operator says: "This forum was designed to give a place to discuss spiritual, personal (please ladies, let's keep it clean) and social issues and problems faced by lesbian women involved with the LDS Church in a friendly and non-threatening atmosphere. This list was not created by the Church and does not have the Church's backing. This is NOT a forum for 'converting' or flaming. These kinds of messages will never make it to the list so don't even bother."

LDS-MORMON-YSA   www.onelist.com/community/lds-mormon-ysa For members of the Church who are generally college age, or around the ages of 18 to 30. The list also welcomes people who generally fit the "Young Single Adult" category, although, says the moderator, "If you're not LDS, married or don't quite fit the age we'll still be nice to you :)" This list operator hopes list members will get in touch with other LDS people, and find out about activities going on in other places.

LDS-MOTHERHOOD   www.onelist.com/community/lds-motherhood A collection of thoughts on Motherhood from an LDS viewpoint. One quote, poem, article, or story is sent out weekly. For more information, contact *<Anita14501@aol.com>*

LDS-NET   The oldest mailing list for LDS discussions. It's often called the Internet First Ward. The list is of a general nature, and includes discussions on social issues, doctrine, scriptures, and general news. It is fairly moderate in tone and volume, though controversies do flair up from time to time. Mostly unmoderated. Subscribe with an e-mail request to *<listproc@mainstream.net>* with the body `subscribe LDS-net your name`.

LDS-NEWS   www.egroups.com/list/LDS-news/info.html LDS NEWS.

LDS-OT   www.egroups.com/list/LDS-ot/info.html LDS study of OT Hebrew. Twenty-two members.

LDS-PHIL   www.nd.edu/~rpotter The LDS Philosophy of Religion list. Primarily for professional philosophers and those with training in philosophy who happen to be Mormon or interested in Mormon theology. The list presents an opportunity to discuss religious issues within the confines of their technical expertise. The list is not moderated, but subscription must be approved. It is a low-volume list. To subscribe, send an e-mail request to *<listserv@vma.cc.nd.edu>* with the message `subscribe LDS-phil <your name>`. Archives are at the Web site.

LDS-POLL   www.egroups.com/list/LDS-poll/info.html LDS Politics. This moderated newsgroup discusses political issues that affect or interest Latter-day Saints. A wide range of political views are encouraged. News and information about pending legislation can also be found here. To subscribe, send an e-mail message to *<LDS-poll@egroups.com>*

LDSPOP   www.onelist.com/community/ldspop This list is for the appreciation of and discussion of the pop culture of the members of the Church of Jesus Christ of

Latter-day Saints (LDS or Mormon). Topics: LDS pop music, current novels, videos, musicals, and culture in general. The list is not for academic debate of theological issues. We just want to visit about the things we like to read, watch, and listen to.

LDSPRIMARY www.panix.com/~klarsen/LDSprimary This is a mailing list for parents, teachers, and administrators in the primary organization. It has discussions dealing with teaching the gospel to children, activities for these children, and finding resources related to these topics. It also discusses the responsibilities of those who have been called to work with the primary organization. Subscribe with an e-mail request to *<LDSprimary@mailing-list.net>* with the body `subscribe LDSprimary`. Archives are at the Web site.

LDSPRODUCTS www.onelist.com/community/ldsproducts This is an announcement list sponsored by an independent LDS Bookstore which provides information on the latest and greatest LDS products available. We are not sponsored by any distributor, vendor, or publisher. Therefore, we have the freedom to select from all the products available in the LDS marketplace today. Keywords: LDS, Church of Jesus Christ of Latter Day Saints, Book of Mormon, Joseph Smith, Mormon. For more information, see www.ldsbooks.com.

LDSPROPHECY www.egroups.com/list/LDSprophecy/info.html Informal group of researchers interested in studying LDS prophecy. The participants on the list analyze prophetic events using the scriptures (The King James Bible, Book of Mormon, Doctrine and Covenants, and the Pearl of Great Price) and the writings of the leaders and members of the Church. Eighty-seven members.

LDSPROZAC www.onelist.com/community/ldsprozac The purpose of this list is to provide a safe forum for current and former members of the Mormon church to discuss issues relating to their Mormon upbringings, heritage, experiences, etc. We will occasionally post different Sunstone articles for all members of the list to review and discuss.

LDS-RESEARCH A mailing list for scholarly discussions on various LDS subjects. It is for serious research on doctrine, history, society, and culture. The list is moderated. Posts are required to include references and quotations relative to the subject being discussed. To subscribe, e-mail a request to *<majordomo@ xmission.com>* with the body `subscribe LDS-research`.

LDSSA www.egroups.com/list/LDSsa/info.html LDSSA Worldwide. Thirty-five members.

LDSSA-L   www.students.uiuc.edu/~sandland/www.aquila.com/niuLDSsa A newsletter and information for the LDS Student Association. This is from the University of Illinois, but may contain information for college students at other institutions that are associated with LDSSA. To subscribe, send an e-mail request to *<Listserv@ po.uiuc.edu>* with the text `subscribe LDSSA-L your name`. Archives are at the Web site.

LDS-SA-LEADERS   www.egroups.com/list/LDS-sa-leaders/info.html LDS Single Adult Leadership Forum. One-hundred four members.

LDSSCRIPTURES   www.onelist.com/community/ldsscriptures This list will be for those who want to read the scriptures as a group and then discuss them. This list has been started and going. Reading a chapter every other day. For more information, contact *<unicorn79@yahoo.com>*

LDS-SEMINAR   www.cybcon.com/~kurtn/exegesis.html Commentary and in-depth discussion on each week's Gospel Doctrine lesson. Includes regular columns, plus postings from other participants. To subscribe, send a message to *<majordomo@ LDSchurch.net>* with the message `subscribe LDSs <yourname@ your.email.address>` or the digest version `subscribe LDSS-D <yourname@ your.email.address>`.

LDSSISWEIGHDN   www.egroups.com/list/LDSsisweighdn/info.html LDS sister weigh down. Forty-eight members.

LDS-SOTD   http://www.onelist.com/community/lds-sotd Receive a scripture a day from the LDS standard works (Bible, Book of Mormon, Doctrine and Covenants, Pearl of Great Price). Scriptures are usually short (1–3 verses) and follow a "theme" to go along with the monthly message from the First Presidency. This is not a discussion list. The list sends out one scripture each day. It is intended to inspire readers—or at least cause them to think. They are also interrelated and cumulative, meaning that they are not just individual verses meant to inspire entirely on their own, but they are all related to each other along the monthly theme, and are meant to support and inspire readers in their scripture studies and contemplation of the First Presidency's message. For more information, seewww.geocities.com/Heartland/Garden/5213/SOTD.html.

LDS-SUNDAY SCHOOL   www.acoin.com/kelly Full text of next week's Sunday school reading assignment. This year's reading assignment is the Doctrine and Covenants. The reading assignment is divided into five messages, one for each weekday. Subscribe by sending your e-mail request to <anderson@itsnet.com>. Archives are at the Web site.

Net Folks

Jean Borde, Port of Spain Trinidad District <jabb@trinidad.net> writes: Sure . . . my wife and I met each other in Y-chat (BYU) and we were sealed in the Washington temple on February 19th, 1999. So it definitely affected us! **:)**

Richard C. Russell, Taylorsville, Utah <lderlore@xmission.com> writes: I can't begin to elaborate on how these last five years on discussion lists have changed me. I have a much widened circle of friends who are important to me and whom I would not have known in any other way. They look me up when in town and I have a face to go with almost all of the regulars.

Lorraine from Salt Lake City <KWDLAD@aol.com> writes: I do get frustrated at times with others on the Internet. I find that it is easy to miscommunicate as you cannot hear another's inflections and tone of voice, and miss the nuances of their real meaning. It is also very easy to push SEND without thinking more about what you wrote. I actually write more long-hand, snail-mail letters to family because it is more personal and means a lot to me when I get one, too.

LDS-TREKKERS www.onelist.com/subscribe/Lds-trekkers A forum for fans of *Star Trek,* science fiction, and fantasy. Church membership is not required to join. For more information, contact the list owner, Phil Musgrave, at home1.gte.net.pmuskrat/LDS/trek.htm

LDS-VERSE www.egroups.com/list/LDS-verse/info.html LDS Scripture Verse. One hundred eighty-two members.

LDS-YOUNGWOMEN www.egroups.com/list/LDS-youngwomen/info.html LDS Young Women. One hundred three members.

LDS-YW LDS-YW is dedicated to the Young Women of the Church and their leaders. It is a way to exchange ideas, testimonies, and experiences. To subscribe, e-mail your request to <majordomo@xmission.com> with the body `subscribe LDS-yw`.

LDS-YWLIST www.onelist.com/community/lds-ywlist This list is dedicated to adult leaders involved in the Latter-day Saint Young Women's program of the Church of Jesus Christ of Latter-day Saints. Topics should reflect the values we strive to teach young women. This is a place for YW leaders to exchange ideas and help one another with anything relating to the young women's program and to share the triumphs and challenges of our lives as YW leaders. For more information, contact <jbuchmil@teleport.com>.

MARYANDMARTHA www.egroups.com/list/maryandmartha/info.html Mary and Martha. Fifty-five members.

M-KABBALAH www.egroups.com/list/m-kabbalah/info.html Mormon Kabbalah Forum. Seventy-one members.

MORM-HIST Thoughtful discussion of Mormon history. Subscription requests should be addressed to *<majordomo@sara.zia.com>* with the message `subscribe morm-hist`.

MORMON www.onelist.com/community/mormon Spanish-language lista de discusion acerca de mormones. For more information, see www.elreino.cjb.net.

MORMON_SINGLE www.onelist.com/community/mormon_single Meet interesting, unmarried LDS members in your area. Find roommates, worldwide pen-pals, clean funny jokes, romance, or just socialize with other single members of the Church. For more information, see www.loveusa.com

MORMONDSMOMMIES www.onelist.com/community/mormondsmommies This is a place for Mormon Mommies of children with Down Syndrome. We have a unique perspective—let's share it.

MORMON-HUMOR Mormon-humor is an e-mail list for telling jokes, puns, and amusing stories and anecdotes about Mormons and Mormonism. Almost all aspects of Mormon culture, activities, events, and people worldwide are fair game. However, racist and sexual jokes and jokes that make malicious fun of others should not be sent to mormon-humor. To subscribe, e-mail a request to *<majordomo@lists.panix.com>* with the body `subscribe mormon-humor`.

MORMON-INDEX www.panix.com/~klarsen/mormon-index List of queries, responses, announcements, and information on Mormon resources on the Internet. If you are looking for information, you can post requests here as well. A very excellent service. To subscribe, send an e-mail request to *<majordomo@lists.panix.com>* with the body `subscribe mormon-index <your@email>`. The list is operated by Kent Larsen. Archives are at the Web site.

Net Folks

Jan Tucker, Lehi, Utah, Lehi 2nd Ward *<tuckete@enol.com>* writes: I belong to several e-mail lists that are "LDS"-oriented and often wonder where some of them get their ideas! But this Church isn't made up of people who all look the same or think the same. I guess that is what makes it so great. There is no such thing as a "typical" Mormon. There are also several who have become good friends. I can't wait to meet them "live." And although I don't think they have ever caused me to change, they have certainly caused me to rethink some things. Most of the time, I have stood firm on my beliefs, but there are some who brought up valid points and caused some minor course corrections.

Maile Hatch, Tucson, Arizona *<maile@azstarnet.com>* writes: I have been uplifted and inspired by the women I have met through the listserv—they are all so strong and so spiritual. . ... Things don't always work out well for our members, and when something goes wrong, the other women are quick to offer love and support. I feel like I am a better person for having had the opportunity to associate with these great people.

MORMON-JOKES www.egroups.com/list/mormon-jokes/info.html Mormon Jokes. Two hundred two members.

MORMON-L Generally considered to be a liberal, active mailing list. Subject matter covers all bases and generates a lot of volume. It's also had a very controversial history. As one of the oldest Mormon mailing lists, it tends to be very widely read. To subscribe, send an e-mail request to *<majordomo@catbyrd. com>* with the body `subscribe mormon-l <your@email.address>`.

MORMONNET www.onelist.com/community/mormonnet Very-low-volume, heavily moderated mailing list for LDS Internet users. Subscribers submit and receive notification of new and substantially upgraded LDS Internet sites.

MORMON-NEWS www.panix.com/~klarsen/mormon-news A mailing list where news about the Church and news articles concerning the Church are posted. No discussions about the articles are posted here. Send a subscription request to *<majordomo@lists.panix.com>* with the body `subscribe mormon-news`. Archives are at the Web site.

MORMONS-ONLY .onelist.com/community/mormons-only Moderated mailing list for members, friends, and investigators to assist one another in lesson and talk preparation, exchange testimonies, share faith-promoting stories, and get to know each other. No religious debate. MORMONS-ONLY was organized in 1996 and now has membership in every inhabited continent and many of the isles of the sea. For more information, see www.geocities.com/Heartland/Lake/4765/mormons.htm.

MORMON-SPANISH www.egroups.com/list/mormon-spanish/info.html Mormon-Spanish List. Seventy-four members.

MORMON-SPEC www.onelist.com/community/mormon-spec For discussing the more speculative aspects of Mormon theology. All are welcome here, no matter what your denominational affiliation. We are not, however, to engage in discussions specifically aimed toward disparaging anyone's belief. Mutual respect is the only rule. If you have an interest in Mormon speculative theology, please join us.

MORMONSTRENGTH www.onelist.com/community/mormonstrength Open discussion without angry debates. Share your stories, respond to stories about the strength and truth of the LDS church. Ask questions and make friends and connect with other Christians.

MORMON-TALK www.onelist.com/community/mormon-talk The moderator writes: "Do LDS mailing lists sometimes get you down? Do you suffer occasional tummy upsets from all the sweetness and light of some? Do you endure the heartburn caused by the wild rantings and anger on other lists? Then try the list that doesn't require 'that pink stuff—try Mormon-talk, designed to benefit both the faith and the reason God gave you!—and see immediate improvement in your outlook on life. Can be taken as many times a day as necessary, with no harmful side effects. (Some persons have noticed an increase in mental ability and strengthening of the heart muscles.) (Two people claim it cured their baldness.) Our slogan is simple—the heart without the brain is merely another bloody muscle. Join us today!" Andrea Stacy and Jeffrey Needle are co-moderators.

MORMONTEENS www.onelist.com/community/mormonteens Mailing list from a Mormonteen. Chat about anything Mormonish!

MORMONTR Mormon Trails discussion list. Subscribe with a request to *<listserv@unlvm.unl.edu>* containing the line `subscribe mormontr`.

MORMON-YOUTH www.onelist.com/community/mormonyouth For people interested in discussing the plan of salvation or who want to know the truth about the Mormon church.

MORMONYOUTH www.onelist.com/community/mormon-youth For Mormons ages 12–18.

NON-READERS www.egroups.com/list/non-readers/info.html This is a "tongue-in-cheek" support group. The moderator writes, "Every trip to an LDS or even a regular bookstore finds me buying books I would like to read, but never get around to. We are looking for people who have read books to make recommendations or create mini book reports to get us reading! Let's start with Readers Picks, Must Haves, Don't Recommends, and Can't Live Without topics. You may endorse certain Scripture forms (quads, large print, standard, etc). Also Reference Works, as Greek or Hebrew Study, Maps and Atlases, or Biographies of Prophets. I am bowled over with books. I have all eight volumes of The Work and the Glory, and have only read the first! Please join us! Buyers of Books Who Don't Read Them." Thirty members.

ORSON-SCOTT-CARD www.wood.net/~khyron/card/cardlist.html A mailing list devoted exclusively to discussion of Orson Scott Card's writings. Orson Scott Card is a well-known science-fiction author and has also authored plays and worked on screenplays. To subscribe, e-mail a request to *<majordomo@wood.net>* with the message `subscribe orsoncard`. Archives are available at the Web site.

PARAGUAY-MISSION www.egroups.com/list/paraguay-mission/info.html Paraguay Asuncion Mission. One hundred six members.

PARENTS A general list for LDS parents. Subscribe by sending an e-mail request to *<majordomo@LDSchurch.net>* with the message `subscribe parents`.

PEACE For Latter-day Saints who need a place to discuss issues relating to depression. No archive, moderated. To subscribe, send a request to *<majordomo@LDSchurch.net>* with the message `subscribe peace <your e-mail address>`.

PIONEER-COOKING www.ldscn.com/pioneer-cooking Discussions, stories, recipes, techniques related to all aspects of pioneer life, with an emphasis on pioneer cooking. Subscribe with an e-mail request to *<majordomo@ldscn.com>* with the message `subscribe pioneercooking`.

PREP www.ldscn.com/prep A list for discussions and information about disaster preparedness, home storage, and emergency planning, from an LDS perspective. To subscribe, send an e-mail request to *<majordomo@ldscn.com>* with the body `subscribe prep`.

RAMHAT www.onelist.com/community/ramhat Reasoning about Mormon history and theology. No out-of-control arguments that do not resolve themselves within a short period of time. This list is open to anyone. The moderator writes: "I will be no respecter of persons, as long as they remain friendly and respectful. Motivation will be the main factor on this list. Let us remember to keep Christ in these discussions. Since there will be those on this list who hold their faith in Joseph Smith, and those who don't it is important to remember that it is the Lord himself who does the drawing, not our intellectual reasoning." For more information, see www.onelist.com/subscribe/RAMHAT.

RAYMCINTYRE www.onelist.com/community/raymcintyre Theological discussion for Mormons and Restorationists.

RULDS2 www.egroups.com/list/ruLDS2/info.html RULDS2? Connecting LDS People Worldwide. One hundred sixty-six members.

SAMU-L For more technical discussions of antiquities and their relationship to Mormonism. Includes frequent discussions about the historical background of Mormon scriptures, archaeology, the Book of Mormon, and historical symbols.

Generally low in volume, and most posts contain quite a bit of information. To subscribe, send an e-mail request to *<pacal@bingvmb.cc.binghamton.edu>* or *<mraish@library.lib.binghamton.edu>*.

SANCTIFY www.ldscn.com/sanctify An e-mail support list for inactive and part-member families. Frequently—and inexplicably—contentious, although several list members work hard to keep it peaceful. Subscribe with an e-mail message to *<majordomo@ldscn.com>* with the body `subscribe sanctify` or contact Susan Malmrose *<susan@ldschurch.net>*.

SCOUTS-LDS www.tagus.com A low-volume list dealing with the scouting program in the Church. Share ideas for activities, describe ways of dealing with youth, or ask advice on handling your calling. To subscribe, send a request to *<scouts-LDS-request@tagus.com>* with the message `subscribe scouts-LDS`. Visit the Web site to review archives.

SCRIPTURE-L www.wnetc.com/scripture-l A discussion of the scriptures. Operated and moderated by Gregory Woodhouse. Volume is moderate. Send subscription requests to *<scripture-l-request@lists.best.com>* with the message `subsingle`. To receive all the day's messages in one post mail, change the message to `subscribe`. Archives available at the Web site.

SEMINARY www.listservice.net/seminary Lesson ideas for teaching seminary, institute, or any other teaching position. Inspiring. A really first-class, useful list. Send your subscription request to *<majordomo@listservice.net>*.

SEM-JOKE www.onelist.com/community/sem-joke People who enjoy good, clean, often religious, particularly Mormon, sometimes computer, humor. Recipients are involved in religious instruction at the high school and college levels.

SISTERS For women to discuss any topic they choose. To subscribe, send an e-mail request to *<maiser@rmgate.pop.indiana.edu>*.

SEEKER www.egroups.com/list/seeker/info.html The Messenger. Thirty-one members.

SPIRIT www.LDScn.com/spirit A mailing list for poems, spiritual thoughts, and stories. Discussions are discouraged, but submissions are welcome. Subscribe with an e-mail request to *<majordomo@seminary.org>* with the message `subscribe spirit`. Archives are maintained at the Web site.

SPIRITUAL_THOUGHTS www.egroups.com/list/spiritual_thoughts/info.html LDS Spiritual Thoughts. Thirty-five members.

STARSHIP-ZION www.egroups.com/list/starship-zion/info.html Starship Zion. One hundred twenty-two members.

STAY-AT-HOME MOMS www.utw.com/~kpearson/homemoms.html A forum for mothers who have chosen to stay at home. Subscribe from the Web page.

TEENS A general list for LDS youth. Subscribe with an e-mail request to *<majordomo@LDSchurch.net>* , with the message `subscribe teens`.

UKLDS www.egroups.com/list/ukLDS/info.html UK LDS Gospel Discussion Forum. Forty-seven members.

WOMENTOO members.aol.com/disciples2/women.htm LDS Women with a same-sex orientation who seek to follow the Church's teachings. Not negative toward the Church. Subscribe with an e-mail request to *<d2moderate@aol.com>*. More information is found on the Web site.

WW-LDS 138.87.151.56/ww-LDS The Church in an international setting. Promotes discussions of the relationship between local cultures, the Church, and Utah Valley culture. It also is for discussing how the ecclesiastical organization and operation is affected by local cultures and the challenges this brings to effective Church service. News about the Church in international settings can also be found here. To subscribe, send a request to *<listserv@acadcomp.cmp.ilstu.edu>* with the message `subscribe ww-LDS <your name>`. Archives are found at the Web site.

WW-LDS www.egroups.com/list/ww-LDS/info.html Worldwide LDS. One hundred eighty-seven members.

Real-time Chats

Me, I'm not a chatter. I used to be, but gave it up after about 20 minutes.

Other people, though, seem to thrive on the genre. They love the noisy, fast-paced, mixed-up conversations that take place in Internet chat rooms, and claim that I'm missing out on the best game in town.

Chatting is the practice of jumping into a live conversation and typing as fast as you can. As soon as you send off a line, other people are reading it and responding to what you wrote. It's all tremendously exciting, and—because the sentences tend to intertwine with the musings of other chat-room participants—it's utterly confusing to new users.

If you're inclined to give it a shot, you'll need to download the free software that makes it all possible. Visit the Web sites in the following chat listings for help getting on line.

HOTLINKS

Affinity LDS Chat
affinity.faithweb.com

#mormon
www.LDS.npl.com/special/irc/
mormon

Mormon Chat
www.mormons.org/chat.htm

#LDSYouth www.inetworld.net/kaos/LDSyouth.html Sometimes heavily used, sometimes empty. In any event, it hasn't been updated in more than a year and on our last visit, the chat room was empty. ★★

#mormon www.LDS.npl.com/special/irc/mormon (See figure 9.6.) This page is dedicated to the many inhabitants of the undernet #Mormon (pronounced "pound Mormon"). A very busy, very popular chat site. Requires special software, but it's all explained at the Web site. ★★★★

#mormon homepage (EFNET) www.irc.mormon.org The first LDS chat forum in Internet History! 📖

#mormon.amigos gemstate.net/friends A new chat area for Spanish-speaking Saints. Spanish isn't one of my languages, so this site is unrated. 📖

#mormon.friends gemstate.net/friends The Mormon Friends chat area. Requires special software. ★★★★

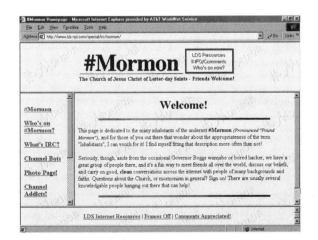

FIG. 9.6

#Mormon: Before you chat, stop here for an introduction.

#mormon.teens www.geocities.com/Heartland/Hills/6850 A fairly new site for teenage chats. News, online dances (really!), and more. Safe, moderated. Requires special software. ★★★★

Affinity LDS Chat affinity.faithweb.com Graphical, interactive Web site. This is the community of the future. Go swimming, dance, play laser tag, have pizza. Participate in monthly socials. Visity the youth den, with music and munchies. Lots more. Java-enabled browsers are OK. I'm very impressed. ★★★★★ ☑

LDS CHAT HISTORY

I run a website called LDS Members on the Internet—ICQ List.

How it all started: The background of how this list happened. I downloaded and installed a program called Internet Phone (IPhone) one day and was setting it up. I noticed an LDS room. I ventured in and found a nice gentleman by the name of Bill Burch. After I talked with him for a bit, he asked if I would like to maintain a list of members of the Church we had met there, and build a database of people to chat with. Well, after trying to build this list for a couple of months and not having very much interest, it kind of just fell by the wayside. I think we had a high of 30 members at one point.

I then found a program called ICQ and started chatting with people. There seemed to be a lot more interest. One day while searching the ICQ Web site, I noticed that it had a place to download information for putting your group or organizations list on their web site. I figured I could move our IPhone list to ICQ. After finding out who would be interested, I moved our list of 15 members to our new ICQ List Home at byondf1.com/icqlist.htm. That was around June 1, 1997, and the list then contained 15 members.

I was then announcing new members to the list by sending a message through ICQ
(continued)

Cumorah's Hill Online Chatting members.aol.com/cumorahhil/chat An unscheduled chat area. You might find someone online, but probably won't. Requires no special software. ★★

Mormon Chat www.mormons.org/chat.htm Scheduled chats take place most evenings. Requires no special software. ★★★★

Real-time chats YCHAT www.ychat.com Site for students and other Latter-day Saints with 18 moderated chat rooms: three for LDS singles, two for gospel discussion, one for sports, one for Brigham Young University alumni, one that is open, and 10 that are semiprivate for two people each. The site also contains a news and weather section and an archive of more than 300 news stories about the LDS Church and BYU collected from newspapers around the country. The new hangout for BYU students and LDS members in cyberspace. Eighteen chat rooms and information on just about anything pertaining to the LDS Church and BYU. 📖

Scott's LDS Chatting Page members.xoom.com/SGRogers Dedicated to helping you find chat sites on the Internet that support LDS standards. 📖

YCHAT www.ychat.com Site for students and other Latter-day Saints with 18 moderated chat rooms: three for LDS singles, two for gospel discussion, one for sports, one for Brigham Young University alumni, one that is open and 10 that are semi-private for two people each. Includes a news and weather section and an archive of more than 300 LDS news stories. A great hangout for BYU students and LDS members in cyberspace. 📖

Newsgroups

Somewhere between the stately pace of e-mail lists and the pure adrenaline rush of real-time chat, lie Internet newsgroups.

Newsgroups are part of a separate portion of the Internet called the UseNet. There are some 20,000 UseNet newsgroups where people debate everything from UFOs to E.coli.

Given the vast number of newsgroups, there are surprisingly few devoted specifically to LDS topics. In fact, only two significant LDS newsgroups exist, one of which is a bit rowdy, and the other of which is a complete madhouse. A third group, focusing on Mormon fellowship, has only a small number of regular participants.

If you're game for a bit of pushing and shoving, open the newsgroup reader on your Web browser (from Navigator, go to the Window menu and click Netscape News. From Explorer, go to the Go menu and click Read News).

If this is your first time reading the newsgroups, you'll need to set some options (call your Internet provider to obtain the appropriate settings for your account), and download the entire list of newsgroups. The process takes about ten minutes on a 28.8-kilobit modem.

(continued)
to everyone on the list each time a new person joined. It soon became apparent that this would become very annoying, so I started a daily newsletter simply to announce our new members. It soon became too much work to put it out daily and it was suggested that it go twice a week. Then people started contributing all kinds of information and suggestions. We soon added the two message boards and the search functions for our list. At that point, it was just a table. But the maintenance was a nightmare. I soon converted it to a database-type program.

Since then, the growth and participation has just astounded me. I never expected it to grow into what it has today. I have been very touched and uplifted by the many members we now have from all around the world. The information and contributions that are sent in help build my testimony daily. Please feel free to contribute at any time, I would love to hear from any of you.

I have found some great friends and heard of some fantastic things happening because of these sites. Things that I could never have imagined, let alone planned. We have an awesome resource of good, caring members out there who are just waiting for the opportunity to help people any way they can. I just provide a means of contact.

Greg A. Anderson, Modesto, California, Fourth Ward <*webmaster@byondf1.com*>

Once you're set up, using newsgroups is a snap. Subscribe to a group (search for the word "mormon" to see a listing), and click on it to read the discussion.

Discussions take place in "threads," where all the discussion on a particular topic keeps the same subject name, and continues for as long as anyone is interested in talking.

The following newsgroups are worth stopping by. Just gird up your loins before you wade in.

alt.religion.mormon   news:alt.religion.mormon Too much bile stored up? Disgorge it all in alt.religion.mormon. You'll fit right in. This newsgroup is the nastiest LDS site on the Web, though the occasional gentle soul tries—for a few days, at least—to inject a word of kindness. (I wish I could claim to be one of those kind people. I'm not. I behave as badly as anyone when I'm in a.r.m.) Don't jump in without reading it for a week or so first. You're unlikely to say *anything* that hasn't been said dozens of times already. ★

alt.religion.mormon.fellowship   news:alt.religion.mormon.fellowship A nice place. A quiet place. Except when nastiness spills over from a.r.m. and infects the generally nice conversations taking place in a.r.m.f. ★★★★

byu.news   news:byu.news For news, discussion, and information related to Brigham Young University. Very little traffic. ★★

msn.forums.religion.latterdaysaint   For Microsoft Network subscribers, this forum is strictly for LDS fellowship. No bashers allowed. I'm not an MSN user, so this site is unrated. 📖

Section 13   The LDS discussion forum on CompuServe and accessible only to CIS members. Moderator Arthur Wilde runs a very thoughtful, very tolerant forum. Type `go:religion`, and log in to section 13. ★★★★★

soc.religion.mormon   Though this group is moderated, it still manages to be tremendously confrontational. Definitely more civilized than the unmoderated a.r.m., however. ★★★★

Web Site Discussion Areas

Finally, we come to the newest sort of discussion group, the Web-based discussion forum.

Using these sites is a simple, almost self-evident procedure. Some sites require you to register (free), some require you to enter a password of your own choosing, and some are just wide open to anyone that stops by.

Some advice, a caution that applies to any discussion group that piques your interest: Before jumping in for the first time, pause to read the existing discussions for at least a day or two. Be sure you understand who's who, and resist the urge to criticize or complain until you've at least introduced yourself and made a couple of positive contributions.

CougarTalk   www.ysite.com/cougartalk The BYU Cougar sports discussion forum. It's talk radio in written form—and the emotions get a little warm. ★★★★

MormonForum   www.homestead.com/mormons Questions about Mormonism are answered by a panel of respondents. Other visitors are also welcome to participate. No registration required, very straightforward. ★★★★★

Nauvoo   www.nauvoo.com Once upon a time, Nauvoo was a forum on AOL. Now everyone can participate—and should. This is easily the best discussion place on the World Wide Web. Orson Scott Card's sponsorship gives it cachet; his *Vigor* newsletter gives it substance. Follow the links to the kids' forum, the Red Brick Store, the Mansion House library, and more. ★★★★★ ☑

The LDS Infobase Message Board   www.enol.com/~infobase/wwwboard This forum has morphed into a strictly Infobase discussion, but it is a lively discussion. Lacks organization, and takes a true bulletin board form, with random, unrelated topics appearing in chronological order. Nevertheless, it has potential as a source of information. ★★★

10
AUXILIARIES

I loved going to my grandparents' house for Sunday dinner. A few times a year, we got to dress up in our nicest clothes, then go to Grandma's, where the grownups sat at their table and all the cousins sat at theirs.

After dinner, we'd all head out to the car to go to sacrament meeting. The building where my grandparents' ward met was a wonderful two-story brick meetinghouse built by my grandpa and my dad and the rest of the ward in the early 1950s. There were pictures of Jesus on the walls of the chapel, and it was an altogether different place from the white cinderblock building in my own town, where I attended Primary on weekday afternoons.

When I turned eight, it seemed natural to ask Grandpa to baptize me. He was happy to do so. He and Grandma drove up from their town for the Saturday-night baptism, and came back the next afternoon for fast and testimony meeting, where Grandpa confirmed me. It was a doubly exciting day, not only because I was being confirmed, but because for once, Grandma and Grandpa got to come to *my* church.

During the testimony meeting, two deacons wandered up and down the aisle holding microphones that they gave to anyone who wanted to stand and bear testimony. Grandma, tearful at the baptism and confirmation of her first grandchild, signaled for a microphone. She stood and bore her testimony, then sat down and handed the microphone to me. I stood, and tried for the first time in my life to speak in front of the whole ward. I was dumbstruck, so Grandma whispered the words in my ear. "I am thankful for my family. . . ." I repeated the words into the microphone. "I am thankful to be baptized. . . ." Nodding to Grandma, I repeated the words. "I am thankful for the Prophet." I nodded and repeated. "And I know this Church is true." I started to repeat, then paused, and said in an embarrassingly loud voice directly into the microphone, "But Grandma, this Church isn't true. *Your* Church is true."

It was many years before I was able to understand why the entire congregation burst into laughter.

In later years, when I was only a little bit smarter, I began hearing a different kind of testimony. For some reason, it became fashionable to stand up in front of a congregation and declare: "Actually, it's not the Church that is true; it's the gospel that is true."

I nodded and started to repeat . . . then paused, and said to myself, "No, I don't think so."

True conversion—to any principle—happens at two levels: the theoretical and the practical. When I believe a thing in theory, but don't act on it in practice, I'm not yet converted; I'm merely persuaded. I might believe in theory that education is important, but if I don't encourage my children to finish their homework, if I fail to show up for school conferences, if I don't get an education myself, then I'm not truly converted to the principle of education.

Likewise, to see the gospel as a thing separate from the Church is to be converted in theory, but not in practice.

The word "gospel" is associated with the Greek word *euaggelizo*, meaning the bearing of good tidings. In the scriptures, the word refers specifically to the glad tidings of the kingdom of God. And what is the kingdom of God, on this earth, if not the Church?

Without a foundation, and without a structure, there is no body of Saints that makes up the Church. There is no means by which we create fellowship. There is no mechanism by which we teach. There is no machinery in place for the perfecting of the Saints.

> Now therefore ye are no more strangers and foreigners, but fellowcitizens with the saints, and of the household of God; And are built upon the foundation of the apostles and prophets, Jesus Christ himself being the chief corner [stone]; In whom all the building fitly framed together groweth unto an holy temple in the Lord: In whom ye also are builded together for an habitation of God through the Spirit.
>
> Ephesians 2:19–22

I love being a Latter-day Saint not only because I love God, but also because I love what God organized. I love the Church. I love all its bits and pieces and personalities and programs and policies and practices. I love the sisterhood of Relief Society, the visiting teaching, the homemaking meetings, the working together that can exist only where there is a structure. I love the Sunday School organization, the reasoning together, the insight that comes from actually, physically, sitting in a class together with other Saints and listening to what they have to say. I love Primary, and

Seminary, and the Youth Programs. I love the programs for priesthood holders and for single adults. None of these programs is theoretical nor could they be. They are part of a living organization that demands much, and gives much in return.

So Grandma, I say this for you—and you know I'm old enough now to mean it with all my heart: I am thankful for my family. I am grateful I was baptized. I am thankful for the Prophet. And I know this Church is true.

This chapter lists resources for the heart of the Church: the auxiliaries. You'll find here Internet listings for the Priesthood, the Primary, the Relief Society, the Seminary program, the Single Adult program, the Sunday School, the Young Men, and the Young Women.

PRIESTHOOD RESOURCES

Helps for priesthood quorums are amazingly difficult to come by on the Internet. In fact, given the ratio of men to women in the LDS online community, the dearth of priesthood resources is downright incredible.

The message? If you're a priesthood holder, and feel compelled to build a Web site, there's a wide-open opportunity to magnify your calling.

The few Priesthood-related sites that do exist do a fine job of covering what they can. You'll find them here:

HOTLINKS

Helping Someone Move
www.virtualpet.com/church/move/move.htm

Home and Visiting Teaching Resource Page
www.absolutesaint.com/resources/htvt.html

HTVT Web Site
members.tripod.com/~hometeaching

Priesthood Organization
www.mormons.org/basic/organization/priesthood

Aaronic Priesthood   www.mormons.org/basic/organization/priesthood/aaronic A collection of articles on topics related to the establishment and powers of the Aaronic Priesthood. Information includes Aaron: Brother of Moses; Aaronic Priesthood: Powers and Offices; Aaronic Priesthood: Restoration; Bishop; Deacons; and History of the Office of Bishop. A Mormons.Org page. ★★★

Combined Index to the Melchizedek Priesthood Study Guides, 1974–1997
Webpages.marshall.edu/~brown/mpsgindx.htm Searchable index of the various Melchizedek Priesthood Study Guides published between 1974 and 1997. ★★★

Dawson Creek Ward Elders   www.geocities.com/heartland/prairie/6333 How one Elders' Quorum stays in touch. Information for home teaching, lessons for Priesthood and Relief Society, some messages, and a lesson calendar for correlation. ★★

Helping Someone Move www.virtualpet.com/church/move/move.htm Personal ideas and tips for an Elders' Quorum involved in helping people move. Very thorough. ★★★

Home Teaching Page www.cnx.net/~kmsiever A resource for Elders' Quorum Presidencies and home teachers of the Church of Jesus Christ of Latter-day Saints. Very slow loading, with little content, but it's making progress. Additional contributions are welcome. ★★★

Home and Visiting Teaching Resource Page www.absolutesaint.com/resources/htvt.html Absolutely great. Mailing list. Talks. Scriptures. Tips. Resources. Daily reminders. This one's a keeper. ★★★★★ ☑

HTVT Web Site members.tripod.com/~hometeaching Dedicated to improving home and visiting teaching. Mailing list, resources, links, ideas, experiences. Submit ideas of your own. Phenomenal (see figure 10.1). ★★★★★ ☑

Leaders to Managers: The Fatal Shift www.farmsresearch.com/nibley/nibley02.html Brother Nibley's brilliant analysis of the need for leadership. Worth visiting repeatedly, even though the material, of course, never changes. 📖

Leadership www.coolcontent.com/familyfun/Leadership An address by Neal A. Maxwell on the qualities of leadership. 📖

Melchizedek Priesthood www.mormons.org/basic/organization/priesthood/melchizedek A collection of articles on topics related to the establishment and powers of the

FIG. 10.1
_____

HTVT Web Site.

Melchizedek Priesthood. Includes information on Melchizedek: LDS Sources; Melchizedek: Ancient Sources; Melchizedek Priesthood: Powers and Offices; Oath and Covenant of the Priesthood; Restoration of the Melchizedek Priesthood; and Apostle. A Mormons.Org page. ★★★

Priesthood Ordinances   www.mormons.org/basic/organization/priesthood/ordinances Articles on the ordinances performed both in and out of the temple. Includes information on Ordinances, Ceremonies, Administration of Ordinances, Baptism, Baptism for the Dead, Confirmation, The Endowment, Priesthood Blessings, Blessings, Blessing of Children, Sacrament, Sealing Power, Cancellation of Sealings, Temple Ordinances, Temple Sealings, and Washings and Anointings. A Mormons.Org page. ★★★

Priesthood Organization   www.mormons.org/basic/organization/priesthood A must-read for all priesthood holders. Articles on Following the Prophets, the Priesthood, Priesthood Offices, Priesthood Ordinances, Melchizedek Priesthood, Aaronic Priesthood, President of the Church, First Presidency, Quorum of the Twelve Apostles, Council of the First Presidency, Succession in the Presidency, Bishopric, Mission Presidents, Assistants to the Twelve, Area Presidency, and Power of the Priesthood. A Mormons.Org page. ★★★

Why Use Olive Oil?   personal.pitnet.net/netty/scripturefiles/whyuseoliveoil.html From Joseph Fielding Smith's Doctrines of Salvation. 📖

PRIMARY

I have a cousin who is the World's Best Mom. She and her husband raise happy, kind, polite children who love one another and are generous and considerate with others.

But when the family moved to Tacoma last year, her seven-year-old son Jonathan had a difficult time of things. Entering a new school with a tough teacher left him despondent, so much so that he withdrew from life, and even began to shy away from other children. It got so bad that my cousin finally decided to remove him from school altogether and teach him at home.

Things got a little better, but at Church he was shy and withdrawn, refusing to speak to anyone or to answer questions in his Primary or Sunday School classes. My cousin, deeply concerned about his happiness, didn't know what to do.

Then along came Sister White.

Everyone's got a testimony of something, and for Sister White, the best—the only—thing about the gospel is the Primary organization. Sister White loves the Primary.

In this particular Primary, there were a handful of "difficult" children. In addition to Jonathan, who refused to speak, there were four tough kids who had scared off a progression of teachers, and a little girl from Russia who spoke no English.

Sister White asked for, and got, a class made up of the six children nobody else seemed able to teach. And she turned them around. Week after week she would visit the children in their homes, read scriptures with them, talk with them, and just generally be their friend.

Somewhere along the line, Jonathan lit up. He began speaking again, started making friends with other children, and developed some self-esteem.

My cousin is so encouraged by the positive changes in his ability to deal with other people that she's decided to re-enroll him in public school. And she gives all the credit to a loving Primary teacher who magnified her calling.

Sister White's not alone in her love for Primary. The following pages were compiled by other Latter-day Saints eager to share their Primary experiences, their sharing time ideas, and their successful activity ideas with other Primary teachers throughout the Church.

Achievement Days Ideas www.primarypage.com/primary/achieve.html From the Primary Page. Lots of great ideas. ★★★

Activity Days Ideas www.primarypage.com/primary/activity.html From the Primary Page. Good list of ideas. ★★★

Cherishing Children www.of-worth.com/cc Theme ideas, poetry, lesson plans, stories, quotes. ★★★★

Christy's Primary Art www.crosswinds.net/~christy/New_Main_Page.html Phenomenal. There's nothing missing. Art, lessons, sharing time, games, international stuff, coloring pages, primary nursery, songs. . . . This site is amazing. It seems to have two home pages, though, so try pw2.netcom.com/pesukone/primary_art.html if you have trouble. ★★★★★ ☑

LDS Today Primary Page www.ldstoday.com/organizations/primary.htm Links to fun ideas for leaders, teachers, and children. Lots of material here, very well organized. ★★★★

HOTLINKS

Christy's Primary Art
www.crosswinds.net/~christy/
New_Main_Page.html

LDS Today Primary Page
www.ldstoday.com/organizations/
primary.htm

LDSPRIMARY
www.panix.com/~klarsen/
ldsprimary.html

Primary Page
www.geocities.com/Heartland/
Prairie/5559/p_container.html

Primary Page
www.primarypage.com

LDSPRIMARY www.panix.com/~klarsen/ldsprimary.html
A mailing list for parents, teachers, and administrators in the Primary organization. Discussions about teaching the gospel to children, activities, and resources. To subscribe, send an e-mail request to *<majordomo@panix.com>* with the message `sub-scribe ldsprimary <your@email.address>`. Highly regarded. More information is available at the Web site. ★★★★

Primarily for Primary People www.uvol.com/www1st/primary/primary.html Very brief selection of ideas, but this page welcomes contributions. ★

Primary Page www.geocities.com/Heartland/Prairie/5559/p_container.html Sharing time, sacrament presentations, activity days, nursery, lessons, music. . . . It's all covered. ★★★★★

Primary Page www.primarypage.com After a hiatus for repairs, this site is back, better than ever. ★★★★

Primary Sharing Time Resources nauvoo.byu.edu/Church/Teaching/SharingTime/underside2.cfm A complete and comprehensive guide to Church-approved materials for Primary Sharing Time. Includes hints and tips. ★★★★

RELIEF SOCIETY RESOURCES

When this book appeared in its first edition, an essay on women and the importance of women's role in the private sphere appeared here. Part of that essay, though, became depressingly political after the book was published. Back before there was any national debate about presidential peccadilloes, I bemoaned what I saw as a growing tendency to separate private from public behavior. I denounced the tendency to glorify public acts while pretending private behavior is inconsequential.

This argument is much deeper than the superficial question of whether to trust leaders suffering from moral schizophrenia. It's significant because in dividing private from public, we also minimize the importance of what people do in private. The honorable, quiet acts of service and charity that make up the lives of most women are diminished when we worship professional athletes and human mannequins; when we seek out the political opinions of movie actors and talk show hosts; when we applaud people who are charitable only when the cameras are rolling; and when we permit braying, self-serving voices to establish the standards of morality.

Sisters who hear these demands for thinner bodies, cleaner homes, fewer children, instant solutions, fascinating careers, unyielding relationships, and pills to solve every problem find their lives unbearably difficult. It is tougher now than ever before to find balance, to live lives of quiet dignity, to remember priorities, or to focus on eternity.

That is why the loving sisterhood of Relief Society is more important now than ever before. In the sisterhood of women is a sweet suggestion of the eternities, a regular reminder that "to every thing there is a season, and a time to every purpose under the heaven" (Ecclesiastes 3:1). Relief Society is where women find birth and death, planting and reaping, death and healing. It's a place where superstitions are broken down, and truth is built up, where the sisters can weep, laugh, mourn and dance together. In the programs of the Relief Society, stumbling stones are cast away, and gospel foundations are built on the rock of truth. We hug, we hold hands, we receive, we give. We exchange clothing, gifts, and talents. We rip, we mend, we listen, we teach. Above all, we learn of the love of Christ, the pain of wrong-doing, the battle against evil, and the sweet peace the gospel brings.

HOTLINKS

Home and Visiting Teaching Resource Page
www.absolutesaint.com/resources/htvt.html

HTVT Web Site
members.tripod.com/~hometeaching

RELIEF_SOCIETY-L
www.zobrist.com/rs

Sego Lily
members.aol.com/perudol1/rs.htm

Relief Society

These general Relief Society sites contain a wealth of ideas and suggestions for women in the Church.

Home and Visiting Teaching Resource Page www.absolutesaint.com/resources/htvt.html Absolutely great. Mailing list. Talks. Scriptures. Tips. Resources. Daily reminders. This one's a keeper. ★★★★★ ☑

HTVT Web Site members.tripod.com/~hometeaching Dedicated to improving home and visiting teaching. Mailing list, resources, links, ideas, and experiences. Submit ideas of your own. Phenomenal. ★★★★★ ☑

Kirkland Washington Second Ward RS Newsletter members.aol.com/Cballd/k2legacy.html Updated monthly. It's much less parochial than the name would imply. It does include this month's birthday listing, but of more general interest are the monthly message from the President, messages from the General Relief Society President, plus other articles local in content but universal in applicability. ★★

Relief Society members.aol.com/cumorahhil/rspage.htm Not a great deal of information, and what's there is irregularly updated. ★

Relief Society www.danvillestake.org/s/danville/rs.html Very thorough list of Relief-Society-related links. ★★★

Relief Society www.of-worth.com/ea/RS.htm Ideas for visiting teaching, homemaking, compassionate service, and Relief Society colors. Inspiring material. ★★★

RELIEF_SOCIETY-L www.zobrist.com/rs Discussion of callings in the Relief Society. Twenty messages a day, and the list stays on topic. To subscribe, send an e-mail message to *<Relief_Society-L-request@ Majordomo.net>*, with the message `Subscribe`. 📖

Reliefsociety.com www.reliefsociety.com This is a fairly new site for the women of the Church. Find here strength, humor, support, and understanding, with material for mothers, homemaking coordinators, and visiting teachers. ★★★

> **TO THE RELIEF SOCIETY**
>
> This is an organization that was established by the Prophet Joseph Smith. It is, therefore, the oldest auxiliary organization of the Church, and it is of the first importance. It has not only to deal with the necessities of the poor, the sick and the needy, but a part of its duty—and the larger part, too—is to look after the spiritual welfare and salvation of the mothers and daughters of Zion; to see that none is neglected, but that all are guarded against misfortune, calamity, the powers of darkness, and the evils that threaten them in the world. It is the duty of the Relief Societies to look after the spiritual welfare of themselves and of all the female members of the Church. It is their duty to collect means from those who have in abundance, and to distribute it wisely unto those in need. It is a part of their duty to see that there are those capable of being nurses as well as teachers and exemplars in Zion, and that they have an opportunity to become thoroughly prepared for this great labor and responsibility.
>
> Joseph F. Smith, *Gospel Doctrine*, p. 385

Sego Lily members.aol.com/perudol1/rs.htm The Sego Lily was selected as the emblem of Relief Society because of its usefulness in sustaining life in the early pioneer settlements. This page offers help and resources for Relief Society members. Of particular note are materials under the categories link, where you'll find outlined the responsibilities of each member of the Relief Society, items on helping new members, callings, preparedness, music and activities. ★★★★

SISTERS A mailing list for women. To subscribe, send an e-mail request to *<MAISER@rmgate.pop.indiana.edu>*.

SISTER-SHARE www.omnicron.com/~fluzby/sister-share/index.htm Page with lots of links to inspirational materials and to the Sister-Share discussion list. The list itself tends to be tremendously chatty, without a lot of depth. If you've got the time. . . . To subscribe, send an e-mail request to *<listserv@psuvm.psu.edu>*. Sisters only. More information is available at the Web site. ★★★

Homemaking

Plastic grapes, wooden wall things, first aid classes. . . . This could be a whole 'nuther book. Just a smattering:

Ask Crafty Cathy www2.deseretbook.com/hm/askcathy Mormon Handicraft responds to your crafting questions online. Ask a question about any type of craft and have it answered quickly online. Brought to you by Mormon Handicraft. $

Christy's Relief Society Art members.tripod.com/~pesukone/rs_art.html (See figure 10.2.) Christy should be canonized. Between this page and her even better pages for Young Women and Primary, these sites are an entire online ward. ★★★★★ ☑

Country Cottage www.osmond.net/osnet/family/ccpals Good links to country crochet, country knits, charity crafts, down home cookin', writing a family history, taking care of kids, and more. ★★★★

Graceful Bee Online Memory Magazine www.gracefulbee.com Scrapbooking ideas online. Not specifically LDS. ★★★

Homemaker Herald www.homemakerherald.com Popular monthly newsletter. Features include: Family Fare (thoughts and tips on feeding the brood), Recipes to

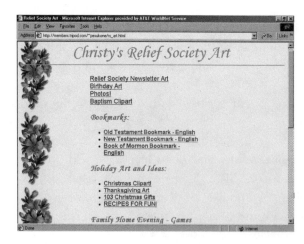

FIG. 10.2

Relief Society Art.

Save, Homemaker Tips (from keeping eggs fresh to ridding your tub of mildew), plus other feature articles. Not specifically LDS. ★★★★

Homemaking Pages   www.geocities.com/Heartland/Oaks/9401/homemaking/recipes.htm
Recipes, fitness, and clutter control. ★★★★

LDS Home   www.ldshome.com A really incredibly well-done magazine for LDS women. Includes a mailing list, many tips for home management, helps for callings, storage, recipes, and much more. ★★★★★ ☑

Organized Home   www.organizedhome.com An online magazine to help declutter, clean, establish routines, and make your house one of order. Subscribe to the twice monthly newsletter from this site. Not specifically LDS. ★★★★

Relief Society Rest Stop   www.mormons.org/rs Links to Morale Boosters, Recipes, Housekeeping Hints, Making a House a Home, and Homemaking Night Ideas. Somewhat useful, although the housekeeping hints would be better located on a Priesthood site. ★★★

> **TO THE SISTERS**
> Rise above the shrill clamor over rights and prerogatives, and walk in the quiet dignity of a daughter of God.
>
> Gordon B. Hinckley, *Cornerstones of a Happy Home,* Jan. 29 1984

Sue's Block of the Month   members.aol.com/sewquilty Enter your quilt block in the Block of the Month contest. Participants work together to build a quilt, all the pieces of which go to the winner of a name drawn from among the participants. Might be worth adopting as a ward project. ★★★★

Women of the WWW 1st Ward, Unite! Not so radical as it sounds www.aiwpgold.com/www1st/sisters Links to crafts, recipes, *A Woman's Touch* online magazine, and *A Woman's Perspective* newsletter for women. ★★

World Wide Quilting Page   ttsw.com/MainQuiltingPage.html Basic quilting techniques, diagrams, and directions for many traditional quilt blocks, a collection of foundations for paper piecing, and the block of the month (actually two new blocks every month). Lots of other stuff here also. So much that it requires, and has, a search engine. Not specifically LDS. ★★★★

SEMINARY

It was more than 20 years ago that I graduated from early-morning seminary. Now I'm driving my own kids to seminary at 5:30 in the morning, and it's not any easier

HOTLINKS

LDS Seminary Files
www.tdholder.com/seminary

Scripture Mastery Games
softdesdev.com/primaryetc/
SMGames.html

SEMINARY
www.listservice.net/seminary

than it was when I was a kid. But believe it or not, my sleepy teenage boys actually look forward to the trip. Why? We leave five minutes early and stop for cocoa.

Seminary teachers are the best-organized people in the Church. The high quality of these seminary resources are good evidence of that.

Brent Hugh's LDS Music Page www.sunflower.org/~bhugh/lds/lds-music.spm Seminary scripture mastery verses set to music. Listen to some songs for free at this commercial site. $

Brother Smedley's burgoyne.com/pages/wes/bspages.htm Scripture mastery lists, seminary calendar, policies, and more. Needs updating. ★★

LDS Seminary Files www.tdholder.com/seminary Tim Holder's tremendous site with discussion forum and teaching resources (see figure 10.3). ★★★★

Seminary Scripture Mastery www.ldstoday.com/lds-resources/mastery.htm Full list, all four years. ★★★

Scripture Mastery Games softdesdev.com/primaryetc/SMGames.html Fantastic collection of games for helping or motivating kids to memorize scriptures. ★★★★

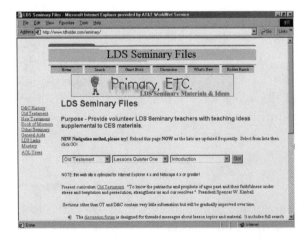

FIG. 10.3

LDS Seminary Files.

SEMINARY www.listservice.net/seminary Lesson ideas for teaching seminary, institute, or any other auxiliary. Inspiring. A really first-class, useful list. Send your subscription request to *<majordomo@listservice.net>* with the message `subscribe seminary`. The list now has more than 1000 subscribers. ★★★★★ ☑

SINGLE ADULT RESOURCES

There's hardly a member of the Church, anywhere, who either hasn't or won't spend some time as a Single Adult. It's no surprise that the Single Adult Internet sites are the most popular, active locations in the entire LDS online community.

In this section you'll find sites for Single Adults, sites specifically for Young Adults, and sites developed by various LDS student associations. None of these sites is specifically focused on dating or courtship; those appear in a separate section in chapter 11.

> **OF SINGLE ADULTS**
> Single adults should join forces. We are mindful that many of our members live alone or with family members who do not share fully their commitment to gospel principles. We encourage them to join together in special home evening groups and to participate in local single adult activities to accomplish these same objectives, always striving to strengthen their family ties with parents, brothers and sisters, and other relatives.
>
> The Teachings of Spencer W. Kimball, p. 345

Single Adults

Both general sites for all single adults and sites strictly for older single adults are included.

Around the Punchbowl www.itstessie.com/sngl/index.cfm LDS Single Adult Resources. A training and leadership forum for LDS Single Adults and ward and stake leaders. Includes worldwide calendar, articles of interest to single adults, and news of the Church. Sister Holladay's site has been the Internet's best Single Adult resource for several years. ★★★★★

AZ Mormon Single Adults www.endure.com LDS Single Adult activities in Arizona and all over the world. ★★★

LDS Single Adult and Young Single Adult Groups www.mich.com/~romulans/ldssaysa.html Links to LDS Single Adult sites throughout the world. ★★★★

LDS Singles Events www.singles.lds.net/eventsconf.html Conferences, dances, hotlines, Web sites and publications. A well-connected resource with lots of listings. ★★★★

HOTLINKS

Around the Punchbowl
www.itstessie.com/sngl/index.cfm

LDS Singles Events
www.singles.lds.net/
eventsconf.html

Monument Park 19th Single Adult Ward   www.aros.net/~wenglund/mp19th.html   Single Adults in Salt Lake City. Features a ward calendar and Bishopric message as well as links to other wards. ★★

Singles Corner   www.mormons.org/singles_corner.htm   Ideas for many kinds of Single Adult program activities. On the young side. ★★★

Young Single Adults

Sites for college-age single adults follow.

Affinity   affinity.faithweb.com   (See figure 10.4.) LDS Singles Stuff at Affinity. Graphical, interactive environment makes a fun, unique online meeting place (free singles listing, too). Go out for "pizza," play games like pong, monthly dances, and more. Rooms for spiritual edification, too. You'll love this one. ★★★★★ ☑

HOTLINKS

Affinity
affinity.faithweb.com

Clovis Young Single Adult Network
members.xoom.com/ysa_sa

LDS-MORMON-YSA
www.onelist.com/subscribe/
LDS-Mormon-YSA

Clovis Young Single Adult Network   members.xoom.com/ysa_sa   Some great links and inspirational stories, plus news for South-Central region singles. ★★★★

LDS-MORMON-YSA   www.onelist.com/subscribe/LDS-Mormon-YSA   E-mail list for members of the Church who are generally college age, or around the ages of 18–30. Also people who generally fit the "YSA" category, or Young Single Adults. Mainly for people to talk and get to know and be in touch with other LDS people, and to find out about activities going on other places. 📖

Melbourne YSA Homepage   yoyo.cc.monash.edu.au/~chompy/ysa   All the YSA activities in Melbourne in an interactive format. YSA News, Fireside schedules, and links. ★★★

Riverside Y.S.A   members.aol.com/cumorahhil/rysa.htm   Local activities. ★★★

Rockhampton: LDS Young Single Adults Page   www.geocities.com/Heartland/3139   Rockhampton (or RockVegas as it is known to the locals) is in the tropical north of Australia. Few LDS Single Adults, but they apparently have fun. Includes links and announcements. ★★★

FIG. 10.4

Affinity LDS Chat.

The Field Is White www.geocities.com/Athens/Acropolis/8825 For the Young Single Adults of the Manchester, England, Stake to let other Young Single Adults around the world know what goes on in the Church in Manchester and the rest of Britain. Well-maintained, good links. ★★★★

Young Single Adults www.wnetc.com/resource/lds/ ysa.html Very brief list of links. Very. ★

Young Single Adults www.geocities.com/Heartland/ 4034/content.html#single Features over 20 links to Young Single Adult sites. ★★

SUNDAY SCHOOL

For teachers of adults and older youth, this list of Sunday School resources will prove invaluable. You'll find here all kinds of lesson resources, including gospel doctrine lesson outlines, reading lists, and several other practical teaching tools. (This section doesn't begin to touch the entire range of scripture study resources. For online scriptures, talks from general authorities, and commentaries, go to "Gospel Doctrine Study Tools" on page 142 in chapter 7. You'll find additional personal scripture study resources beginning on page 279 in chapter 12.

HOTLINKS

Daniel Rona's Old Testament Gospel Doctrine Study Guide
www.israelrevealed.com/gospel/ index.html

Gospel Doctrine Class
members.tripod.com/beardall/ gospdoct.html

Gospel Doctrine Weekly Reader
www.dancris.com/~gregor/gdlist

Latter-day Saint Seminar
www.cybcon.com/~kurtn/ exegesis.html

LDS-GEMS columnists
www.lds-gems.com/archive/nt

Daniel Rona's Old Testament Gospel Doctrine Study Guide www.israelrevealed.com/gospel/index.html Gospel doctrine lesson plans and insights from Jewish convert and Israel tour guide Daniel Roma. ★★★★

Gospel Doctrine Class members.tripod.com/~beardall/gospdoct.html Notes and quotes from The Gospel Doctrine Class taught in Sunday School. Handouts, lesson schedules, history, and more for a ward in Federal Way, Washington (see figure 10.5). Tremendous! ★★★★★ ☑

Gospel Doctrine Lessons www.uvol.com/www1st/barton/index.html Extremely thorough research. Good background for teachers. This site moves from time to time. Check the listings at www.mormontown.org if you're having trouble locating it. ★★★★

GOSPEL DOCTRINE *<gosdocteachers-subscribe@makelist.com>* A discussion list for gospel doctrine teachers. 📖

Gospel Doctrine Weekly Reader www.dancris.com/~gregor/gdlist Gregor McHardy's read-only list with links to the scriptures, lesson, scripture chains, and helps for families, delivered in small doses throughout the week. This is the list I use most. ★★★★★

LDS Teachers' Resources on the Internet www.lds.npl.com/special/teachers A small collection of stories and class handouts arranged by topic. ★★★

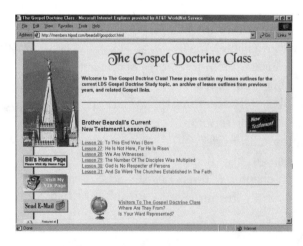

FIG. 10.5

The Gospel Doctrine Class.

LDS-GEMS Columnists www.lds-gems.com/archive Search the archives for scripture columnists who write supplementary materials for Gospel Doctrine. The New Testament archive is at www.lds-gems.com/archive/nt. ★★★★★

Latter-day Saint Seminar www.cybcon.com/~kurtn/exegesis.html Kurt Neumiller's extensive commentaries on Isaiah, the Old Testament, and the New Testament, along with numerous D&C commentaries and links. Worth bookmarking. Includes a mailing list, LDS-SEMINAR, with commentary and in-depth discussion on each week's Gospel Doctrine lesson. Includes regular columns, plus postings from other participants. To subscribe, send a message to *<majordomo@ldschurch.net>* with the message `subscribe ldss <yourname@ your.email.address>` or the digest version `subscribe ldss-d <yourname@your.email.address>`. The first edition promised this site five stars for better organization. Brother Neumiller did the organization. Here are the solid five stars: ★★★★★ ☑

LDS-SSRL www.acoin.com/lds-ssrl.htm The LDS Sunday School Reading List. Receive the full scriptural text for next week's LDS Sunday School lesson every weekend. 📖

LDS-SUNDAY SCHOOL www.acoin.com/kelly Full text of next week's Sunday School reading assignment. This year's reading assignment is the Doctrine and Covenants. The reading assignment is divided into five messages, one for each weekday. Subscribe by sending your e-mail request to *<anderson@itsnet.com>*. Archives are at the Web site. ★★★★★

SCRIPTURE-L www.wnetc.com/scripture-l A discussion of the scriptures. Operated and moderated by Gregory Woodhouse. Volume is moderate. Send subscription requests to *<scripture-l-request@lists.best.com>* with the message `subsingle`. To receive all the day's messages in one post mail, change the message to `subscribe`. Archives available at the Web site. 📖

YOUNG MEN

Thonk, thonk, thonk. . . . Is that a basketball I hear?

If you're looking for something *different* for your Young Men's program, turn to these Internet sites for ideas.

Better yet, take the, ahem, ball into your own hands, and consider letting the Young Men in your ward build a site of their own. You'll find additional helps under "The Scout Committee" on page 253 in chapter 11.

Holladay Third Ward Priests Quorum burgoyne.com/pages/r_tate/priests The Holladay Third Ward Priests Quorum Homepage. The young men know where they're going. See similar pages for other young men's priesthood quorums at www.expage.com/page/ebteachers (the Emerald Bay Teachers Quorum Homepage) and www.freeyellow.com/members2/wwvarsity551 (the Westwood Arizona Ward Young Men Homepage). ★★★

LDS-Activity-Scoope members.aol.com/ldsscoope/welcome.htm Ideas for Young Men's program activities, compiled by German member Thomas Mueller. ★★★★

Providence, Rhode Island, Stake YM www.geocities.com/heartland/1948 Providence, Rhode Island, Stake Young Men's Home Page. One of the best auxiliary-created sites on the Web. Very nicely done and worth emulating for your own stake or ward. ★★★★

Young Men Mutual Activities nauvoo.byu.edu/Church/Teaching/ymma/underside2.cfm (See figure 10.6.) This book helps keep mutual activity ideas flowing for both youth and their leaders. Use the ideas found in this book to plan fun, meaningful, mutual activities of many kinds. Wow. ★★★★★ ☑

Young Men and Scouts www.danvillestake.org/s/danville/ym-scout.html One stake's very thorough selection of YM and scouting resources. A good link list. ★★★

Young Men's Corner www.mormons.org/ymc Gives YM leaders a starting point on the Web and ideas for planning. Wish there was more here. ★★

YOUNG WOMEN

These sites provide resources for leaders in the Young Women's program.

ActivitEase members.tripod.com/laugh_lines/activitease Activity Ideas for Young Women, plus a few for Relief Society and youth in general. Site includes skits,

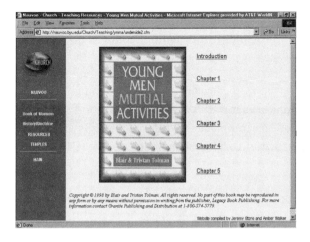

FIG. 10.6

Young Men Mutual Activities.

musicals, Firesides, lesson plans, homemaking ideas, and more. Scripts included. ★★★★

Defenders of Zion www.of-worth.com/yw Links to all the values with a wide variety of helps, including scriptures, stories, activities, object lessons, poems, etc. ★★★

Especially for Young Women www.geocities.com/Heartland/Prairie/5559/yw_container.html Girls' Camp ideas, thoughts for teachers, Laurel projects, etc. A great resource for the young women of the Church. ★★★

LDS Young Women www.angelfire.com/ut/ldsyw This site is Laurel project, but it's as well done as any of the adult-generated sites in this list. Quotes, activity ideas, and more! ★★★★

LDS-YW LDS-YW is dedicated to the Young Women of the Church and their leaders. It is a way to exchange ideas, testimonies, and experiences. To subscribe, e-mail your request to *<majordomo@xmission.com>* with the body `subscribe lds-yw`. 📖

LDS-YWLIST www.onelist.com/subscribe/LDS-YWList Dedicated to adult leaders involved in the Young Women's program. Topics reflect the Young Women's values. A place for leaders to exchange ideas and help

HOTLINKS

ActivitEase
members.tripod.com/laugh_lines/activitease

LDS Young Women
www.angelfire.com/ut/ldsyw

Lorrie's Young Women's Page
members.xoom.com/LBlake/ideas.htm

Young Women Mutual Activities
nauvoo.byu.edu/Church/Teaching/ywma/underside2.cfm

Young Women Resources
nauvoo.byu.edu/Church/Teaching/YoungWomen/main.html

Young Women
softdesdev.com/primaryetc/ywpage.htm

one another with anything relating to the program and to share the triumphs and challenges of our lives as YW leaders. For more information, contact *<jbuchmil@ teleport.com>*. 📖

Marquette Branch Young Women   members.tripod.com/~1Molly/Mormon.html A sweet page of doctrine and background material produced by the Marquette Branch program. Similar pages are located at hometown.aol.com/mdavis1175/links (Riverton Utah Twentieth Ward) and www.geocities.com/Heartland/Valley/5224 (Cincinnati Fourth Ward). ★★★

Young Women Ideas   members.xoom.com/LBlake/ideas.htm Tons of great ideas and activities for Young Women leaders. Post your own or get a few new ideas here. ★★★★

Young Women Resources   nauvoo.byu.edu/Church/Teaching/YoungWomen/main.html A guide to LDS Church-approved resources illustrating the seven young women values. Spend more time preparing and less time scrounging around the library for materials. ★★★★

Young Women Mutual Activities   nauvoo.byu.edu/Church/Teaching/ywma/ underside2.cfm This book helps integrate the seven values into mutual activities for the Young Women Program. Another great site from the Tolmans. But most of the Young Women's sites are great, so this one doesn't shine so brightly as the companion Young Men's site does. ★★★★

Young Women Sites   softdesdev.com/primaryetc/ywlinks.html Debra Woods' great list of Young Women's links. ★★★

Young Women   softdesdev.com/primaryetc/ywpage.htm Dozens of well-presented activities for the Young Women's program. ★★★★

Young Women   www.mormon.com/html/young_women.html A relatively brief page of Young Women's activities. ★★★

Young Women   www.uvol.com/www1st/youngwomen/youngwomen.html The Young Women's Pledge/Oath, along with handful of references on ideas for activities, faith, individual worth, and other subjects. Lots of room for expansion. ★★

Young Women's Corner   www.mormons.org/ywc Ideas relating to young women and the Young Women's program. Includes leaders, activities, New Beginnings, standards night, Firesides, dates, camp, and good clean fun. A tremendous resource. ★★★★★

11

INTEREST
GROUPS

For Latter-day Saints, religion isn't just something to join, and Church isn't just something to attend. Church, religion, faith, action, work, and life are all inter-twined, one giving substance to the other. Devout Mormons believe—and live—the scriptural injunction that faith, without *work,* is dead.

For Latter-day Saints, it is part of one's duty to God to be anxiously engaged in parenting, in marriage, in temple work, in callings, in service, and in the commu-nity. Indeed, the Saints try to follow the example of King Benjamin, who in his last great address reminded his people: "And even I, myself, have labored with mine own hands that I might serve you, and that ye should not be laden with taxes, and that there should nothing come upon you which was grievous to be borne. . . . I do not desire to boast, for I have only been in the service of God. . . . Behold ye have called me your king; and if I, whom ye call your king, do labor to serve you, then ought not ye to labor to serve one another?" (Mosiah 2:14–18)

Labor is a part of every moment of LDS life. Whether it's Scout leaders, choir directors, sisters working to build fellowship, or youth who socialize in school and other activities, Mormons make a life's work out of life's work.

Chapter 10 described a number of Internet resources related to the auxiliary organizations of the Church. In this chapter, you'll be introduced to resources for

Saints working to blend their religion, their families, their callings, their employment, and their personal interests into one great whole.

The first section covers Youth resources, much of which will be of interest to Youth leaders. That's followed by a separate section on Dating and Courtship. The next section covers Internet resources to help in various Church callings, including Scouts, Music, Activities Committee, Public Communications/Ward Newsletter, and Teaching. Then come sections on resources for Women, for Professionals, for Home-schoolers, for Disabled Saints, and for Saints dealing with same-sex attraction. The final section in this chapter is a list of commercial sites selling products and services designed for Latter-day Saints.

Ready? Then let's Do It.

LDS YOUTH RESOURCES

I was a good teenager. Really. I was respectful, hard-working, clean, and sober. I got good grades, I participated in dozens of organizations and activities at school, I was the president of my Laurel class, I had a part-time job, and I ran the stake dance committee. I got up early every morning all on my own and found my own ride to Seminary. In short, my children hate me.

Despite all my otherwise good behavior, I had an inexplicable need to "hang" with my friends. Where I grew up, "hanging" meant driving to the next town and cruising in endless slow circles around the "loop," an eight-block rectangle in the center of town. Somewhere around midnight, the police would block the streets, at which time everyone would head toward the parking lot at Jack-in-the-Box, and stand around eating French fries 'til the wee hours.

And that's what the *good* girls did.

That's why I'm glad my own kids have an alternative—a place to "hang" with good kids who love the Church, who are excited about the gospel, who want to be the best people they can be.

Here's where you'll find them:

#LDSYouth   www.inetworld.net/kaos/ldsyouth.html Sometimes heavily used, sometimes empty. In any event, it hasn't been updated in more than a year and on our last visit, the chat room was empty. ★★

#mormonteens IRC teen chat channel members.xoom.com/mormonteens #mormonteens is a teen chat channel for kewl teens. Come on in and enjoy clean chat! ★★

Affinity LDS Chat affinity.faithweb.com This may be the most fun you can have on the Internet. Affinity is a graphical, interactive chat site. Go swimming, dance, play laser tag, have pizza. Monthly socials, Youth Den with music and munchies, lots more. Java-enabled browser OK. ★★★★★ ☑

Darbie's Webpage www.geocities.com/SouthBeach/Lagoon/3550/darbie2.html The life and times of Darbie as they were when she was 14. Darbie appears to have moved on to new adventures as her Web page hasn't been updated in a while. ★★

EFY Memories users.vnet.net/rabbanah EFY Memories is a collection of pictures and descriptions from participants in Especially For Youth. Accepts submissions. Register to receive e-mail updates. ★★★

HOTLINKS

Affinity LDS Chat
affinity.faithweb.com

For the Strength of Youth
www.npl.com/~jradford/soy/strength.html

John Bytheway
www.deseretbook.com/bytheway/btwhome.html

LDS Chat
www.ldschat.com

LDS Youth Homepage
www.inconnect.com/~bytheway

Peter D. Coyl
www.geocities.com/heartland/plains/2999

Elder Gene Cook www.xmission.com/~dkenison/lds/lds_quo/grc_jagg.html Talk given by Elder Gene Cook at Ricks College in 1988 about a visit with Mick Jagger on an airplane. 📖

Especially For Youth coned.byu.edu/yp/efy Home page for BYU's Especially for Youth program. In addition to specific information concerning the current BYU-EFY program, it also includes links to other youth-oriented sights. ★★★

For the Strength of Youth www.npl.com/~jradford/soy/strength.html Text of the pamphlet on standards. 📖

How to Write a Sacrament Meeting Talk www.dayton.net/~dalleyj/bvrcrkward/talk1.htm An inspirational essay—serious in tone—about speaking at sacrament meeting, covering four basic principles. Also tacked on is a humorous piece: Recipe for Cooking Up a Sacrament Meeting. ★★★

John Bytheway www.deseretbook.com/bytheway/btwhome.html A delightful diversion featuring at its core a positive and upbeat message for youth. Bytheway successfully straddles the line between being overly preachy and overly irreverent with a fun-loving approach that only the Grinch could object to. ★★★★★

LDS Chat   www.ldschat.com Two rooms for teens . . . very heavily populated (see figure 11.1). Includes the ability to conduct private conversations. Not particularly safe, though. Although there's a moderator aboard, the talk is too fast to moderate, private chats are completely unmoderated, and anyone can crash. But if your kids are generally reliable and sensible, send 'em over. My 16-year-old loves it. ★★★★

LDS Youth Homepage   www.inconnect.com/~bytheway Ben Bytheway's youth-oriented page with thought of the day, Seminary scripture, mastery scriptures, discussions, and more. ★★★★

LordBryan's Homepage   www.cyberjunkie.com/LordBryan Lord Bryan Mulholland is a choral education major at BYU. In addition to listing the contents of his closet, this Web site includes a page dedicated to LDS issues. Included are links to the testimonies of the Book of Mormon, the Articles of Faith, and more. What youth can look forward to when they get to college. ★★

MormonTeens   www.onelist.com/subscribe/MormonTeens Mailing list from a Mormonteen. Chat about anything Mormonish! 📖

Mormonyouth   www.onelist.com/subscribe/Mormonyouth Newsletter/Club for LDS youth, ages 12–18. 📖

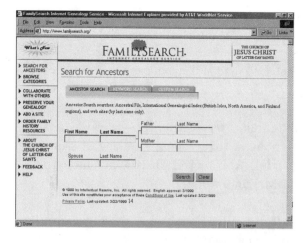

FIG. 11.1

LDS Chat.

Peter D. Coyl Homepage   www.geocities.com/heartland/plains/2999 Peter's a high school student who's built a fine page with information of interest to other youth. Continues to be regularly updated. ★★★★

Teenwantbemormon   www.onelist.com/subscribe/Teenwantbemormon For teenaged investigators and their friends. Talk about being an LDS teen. 📖

What We Do for Fun   members.tripod.com/~1Molly/Fun.html A very nice list of fun youth activities. ★★★

SENIORS

Possibly the fastest-growing group on the Internet, seniors are leading gospel discussions, doing missionary work online, and finding communities of peers. These sites will be of particular interest to senior Saints.

Elderly and Frail Elderly   www.ce.ex.state.ut.us/cdbg/cp-4.htm Populations with Special Needs. A government report on Utah's senior population, along with nursing facilities around the state. 📖

HOTLINKS

LDS Travel Network
www.ldstravel.com
Seniors
www.lds.net/ldslife/elderly

LDS Travel Network   www.ldstravel.com Travel the world or your own state! Stay in safe, clean, LDS homes inexpensively or even for free. Host LDS families from around the world and make new friends. Very cheap, very well done. This is a great idea. ★★★★

Seniors   www.lds.net/ldslife/elderly An LDS community for senior Saints. Dating ideas, grandparenting, volunteering, share your testimony, resources and links for seniors, and a senior chat room. ★★★★★ ☑

To the Elderly in the Church   www.xmission.com/~dkenison/lds/lds_quo/etb_eld.html An address by Ezra Taft Benson. 📖

Why Every Member a Missionary?   www.lds.org/en/3_General_Conference_en/01997en/01997en_2_8_Scott.html Elder Scott's call-in October '97 conference for every member to do missionary work. Includes a discussion of the urgent need for missionary couples. 📖

LOVE AT FIRST BYTE

This is the true story of two lost souls who found each other, as well as the Church, on the Internet.

Both of us had endured the dilemma of being single parents in the Church. We both agreed that after enjoying the blessings of the Church with our complete families, we felt like outsiders when we tried to remain active as single parents.

LuJane went through a bitter divorced twelve-plus years ago. She found herself forced to become a working mother with three young children, and finding time to adequately participate in church activity seemed impossible. She struggled for about seven years before inactivity eventually became the norm in her daily life.

Bear suffered the pains of divorce while his two grown sons were on their missions. He struggled to raise his adopted 13-year-old son as a single parent. When he lost Neal in a tragedy, he became completely inactive.

Both of us held to only two principles of the gospel: We both searched our scriptures and prayed unceasingly. And with a little help from the Internet our efforts were rewarded.

Bear had been surfing the Net, looking for information to use in a magazine article he was writing. He accidentally landed at "LDS Friends Worldwide." For reasons unknown to himself, he bookmarked the site and went on researching his article, returning to the site a few hours later. That's when, he says, he received the second testimony of his life. The first was when he prayed on the Book of Mormon, and the second when he saw LuJane's personal. He was overcome by the same Spirit.

DATING AND COURTSHIP

Lots of resources here, some for teens, some for single adults. I long for the day when somebody builds a dating and courtship site designed for Happily Married Men.

Youth Oriented

The how-tos and the wherefores of teenage dating for Latter-day Saints.

HOTLINKS

Dates
www.mormons.org/ywc/dates/dates.htm

LDS Youth
www.ldsyouth.com

Dates www.mormons.org/ywc/dates/dates.htm A teen-oriented site with good reading on Answers to Dating Questions, Invitations, and Places to Go and Things to Do. Lots of information here. ★★★★

Dating Ways members.aol.com/cumorahhil/dateway.htm How to (eeekkk!) ask someone out on a date. Lots of fun suggestions. ★★★

Good Clean Fun www.mormons.org/ywc/gcfun/fun.htm Younger and more friends-oriented, but lots of good ideas for group activities. ★★★

Bear says he never intended to find a wife and children again. "I had no intention of fighting my way back to activity in the Church," he says. "I just happened upon LuJane's personal and immediately knew that she was the one—the only one—for me."

LuJane was quite surprised to get her first e-mail from Bear, as she received it just as she was done posting her personal. "It was as if he was just waiting for me to post so he could contact me," she says. "I had three teenagers and three adopted young boys, the youngest being only three years old. I had basically given up looking for a worthy priesthood holder who would be willing to take on a family of six kids and a headstrong wife who doesn't want to give up her newspaper business and extremely active lifestyle. . . .

After a two-week visit by Bear, in which much time was spent in family prayer and scripture searching, we were wed at the Potlatch, Idaho, Branch and are now looking forward to our sealing in the Seattle Temple, hopefully next April.

Let no man or woman disclaim the words of the Prophets. Modern-day technology is leading many lost souls back into Heavenly Father's blessings, and Internet services such as LDS Friends Worldwide are His tools to bring out miracles like we have experienced. Just ask us if this isn't so.

Brujo Bear and LuJane Nisse, Palouse, Washinton <lujane@palouse.com>
Publishers, *Boomerang!*
www.palouse.com/business/boomerang

LDS Teens   A mailing list for, well, LDS teens. The list started in January 1997, and sees daily traffic of about three messages. E-mail subscription request to <karlp@slcolubs.com>. 📖

LDS Youth   www.ldsyouth.com Dating. Dating. More dating. Also some thoughts, poetry and chat. And dating. ★★★★

Single Adult Oriented

Bemoaning the lack of marriageable singles in your area? Problem solved.

The Internet not only expands your opportunities for meeting the love of your life; it also improves the chances that you'll be able to create a good marriage when you do. E-mail is a boon to relationships, a far better method for sharing and learning about another person than anything that has ever gone before. Grandma and Grandpa mailed long letters; Mom and Dad courted over the telephone; older siblings hung their heads in shame and met at discos and more disreputable places, rationalizing that they'd be able to "make over" the mates they found there. Modern courtship, online, is the best of all worlds: the real sharing and permanence of letters, the immediacy of the telephone, and the shelter— and enforced distance—of online communications. In that environment, real, honest, deep, and eternal love blooms.

HOTLINKS

Affinity
affinity.faithweb.com

LDS Friends Worldwide
www.ldsfriends.com

LDS Singles Connection
www.singles.lds.net

LDS Singles Online
www.ldssingles.com

Mormon Matchmaker
www.lds.email.net

Some advice to those who are corresponding over the Internet, from someone who's been there, and who is now happily married because of it: Be completely honest. Be tremendously careful if you find you're corresponding with someone who is *not* completely honest. If you're uncomfortable, trust your feelings. Be open to the promptings of the Spirit.

But while you're being careful, be happy. Ignore people who think it's shocking that you'd correspond with someone as part of a courtship. Remind them that until a few years ago, that's the way all permanent relationships began. Enjoy the opportunity for developing real emotional intimacy with another person. And save all those letters!

Affinity   affinity.faithweb.com This may be the most fun you can have on the Internet. Affinity is a graphical, interactive chat site. Go swimming, dance, play laser tag, have pizza. Monthly socials, Youth Den with music and munchies, lots more. Java-enabled browser OK. ★★★★★

Dating and Courtship   www.mormons.org/daily/dating A collection of articles on dating. Includes *For the Strength of Youth,* Dating and Courtship, Dating Nonmembers, Teaching Adolescents: From Twelve to Eighteen Years, Mature Intimacy: Courtship and Marriage, and President Benson's Teachings About Dating. A Mormons.Org site. ★★★★

LDS Friends Worldwide   www.ldsfriends.com (See figure 11.2.) Claims to have had nearly a million visitors since 1995. Could be. In any event, this site is very popular. ★★★★

LDS Singles Connection   www.singles.lds.net A big bride and groom picture on the opening page assure you that success means marriage. The site is free, the questions are extensive, and the search tool is thorough. And pen pal hunters are welcome. For the curious—and for your amusement—the site does post true success stories from clients. Features e-mailed profiles, user-defined levels of importance, user-defined visibility screening, as well as other premium features. Registration for the connection service is free. A chat service is available for a small fee. Regularly updated and fun to read. ★★★★★

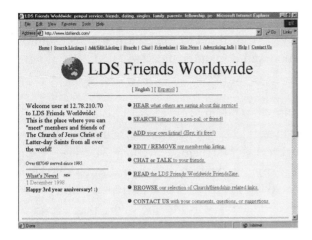

FIG. 11.2

LDS Friends: Meet, greet, have a seat.

LDS Singles Online   www.ldssingles.com Basically the same as the LDS Singles Connection except there are 33,000+ members. Offers cheap rates for a longer-term commitment, but prices are reasonable for any period. Search for free, but you've got to pay to play. $

Mormon Matchmaker   www.lds.email.net A site designed to help members cope with the demands of everyday life and the desire to meet a suitable partner. ★★★

MORMON_SINGLE   www.onelist.com/subscribe/mormon%5Fsingle Mormon and Single? Looking for a temple-worthy person to love? Get introduced to interesting, unmarried LDS members in your area. Find roommates, worldwide pen pals, clean funny jokes, romance, or just socialize with other single members of the Church. ★★★

Of Souls, Symbols, and Sacraments   advance.byu.edu/devo/holland88.html Elder Jeffrey R. Holland, then President of Brigham Young University, discusses why sexual relations are so sacred. 📖

Personal Purity and Intimacy   coned.byu.edu/cw/cwwomens/watson99.htm Dr. Wendy L. Watson's address to the 1999 Women's Conference. 📖

Single Mingle   www.ysite.com/singles Made up primarily of five sections: The Mingle (browse the home pages of many Latter-day Singles), the Barter Board (an online classified Ad Board especially for singles), the Chatter Box (an LDS singles forum), the Funny Bone (a daily dose of humor and inspiration), and Singles

Travel (a discount travel center for LDS singles). There's a lot of material to read. Participation requires registration and a maintenance fee of $1.50 a month. ★★★

Teachings About Marriage www.mormons.org/basic/family/marriage LDS beliefs about marriage. Articles include Eternal Marriage, Covenant Marriage, John and Mary, Beginning Life Together, Plural Marriage, Social and Behavioral Perspective of Marriage, Divorce, and Celibacy. A Mormons.Org page. ★★★

Teachings About Sexuality www.mormons.org/daily/sexuality This page offers links to the LDS perspective on such topics as Procreation, Abortion, Adultery, and Birth Control. Mostly quotes from the *Encyclopedia of Mormonism.* ★★★

MANY ARE CALLED

Many, many are called, actually. It's the best thing about the organization of the Church. Whatever your calling, you'll find in this section some tools to help out. Here you'll discover resources for Scouting, music, activities committees, the ward newsletter, and teachers. (Separate sections for each of the auxiliaries are found in chapter 10, beginning on page 223.)

A More Determined Discipleship www.lib.ricks.edu/reserve/tod_hammond/bs1140n227.htm Elder Neal A. Maxwell's address on discipleship and foreordination. ★★★

Called to Serve www.lds.org/en/3_General_Conference_en/01997en/01997en_1_2_Packe.html "The willingness of Latter-day Saints to respond to calls to serve is a representation of their desire to do the will of the Lord." Elder Boyd K. Packer's October '97 address on fulfilling callings. 📖

Church Callings www.shire.net/mormon/callings.html How much to ask? How much to accept? Allen Leigh attempts to strike a balance between meeting the demands of callings and being reasonable. In other words, if you kill yourself today, you ain't gonna be much good tomorrow. So relax, pace yourself, and do what you can without compromising your own ability to prosper. ★★★

Feed My Lambs www.lds.org/en/3_General_Conference_en/01997en/01997en_5_7_Eyrin.html Elder Henry B. Eyring's October '97 general conference address on caring for one another and fulfilling callings. 📖

Sacred Treasures www.geocities.com/Heartland/Acres/ 1756/madsen.html An address by Truman G. Madsen. How do we make the best use of our talents? Dr. Madsen offers some practical suggestions in this address delivered at BYU. 📖

Stewardship www.mormons.org/daily/activity/stewardship_eom.htm J. Lynn England's commentary on the responsibility given through the Lord to act on behalf of others. ★★★

Set Apart members.aol.com/perudoll/call1.htm What you need to know about being set apart. ★★

The Scout Committee

My middle son recently had his first taste of Scout camp. It was a few days before his twelfth birthday, so he didn't get to sleep over. So guess who got to make the twice-a-day trip out to Camp Farfaraway, to pick him up and drop him off?

I'm glad I did. It was a real treat to see a group of fine, sturdy young men—the same crowd of rowdy 12-year-olds I teach in Sunday School—pulling together, working as a team, and getting their first real experience at becoming young men.

I have a real tender spot in my heart for the fine scoutmasters who have worked so hard with my own boys, training them, teaching them, demanding their best.

For all of you hard-working scoutmasters, here's some help:

HOTLINKS

Cub Scouts and 11-Year-Old Scouts
www.primarypage.com/primary/cubs.html

LDS Scouting Resources
gemstate.net/scouter/ldsplus.htm

Mike Pearce's LDS Scouters Resource Page
www2.dtc.net/~mpearce/scouts/scouts.htm

Ward Scouting Job Descriptions
www.mormonscouting.com

Brad's Book pages.prodigy.com/PHJF79A/scouts.htm Excerpts from the book on Scouting written by Brad W. Constantine. Chapter 10: Does Scouting Work Better Inside or Outside the Church? ★★

Camping in a Hammock www.shire.net/mormon/hammock.html Hey, ever done it? Allen Leigh tells you how. ★★★

Cub Scouts and 11-Year-Old Scouts www.primarypage.com/primary/cubs.html A very nice Web site full of ideas and resources for LDS Cub packs. One reviewer says: "An excellent source of links and information for both the novice and the experienced. Leadership at every level would benefit from a careful reading of how the Cub program must be managed to be in compliance with the Church Handbook of Instructions." See a corresponding page at www.primarypage.com/cubscouts. ★★★★

LDS Scouting Resources www.gemstate.net/scouter/ldsplus.htm Quotes from general authorities, training and orientation topics, LDS units/resources, LDS patches, LDS/BSA history, articles on Scouting, and more. ★★★★★ ☑

Mike Pearce's LDS Scouters Resource Page www2.dtc.net/~mpearce/scouts/scouts.htm Includes links to scoutmaster minutes and other inspirational messages, leadership helps and ideas, games, stories and poems, songs, spiritual material, and additional Scout links (see figure 11.3). Generally considered one of the best Scouting resources on the entire Net. ★★★★★

National Council Announces Program Change www.exploring.org/change.htm The least you should know about the new Venturing program. 📖

Planning an Eagle Project www.shire.net/mormon/eagle.html A true experience with fictitious names. Allen Leigh describes the exhausting process. 📖

Scout Links www.daimi.aau.dk/~arne/ScoutLinks Sorted alphabetically, by nationality, newsgroups, new sites, and the ability to request that sites be included among the links. Over 500 Scout-related sites. ★★★

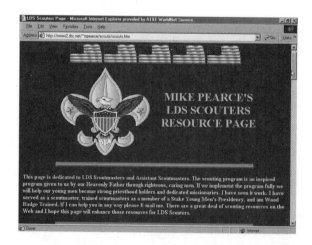

FIG. 11.3

Mike Pearce's LDS Scouters Resource Page: Endless help for scoutmasters.

Scouting in Utah www.uvol.com/scouts/homepage.html This one's sure changed since it was first posted! Lots of links helpful to members in or out of Utah. ★★★★

SCOUTS-LDS www.tagus.com A low-volume list dealing with the Scouting program in the Church. Share ideas for activities, describe ways of dealing with the youth, or ask advice on handling your calling. To subscribe, send a request to *<scouts-lds-request@tagus.com>* with the message `subscribe scouts-lds`. Visit the Web site for additional information. ★★★

The Telegraph www.thetelegraph.org A Sea Scouting newsletter published by Bill James, a Latter-day Saint in New Jersey. ★★★★

Venturing Program Ideas www.trappertrails.org/francispeak/images/venturing_program_ideas.htm Eight bajillion program suggestions. The eighth area, missionary prep, is particularly notable. Never brainstorm again. ★★★★

Ward Scouting Job Descriptions www.mormonscouting.com The nuts and bolts of ward Scouting job descriptions. Who must do what to make the ward Scouting program successful. ★★★★

Youth Advancement and Activity Software for LDS Stakes, Wards, and Families home.utah-inter.net/sbf/sb01001.htm Advancement and Activity Software for Cub Scouting, Boy Scouting, Varsity Scouting, Explorers, Sea Explorers, and the YW advancement programs of the LDS church. A commercial site. $

The Music Chairman

When I was in the first grade, my younger sister and I came home one day to find a huge piano in our living room. We danced around it in excitement, wondering aloud what it was. As I lifted the lid to look at the strings, my sister made a triumphant shout. "It's *mine*," she announced, waving the red John Thompson beginner's manual my mother had purchased. "See? It came with a Kindergarten book!"

A year's worth of piano lessons later, as the piano became more of a chore than a joy, my grandma caught me plodding, grudgingly, through the second-grade book of piano lessons. "You don't have to be a concert pianist," she whispered in my ear. "Just be good enough to play Church hymns."

> If thou art merry, praise the Lord with singing, with music, with dancing, and with a prayer of praise and thanksgiving.
>
> *Doctrine & Covenants* 136:28

So much for my mother's dream of raising brilliant children.

AMA Report Card   www.ama-assn.org/ad-com/releases/1996/vvcard.htm Discussion of the role of violence in the media (including music) and real-life violence. 📖

Basic Music Theory   www.jazclass.aust.com/bt1.htm How does anyone make a living when all this stuff is online for free? An entire college course in music theory. When you finish part 1, go to part 2. www.jazclass.aust.com/bt2.htm, then part 3 www.jazclass.aust.com/bt3.htm. When you finish all that, start learning about jazz, blues, and other musical styles. Not specifically LDS. ★★★★

HOTLINKS

Basic Music Theory
www.jazclass.aust.com/bt1.htm

Christian Music
members.tripod.com/wisealma

Free Music Lessons
www.mysheetmusic.com/free_music_lessons.htm

LDSPOP
www.onelist.com/subscribe.cgi/ldspop

Music and the Spoken Word
www.ksl.com/TV/word.htm

MUSIC
www.ldscn.com

Selected Transcripts
coned.byu.edu/cw/cwchmusi/talks.htm

Teaching Tips!
members.tripod.com/~noteworthy/ttips.htm

Children's Songbook   www.uleth.ca/~anderson/csb.htmlx The Children's Songbook MIDI page. Sound files of some of the Primary songs. New selections are being added. ★★★

Children's Song Book   elders.web-home.net/primary.html This page contains songs from the LDS Children's Songbook in MIDI format. ★★

Christian Classics Ethereal Library   ccel.wheaton.edu Collection of words to the Protestant Episcopal Hymnal of 1916, John Wesley's "Collection of Hymns, for the Use of the People Called Methodists," other collections, and 200 sound files. Vast library of online books and texts, all Christian classics. ★★

Christian Music   members.tripod.com/wisealma If you already own these Mormon Tabernacle Choir songs, you may download a computer-playable version here. Quotes, links, lots of good stuff. Some 40 songs to choose from. ★★★★

Cyber Hymnal   tch.simplenet.com Free site with more than 1,600 Christian hymns and gospel songs from many denominations. It includes lyrics, background information, photos, links, MIDI sound files, and scores for downloading. ★★★★

Danish Tabernacle Choir Society   www.mtc.dk A musical association with the object of diffusing knowledge of the Mormon Tabernacle Choir. This is a history tour. Very informative. Roll up, roll up for this history tour. But purchase the CDs listed if you plan on hearing music. ★★★★

Eastern Catholic Liturgical Music   www.homestead.com/Easterncatholichymns/SpasiHospodi.html Hymns and other music from the Syrian, Armenian, Coptic, Chaldean, and other Eastern churches. Very not LDS. ★★★

Elder Richard Scott   advance.byu.edu/devo/ScottSu97.html Explanation of how good music is important for spiritual development. 📖

Free LDS Sheet Music   www.petriefamily.org/ldsmusic Craig Petriea's hymn arrangements and original songs. ★★★

Free Music Lessons   www.mysheetmusic.com/free_music_lessons.htm Piano lessons online, from Daly Music. Basic, but you can print out the lessons for distribution to a group. ★★★★

Hatch Music   www.hatchmusic.com Music composed by Senator Orrin Hatch. $

LDS Hymns   www.uleth.ca/~anderson/midi.htmlx An LDS Hymns MIDI page. Over 300 Hymns are now available from this site. Good selection. ★★★★

LDS MIDI Archive   www.betz.demon.co.uk/midi.htm A collection of MIDI files downloaded from other sites on the Internet. All files are assumed—with no apparent basis—to be public domain. ★★★

LDS Music Source   members.xoom.com/dadstone/links.htm Links for and about music. ★★

LDS Music Web Ring   members.tripod.com/mormmom/LDSmusic.htm A ring of Web sites related to LDS Music. ★★

LDS Music   www.g-web.net/mrkh Web site operated by LDSPOP list owner Mark Hansen. Features powerful, thought-provoking, meaningful, and spiritual music with a backbeat you can dance to. Every month, or so, a new song is available for download. ★★★

LDS-Music   www.lds-music.com A commercial site with patriotic and Book-of-Mormon-inspired music. $

LDSPOP www.onelist.com/subscribe.cgi/ldspop List owner Mark Hansen writes: "This list is for the appreciation of and discussion of the pop culture of the members of the Church. Topics: LDS pop music, current novels, videos, musicals, and culture in general. The list is not for academic debate of theological issues. We just want to visit about the things we like to read, watch, and listen to." 📖

Mom's Music www.geocities.com/Heartland/Prairie/9844/mommusic.html Scores of LDS MIDI files and Zip files for download. Created by Mary Brownell. ★★★

Music and the Spoken Word www.ksl.com/TV/word.htm A weekly address delivered from the Tabernacle on Temple Square in Salt Lake City. ★★★★

Music Matters www.homestead.com/fromjanesbrain/music.html Jane Dumont's page on the Fundamentals of Conducting, Relief Society Music, and Staff Notes. Under construction last time we looked, but Jane has a reputation for hard work, so expect great things. ★★

Music to Heal the Soul www.geocities.com/Heartland/Hills/7404/music.html Sheryl Bagwell's uplifting collection of hymns and other music. Requires a sound card. ★★★★

MUSIC www.ldscn.com A mailing list dedicated to the discussion of all aspects of music from an LDS perspective. Subscribe with an e-mail request to *<majordomo@ldscn.com>* or go to the Web site and find music on the scroll-down list. 📖

Portland Regional Music Workshop lds.miningco.com/library/blmusic.htm Information for the Portland Regional Music Workshop, with information for upcoming LDS musical events in the area. ★★★★

Roxanna Glass Homepage www.geocities.com/Paris/LeftBank/9629 Memorial to Sister Roxanna Glass contains free religious and instrumental music in both audio and sheet music formats, as well as a scholarship application. Features LDS Music, psalms, links, scholarship information, and articles on how to cope with traumatic life experiences. ★★★

Russ Josephson's Mormon Tabernacle Choir Discography www.geocities.com/SunsetStrip/7158/mtchoir.htm All about the Mormon Tabernacle Choir. Look for late-breaking news concerning appearances and personnel changes. A discography is also available. ★★★

Sally DeFord Music   members.aol.com/defordm1 LDS choral, duet, solo and instrumental sheet music. Download, print, and copy as many selections as you wish. ★★★

Selected Transcripts   coned.byu.edu/cw/cwchmusi/talks.htm Transcripts of some inspiring addresses from BYU's annual Workshop on Church Music. Sister Perry's 1998 address on simplicity and hymns is particularly worthwhile. ★★★★

Teaching Tips!   members.tripod.com/~noteworthy/ttips.htm Brother Carl Stoddard offers teaching tips to music teachers, which can be adapted to choirs and other groups. See his Articles of Faith music links at the same. ★★★★

Tonal Center   dspace.dial.pipex.com/andymilne A great music theory site with thorough descriptions of scales, chords, cadences, modulation, and tonality. Not specifically LDS. ★★★★

Traditional Catholic MIDI files   www.homestead.com/midicatholic/Catholicinformation.html A collection of traditional hymns from the Catholic faith. ★★★

Utah Valley Children's Choir   www.utahchoir.com The homepage of the Utah Valley Children's Choir. Includes historical information, the current schedule, pictures and highlights, ordering information, and sample sound bites. $

Ward Music Committee   www.mormon.com/callings/html/music.html#wcd Beginnings of a list of ideas for music people in the ward. Keep your fingers crossed, because there's not much there yet. ★★

The Activities Committee

"May the road rise up to meet you, may the wind be at your back, and may you never have to serve on an activities committee" (An old Lamanite prayer).

Here you'll find activities for the whole ward, as well as a few sites that list activities for several auxiliaries of the Church.

Activities Committee   www.mormons.org/actcomm.htm Fun ideas for your ward. A very helpful collection. ★★★★

Becky's World of "Son" Shine   members.aol.com/CWS38/ideas3.html Leaders from every auxiliary will find much to do here. Lots of activities, but not much for the entire ward. Still, you'll be able to generate new ideas from this list. ★★★

HOTLINKS

Activities Committee
www.mormons.org/actcomm.htm

Becky's World of "Son" Shine
members.aol.com/CWS38/
ideas3.html

Jump.com
www.jump.com

Christmas and New Year Traditions in the UK www.rmplc.co.uk/eduweb/sites/wickham/xmas/xmastory. html A wonderful page describing English holiday traditions. Some ideas worth contemplating (not an LDS page). ★★★

Church Activities Page softdesdev.com/primaryetc/ activity.htm A small collection of ideas for ward activities. ★★★

Jump.com www.jump.com Tremendous resource for putting your ward calendar on line. Not specifically LDS. ★★★

Ward Activities Committee www.mormon.com/callings/ html/wac.html A handful of ideas and the site is soliciting more. ★★★

Ward Activities www.uvol.com/www1st/perfect/wardact.html Very abbreviated collection of successful ward activities. This site welcomes reader input. ★★

The Newsletter Editor/Public Communications Specialist

Some time back I was walking down the hallway at Church when a member of the mission presidency—someone with whom I regularly exchange e-mail jokes—stopped me to explain how to get in touch with a third person we'd been discussing. "Just e-mail me his contact," I said. He nodded, then paused a moment, looked me dead in the eye and said with a smile, "You know, Laura-Maery, there are some people in this world who actually don't have e-mail."

While I don't expect there'll ever be a thing we call the paperless office, the time is coming when units of the Church will begin publishing their newsletters on line. If you're not quite there yet, you can at least use these online resources to do a better job at the low-tech paper newsletter you still publish.

Nearly all the sites in this section are exceptionally well done, so you'd do well to visit the entire list.

Artwork from the Life of Christ www.itstessie.com/christ Beautiful collection of artwork from the life of the Savior. Arranged in categories: The Pre-mortal Christ, Annunciation, Nativity, Adoration of the Shepherds, Adoration of the Magi, The Holy Family, Youth, Ministry, Children, Parables, Healing, Apostles, Miracles, Mary, Gethsemane, Crucifixion, Ministry in the Spirit World, Resurrection, Appearance in the Americas, Restoration, Last Judgment. Stunning. ★★★★★

Highland Graphics   www.itsnet.com/~highland LDS images have been removed in favor of generically Christian artwork. Over 150 images; specializes in religious and holiday themes. ★★

Homestead   www.homestead.com Want to put your ward newsletter on the Web? Here's one of several sites on the Web that give away free homepages. Homestead is my favorite because in addition to providing free space and great page-building tools, it also has the power to permit several people to work on the same page. And there are no pop-up ads and no long URL requirements. Other places that permit you to build your own Web page for free include www.maxpages.com, www.angelfire.com, www.tripod.com, and www.geocities.com. ★★★★

Inspire Graphics   www.inspiregraphics.com/lds Find great LDS computer clip art for all of your church projects, ward bulletins, newsletters, Young Women, Scouting, and more. Also tips for creating attractive projects from professional designers. ★★★★

Jim Radford's LDS Art Gallery   www.npl.com/~jradford/lds/artgallery.html A large collection of LDS-related artwork and images (see figure 11.4). Tons of stuff. ★★★★

Mike Pearce's LDS Graphics   www2.dtc.net/~mpearce/graphics.htm Pictures of Jesus, prophets, general

HOTLINKS

Artwork from the Life of Christ
www.itstessie.com/christ

Homestead
www.homestead.com

Inspire Graphics
www.inspiregraphics.com/lds

Onelist
www.onelist.com

FIG. 11.4

Jim Radford's LDS Art Gallery: Page through the list of graphics.

authorities, temples, artwork, scriptures (categorized by book), Scouting, historical pictures, and much more. ★★★★★

New Church Logo Announced   members.aol.com/cumorahhil/newlogo.htm Text explaining/announcing the new logo. It is not a graphics download area. The logo does not even really exist on this page to be captured; it's superimposed over a picture of Jesus Christ. ★★

Onelist   www.onelist.com If you want to communicate with your ward via e-mail, this is your best option. Great features, very reliable, and very configurable. And it's free. If you want other choices, consider www.egroups.com, www.coollist.com, or www.listbot.com, all very nice, very free, mailing list services. ★★★★

Primarily Speaking: LDS Clip Art   www.tdsi.net/sunstone/113.html For scripture stories, gospel principles, nature, home and family, music, calendars, invitations, announcements, and much, much more! Commercial site. $

Tips   www.inspiregraphics.com/lds/html/tips.html Advice for editors of ward programs, newsletters, calendars, or other bulletins or flyers. Pointers on how to help your creations look great. ★★★★

Welcome to My Planet   www.davejennings.freeserve.co.uk/home.html Lots of free LDS artwork here. Artist Dave Jennings has created dozens of animated GIF files and clipart images and an LDS art gallery for contributors. ★★★★

Teaching: No Greater Call

I must be a particularly difficult child of God, for the lessons I learn are hard won. Too often I spend months, even years, puzzling over a particular idea, and then, suddenly, while I am doing something simple such as preparing a lesson for my Sunday School class, the answer comes to me in a flash of understanding.

For example, for me, one of the most difficult scenes in the New Testament has always been that of Jesus, whom I know as a loving, gentle Savior, clearing the temple. This same person who wrote in the dust with his finger when confronted by angry accusers; who called the little children to his side; who wept at the sorrow of his friends—I'd never been able to reconcile that with the Jesus who cleared the temple of money changers and overturned tables.

Fortunately, these bouts of stupidity on my part always find resolution and usually do so accompanied by a loud, heart-pounding clang.

While I was preparing this week's Sunday School lesson, the answer hit me hard. There it is, in the third chapter of Malachi, the prophecy of the Messiah purifying the temple, refining the sons of Levi "till they present right offerings to the Lord" (Malachi 3:1–7). Symbolism, prophecy, righteousness, firm correction, the central role of the temple in true worship, and the truth of Jesus as the Christ . . . they all came together right there in one small section of scripture.

That is why I love teaching.

You'll find additional resources for specific auxiliaries in chapter 10, beginning on page 223.

HOTLINKS

Called to Serve
www.homestead.com/called

Church Lessons
www.mormontown.org/
church_lessons

Gospel Doctrine Class
members.tripod.com/~beardall/
gospdoct.html

LDS Seminar
www.cybcon.com/~kurtn/
exegesis.html

Called to Serve www.homestead.com/called A resource site for every teacher in the Church. Separate sections for Gospel Doctrine, Gospel Principles/Gospel Essentials, Missionary Lessons, Priesthood, Primary, Relief Society, Seminary, Youth, General Teaching Resources, and Scriptures Online. Lesson plans, tips, resources, and much more. ★★★★

Church Lessons www.mormontown.org/church_lessons The primo LDS teacher's resource on the Internet. Lessons for gospel doctrine, priesthood, Relief Society, and genealogy, with plans for music, missionaries, Scouts, and primary on the way. ★★★★

Get an Idea www.geocities.com/Heartland/Shores/9767/List.htm Several dozen lesson ideas for teaching youth. ★★★

Gospel Doctrine Class members.tripod.com/~beardall/gospdoct.html Notes and quotes from the Gospel Doctrine class taught in Sunday School. Handouts, lesson schedules, history, more for a ward in Federal Way, Washington. Tremendous! ★★★★★ ☑

Gospel Doctrine www.ldscn.com/lynne/gd.html Comprehensive resource for Gospel Doctrine teachers. Online resource for LDS persons who are studying the scriptures. The archive is maintained with Kurt Neumiller's online teaching guide, with information useful to any gospel teacher. Includes an extensive collection of Isaish commentaries, scripture discussions corresponding with the numbered gospel doctrine lessons, discussions of various doctrinal issues related to particular portions of scripture, and much more. A tremendous resource that would be even more useful with a search tool. ★★★★

Latter-day Saint Seminar www.cybcon.com/~kurtn/exegesis.html Kurt Neumiller's extensive commentaries on Isaiah, the Old Testament, and the New Testament, along with numerous D&C commentaries and links. Worth bookmarking. Includes a mailing list, LDS-SEMINAR, with commentary and in-depth discussion on each week's Gospel Doctrine lesson. Includes regular columns, plus postings from other participants. To subscribe, send a message to *<majordomo@ldschurch.net>* with the message `subscribe ldss <yourname@your.email.address>` or the digest version `subscribe ldss-d<yourname@your.email.address>`. The first edition promised this site five stars for better organization. Brother Neumiller did the organization. Here are the solid five stars: ★★★★★

LDS Games angelfire.com/mn/ldsgames Downloadable shareware games inspired by Primary songs, pioneers, apostles, and more. A fun, interactive way of learning about the gospel. ★★★

LDS Teachers' Resource on the Internet www.lds.npl.com/special/teachers Links related to America, Christmas, Christ, history, human relations, humor, inspirational, integrity, LDS focus, miscellaneous, and missionary service. Not updated recently. ★★

Modular Teaching www.shire.net/mormon/teach.html You don't have to teach everything in the manual, right? Here's how one teacher picks and chooses his materials to suit his class. ★★★

Sunday School Teachers www.mormon.com/callings/html/ss_teachers.html Need an idea or tip for your calling? If other members have shared their tips or ideas you'll find them on this callings page. Not much here yet. ★★

Tips and Tricks www.davejennings.freeserve.co.uk/ldstips.html You'll particularly enjoy the suggestion for handling a class of rowdy teenagers. ★★★

RESOURCES FOR WOMEN

You may have noticed that chapter 10 had substantially more Relief Society–sponsored sites than Priesthood-sponsored sites.

This is the Resources for Women section. Guess what? The corresponding Resources for Men section

HOTLINKS

Errand of Angels
www.of-worth.com/ea

LDS Home
www.ldshome.com

LDS Women's Forum
ldschurch.net/f/fowkes

Women's Conference
coned.byu.edu/cw/womens.htm

consists of exactly no sites. Get busy, boys. The ladies are running you off the road.

Arta Johnson's Home Page   www.ucalgary.ca/~ajohnson A good index of publications by and about Mormon women. Hasn't been updated for a very long time. ★★

Errand of Angels   www.of-worth.com/ea To support and encourage all women, but especially those belonging to the Church of Jesus Christ of Latter-day Saints. Includes teaching moments, humor, teenagers, pioneers, cleaning and organizing tips, holidays, and much more. ★★★★

For the Sisters   members.visi.net/~atom/totally/Sisters.html An essay by Krista Holle on her perceptions of the role of women in the Church. ★★

LDS Home   www.ldshome.com A really incredibly well-done magazine for LDS women (see figure 11.5). Includes a mailing list, many tips for home management, helps for callings, storage, recipes, and much more. ★★★★★ ☑

LDS Moms @ Home   www.geocities.com/Heartland/Prairie/1139/moms.html A ring of sites for LDS Moms who either stay at home or work at home with their children. A support group composed of others who share a career and a faith, and a Web ring composed of child- and family-safe sites. As with most rings, quality varies wildly. ★★★

LDS Stay-Home-Moms Home Page   www.utw.com/~kpearson/ldshomemoms An e-mail group for mothers who have decided to stay home with their children. Supportive. ★★★

FIG. 11.5
_____

ldshome.

LDSFoyer www.onelist.com/viewarchive.cgi?listname=LDSFoyer A place for LDS women to share ideas for callings, help each other through life, make new friends, visit, and have fun. Plop on the couch and visit in the foyer! 📖

LDS Women's Forum ldschurch.net/f/fowkes Lots of writer-ly resources, and a good place to share essays, poetry, and thoughts. ★★★★

LDS-Sisters www.geocities.com/Heartland/Meadows/2528/LDS_Sisters.html E-mail list to help and give support to the sisters of the Church. 📖

Peg's Working Moms www.geocities.com/Wellesley/3212 Devoted to working mothers with tips on balancing home and work, housework, cooking, childcare, church callings, and personal time. Rather cluttered, but then, so is a working mom's life, right? ★★★

Relief Society.com www.reliefsociety.com Less about Relief Society and more about items of particular interest to women. Homemaking, speaking, recipes, poetry, motherhood, charity, and more. Affiliated with the Osmond family. ★★★

SISTER-SHARE www.omnicron.com/~fluzby/sister-share/index.htm Page with lots of links to inspirational materials and to the Sister-Share discussion list. Tends to be tremendously chatty, without a lot of depth. If you've got the time. . . . To sub-scribe, send an e-mail request to *<listserv@psuvm.psu.edu>*. Sisters only. More information is available at the Web site. ★★★

Women's Conference coned.byu.edu/cw/womens.htm An excellent site from BYU's annual Women's Conference. The Transcripts section features selected talks about time management, becoming a disciple of Christ, searching diligently in the light of Christ, and much more. Talks here are archived through to 1997. A search engine would be helpful. ★★★★★ ☑

LDS PROFESSIONAL GROUPS

When I lived in Hong Kong, a few of the male members of the Victoria Ward organized a thing they wanted to call the LDS Businessmen's Group—until the two women in the Ward who wanted to attend the meetings raised some objec-tions. So then it became the LDS Professionals Organization, or the LDS Busi-ness Council, or the Mormon Business Group—depending on who typed up the Ward bulletin that week. Never mind. Not much business was ever conducted. But I'm here to tell you, it was a really good lunch.

Fortunately, there are some real LDS professional organizations where the members have more in common than close proximity to a great restaurant.

Academy of LDS Dentists   coned.byu.edu/cw/cwdentis Organized in 1978 to provide dentists with opportunities to enhance their professional endeavors. Sponsors educational service projects and provides scholarships to deserving dental students. ★★★

AMCAP   www.amcap.net   Wa-hoo! Finally, the Association of Mormon Counselors and Psychotherapists, the last organized group in the free world to discover the Internet, is on the Web. AMCAP is an international organization of counselors, psychotherapists, and others in helping professions, who share in the principles and standards of the Church. The site is already outdated, but at least there's something there. Campaign for AMCAP to post its papers and proceedings to this site. ★★

Association of Latter-day Saint Public Relations Professionals   www.aldsprp.org Founded in 1992, the Association of Latter-day Saint Public Relations Professionals was established to create a network of skilled communicators capable of lending expertise to the Public Affairs Department of the Church. The association is a nonprofit organization of public relations professionals and students. Although its primary goal is to assist the Church, the association also encourages interaction among professionals with similar beliefs and values. The association meets in an annual conference, typically held in Salt Lake City. ★★★

Collegium Aesculapium   bioag.byu.edu/collegium/ca.html A professional association for LDS physicians, health professionals, and students who approach medical service with high ethical and moral values and with open hearts. It welcomes members of The Church of Jesus Christ of Latter-day Saints, alumni of BYU, and other interested persons who desire to grow in mind and spirit as they partake of opportunities to improve human health. The association publishes *The Journal of Collegium Aesculapium,* which focuses on articles dealing with moral, ethical, and religious issues. A very readable page. ★★★

International Society   fhss.byu.edu/kenncent/International_Society In 1989, Bill Atkin and Lee Green, LDS attorneys who were living in Taipei, worked with the David M. Kennedy Center at BYU to organize an association of working profes-

HOTLINKS

Collegium Aesculapium
bioag.byu.edu/collegium/ca.html

International Society
fhss.byu.edu/kenncent/
International_Society

LAMPS
cpms.byu.edu/cpms/talmage

sionals with international interests, who are members or friends of the LDS community. The International Society sponsors an annual summer conference and supports students and professionals living and working overseas. ★★★

J. Reuben Clark Law Society   www.law.byu.edu/JRCLS An association of LDS legal professionals. Page includes links to the National Committee, fund-raising. Law Society Chapters, Law Society Handbook, calendar of events, the publication *Clark Memorandum,* and a member directory. Also of interest will be JRCLS, an Internet e-mail list for members of the J. Reuben Clark Society. To subscribe, send an e-mail request to *<listserv@lawgate.byu.edu>* with the message `subscribe jrcls-l <your name>`. 📖

Latter-day Saint Association of the Mathematical & Physical Scientists (LAMPS) cpms.byu.edu/cpms/talmage The Latter-day Saint Association of Mathematical and Physical Scientists (LAMPS). A group publishing information about LDS scientists and issues related to science and religion. Chatty. Science Departmental. Sometimes Valuable. ★★★★

Management Society   msm.byu.edu/alumni An organization of individuals from a wide variety of businesses and professions. The Society is associated with the Marriott School of Management at BYU. ★★★

HOMESCHOOLING

A couple of years ago I overheard my then nine-year-old sitting in the back seat of the car talking to his brothers. It had been a bad week anyway, with one kid in tears because he'd misunderstood a homework assignment, and spent hours doing the wrong thing, another kid making friends with kids who were having a very bad influence on her, and yet another kid living in fear of being beat up at school. So it wasn't a good day to hear my nine-year-old say to his brother, "Hey, man . . . wanna toke of this?" I pulled the car over to the side of the road, whirled around in my seat and asked where he'd heard that phrase.

"Um, at school," he said.

"Where?"

"Um, Officer Bob taught it to us today in DARE. We learned all kinds of words, Mom." He then proceeded to rattle off a list of drug slang, the names of various sorts of drug paraphernalia, and the locations in town where most drug transactions take place.

I asked him if he'd learned anything else in school that day.

He couldn't think of a single thing.

That night we sat down and decided to start homeschooling. It's a decision I've not regretted. In my case, the school was very cooperative, and was even willing to supply textbooks and permit the kids to continue participating in various school programs. I've since learned that some other parents have a tougher time of it, but I'm persuaded that no child is harmed by increased parental involvement in education.

Fortunately, the Internet is replete with resources for parents who want to enrich their children's education. History, math, languages, music, science . . . there's nothing educational that's not available for free on the Internet.

Here are some of the best LDS sites for homeschoolers.

HOTLINKS

Homeschool Teacher's Lounge
www.geocities.com/athens/oracle/4336

LDS Homeschooling Page
home1.gte.net/shannon2

LDS Homeschooling
www.midnightbeach.com/hs/lds.htm

Center for Educational Restoration   www.cerlink.com Homeschool curriculum written by Dr. Glenn Kimber and his wife, Julianne Kimber. Also offers a chat room with scheduled chats as well as a forum to post questions. Commercial site. ⑤

Education and Homeschool   www.olypen.com/wng/hs.htm A wonderful resource from Ladybug Links. Curriculum materials, many free, broken out by subject. ★★★★

HearthSpun Publishers and Polly Block   www.ldschurch.net/f/blockp A collection of short stories and articles for young Latter-day Saints, helpful in teaching LDS principles. ★★★★

Homeschool Is Cool   www.geocities.com/Heartland/Farm/3182/homeschl.html Tons of links, activities, projects, and other goodies for homeschooling families. A great resource. ★★★

Homeschool Teacher's Lounge   www.geocities.com/athens/oracle/4336 Very well-written articles on homeschooling from an LDS mom. Includes help for teaching reading, creative writing, Web page teaching, history, writing reports, and more. Updated about weekly. ★★★★★

Iron Rod Enterprises   www.geocities.com/Athens/Troy/5371 Homeschool curriculum developed to teach from the scriptures. Commercial site. ⑤

Izu Early Childhood Education   www.netcom.com/~toniaizu/eiedu.html AJKJJ site for homeschoolers. Owner Tonia Izu writes: "Individuals have often asked why and how our children were able to begin first grade when they were four years old. This page explains our family educational philosophy." Brilliant. ★★★★

Latter-day Family Home Educators Support Page   members.xoom.com/ldfhe A very busy-looking site to support LDS and other homeschoolers. Includes a monthly newsletter, chat room, links, and a list of LDS homeschoolers in your area. Some links are dead, others are outdated. ★

Latter-day Family Resources   www.ldfr.com Commercial site, with links to other LDS homeschooling families. See the online catalog of homeschooling resources offered by this LDS homeschooling family. Also find free newsletter, bulletin boards, and chat. $

LDS Homeschooling Page   home1.gte.net/shannon2 Another great page on LDS homeschooling resources. Includes articles on subjects related to homeschooling, including parenting, socialization, dealing with criticism of homeschooling, and a history of education; LDS homeschooling organizations, curriculum resources, and regional contacts; quotes from the Brethren on education, public schools, parental responsibility, socialization, and more. ★★★★★

LDS Homeschooling   www.midnightbeach.com/hs/lds.htm This site strongly advocates homeschooling for everyone. A good resource for LDS-oriented links, it includes an excellent list of homeschooling information and links to support groups, Web pages, mailing lists, and curricula. ★★★★★

LDSHOMEED   www.utw.com/~kpearson/ldshomeed The LDS Home Education e-mail group is for parents who want the joy of watching their own children grow and learn. Good resources. Fairly active, conservative list. ★★★

Tightwad Gazette Fan Club   users.aol.com/maryfou/tightwad.html If you're going to stay home and teach your kids, you've got to be able to make ends meet. Here's how. Not specifically LDS, but the links are certainly akin to the unofficial pioneer mantra "Use it up, wear it out, make it do, or do without." ★★★

DISABILITY, MEDICAL, AND COUNSELING RESOURCES

There's an unfortunate dearth of LDS-oriented Internet information for people dealing with various disabilities. Fortunately, these few sites are unusually well done.

Ability, Achievement, Action, Artistry home.rmci.net/ porter1/fce FCE is a nonprofit foundation promoting 3-D animation, music, multimedia, and art from disabled artists. $

Camp Liahona www.dhlcc.org/campliahona A unique summer camp for hearing-impaired or deaf children or teens that gives them opportunities to learn life skills in an LDS standards setting. A not-for-profit organization. The Web site is nicely done; one imagines the camp is, too. 📖

HOTLINKS

Heart t' Heart
www.heart-t-heart.org

LDS Deaf Connection
www.gutches.net/ldc

Living Beyond Loss
adrr.com/living

Heart t' Heart www.heart-t-heart.org There's probably nobody who couldn't benefit from this site. Period. Think not? Try reading through the 12 Steps of Heart t' Heart at www.heart-t-heart.org/12steps.html, and see whether you come up clean. ★★★★

LDISABLED For members of the Church who are disabled or chronically ill in any way, and their families and friends. To subscribe, send an e-mail request to *<listserv@home.ease.lsoft.com>* with the message `subscribe LDISABLED <your name>`. 📖

LDS Deaf Connection www.gutches.net/ldc A tremendously well-done site, with helpful resources for deaf members (see figure 11.6). Features include a message board, news, visitors center, and mission information. ★★★★★ ☑

FIG. 11.6

LDS Deaf Connection: Resources for Deaf members of the Church.

LDS DIVORCE   www.flash.net/~poly/lds-divorce.html A list for LDS members who have experienced or who are in the midst of divorce. Administrative address: <lds-divorce-request@mLists.net>, list address: <lds-divorce@mLists.net>, contact: <Bill Polhemus<poly@flash.net>. Bill Polymous' list. Tends to be less wishy-washy than similar lists. Whiners are assisted in adjusting their attitudes. Good stuff. ★★★★

LDS_TOURETTES   www.onelist.com/subscribe/LDS%5FTourettes An LDS e-mail list for people with the neurological disorder Tourettes or their family members. Exchange ideas about this problem. Address questions to <angelalauraem@sprintmail.com>. 📖

Little Ones Lost   home.sprintmail.com/~adamszoo A fairly new site dedicated to helping LDS parents cope with miscarriage, stillbirth, SIDS, infertility, and related losses. Parents can share their stories at this site by submitting them to the Webmaster. Owner Linda Adams writes: "It is hoped that this way we can bear one another's burdens and help others to work through their grief, by sharing our own as well as our faith and hope." Contains useful links and resources. ★★★★

Living Beyond Loss   adrr.com/living How to cope and make it through losses of loved ones in life. A home page for Stephen R. Marsh, a father who lost three of his four daughters to illnesses. Brother Marsh advocates for the use of love and charity for solving problems, healing from grief, resolving anger, and becoming more spiritual. Of particular note is his Ethesis page adrr.com/living/e01.htm. ★★★★★

Materials for the Blind and Deaf   www.mormons.org/daily/health/Deaf_Materials_EOM.htm An article about materials available to disabled Saints. 📖

MORMONDSMOMMIES   www.onelist.com/subscribe/MormonDSMommies For the mothers of children with Down Syndrome. 📖

PEACE   www.ldscn.com A mailing list for Latter-day Saints who need a place to discuss issues relating to depression. No archive, moderated. Subscribe directly from the Web site. A moderately active list. ★★★

SANCTIFY   www.ldscn.com/sanctify An e-mail support list for inactive and part-member families. Frequently—and inexplicably—contentious, although several list members work hard to keep it peaceful. Subscribe with an e-mail message to

<majordomo@ldscn.com> with the body `subscribe sanctify` or contact Susan Malmrose *<susan@ldschurch.net>*. ★★

Springs of Water www.springsofwater.com A refuge for people struggling with nearly every sort of difficulty. And if there's not a forum linked to the site, talk to owner Rex Goode *<sowater@springsofwater.com>*, and he'll consider building one. ★★★

Stress Relief Page www.jefflindsay.com/stress.html Feeling stressed about life? Overcome with guilt? These scriptures are worth contemplating. ★★★

RESOURCES FOR SEXUALITY ISSUES

There's a wide range of material here dealing with what is, essentially, the same subject: nonmarital sexual relations. You'll find in this section materials dealing with every sort of nonmarital sexual issue: abuse, adultery, same-sex attraction, addictions, and compulsions.

Most of the sites are tremendously supportive of the policies and doctrines of the Church. Some are more political, and argue against policies and doctrines. The upside? No matter where you stand on the politics of sexuality, you're sure to find help here in dealing with personal struggles. These sites are all worth knowing about if for no other reason than to point to as a resource when you encounter others who are struggling.

HOTLINKS

CLEAN-LDS
members.tripod.com/RexGoode/
Clean.html

DISCIPLES
users.aol.com/disciples2

Evergreen International
members.aol.com/evergrn999

Healing the Heartache
www.itstessie.com/heart

Latter-day Sexual Recovery
www.ldsr.org

Affirmation www.affirmation.org Sometimes militant, often angry, but very well-known affiliation of people associated—often loosely—with the Church and concerned in various ways with the issue of same-sex attraction. This site frequently takes on the Church and its leaders in an adversarial manner. I'm not neutral about the mission of Affirmation, so consider this rating only a representation of the quality of the Web site and not an evaluation of the material it contains or the politics it espouses. ★★★★

CLEAN-LDS members.tripod.com/~RexGoode/Clean.html Support list for members of the Church who struggle with pornography addiction. Membership in the list is not restricted to members, but topics will be consistent with LDS teachings.

> Thou shalt love thy wife with all thy heart, and shalt cleave unto her and none else.
>
> And he that looketh upon a woman to lust after her shall deny the faith, and shall not have the Spirit; and if he repents not he shall be cast out. . . .
>
> But he that has committed adultery and repents with all his heart, and forsaketh it, and doeth it no more, thou shalt forgive;
>
> *Doctrine & Covenants 42:22–25*

Use of clean language is mandatory. All subscription requests must be sent directly to *<rexg@coil.com>*, after reading the requirements at the Web site. A sister list, CLEAN-SUPPORT, helps family members of Saints trying to overcome the practice. Subscribe to either list with a request to *<rexg@coil.com>* after reading the requirements at the Web site. Very well moderated, appears to be a tremendous strength to its members. ★★★★★

DISCIPLES   users.aol.com/disciples2 A mailing list for those who grapple with issues of same-sex attraction but are committed to obedience to the gospel of Jesus Christ and the teachings of modern apostles and prophets. Anonymous participation is permitted. Charter is strictly enforced, as is confidentiality. The list welcomes parents, spouses, priesthood leaders, and counselors. Subscribe with a request to *<d2moderate@aol.com>*. Charter is at the Web site. ★★★★

Evergreen International   members.aol.com/evergrn999 A Web page for the Evergreen International organization. It tries to help members who struggle with homosexuality. Includes articles on Finding Forgiveness, Finding the Way Back, Healing Your Damaged Life, Obtaining Help from the Lord, Same Gender Attraction, To Be Healed, Trust in the Lord, Happiness. ★★★★

FAMILIES   members.aol.com/disciples2/families.htm A discussion list for families of LDS members dealing with same-sex orientation. Not negative toward the Church. Subscribe with an e-mail request to *<d2moderate@aol.com>*. More information is available at the Web site. ★★

FAMILYFELLOWSHIP   www.arcticmen.com/familyfellowship Family Fellowship is an Affirmation-affiliated group, a support group of LDS families. The group subscribes to the philosophy that gay and lesbian Saints can be great blessings in the lives of their families, and that families can be great blessings in the lives of their gay and lesbian members. Subscribe at www.onelist.com/subscribe/FamilyFellowship. Web site is only moderately well-down, and not updated regularly. ★★

GAYMORMON   www.geocities.com/Athens/Academy/6261 A place for Latter-day Saints with same-sex attraction. Note that I don't say "struggling with." People on this list are generally opposed to the notion of changing or overcoming sexual orientation. Moderator says: "This is a positive place: a place of tolerance, of acceptance, and of holiness. We do not condemn same-sex attraction (neither the attraction nor the sex) nor do we condemn the Church." Members who wish to maintain confidentiality will have their privacy guaranteed. Subscribe at www.onelist.com/subscribe/Gaymormon. Or subscribe to an identically named list for same-sex attracted Saints who are trying to become part of the gay community with an e-mail request to <nephi@netcom.com>. 📖

Healing the Heartache www.itstessie.com/heart A help for Saints recovering from adultery and adulterous marriages. An excellent, thorough, resource for Latter-day Saints and other Christians who are coping with the heartache of infidelity. Includes links to marriage sites, sermons, support groups, etc. Focus is on repentance and reconciliation. ★★★★

Latter-day Sexual Recovery www.ldsr.org A place of help, hope and healing for LDS Church members caught up in sexual addiction and compulsion. Many well-written articles, lots of thoughtful information. Recommended. ★★★★★

LDS-L www.onelist.com/subscribe/Lds-l LDS Lesbians was created for lesbian women who are current or former members of the Church, as well as other interested parties. Similar in tone to the GAYMORMON lists, this forum was designed to give lesbian women a place to discuss spiritual, personal, and social issues in a friendly and nonthreatening atmosphere. This list was not created by the Church and does not have the Church's backing. 📖

LDS_SSA Channel on IRC www.geocities.com/SoHo/Cafe/9775 A special meeting place for Latter-day Saints dealing with same-sex attraction on Internet Relay Chat with twice-weekly meetings and the opportunity to meet friends anytime and have a safe place for mutual support. 📖

ON SEXUAL ADDICTIONS

My name is Nick, and I am a sex addict who has been in recovery for two years. My main addiction is linked to pornography. About a year ago I stumbled across a site called Clean LDS. I was a little leery of what I would find or get connected with. What I found was an e-mail group that allowed me to learn from the experiences of others dealing with sexual addiction. I am learning to modify my behaviors. I am still learning to lay my burdens at the Lord's feet and then not try to take them back when He sets my life in order. Originally, I was lead to a counselor specializing in sexual addiction, who recommended that I check myself into a sexual addiction recovery unit in a psychiatric hospital. What you must understand is that by the time I got to the hospital I had reached a low so low that the pain of the addiction far exceeded the pain of any form of recovery. I had one step lower that I could go and that was to end my life. I could not do that knowing what I know about the Lord and His teachings. When I got together with others who had gotten into a recovery program I learned that with the help of my Heavenly Father I could find my way home. The road is long and I still have a lot to learn, but I take each day and try to make the best of it. There is hope, I have found some. Each day I try to find more ways to improve my life, to change from the unhealthy person that I was. Today with the help of the list and support groups I can hold my head up and even look in the mirror at myself and not feel ashamed of where I am and who I am.

God bless, Nick

Q-SAINTS E-mail list for lesbian, gay, and bisexual people who come from a Mormon or Restoration background. Family members are welcome. Often takes an adversarial position toward the Church. Sponsored by Affirmation. Subscribe with an e-mail request to *<majordomo@vector.casti.com>* 📖

Ruth and Esther members.aol.com/readmin E-mail list for Mormon women who have had to deal with sexual abuse in their lives, which welcomes women of all faiths who have been affected by sexual abuse, whether it happened to them or to a friend or family member. Anonymous posting available. Contact Susan Anderson or Kim Mack *<REadmin@aol.com>*. Tends to work within gospel principles. 📖

Same-Sex Attraction members.aol.com/sykobabbel/#ssa Another leader in the movement to encourage SSA-Saints to adhere to gospel standards, Kim Mack has developed a thought-provoking collection of resources and essays about her own experiences and decisions. Awe-inspiring, principled, and worth reading. ★★★★

Stephen Rex Goode www.coil.com/~rexg Among his many interests, Rex has become a fairly prominent leader in the movement for adhering to gospel standards in the struggle with same-sex attraction. This page contains some of his excellent essays on the subject. ★★★★

VOICINGS members.aol.com/disciples2/women.htm Moderated support list for LDS women with same-sex orientation who seek to follow the Church's teachings. Not negative toward the Church. Anonymous posting is available. Tends to work within gospel principles. Subscribe with an e-mail request to *<d2moderate@ aol.com>*. More information is found on the Web site. 📖

HOTLINKS

LDS Yellow Pages
www.ldsyellowpages.com
LDS-related Commercial Sites
www.danvillestake.org/s/danville/
commerce.html

COMMERCIAL SITES FOR LDS PRODUCTS AND SERVICES

Pull out your credit cards, boys and girls. Electronic commerce is here to stay. Here you'll find links to LDS bookstores and a mind-numbing array of products designed for a Mormon audience.

Commercial Sites www.geocities.com/Heartland/Plains/5159/gen.htm#COM Brief list of sites related to genealogy products. ★

Commercial Sites   www.wnetc.com/resource/lds/commercial.html Links to 24 commercial sites, including MTC Cookies, Deseret Book, Covenant Books, LDS Music in Spanish, and more. ★★

LDS Business Sites   www.mormons.com/search/LDS_Business_Sites Lots of links to LDS-related businesses. $

LDS Commerce   www.ldstoday.com/commerce/commerce.htm Nada. Not much here. ★

LDS Retailer Search   www.deseretbook.com/retail_search.html A Deseret Book list of retail outlets for LDS products. ★★

LDS Yellow Pages   www.ldsyellowpages.com Several LDS-owned businesses with a search tool. Organized by category or geography. ★★★★

LDS-related Commercial Sites   www.danvillestake.org/s/danville/commerce.html Probably the best collection of LDS-owned and -operated businesses on the Net. Or is that a tautology? ★★★★

Mormon Commercial Sites   www.shire.net/mormon/stores.html Dozens of commercial LDS sites categorized by product line. ★★★

12

PURSUIT
OF EXCELLENCE

The pursuit of excellence. If it wasn't a Latter-day Saint who coined the term, it was certainly a large body of Latter-day Saints who made it popular. We learn from an early age to pursue excellence in all our endeavors. To strive to be the very best people we can be, to contribute to our families, our communities, our Church, and our world. To serve God in serving others. We take as our example not only Christ, from whom we learn service and charity, but also King Benjamin, who labored all his days among his people, building and creating, and serving God.

In this chapter, we use the Internet as a resource in several areas of the pursuit of excellence. The first, and largest, section looks at Internet tools for personal scripture study. In the second section, we cover Mormon arts and letters, the literature and fine arts that help define us as a community. We wouldn't be excellent people if we couldn't keep ourselves in perspective; the third section provides some great resources on Mormon-oriented humor. Finally, we address the last temporal concern: emergency preparedness.

SCRIPTURE STUDY

The Internet is a fantastic tool for studying the scriptures. Not only will you find the complete text of all the standard works online; you'll also find commentary,

HOTLINKS

Book of Mormon
www.new-jerusalem.com/scripture/bom/contents.htm

Book of Mormon Lecture Series
www.farmsresearch.com/bomlectures

Book of Mormon:
Another Testament of Jesus Christ
www.mormons.org/basic/bom

Journal of Book of Mormon Studies
www.farmsresearch.com/jbms

Mormon's Story
www.enoch.com/voicesfromdust/mormonstory/mormonstory.html

Rabbi Yosef's Jewishness
of the Book of Mormon
www.itstessie.com/jewishbom

criticism, history, and other insights that can expand your understanding of the gospel. Latter-day Saints are often advised not only to read the scriptures, but to search them and ponder them, to "feast" on the words of Christ.

In this section, we look at Internet resources that are suitable for personal scripture study, but probably go beyond the scope of Gospel Doctrine class. Here each book of scripture has its own heading. The Book of Mormon tools warrant three heads: Book of Mormon Study Tools, Responses to Critics of the Book of Mormon, and Chiasmus Studies. Following the Book of Mormon sections are sections on the Bible, the Doctrine and Covenants, the Pearl of Great Price, and multiple books of scripture.

Book of Mormon Study Tools

In chapter 6, page 99, we introduced the Book of Mormon for investigators and new members. Chapter 7, page 143, contains links to the text of the Book of Mormon. You'll find historical Book of Mormon links on page 322 in chapter 13. In this section, you'll find scholarly commentary and textual analysis of the text of the Book of Mormon.

Walk through the following sites for a taste of the Book of Mormon insights available on the Internet:

2 Nephi 25 www.jefflindsay.com/2Nephi25.html Describes Nephi's prophetic vision of the Messiah, and the relationship between Grace and Works. Includes links to an introduction to the Book of Mormon, and Jeff Lindsay's discourse on Faith and Works. ★★★

3 Nephi 11 www.jefflindsay.com/3Nephi11.html Christ visits the Americas. Includes useful background information lending context to the chapter. Full text of chapter 11. ★★★

Alma 32 www.jefflindsay.com/Alma32.shtml Alma's missionary text. Background information lends good context to the quoted material. ★★★

Alma 36 www.jefflindsay.com/Alma36.html Alma's beautifully told conversion story. One of the most poetic Book of Mormon passages, this passage is one of the best examples of Chiasmus. The page contains interesting background material and the full text of the story. ★★★

Atonement in the Book of Mormon www.farmsresearch.com/bomlectures/mil-vt4.html Text of an essay by Robert L. Millet, wherein he says it's not possible to appreciate the salvation of Christ until you know why you need Christ. And the Book of Mormon helps establish that. 📖

Authorship of the Book of Mormon www.farmsresearch.com/transcripts/rey97.html A slide presentation minus graphics, of a 1997 report on the authorship of the Book of Mormon by Noel B. Reynolds. 📖

Book of Mormon www.new-jerusalem.com/scripture/bom/contents.htm New Jerusalem offers the entire Book of Mormon on bright, easy-to-read Web pages. Click on the chapter to read. Also included is "Twenty-three Questions Answered by the Book of Mormon." This section quotes specific passages to answer common questions. A Book of Mormon word search allows you to find specific words and phrases easily. ★★★★

> **PRESIDENT BENSON ON THE BOOK OF MORMON**
> There are three ways in which the Book of Mormon is the keystone of our religion. It is the keystone in our witness of Christ. It is the keystone of our doctrine. It is the keystone of testimony.
>
> *Teachings of Ezra Taft Benson*, p. 53

Book of Mormon Geography www.mormonlands.com A page on Book of Mormon geography, lands, and predicted evidence. Specific geographic discoveries addressed in the Book of Mormon, along with new insight for the identification of an actual Book of Mormon setting. ★★

Book of Mormon Lecture Series www.farmsresearch.com/bomlectures A resource from the Foundation for Ancient Research and Mormon Studies containing important lectures on the Book of Mormon (see figure 12.1). Catalog-y, but includes full text of Richard Anderson's "Book of Mormon Witnesses"; Dahl's "Faith, Hope and Charity"; Susan Easton Black's "Christ in the Book of Mormon"; James Faulconer's "How to Study the Book of Mormon"; Ludlow's "The Covenant Teachings of the Book of Mormon"; Millet's "The Nature of God in the

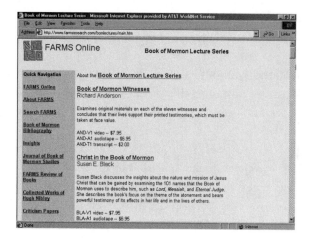

FIG. 12.1

Book of Mormon lecture series: Text from several of FARMS' best lectures.

Book of Mormon," "The Fall As Taught in the Book of Mormon," "The Doctrine of the New Birth," "The Atonement in the Book of Mormon," and "The Destiny of the House of Israel"; Nyman's "Is the Book of Mormon History?"; Ed Pinegar's "Missionary Work and the Book of Mormon"; Stephen Ricks' "The Translation and Publication of the Book of Mormon"; Royal Skousen's "The Critical Text of the Book of Mormon"; James E. Smith's "A Study of Population Size in the Book of Mormon"; Sorenson's "The Book of Mormon in Ancient America"; Catherine Thomas' "Zion and the Spirit of At-one-ment"; and Tvedtnes' "Hebraisms in the Book of Mormon." You can order these and other items in the series through FARMS. Hasn't been updated in a couple of years. ★★★★

Book of Mormon: Another Testament of Jesus Christ   www.mormons.org/basic/bom
Very well done collection of articles on Book of Mormon topics. Includes Come Unto Christ, An Overview, Biblical Prophecies About the Book of Mormon, Government and Legal History, History of Warfare, Authorship, the Book of Mormon in a Biblical Culture, Chronology, Commentaries, Economy and Technology, Editions (1830–1981), Geography, Language, Literature, Manuscripts, Names, Near Eastern Background, People in the Book of Mormon, Plates and Records, Religious Teachings and Practices, Studies, Translation by Joseph Smith, Translations, Witnesses, Allegory of Zenos, Anthon Transcript, and Archaeology. A Mormons.Org page. ★★★★★

Book of Mormon—Artifact or Artifice? By Orson Scott Card   www.nauvoo.com/library/bookofmormon.html Adapted from a speech he gave at the 1993 BYU Symposium on Life, the Universe, and Everything. An eye-opening commentary on the Book of Mormon as an impossible work of fiction by someone who should know. It'll permanently alter the way you understand the Book of Mormon. 📖

Brant Gardner's Self-Published Papers Page www.highfiber.com/~nahualli A collection of essays about Mesoamerican issues (Quetzalcoatl's "Fathers" and "The Impact of the Spanish on our Record of Native Oral Tradition") and commentary on the Book of Mormon, along with other interesting essays. Lacks authority, but the thinking is worth a read. ★★★

Chronology of the Book of Mormon werock.com/granite15/bom-chrn.htm Very cool hyperlinked chart with a timeline and a description of what was going on at any given time in the Book of Mormon. ★★★

Historicity of the Book of Mormon www.math.byu.edu/~smithw/Lds/LDS/Oaks-on-BoM-critics Elder Dallin H. Oaks discusses the Book of Mormon's historical context in this 1993 address to the Foundation for Ancient Research and Mormon Studies. For another transcript, see www.farmsresearch.com/transcripts/dho-93.html. 📖

Journal of Book of Mormon Studies www.farmsresearch.com/jbms Contents for every issue of the *Journal*, but only a handful of full-text articles are available online. Unfortunately, there's no easy way to view a single listing of all the online articles. Click through the contents links to find hyperlinks to the online text of Lehi's Jerusalem and Writing on Metal Plates; Three Days of Darkness; The Prophetic Laments of Samuel the Lamanite; The Design of the Liahona; Notes on Korihor and Language; The Mortal Ministry of the Savior; The Jewish Lectionary and Book of Mormon Prophecy; New and Old Light on Shawabtis from Mesoamerica; The Historiography of the Title Page; The Economics of the Book of Mormon; The Tree of Life; The Book of Mormon; Life, Historicity and Faith; Thus Saith the Lord; Secret Combinations Revisited; Joseph Smith's Receipt of the Plates and the Israelite Feast of Trumpets; The True Points of My Doctrine; Translation of the Book of Mormon; Others in the Book of Mormon; Comments on Nephite Chronology; The Jaredite Exodus; Destruction at the Time of the Crucifixion; Jewish and Other Semitic Texts Written in Egyptian Characters; The Influence of Lehi's Admonitions; and The Plan of Redemption as Taught in the Book of Mormon. Sterling research, but the table of contents is rather unorganized. ★★★★

King Benjamin's Farewell Address www.jefflindsay.com/KBenjamin.html If you had to choose one section of the Book of Mormon to send out to all the world, this would be it. Brother Lindsay includes some background information that puts the discourse into its historical context. The full text follows. ★★★

Mormon's Story www.enoch.com/voicesfromdust/mormonstory/mormonstory.html The text of the Book of Mormon in a simpler English (see figure 12.2). While I'm a great fan of reading scriptures in their original form, I'm an even greater fan of understanding the scriptures—in whatever form generates understanding. Timothy Wilson's rewrite of the Book of Mormon is beautifully done, and it's all available online at this Web site. If this is the kind of simplification it takes to get a child, a poor reader, a non-native English speaker, or a new reader through the Book of Mormon for the first time, it's a worthwhile venture. ★★★★★ ☑

People in the Book of Mormon www.mormons.org/basic/bom/people Articles on prominent people in the Book of Mormon, including Book of Mormon Peoples; Abinadi; Alma the Elder; Alma the Younger; Amulek; Benjamin, Brother of Jared; and Moroni, Son of Mormon. A Mormons.Org page. ★★★★

Rabbi Yosef's Jewishness of the Book of Mormon www.itstessie.com/jewishbom Page maintained by a Jewish rabbi who believes the Book of Mormon has Semitic origins. The page demonstrates connections linking the Book of Mormon and Judaism for Messianic Jews. ★★★★★

Record Keepers of the Book of Mormon members.aol.com/jhardy355/bomrec.htm Joel Hardy's accounting of who was whom among writers of the Book of Mormon. A graphic representation of the keepers of the Book of Mormon. ★★★

SAMU-L *<pacal@bingvmb.cc.binghamton.edu>* This group is for more technical discussions about antiquities and how they relate to Mormonism. There are frequent discussions about the historical background of Mormon scriptures,

FIG. 12.2

Mormon's Story: An easy-to-read retelling of the Book of Mormon.

archaeology and the Book of Mormon, and historical symbols. Generally low in volume, and most posts contain quite a bit of information. To subscribe, send an e-mail request to *<pacal@bingvmb.cc.binghamton.edu>* or *<mraish@library.lib. binghamton.edu>* 📖

Unrolling the Scrolls www.math.byu.edu/~smithw/Lds/LDS/Hugh-Nibley/Nibley-Unrolling-the-Scrolls.html A Hugh Nibley white paper from 1967, in which he expounds on the possibilities contained in unexplored documents of the ancient world. 📖

Variations Between Copies of the First Edition of the Book of Mormon www. farmsresearch.com/transcripts/jen-73.html Janet Jenson (1973). A consideration of variations between copies of the first edition of the Book of Mormon. 📖

Who's Who in the Book of Mormon www.srv.net/~rlo/bomchar.html Rick Owen's list of all the people in the Book of Mormon with biographical sketches. Very helpful. A similar page by Joel Hardy is found at members.aol.com/jhardy355/boma2z.htm ★★★

Years of the Jaredites www.farmsresearch.com/transcripts/sor-69.html The Years of the Jaredites is a summation of John L. Sorenson's efforts to construct the chronology of the Jaredites by comparing Book of Mormon references to current (1968) archeological records of ancient American civilizations. This article originally appeared in BYU Today in September of 1968. 📖

Responses to Critics of the Book of Mormon

Some of the most heated discussion in the LDS online community surrounds the Book of Mormon: its truthfulness, its historicity, its meaning.

As the keystone of our religion, it is perhaps natural that the Book of Mormon should be the focus of a great deal of discussion, both within the Church, and from without.

Latter-day Saint defenders of the Book of Mormon have produced a remarkable volume of literature in support of the book, responding with scholarly and disciplined answers to each issue raised by detractors.

A good number of the best, most scholarly responses to critics come from the Foundation for Ancient Research and Mormon Studies—FARMS.

> **RICHARD CRACROFT ON MARK TWAIN'S BURLESQUE OF THE BOOK OF MORMON**
>
> If Twain read the Book of Mormon at all, it was in the same manner that Tom Sawyer won the Sunday School Bible contest—by cheating.
>
> Richard H. Cracroft, *BYU Studies*, Vol. 11, No. 2, p. 119.

Accordingly, FARMS studies are well represented in this list of responses to critics of the Book of Mormon. While FARMS also publishes reviews of LDS-authored books on its Web site, the responses to critics are, quite frankly, more interesting, and so are documented here individually.

While the battle continues to rage, the following sites continue to provide good clean help for readers who need additional background on the Book of Mormon.

Alma 7:10 and the Birthplace of Jesus Christ www.farmsresearch.com/criticism/critic02.html Was it really a translation error on Joseph's part when he placed Christ's birth "at Jerusalem which is the land of our forefathers?" FARMS' favorites Peterson, Roper, and Hamblin respond to critics who claim Alma 7:10 impugns Joseph Smith. ★★★

Apparent Book of Mormon Problems www.jefflindsay.com/LDSFAQ/FQ_BMProblems.shtml Responds to objections about the weight of the plates, coins, the use of the word "adieu," metals, and more. Very thorough answers to questions commonly raised by critics of the Church. ★★★★

Archaeology and Book of Mormon Evidence www.jefflindsay.com/LDSFAQ/FQ_BMEvidence.shtml Jeff Lindsay's thoughtful responses to questions on archaeology and the Book of Mormon. Responds to sixteen real queries from readers. Covers questions such as: Have non-LDS scholars confirmed that the Book of Mormon is true? Does the Book of Mormon have the expected level of historical confirmation for true scripture? Is there evidence that Lehi existed? Why is there lots of archaeological evidence for the Bible but little for the Book of Mormon? Why hasn't a single Book of Mormon site been identified? Is there evidence that the golden plates ever really existed? How can we believe the Book of Mormon without having the original plates? Haven't archaeologists and geneticists

HOTLINKS

Basic Methodological Problems
www.farmsresearch.com/criticism/critic04.html

Book of Mormon and Archaeology FAQ
www.teleport.com/~arden/mormfaq.htm

Book of Mormon Answerman
www.new-jerusalem.com/boma

Evidences for the Book of Mormon
www.jefflindsay.com/BMEvidences.shtml

Foundation for Ancient Research and Mormon Studies
www.farmsresearch.com

Mormonism Researched
www.cyberhighway.net/~shirtail/mormonis.htm

Reformed Egyptian
www.farmsresearch.com/criticism/critic01.html

refuted the Book of Mormon? Hasn't it been proven that all Native Americans are of Asian (Mongolian) origin, not Jewish origin? Brother Lindsay's responses are always well documented and thorough. ★★★★

Basic Methodological Problems   www.farmsresearch.com/criticism/critic04.html A discussion of the basic methodological problems with the anti-Mormon approach to the geography and archaeology of the Book of Mormon. Addresses the Nature of "Proof," Misconceptions, Witnesses, Understanding of Arabia, Book of Mormon Names, Hebrew Writing Styles and Idioms, Chiasmus, Annual Great Assembly, Modern Stylemetry Analysis, Claims for Origin of Book of Mormon, Discussions About the Book of Mormon, and Additional Sources of Information. Critics of the Church and of the Book of Mormon often use a questionable set of assumptions. Bill Hamblin takes a look at the arguments and patterns of assumptions. ★★★

Book of Mormon an Ancient Book?   www.comevisit.com/lds/bom-evid.htm An answer to critics who would contend that the Book of Mormon is of modern origin. Among the dozens of subjects addressed are authorship, gold plates, and temple building. ★★★

Book of Mormon and Archaeology FAQ   www.teleport.com/~arden/mormfaq.htm Arden Eby's collection of responses to questions raised about Book of Mormon archaeology. Includes a beautiful retelling of the Mayan creation story. Worth a visit. ★★★

Book of Mormon and Metal Plates   www.jefflindsay.com/LDSMetal.shtml Research conducted by William J. Hamblin for FARMS provides powerful modern evidence for the authenticity of the Book of Mormon. ★★★

Book of Mormon Answerman   www.new-jerusalem.com/boma BOMA, which as of mid-1999 had 179 members, provides the answers concerning questions of faith, propriety, and the Book of Mormon. Interested people from around the world provide the questions. ★★★★

Book of Mormon Challenge   www.jefflindsay.com/BOMchallenge.shtml Hugh Nibley's challenge to critics. The title is the same as the site below; the content is entirely different. ★★★

Book of Mormon Challenge   www.ychat.com/murat/challan.html One of those lists that gets passed around Sunday School without attribution. If anyone asks, it seems to be inspired by a much-better-written text from Hugh Nibley. In any event, it's an interesting way to view the Book. ★★

Book of Mormon Issues: Archaeology, History & Thought www.cyberhighway.net/ ~shirtail/mormonis.htm#BookofMormon Dozens and dozens of scholarly articles responding to critics of the Book of Mormon. External and internal evidences of the authenticity of the Book. ★★★★

Changes in Early Texts of the Book of Mormon www.flash.net/~mdparker/ BofMChanges.htm An *Ensign* article concerning this worn-out claim by those that oppose the Church. 📖

Changes in the Book of Mormon? www.jefflindsay.com/LDSFAQ/FQ_changes.shtml A lengthy examination of changes made in various texts of the Book of Mormon. Author Jeff Lindsay considers various explanations for each kind of change. Includes a well-done summary of textual changes in a table format. Demonstrates that assertions of "thousands" of changes are overwrought. ★★★

Comments on the Book of Mormon Witnesses: A Response to Jerald and Sandra Tanner www.farmsresearch.com/criticism/critic03.html Tremendously well-documented article by Matthew Roper that challenges the Tanners' representations about the witnesses of the Book of Mormon. ★★★

Did Joseph Copy the Names Moroni and Cumorah? www.geocities.com/Athens/ Forum/5499/bom/comoros.html A credible response to those who suggest the ancient names were copied from modern documents. Part of the LDS Evidences site. ★★

Evidences for the Book of Mormon www.jefflindsay.com/BMEvidences.shtml Jeff Lindsay is the Energizer Bunny of the Mormon Internet. In this page of responses to questions posed by readers, Brother Lindsay describes Excellent Printed Resources; Geography of the Arabian Peninsula; Writing on Metal Plates; Writing in Reformed Egyptian? Mulek, Son of King Zedekiah? The Use of Cement in Ancient America; Chiasmus in the Book of Mormon; Olive Culture; Wars in Winter? Mesoamerican Fortifications; Numerous Hebraic Language Structures; Names in the Book of Mormon; "The Land of Jerusalem" question; and a new page, The Great Catastrophe: Volcanism in Book of Mormon Lands. ★★★★

Foundation for Ancient Research and Mormon Studies www.farmsresearch.com FARMS is a nonprofit educational foundation that encourages and supports research about the Book of Mormon and other ancient scriptures independent of all other organizations. Research areas include ancient history, language, literature, culture, geography, politics, and law relevant to the scriptures. As a service to teachers and students of the scriptures, research results are distributed both in scholarly and popular formats. ★★★★★

Is the Book of Mormon a Fraud? www.jefflindsay.com/nibley_bom_fraud.html Interesting passages from the works of Hugh Nibley. ★★★

Just the Facts Please www.farmsresearch.com/review/6_2/bushman.html Joseph Smith scholar Richard L. Bushman's evaluation of Marquardt and Walters' *Inventing Mormonism: Tradition and the Historical Record.* Excellent. ★★★

Look at Book of Mormon Authorship www.farmsresearch.com/review/1/norwood.html L. Ara Norwood's dispassionate review of Holley's *Book of Mormon Authorship.* Very readable, void of polemics. 📖

Look at Covering Up the Black Hole www.farmsresearch.com/review/5/nibley.html Tom Nibley's rather amusing dismissal of Jerald and Sandra Tanner's 1990 book. 📖

Metals, Weapons, and the Book of Mormon www.jefflindsay.com/LDSFAQ/FQ_metals.shtml Responds to queries about steel in ancient America, swords, weight of the plates, size of the plates, brass, sources of metals, ancient writing on metal plates, and more. There's no end of possible responses. Jeff Lindsay covers the basics. ★★★

Modern Malleus Maleficarum www.farmsresearch.com/review/3/dcp.html Daniel C. Peterson's review of *The Best Kept Secrets in the Book of Mormon,* a polemic he describes as "New Age anti-Mormonism." ★★★

Mormonism Researched www.cyberhighway.net/~shirtail/mormonis.htm Kerry Shirts' new page of essays on the Book of Abraham, the Bible, the Book of Mormon, and archaeology. Extensive. Combative. ★★★★★ ☑

New Approaches www.farmsresearch.com/review/6_1/bitton.html Reviews of Brent Metcalfe's *New Approaches to the Book of Mormon: Explorations in Critical Methodology.* Responses from Davis Bitton. See additional pages by various authors at the following sites: John A. Tvedtnes www.farmsresearch.com/review/6_1/tvedtnes.html, and Daniel C. Peterson www.farmsresearch.com/review/6_1/text_c.html. 📖

Plagiarism and the Book of Mormon   www.jefflindsay.com/LDSFAQ/FQ_BMProb3.shtml
If you're a nonbeliever, it's tough to account for the Book of Mormon. Critics go to extraordinary lengths to find nondivine sources for the text. This page responds to common charges that the Book of Mormon was plagiarized. Answers three questions: Did Joseph Smith plagiarize from *View of the Hebrews?* Did Joseph Smith plagiarize from Shakespeare? Did Joseph Smith plagiarize from the King James Bible? ★★★

Plants and Animals in the Book of Mormon   www.jefflindsay.com/LDSFAQ/FQ_BMProb2.shtml Jeff Lindsay's answers to objections raised by critics regarding seeming anachronisms in the Book of Mormon. Good introductory material and thorough responses to several specific questions. ★★

Problems with the Book of Mormon?   geocities.com/Athens/8020/whtprobs.html A list of possible solutions. Melissa Birkholz responds to a long list of Book of Mormon criticisms. ★★★★

Reformed Egyptian   www.farmsresearch.com/criticism/critic01.html William J. Hamblin's response to critics who maintain that there is no language known as "reformed Egyptian." See a related site, **Cuneiform.** mahan.wonkwang.ac.kr/lecture/ancient/meso/cuniform/cunei.htm Not an LDS site, but worth contemplating for its brief explanation of Cuneiform, one of the earliest writing systems devised. Developed by the Sumerians in Mesopotamia as a picture writing and handed down to the Jews. ★★★★

Response to the Smithsonian Institution's 1996 Statement Regarding the Book of Mormon   www.jefflindsay.com/LDSFAQ/smithsonian.shtml A Jeff Lindsay page dealing with sloppy, but widely circulated, statements made by a department at the Smithsonian Institution, without the benefit of adequate knowledge of either Mesoamerica or the Book of Mormon. The Smithsonian Statement is embarrassingly out of date and needs significant revision. Many issues are covered, including transoceanic voyaging and allegedly missing items such as silk. ★★★

Review of *A Sure Foundation: Answers to Difficult Gospel Questions*   www.farmsresearch.com/review/2/gillum.html This review includes fourteen of the questions and answers in the book. Worth a read. 📖

Review of *Are the Mormon Scriptures Reliable?*   www.farmsresearch.com/review/2/wirth.html Diane E. Wirth's examination of the Ropp and Walters' text. She writes: "This book is, perhaps, rather better than the average anti-Latter-day-Saint book."

The review responds to oft-repeated allegations about Mormon Christianity, archaeology, reformed Egyptian, Kinderhook, geography, textual changes and inconsistencies, plural marriage, Book of Abraham, scriptural interpretation, and quality of scholarship. 📖

Review of Ethan Smith's *View of the Hebrews* www.farmsresearch.com/review/9_1/hedges.html Be ready to wave this one next time someone says the Book of Mormon was plagiarized. 📖

Review www.farmsresearch.com/review/2/dcp.html Daniel C. Peterson's assessment of Bartley's *Mormonism: The Prophet, the Book and the Cult*. He describes Bartley's haphazard scholarship. (Bartley at one point quotes Brigham Young from a nineteenth-century novel as though the prophet had actually spoken the fictionalized words.) 📖

Review www.farmsresearch.com/review/2/norwood.html L. Ara Norwood persuasively refutes David Persuitte's *Joseph Smith and the Origins of the Book of Mormon*, in which Persuitte alleges a *View of the Hebrews* origin for the Book of Mormon. 📖

Review www.farmsresearch.com/review/8_1/dcp1.html Daniel C. Peterson's well-written review of Van Gorden's *Mormonism*. Responds to the usual critical controversies such as archaeology, coins, hieroglyphics, birthplace of Christ, Professor Anthon, witnesses, and priesthood. 📖

> ## ON EVIDENCES
> The Book of Mormon, indeed a marvelous work and a wonder, is rich beyond our present appreciation. Examples are the apparent presence of Jewish festivals in the Book of Mormon, and extensive and precise chiasmus. When Joseph was translating the record, he could not have known of such things. Once he even inquired of Emma as to whether there were walls around Jerusalem! He simply did not know.
>
> Neal A. Maxwell, *A Wonderful Flood of Light*, p. 32

Secret Combinations Revisited www.farmsresearch.com/jbms/1_1dcp.html Daniel C. Peterson article originally published in *Journal of Book of Mormon Studies*, wherein he responds to allegations that the term "secret combinations" casts doubt on Book of Mormon authorship. 📖

Various Editions of the Book of Mormon www.new-jerusalem.com/bom-answerman/changes.html A New Jerusalem site. Text from an *Encyclopedia of Mormonism* article comparing editions. 📖

Chiasmus Studies

A new and fascinating line of inquiry into the Book of Mormon is the field of Chiasmus Studies. Chiasmus is an ancient poetic and structural form found in both the Old and New Testament, as well as in the Book of Mormon and the Doctrine and Covenants. Its presence in the Book of Mormon is considered by many to be evidence of the Book of Mormon's divine origin.

Several Web sites address the issue of Chiasmus, in particular, as it relates to comparisons between the Book of Mormon and the Bible.

Alma 36   www.jefflindsay.com/Alma36.html One of the most poetic Book of Mormon passages. Author Jeff Lindsay claims this passage is one of the best examples of the Hebrew poetic form called Chiasmus in all of ancient literature. ★★★

Chiasmus in the Book of Mormon   www.jefflindsay.com/chiasmus.shtml A satisfyingly thorough beginner's guide to Chiasmus (an ancient poetic structure) and its appearance in the Book of Mormon. Another Jeff Lindsay page, with careful explanations of how Chiasmus is structured. Contains many examples of the form. ★★★★

Chiasmus on the Brass Plates   www.mormonism.com/chiasmus.htm A brief introduction to Chiasmus. ★★

Criteria for Identifying and Evaluating the Presence of Chiasmus   www.farmsresearch.com/jbms/4_2/welch.html John W. Welch offers a careful consideration of the structure of Chiasmus. ★★★

Davidic Chiasmus and Parallelisms   www.geocities.com/CapitolHill/3500 A governing literary structure for messianic literature. Here you'll find more than 100 examples of chiastic patterns. The page describes the chiastic structure and illustrates it through many examples. Some of the chiastic structures here are controversial, so ponder it carefully. ★★★★

Mosiah 3 Chiasmus   www.cybcon.com/~kurtn/mosiah3x.txt Kurt Neumiller considers this Book of Mormon passage as a chiasmic form. Very little commentary. ★★

Structure and Outline of Zephaniah   www.berith.com/English/ZEPH001.html Certainly not a Book of Mormon site, but nevertheless a very compelling resource on

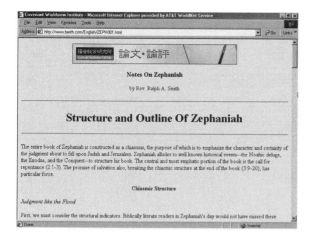

FIG. 12.3

Structure and Outline: The Old Testament book of Zephaniah exhibits the chiasmic structure.

chiasmic structure, as illustrated in the book of Zephaniah (see figure 12.3). Compiled by a Rev. Ralph A. Smith, who writes: "The entire book of Zephaniah is constructed as a chiasmus, the purpose of which is to emphasize the character and certainty of the judgment about to fall upon Judah and Jerusalem. Zephaniah alludes to well-known historical events—the Noahic deluge, the Exodus, and the Conquest—to structure his book. The central and most emphatic portion of the book is the call for repentance (2:1–3). The promise of salvation also, breaking the chiasmic structure at the end of the book (3:9–20), has particular force." ★★★★

Types of Scriptural Poetry www.cybcon.com/~kurtn/scrippoetry.txt Clark Goble's compilation of various Hebraic poetical forms, along with examples from the entire cannon of scripture, is tremendously enlightening. Begin discerning poetical forms and find your testimony increase with regard to the inspired nature of scripture. This is a great starting point for further contributions. ★★★★

Bible Commentaries

A Bible site, a Bible site. We have got a Bible site. And there cannot be any more Bible sites.

The following Bible commentaries are, primarily, from Protestant sources and so may or may not be doctrinal. To compare these sites and to determine the bias of various biblical commentaries, we looked at a biblical verse that has a great deal more meaning for Latter-day Saints than it has for most other Christians: 1 Cor. 15:29, "Else what shall they do which are baptized for the dead, if the dead rise not at all? why are they then baptized for the dead?"

Here's a sampling of what we found. (Additional commentaries from more specifically LDS sources are included in the listings under the "Multiple Books of Scripture" heading, later in this chapter).

Bible Comments on Resurrection and Annihilation

www.cybcon.com/~kurtn/anihil.txt Part of Kurt Neumiller's LDS-Seminar site, where he examines the question of whether there is a physical resurrection. ★★★

Blue Letter Bible Project

www.khouse.org/blueletter Multiple commentaries, some very well done. Commentator Ray Stedman provides tremendous context for 1 Corinthians, but avoids the baptism for the dead issue altogether. "If Jesus Christ was not raised from the dead, then, as the apostle says in this chapter, we are hopeless, and not only that, we are the most to be pitied of all people—we are nuts, we are fools, we ought to be locked up somewhere, if Christ be not raised from the dead." Stedman is very readable. Another commentator, Chuck Smith, goes for the jugular: "Baptism for the dead is a practice that was common in the pagan religions of Greece and is still practiced today by some cults; but it doesn't change a person's sentence, for that is determined while he lives." (Yeah, sez you!) And the last, David Guzik, prefers the "best defense is a good offense" strategy: "What was being baptized for the dead?" he asks. "It is a mysterious passage, and there have been more than thirty different attempts to interpret it. i. The plain meaning of the Greek in verse 29 is that some people are being baptized on behalf of those who have died—and if there is no resurrection, why are they doing this? ii. Either Paul is referring to a pagan custom (notice he uses they, not 'we'), or to a superstitious and unscriptural practice in the Corinthian church of vicarious baptism for believers who died before being baptized. iii. Either way, he certainly does not approve of the practice; he merely says that if there is no resurrection, why would the custom take place? The Mormon practice of baptism for the dead is neither scriptural or sensible." (Choice i. works for us. Occam's razor gives a pretty close shave.) Overall, the site is a bit difficult to use. But it's worth visiting if only for the Ray Stedman backgrounders. ★★

Concise Matthew Henry Commentary

ccel.wheaton.edu/henry/mhc/mhc.html Regarding 1 Cor. 15:29, the author says: "What shall those do, who are baptized for the dead, if the dead rise not at all? Perhaps baptism is used here in a figure, for afflictions, sufferings, and martyrdom, as Matthew 20:22,23. What is, or will become of those who have suffered many and great injuries, and have even lost their lives, for this doctrine of the resurrection, if the dead rise not at all? Whatever the meaning may be, doubtless the apostle's argument was understood by the Corinthians." Yeah, doubtless. Lots of good stuff anyway. ★★★★

Easton's Bible Dictionary   ccel.wheaton.edu/easton/ebd/ebd.html Here's Easton's take on baptism for the dead: "This expression as used by the apostle may be equivalent to saying, 'He who goes through a baptism of blood in order to join a glorified church which has no existence [i.e., if the dead rise not] is a fool.' Some also regard the statement here as an allusion to the strange practice which began, it is said, to prevail at Corinth, in which a person was baptized in the stead of others who had died before being baptized, to whom it was hoped some of the benefits of that rite would be extended. This they think may have been one of the erroneous customs which Paul went to Corinth to 'set in order.'" Or maybe not. Quite a number of useful definitions, nevertheless. ★★

Executable Outline Series   ccel.wheaton.edu/contrib/ exec_outlines A very well organized series of documents describing the history and text of books of the Bible. Not LDS, but useful nevertheless. The 1 Cor. verse on baptism is glossed over completely. ★★★

Lightfoot's Commentary on the New Testament www.mv.com/ipusers/butterfly/comment/00index.htm John Lightfoot, writing in the 17th century, provides a tremendously useful commentary from the Talmud and Hebraica on the four gospels as they would have been understood at the time of their writing. ★★★★

Bible Study Tools

Two subjects compete for the title of Taking Up the Most Space on the Internet: Religion and Pornography. Naturally, then, there's no shortage of information to be found on biblical topics—or antibiblical ones, if that's your inclination. In this section, we list some of the Bible-oriented sites that have a particular interest to LDS readers, but remind you that if you're searching, you'll find literally hundreds of Bible sites of a more general nature.

BRIGHAM YOUNG
ON BIBLE STUDY

The Bible is true. It may not all have been translated aright, and many precious things may have been rejected in the compilation and translation of the Bible; but we understand, from the writings of one of the Apostles, that if all the sayings and doings of the Savior had been written, the world could not contain them. I will say that the world could not understand them. They do not understand what we have on record, nor the character of the Savior, as delineated in the Scriptures; and yet it is one of the simplest things in the world, and the Bible, when it is understood, is one of the simplest books in the world, for, as far as it is translated correctly, it is nothing but truth, and in truth there is no mystery save to the ignorant. The revelations of the Lord to his creatures are adapted to the lowest capacity, and they bring life and salvation to all who are willing to receive them.

Discourses of Brigham Young, p.124, 14:135

HOTLINKS

Bible Browser Advanced Home Page
goon.stg.brown.edu/
bible_browser/pbform.shtml

Bible Gateway
bible.gospelcom.net/bible

Goshen Net
www.biblestudytools.net

Harmony of the Four Gospels
www.wwnet.net/~farmer/bible

Holy Bible
www.mormons.org/basic/bible

LDS Bible Dictionary
www.geocities.com/Heartland/
Lane/2536/bd/bd.htm

Medieval Manuscripts
www.utah.edu/umfa/
mmgenintro.html

New Testament Study Aids
www.lds-gems.com/archive/nt

The following sites contain various sorts of tools that will help you in your study of the Old and New Testaments.

At Home with Hebrew www.hebrewresources.com Hebrew lessons online, many free of charge. Fascinating stuff here, particularly the Hidden Hebrew entries. $

Bible Browser Advanced Home Page goon.stg.brown. edu/bible_browser/pbform.shtml A tremendously useful comparison of nine popular versions of the Bible (see figure 12.4). This site contains the text for the *American Standard Version* (1901), *Bible in Basic English* (1965), *Darby* (1884/1890), *Jerome's Latin Vulgate* (405 C.E.), *Noah Webster* (1833), *Revised Standard Version, Weymouth New Testament* (1909), and *Young's Literal Translation* (1898). Altogether easy to use, with useful background information on each version. ★★★★★

Bible Gateway bible.gospelcom.net/bible Another good page for comparing various editions of the Bible. This one compares the *New International Version* and *New American Standard Bible*, plus the same RSV, KJV, Darby, and YLT versions as above. Includes a

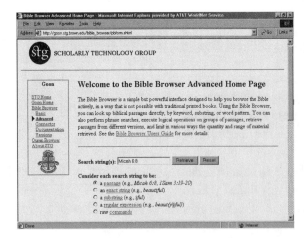

FIG. 12.4

The Bible Browser: Use the Bible Browser to compare nine versions of the Bible.

topical search tool. Lacks the background material found on the Bible Browser site, but still worth investigating. ★★★★

Bible Study FAQ www.storm.ca/~sabigail/youth.htm Answers to questions about how to study the Bible effectively. Assumes Biblical inerrancy, and works hard to account for textual contradictions. ★

Bibles, Bible Resources, and Commentaries www.igs.net/~vfl/bible-resources.html Good links to Bible translations. ★★

Bibles www.newcreation.org/tcbible.html List of links to Bibles in various languages. ★★

Biblicality of the Doctrine of Exaltation www.cybcon.com/~kurtn/biblexlt.txt Another tremendous insight from LDS-Seminar. ★★★

Goshen Net www.biblestudytools.net Media Management's GOSHEN (Global Online Service Helping Evangelize Nations) is a powerful database search tool that makes it easy to explore Bibles and related text. There is a long list of documents available to users of this site including, but not limited to, The New American Standard Bible, two versions of the King James Bible, and the Douay-Rheims Bible. Extensive Bible study resource site includes searchable versions of several dictionaries, concordances, commentaries, and Greek and Hebrew lexicons. Voluminous. ★★★★

Great are the Words of Isaiah www.farmsresearch.com/nibley/1/isaiah.html The text of a lecture given by Hugh Nibley at BYU's sixth annual Sidney B. Sperry Symposium on January 28, 1978. 📖

Harmony of the Four Gospels www.wwnet.net/~farmer/bible An ambitious project to combine the gospels of the apostles with maps and pictures. The end result is a unifying vision of the life of Christ and of the times in which he lived. See a visually challenging LDS version of the same material, correlated with Latter-day scriptures, at www.geocities.com/Heartland/Lane/2536/bd/harmony.htm. ★★★★

Hebraeus Foundation www.vcaa.com/hebraeus Excerpts from the Isaiah studies of LDS scholar Avraham Gileadi. Minimal content. ★★

Holy Bible www.mormons.org/basic/bible (See figure 12.5.) A collection of LDS teachings on the historicity and role of the Bible. Includes articles on the Bible,

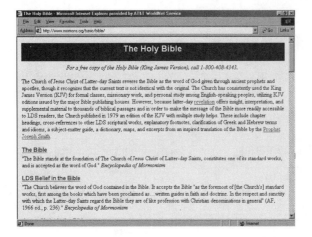

FIG. 12.5

The Holy Bible.

LDS Belief in the Bible, King James Version, People in the Bible, LDS Publication of the Bible, Bible Dictionary, Bible Scholarship, Abrahamic Covenant, the Beatitudes, Biblical Prophets, Covenants in Biblical Times, Fall of Adam, The Creation, and the Prophesies of Daniel. A Mormons.Org page. ★★★★

LDS Bible Dictionary   www.geocities.com/Heartland/Lane/2536/bd/bd.htm For teachers and students who require a concise collection of definitions and explanations of items that are mentioned in or are otherwise associated with the Bible. It is based primarily on the biblical text, supplemented by information from the other books of scripture. ★★★★★

Living by Faith Ministries   web.infoave.net/~tracymelody/textusreceptus.html A Christian organization that supports continued use of the King James version of the Bible. Interesting historical information about the various manuscripts used in translations, and the current debate among theologians about whether or not to scrap the King James version. Not LDS, which, in this case, makes it an even better read. ★★★

Medieval Manuscripts   www.utah.edu/umfa/mmgenintro.html The illuminated manuscript—a handwritten book with pictures and decoration painted or drawn in bright colors, illuminating, or lighting up, the page—was a major form of artistic expression in medieval times. Here's how your scriptures were maintained for a time. ★★★

Navigating the Bible   bible.ort.org Read, study, and enjoy the Jewish Bible. The program is available in English, Russian, and Spanish. ★★★

New Testament Study Aids www.lds-gems.com/archive/nt Expect this LDS-GEMS site to change addresses as additional books of scripture are added. Find the general archive at www.lds-gems.com/archive. Good study aids to prepare for your Sunday School lesson. ★★★★

Original Bible Project www.centuryone.com/obp.html An interesting translation and explanation of why the text is being translated in this manner. ★★★

People in the Bible www.mormons.org/basic/bible/people A collection of articles on biblical people whose lives had a significant impact on the ancient Church. A Mormons.Org page. ★★★

Tanach Study Center www.tanach.org Hasidic Jewish (Orthodox) Web page based in Israel, archived commentaries on the weekly Torah portions, and some on the Prophets. Read and see whether it doesn't illuminate your understanding of the latter-day temple ordinances. ★★★

TC: A Journal of Biblical Textual Criticism scholar.cc.emory.edu/scripts/TC/TC.html TC exists for the serious scholar. The TC site is dedicated to the study of Jewish and Christian biblical text. Published works dating back to 1996 are available for viewing. Of course, these sorts of things tend to be self-congratulatory, and to deny revelation, so take it all with a grain of salt. ★★★

Ten Commandments www.danvillestake.org/s/danville/the10.html In case you couldn't remember whether or not it's ok to covet your neighbor's lawnmower. Seriously, it's tough to pick the ten out of the Exodus verses. This site clarifies, and it's actually pretty well done. ★★★

Use of KJV English Rhetoric in the LDS Cannon www.cybcon.com/~kurtn/KJVisms.txt Fascinating analysis, with contributions from several editors. ★★★

Who Wrote the Pentateuch? www.cybcon.com/~kurtn/whowrotetorah.txt Argues for Moses as author, against the arguments of some academics. See an interesting counterpoint at www.religioustolerance.org/chr_tora.htm. ★★★

Doctrine and Covenants Study Tools

Because it's all so braided into Church history, most of the sites that might otherwise be Doctrine and Covenants–related are actually found in chapter 13: "The Glory of God Is Intelligence"—Church History section.

HOTLINKS

Changes in the Book of Commandments
www.flash.net/~mdparker/
BoC_Changes.htm

Doctrine & Covenants Resource Page
www.geocities.com/Heartland/
Lane/2536/dc_main.htm

Doctrine and Covenants
www.mormons.org/basic/
doctrines/scripture/dc

In this section you'll find study tools specifically related to the text of the Doctrine and Covenants.

Book of Commandments church-of-christ.com/Book%20of%20Commandments%20Main.htm The complete text of the 1833 edition of Joseph Smith's early revelations, posted on the Internet by the Church of Christ at Temple Lot, an LDS splinter group. (Mike Parker's critical edition of the text, a work in progress, is available at www.flash.net/~mdparker/BoC_Index.htm.) ★★★

Changes in the Book of Commandments www.flash.net/~mdparker/BoC_Changes.htm A master's thesis called *Study of the Nature of and the Significance of the Changes in the Revelations as Found in a Comparison of the Book of Commandments and Subsequent Editions of the Doctrine and Covenants.* The thesis was written by Melvin J. Petersen in 1955 under the supervision of Sidney Sperry, and posted on line by Mike Parker. ★★★★

Doctrine & Covenants Resource Page www.geocities.com/Heartland/Lane/2536/dc_main.htm Andy Hobbs has an impressive collection of links, reference papers, and other works on the history and development of the D&C. ★★★

Doctrine and Covenants Mastery Scriptures www.inconnect.com/~bytheway/dcmast.html Scripture mastery selections from the Doctrine and Covenants, assembled by John Bytheway. ★★

Doctrine and Covenants Vocabulary Guide nauvoo.byu.edu/Church/ChurchHistory/DC_Guide/main.cfm What it says. Get the skinny on word usage in the modern scriptures. Quite a short list. ★★

PRESIDENT BENSON ON THE D&C
The Book of Mormon is the "keystone" of our religion, and the Doctrine and Covenants is the capstone, with continuing latter-day revelation. The Lord has placed His stamp of approval on both the keystone and the capstone. (CR April 1987, Ensign 17 [May 1987]: 83.)

Teachings of Ezra Taft Benson, p. 41

Doctrine and Covenants www.mormons.org/basic/doctrines/scripture/dc Articles related to studying the D&C. Includes an Overview, Doctrine and Covenants Commentaries, Doctrine and Covenants Editions, Doctrine and Covenants as Literature, and Book of Commandments. A Mormons.Org page. ★★★

Second Comforter of Promise and the Second Comforter of Presence
webpages.marshall.edu/~brown/dc88-1-4.htm A Commentary on Doctrine and Covenants 88:1–4 by Lisle Brown. ★★

Some Historical Notes webpages.marshall.edu/~brown/dc107.htm Selected verses in Doctrine and Covenants 107. Notes on the amalgamation of this revelation between 1831 and 1835. Good background. ★★★

Word of Wisdom www.jefflindsay.com/WWisdom.shtml Background information and full text of the Word of Wisdom. Little you haven't seen before. ★★

The Pearl of Great Price

The smallest book of the canonized LDS scripture, the Pearl of Great Price was compiled and published by Elder Franklin D. Richards, of the Council of the Twelve Apostles, when he was in Liverpool, England, in 1851. Elder Richards was at the time presiding over the British mission.

Elder Richards collected together the items that comprise the Pearl of Great Price: the Book of Abraham; the Book of Moses; the account of the First Vision and the History of the Prophet Joseph Smith; and the Articles of Faith, along with some additional material. He published them in a single volume.

That small book has since been the subject of a great deal of study and thought. Some of the best research is available on the Internet.

HOTLINKS

Book of Abraham Project
www.boap.math.byu.edu

Book of Abraham
www.mormons.org/basic/
doctrines/scripture/abraham

Questions About the Book of Abraham
www.jefflindsay.com/LDSFAQ/
FQ_Abraham.shtml

Abracadabra, Isaac and Jacob www.farmsresearch.com/review/7_1/gee1.html A John Gee response to Ashment's *The Use of Egyptian Magical Papyri to Authenticate the Book of Abraham*. From FARMS Review of Books. Clarifies much controversy. ★★★

Ancient History Page www.math.byu.edu/~smithw/Lds/LDS/Ancient-history-items/Book-of-Abraham Book of Abraham in plain text, as originally published in the periodical, *Times and Seasons*, beginning in March 1842. Also find the three facsimiles in EPS format. 📖

Book of Abraham Links www.geocities.com/Athens/Parthenon/2671/Abraham.html A page of links to Book of Abraham resources. A worthwhile short-cut if you're doing Book of Abraham research. ★★★

Book of Abraham Project www.boap.math.byu.edu The nonprofit Book of Abraham Project includes scholarly analysis, documentation, and supporting texts and links to relevant sites. One of its best projects is the downloadable Joseph Smith Commentary on the Book of Abraham. ★★★★

Book of Abraham www.math.byu.edu/~smithw/Lds/LINKS.html A list of links to Book of Abraham sites and a sign-up link for a Book of Abraham mailing list. ★

Book of Abraham www.mormons.org/basic/doctrines/scripture/abraham Facsimile, plus articles on the subject of the Book of Abraham. A Mormons.Org page. ★★★★

Book of Moses www.mormons.org/basic/doctrines/scripture/moses_eom.htm The Book of Moses is an extract of several chapters from Genesis in the Joseph Smith Translation of the Bible, and constitutes one of the texts in the Pearl of Great Price. An *Encyclopedia of Mormonism* text. 📖

Critics and the Book of Abraham www.math.byu.edu/~smithw/Lds/LDS/critic.html A response to textual criticisms of the Book of Abraham. 📖

How to Memorize the Articles of Faith www.geocities.com/EnchantedForest/4438 Learn the secret to memorizing the Articles of Faith. Links to other sites and some fun and games make this a site worth investigating. ★★★

Hugh Nibley—Ancient Documents and Mormonism www.math.byu.edu/~smithw/Lds/LDS/Hugh-Nibley/NIBLEY.html Nibley's writings on the Book of Abraham. Includes "The Three Facsimiles of the Book of Abraham" and "Unrolling the Scrolls." ★★★★

Questions About the Book of Abraham www.jefflindsay.com/LDSFAQ/FQ_Abraham.shtml Jeff Lindsay responds to questions about the Book of Abraham, its sources, content, and historicity. An excellent resource. Massive. ★★★★

Tragedy of Errors www.farmsresearch.com/review/4/gee.html John Gee's review of Larson's critical work, *By His Own Hand upon Papyrus: A New Look at the Joseph Smith Papyri*. A FARMS publication. 📖

Multiple Books of Scripture

In this list, you'll find study tools related to all or most of the standard works. Links to the full text of the scriptures are listed beginning on page 146 in chapter 7.

Bible and the Book of Mormon members.xoom.com/Max_Frankie A content-rich site by Massimo Franceschini. Carefully considered. This site contains thought and comments on The Bible and the Book of Mormon, Satan's Devices, Resurrection, Adam, Lost Books, The Book of Abraham, and much more. ★★★★

Daniel Rona's New Testament Gospel Doctrine Supplements www.israelrevealed.com/studies.htm Daniel Rona has put together some excellent Gospel Doctrine supplements for every week. The supplements for the New Testament and Old Testament are both available. ★★★★

Latter-day Saint Seminar www.cybcon.com/~kurtn/exegesis.html Kurt Neumiller's extensive commentaries on Isaiah, the Old Testament, and the New Testament, along with numerous D&C commentaries and links. Worth bookmarking. Includes a mailing list, LDS-SEMINAR, with commentary and in-depth discussion on each week's Gospel Doctrine lesson. Includes regular columns, plus postings from other participants. To subscribe, send a message to *<majordomo@LDSchurch.net>* with the message `subscribe ldss <yourname@your.email.address>` or the digest version `subscribe ldss-d <yourname@your.email.address>`. The first edition promised this site five stars for better organization. Brother Neumiller did the organization. Here are the solid five stars: ★★★★★

LDS Scriptures Study Room python.cs.byu.edu/~lehmann/ref.html A very well executed search engine for finding scriptural terms in context. It currently supports responses in English and French. Includes a mailing list, *LDS-SEMINAR*, with a commentary on each week's Gospel Doctrine lesson. The posts are open to exegesis, textual analysis, historical issues pertinent to the context or application of the scriptures, life applications, and "likening the scriptures unto us" issues. Includes regular columns, plus postings from other participants. Subscribe from the Web site, or by sending a message to *<majordomo*

HOTLINKS

Bible and the Book of Mormon
members.xoom.com/Max_Frankie

Daniel Rona's New Testament Gospel
Doctrine Supplements
www.israelrevealed.com/
studies.htm

Latter-day Saint Seminar
www.cybcon.com/~kurtn/
exegesis.html

Scriptural Writings
www.mormons.org/basic/
doctrines/scripture

SCRIPTURE-L
www.wnetc.com/scripture-l

@ldscn.com> with the message `subscribe ldss <yourname@your.email.address>` or the digest version `subscribe LDSS-D <yourname@your.email.address>`. The first edition promised this site five stars for better organization. Brother Neumiller did the organization. Here are the solid five stars: ★★★★★

LDS Scriptures Study Room   python.cs.byu.edu/~lehmann/ref.html A very well executed search engine for finding scriptural terms in context. It currently supports responses in English and French. ★★★

Miller Eccles Study Group Page   www.geocities.com/Athens/2245 Directions and contact information for a study group conducted in La Canada, California. ★

Richard M. Kettley's Give-Away Site   www.kettleymedia.com/rmk The LDS Scripture Study System is available as a free download that can be used as a scheduler for studying scripture. Features include a reading checklist, important quotes, and a scripture crosswords puzzle. ★★★★

Scriptural Writings   www.mormons.org/basic/doctrines/scripture A collection of pages for each of the canonical works, and more. Includes The Book of Mormon: Another Testament of Jesus Christ; The Holy Bible; The Doctrine and Covenants; The Book of Moses; The Book of Abraham; Apocalyptic Texts; Apocrypha and Pseudepigrapha; and Scriptual References to Astronomy. A Mormons.Org page. ★★★★

SCRIPTURE-L   www.wnetc.com/scripture-l This is the companion site to Gregory Woodhouse's SCRIPTURE-L discussion list. Subscribe from the Web site, or with an e-mail request to <scripture-l-request@lists.best.com> with the message `subsingle`. To receive a digest version, with all the day's messages in one post, change the message to `subscribe`. Archives available at the Web site, along with other scripture commentaries and resources. ★★★★

Scriptures   www.mormon.com/html/scriptures.html This is Mormon.com's LDS Scripture search engine. ★★

MORMON ARTS AND LETTERS

If we didn't have a culture, we wouldn't be a People. Nothing creates a culture, describes a culture, inculcates a culture so thoroughly as its visual art, its music, and its literature.

As you might hope, the Mormon arts and letters Internet sites are about the most civilized in the entire LDS online community.

For that, credit goes to two people: Benson Parkinson, moderator of AML-List, and Keith Irwin, moderator of LDS-Bookshelf. AML-List, a discussion group for LDS literature, is peopled largely by writers, but also by fans of Mormon literature. AML-List is a model of what an online community ought to be: intelligent, inspired, and entertaining.

Keith's LDS-Bookshelf has generated a whole new level of awareness and appreciation for "the best books," old and rare volumes of Mormon literature.

In this section you'll find plenty of other resources related to the Mormon fine arts. See additional music-related resources in chapter 11, under the "Callings: Ward Music Chairman" heading.

AML-LIST cc.weber.edu/~byparkinson/aml-list.html A discussion list for members of the Association for Mormon Letters. Welcomes all scholars and fans of Mormon literature. Maximum volume is 30 posts per day. Send subscription request to *<aml-request@ cc.weber.edu>* with the message `subscribe aml-list "Your Name in Quotes"` *<your@address. in.brackets>*. Benson Parkinson moderates the list. The Web site is a tremendous resource for LDS writers. Also available in digest form, and low-volume magazine form. ★★★★★ ☑

American Night Writers Association www.netzone.com/ ~pegshumw ANWA is a support group for LDS women who love to write. Includes a list of authors and other material of interest to members. ★★★

HOTLINKS

American Night Writers Association
www.netzone.com/~pegshumw

AML-LIST
cc.weber.edu/~byparkinson/
aml-list.html

Author Guidelines
www.nauvoo.com/hrp/
guidelines.html

Hatrack River
www.hatrack.com

Kristen Randle's Mailing List
www.kristen.randle.com

LDS Women's Forum
ldschurch.net/f/fowkes

LDS-BOOKSHELF
www.wenet.net/~kirwin/
bshelf.html

LDSF
www.zfiction.com/ldsf

Mormon Arts Foundation
www.thewatchmen.com/ma

Mormon-J: The LDS Journal-List
www.writerspost.coml/mormonj

Steven Kapp Perry Music Page
www.stevenkappperry.com

Attitudes Toward the Arts www.mormons.org/daily/arts
A collection of articles on the subject of Mormonism and the arts. Illustrates the importance of arts and letters in LDS lives. ★★★

Author Guidelines www.nauvoo.com/hrp/guidelines.html Author guidelines for Hatrack River Publications, a publishing endeavor by author Orson Scott Card. If you meet his criteria, it might be worth submitting a manuscript. ★★★★

Crossroads www.zyx.net/~andrea Andrea Williams' page of poetry, images, and literature. Includes several Mormonads. ★★

CS Lewis Home Page cslewis.drzeus.net Yeah, yeah, so he wasn't technically LDS. But his personal theology continues to speak to LDS beliefs to such a degree that he certainly deserves the status of honorary member. This Web site introduces Lewis' works, along with anecdotes, studies, photographs, and much more. Worth diving into. ★★★★

Cumorah's Hill angelfire.com/ny/FromCumorahsHill A collection of verse inspired by the cantata of the same name by Steven Kapp Perry and Brad Wilcox. ★★★

Garden Musical www.thegardenmusical.com Homepage for The Garden, a "play within a play." The site includes history, synopsis, location and ticket information, and photos. ★★

Hajicek Mormonism.com www.mormonism.com/Portrait.htm A site for collectors of rare LDS books. $

Hatrack River www.hatrack.com The official Web site of author Orson Scott Card. Includes helpful links to writers groups for adults and youth. ★★★★

Holyoak.com Art Gallery www.holyoak.com/gallery Trevor Holyoak's commercial site with some religious artwork. $

JOYFULNOISE www.onelist.com/subscribe/Joyfulnoise A mailing list for those interested in hearing when a new single is released on Mark Hansen's "A Joyful Noise" Web site. Mark makes spiritual, uplifting, LDS-oriented rock music. 📖

Kristen Randle www.kristen.randle.com Award-winning LDS author Kristen Randle's page includes discussions of her books and a short bio. The site, nice as it is, doesn't do justice to the quality of her books and other writing. (But if you introduce yourself, and ask nicely, Kristen may add you to a private list she operates that consists primarily of beautifully written essays on her life and her family. The list, not the site, earns this rating :) ★★★★★

LDS Creations www.ldscreations.com Online gallery exhibiting fine art by Latter-day Saint artists from around the world. $

LDS Culture and the Arts www.ldsworld.com/links/culture.html Abbreviated list of links. ★

LDS Hymns MIDI Page   www.uleth.ca/~anderson/midi.htmlx Music from hymns, LDS songs, and other musical works. Requires a speaker and sound card. ★★★

LDS Women's Forum   ldschurch.net/f/fowkes Stories, essays, and poetry written with an LDS perspective by Sisters from around the world. Uplifting. ★★★★

LDS_BOOKCLUB   www.onelist.com/subscribe/LDS_Bookclub The LDS_BOOK-CLUB is intended for members of the Church. Books are submitted for recommendation to the entire membership. ★★

LDS-BOOKSHELF   www.wenet.net/~kirwin/bshelf.html A mailing list designed for those who collect or have a serious interest in collectible books related to Mormon Americana. Subscribe with an e-mail request to *<majordomo@xmission.com>* with the body `subscribe lds-bookshelf`. List operators are Keith Irwin and Hugh McKell. Archives are maintained at the Web site. Great resources. ★★★★

LDSF   www.zfiction.com/ldsf Sci-fi writer Thom Duncan's LDS Science/Speculative Fiction list. The list isn't limited to Mormon authors of science fiction, but includes discussions of other books related to Mormon literature. ★★★

LDSPOP   www.onelist.com/subscribe/ldspop LDSPOP is a free mailing list. The conversation is kept light—no academic debates of theological issues here. Topics include: LDS pop music, current novels, videos, musicals, and culture in general. ★★

Liahona Developmental Systems   www.liahona.com Promoting LDS Literacy. Collection of LDS literature and learning resources for Spanish-speaking members. Guidelines for using forwarding agencies to distribute LDS products across borders. $

Marvin Payne   members.aol.com/yompayne Homepage of Marvin Payne, Mormon actor, wordsmith, songwriter, and maker of children's media. Highlights include links to Marvin's poetry. ★★★

Mormon Arts Foundation   www.thewatchmen.com/ma A festival held each year near St. George, Utah. The Web site focuses on dance, theater, music, literature, film and media, and visual arts. The page includes an art gallery, contest information, and transcripts from previous festivals. A very readable page. ★★★★

Mormon Literature Links   humanities.byu.edu/MLDB/mlithome.htm The BYU Humanities Department's site dedicated to the study and research of literature by, for, and about Mormons. ★★★★

Mormon Literature Web Site   128.187.38.118/MLDB/mlithome.htm   Gideon Burton's comprehensive links to LDS literature. Includes a Mormon literature sampler, a bibliography of Mormon literature, information on Mormon criticism, a "Who's Who," and a "What's Where" of Mormon literature. ★★★★

Mormon Literature   www.wnetc.com/resource/lds/literature.html   Very brief list of literature links. ★

Mormon Tabernacle Choir Discography   www.geocities.com/SunsetStrip/7158/mtchoir.htm   A list of Mormon Tabernacle Choir recordings and related resources. Very, very thorough. ★★★

Mormon-J: The LDS Journal-List   www.writerspost.com/mormonj   A resource page for LDS journalists, journal-keepers, and other historians. Differs from the literature pages in its emphasis on the journalism profession and the role of journalists as historians. A really great page. But then, I can say that. It's my own site. View this rating with suspicion: ★★★★★

Museum of Art   www.byu.edu/moa   Durned copyright laws (except when they benefit me). Wouldn't it be great if this page actually contained some art? Ah, well. The background information on museum exhibits make it a worthwhile stop. ★★

Music   www.byu.edu/music   The BYU School of Music Homepage. ★★

Once More   www.kna.to/brent_gardner   Brent Gardner's contact and information page. Brent is a songwriter and inspirational speaker. ★★

ORSON-SCOTT-CARD   wood.net/~khyron/card/cardlist.html   A mailing list devoted exclusively to discussions of Orson Scott Card's writings. Orson Scott Card is a well-known science fiction author who has also authored plays and worked on screenplays. To subscribe, e-mail a request to *<majordomo@wood.net>* with the message `subscribe orsoncard`. Archives are available at the Web site. ★★★

Poet's Paradise   angelfire.com/va/vjennings   A home for inspired poetry. Read, submit, or follow the links to related sites. ★★★

Power and the Glory   www.celestial-visions.com   Over 400 musicians were required to create this powerhouse version of LDS songs. $

Rachel Ann Nunes   www.ranunes.com   Site of the best-selling author of the Ariana series, LDS contemporary fiction. Read sample chapters of her LDS work and her national science fiction, complete a survey, and join the mailing list. ★★★

Repartee Group   www.rggallery.com/gospir.html Commercial site offering beautiful LDS-themed art, much of it related to the life of Christ. Serious art for serious collectors. Includes thumbnail pictures. Worth visiting to discover the collections of leading LDS artists. $

Review of Orson Scott Card's Science Fiction   www.farmsresearch.com/review/2/england.html What a treat! Eugene England reviews the science fiction of Orson Scott Card. If you're a fan of either writer, you'll want to read this review. 📖

Roger and Melanie Hoffman's Music Site   www.hoffmanhouse.com A collection of fine LDS music for both the adult soul and the child's. Recording and musical services, video, and a wealth of information delightfully assembled. ★★★

Saints in Review   www.writerspost.com/review Reviews of LDS-authored books, and books on LDS topics. This page is affiliated with Mormon-J: The LDS Journalist. ★★★★

Steven Kapp Perry Music Page   www.stevenkappperry.com A collection of LDS music, lyrics, stories behind the songs, some downloadable free stuff, what's in production now, and thoughts on songwriting. Fans of the Perry family will really enjoy this site, and the free downloadable choir music is a real bonus. ★★★★

STUDENT REVIEW   Low-volume general discussion list for alumni of *Student Review* (unofficial magazine at BYU), about *Student Review* and about the Church. Digest available. To subscribe, send an e-mail message to *<majordomo@panix.com>* with the message `subscribe student-review <your name>`. 📖

Tom Roulstone's Homepage   www.ldschurch.net/f/roulstone Tom Roulstone is the author of two LDS historical novels: *One Against the Wilderness* and *Fleeing Babylon.* ★★

Tracy Hickman Homepage   www.trhickman.com LDS science-fiction and fantasy Author Tracy Hickman's Web site, including mission experiences and testimony. ★★★

Utah Contemporary Dance Theatre   www.ucdt.org A Utah-based dance group operated by BYU professor Derryl Yeager. The group has a national following. ★★★

Watchmen Institute   www.thewatchmen.com Committed to producing and promoting the best of performance, media, and fine art. Most of the people involved are

LDS. The Institute sponsors The Mormon Arts Foundation, UCDT, and more. ★★★

Zion's Fiction www.zfiction.com Electronic publishers of LDS science fiction. Operated by author Thom Duncan. The site provides downloadable LDS speculative fiction. Fascinating stuff. $

MORMON HUMOR

Anyone who thinks Mormons lack a sense of humor hasn't listened to a gloomy congregation singing "There Is Sunshine in My Soul Today."

Latter-day Saints have a great tradition of humor. Sometimes it's spontaneous, as anyone who has listened to President Gordon B. Hinckley—or many of the past presidents of the Church—will attest.

Other times, it's a great setup. Latter-day Saints love to retell stories of their favorite humorist, J. Golden Kimball, the son of President Heber C. Kimball. The colorful general authority is reputed to have said, among other things, that he couldn't go to hell for swearing, because he repents too damn fast.

Latter-day Saints on the Internet continue to carry on that tradition of Mormon humor, with their own Web sites replete with cartoons, jokes, and amusing stories.

The following sites contain some of the best—and cleanest—humor on the Internet.

HOTLINKS

ALPHA
www.ldscn.com/alpha

Humble Humor Hut
www.jefflindsay.com/
MyPages.shtml#humor

Latter-day Lampoon
www.latterdaylampoon.com

LDS Humor
www.mormons.org/humor

The Wasp
www.xmission.com/~estep

ALPHA www.ldscn.com/alpha Did you know that the Book of Mormon saved a man's life? He carried it in his shirt pocket over his heart. During the war a piece of shrapnel hit the book, but stopped at 2 Nephi. Alpha is the home page for the alpha mailing list of nonoffensive humor hosted by LDSCN. The list operators are not LDS, but the humor appeals. ★★★★

Facetious (?) Questions www.jefflindsay.com/LDSFAQ/ FQ_Facet.shtml Includes discussions of Mormon ownership of Pepsi, planets, polygamy, and more. Author Jeff Lindsay has written numerous pages of answers to questions about the Church. The answers on this page respond—often flippantly—to questions too bizarre for the serious pages. Good fun. ★★★

Humble Humor Hut www.jefflindsay.com/MyPages.shtml#humor Jeff Lindsey's cracked crack-ups. All sorts of amusing thoughts loosely related to Mormonism. Includes the CultMaster 2000 software, "All the power you need to prove that you're the only real Christian around" (see figure 12.6). Irresistible. But then, I've been hearing a little too much of the "C" word lately. Articles on National Lawn Care Now! Commercial Ninja Services, The Citizens Union for Safe Smoking, The Higher Institute for Safe Shooting, Sci-Cops, and More. A crack-up. ★★★★

Humor, Jokes, Urban Legends, and Myths www.xmission. com/~estep/humor.html Mostly funny stuff. The unfunny stuff makes jokes at the expense of non-Mormons. ★★★

Humor/Story Center www.igoshopping.com/fun G-rated Web site that features shopping and a searchable humor database. A mailing list option is available. Not specifically LDS. ★★★

Latter-day Lampoon www.latterdaylampoon.com Ouch. Wicked, biting humor. Not for the faint-hearted. Mormon culture parody and inside humor, including headline news, spiritual roulette interactive games, gossip, science and religion updates, top ten lists, virtual patriarchal blessings, and testimony contests. Subscribe and receive a biweekly e-mail magazine containing all the posts, news, and nonsense from the site. ★★★

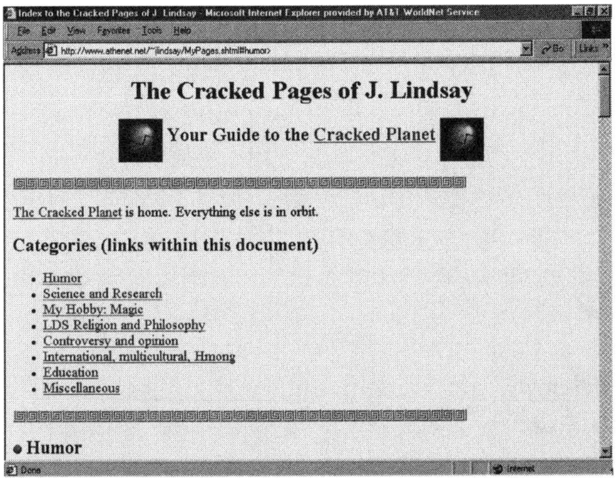

> **MODERN PIONEER**
> None of us can really imagine for a moment that which [the pioneers] endured. I've been on the trail they followed a number of times now, when the weather was good, when it was comfortable, in an air-conditioned car—just like any other sissy would do who was trying to honor his pioneer forebears.
>
> President Gordon B. Hinckley, July 24, 1999, at the dedication of the Handcart Pioneer Memorial at the This Is The Place Monument.

FIG. 12.6

The Cracked Pages of J. Lindsay.

LDS Humor www.of-worth.com/ea/humor.htm Lots of amusing stories and anecdotes from Errand of Angels. ★★★

LDS Humor www.mormons.org/humor Includes Bible Humor, Book of Mormon Humor, Mormon Culture Humor, and General Religious Humor. You'll find, among other items, a top ten list of How the Bible Would Have Been Different If Written by College Students: "Five commandments, but double-spaced and written in a large font, they look like ten" and four-year-old Jonathan's 2,000 Stricken Lawyers. And who can resist: "An Agnostic and an Atheist were married and had a real moral problem on their hands. You see, they couldn't decide which religion not to raise their children in." ★★★★

Lightness Challenge Page www.sas.upenn.edu/~dbowie/armlc/armlc.html Chill out with amusing posts from the two major LDS newsgroups, alt/soc.religion.mormon. Twice a year, site owner David Bowie (no, they're not related) conducts a vote for the best postings on the two newsgroups. The messages are always funny, sometimes caustic. ★★★

Mormon Culture www.mormons.org/humor/culture.htm Jokes that shouldn't be funny. "*Joe:* My home teacher is so good he comes on the first day of every month! *Henry:* Oh Yeah? My home teacher is so good he comes the day before that!" ★★★

Mormon Humor members.tripod.com/~jeider/joke.htm Features one-liners, true stories, and missionary humor. Accepts suitable submissions. ★★★

MORMON-HUMOR A new e-mail list for telling jokes, puns, amusing stories, and anecdotes about Mormons and Mormonism. At press time, the list was just getting under way. List owner Kent Larsen says: "Almost all aspects of Mormon culture, activities, events, and people worldwide are fair game. However, jokes that are racist, sexual, or make malicious fun of others should not be sent to mormon-humor. Be prepared to take a lighthearted look at Mormonism and put up with a swear word or two. Don't take offense easily, and we'll all be better off." A once-a-week digest version of the list will also be available. To subscribe, send an e-mail request to *<majordomo@lists.panix.com>*. In the body of the message write `subscribe mormon-humor`. To subscribe to the digest, write `subscribe mormon-humor-digest`. This list is great fun, except when participants debate whether something is funny. ★★★★

On the Bright Side www.desnews.com/cgi-bin/libheads_reg?search=%22 On+the+bright+side%22&limit=999&x=49&y=12 A collection of humorous stories that run in the *Church News*. Cute. ★★★★

Starship Troopers filmovy.seznam.cz/pechota/pics/fx_94lo.jpg Still frame from the science fiction film *Starship Troopers* that shows the Angel Moroni on top of a building on another planet. The filmmakers made use of additional Mormon imagery. ★

The Wasp www.xmission.com/~estep Words of inspiration, counsel, and guidance: Christoper Estep's LDS Journal of news, humor, links, and more! A delightful read. ★★★★★

HEALTH AND FITNESS

Oh that I were an angel . . . perhaps then I could stop wishing I were in better shape.

Here you'll find Internet resources to help you in caring for that temple that is your body.

Attitudes Toward Health, Medicine, and Fitness www.mormons.org/daily/health The Mormons.org collection of resources on every health subject from abortion to vegetarianism. An excellent resource. ★★★★

HOTLINKS

Attitudes Toward Health, Medicine, and Fitness
www.mormons.org/daily/health

Word of Wisdom
www.wipd.com/~westra/WordofWi.htm

Coaching (Running) on the Internet www.shire.net/mormon/run.html A former marathoner, Brother Leigh, discusses his philosophy for getting in shape and exercising. ★★★

Health and Well-Being www.lds-index.org/health.htm Links to numerous sites related to health and fitness for Latter-day Saints. ★★★

LDS Word of Wisdom www.jefflindsay.com/WWisdom.shtml The scripture, along with commentary and documentation of the health benefits of adherence to the principals. ★★★

Word of Wisdom www.lds.net/research/basics/4-07.html A reasonable, if undocumented, explanation of the principles of the Word of Wisdom. Find a much better-documented discussion at www.mormons.org/daily/health/Wisdom_EOM.htm. ★★★

Word of Wisdom www.wipd.com/~westra/WordofWi.htm Great stories, quotes, and links to resources on the Word of Wisdom. Ought to settle any discussion on the controversial issues, but it probably won't. ★★★★

EMERGENCY PREPAREDNESS

The sites found here can be of help only *before* the emergency—unless, of course, you're already set up with a generator for your PC and a ham-radio-based modem. Yeah, like you'd then use it to browse the Web, right?

Emergency Communications

It's what to do if the phone goes out.

Amateur Radio Emergency Service Organizations www.geocities.com/Tokyo/3273/hamemergency.html Great explanation of how various radio networks, including those affiliated with the Church, are employed. ★★★★

HOTLINKS

Amateur Radio Emergency
Service Organizations
www.geocities.com/Tokyo/3273/
hamemergency.html

Communications
www.mormon.com/epm/
communic.htm

Communications www.mormon.com/epm/communic.htm Thorough-going materials on the Emergency Response Radio System, amateur (ham) radio, CB radios, walkie-talkies, and cellular phones. ★★★★

Corvus Radio www.corvusradio.com Modified radios let you listen to devotionals, Conference reports, contemporary music, Church news, and BYU sports. $

Ham Radio Outlet www.hamradio.com Supplier of amateur radio equipment. $

W3BNR's Home Page www.worldlynx.net/w3bnr Excellent amateur radio links. Amusing links to conspiracy theories. (One hopes the site author also finds them amusing, but given the nature of the subject matter, that's not likely.) ★★★★

Disaster Preparedness

When my grandma passed away a few years back, I had to fight hard not to inherit the cans of dried cheese and Textured Vegetable Protein she stored under her bed. Um, yummy. TVP: the perfect filling for tacos, lasagna, and road surfaces. Finally, a noble cousin squared her shoulders and took on the task.

It turns out my grandma's food storage was actually a disaster prevention program. As we hauled out the cans and boxes, we realized that, more than anything, food storage kept the bed from falling down.

Emergency and Disaster Preparedness www.ci. anchorage.ak.us/Disaster Courtesy of the Municipality of Anchorage, Alaska. Brief instructions for what to do in the event of an emergency—at which time you'd probably find an online list inaccessible. ★★

Emergency and Family Preparedness www.ldschurch.net/ s/danville/prepare.html Fantastic page designed for members of a Northern California stake, with preparedness info useful to anyone. ★★★★

Emergency Essentials www.beprepared.com Mostly commercial, with products for preparedness equipment, camping supplies, and food storage. But it's worth visiting regularly for the Insights column. ★★★★

HOTLINKS

Emergency and Family Preparedness
www.ldschurch.net/s/danville/
prepare.html

Emergency Essentials
www.beprepared.com

Emergency Preparedness Manual
www.mormon.com/epm

FEMA
www.fema.gov

PREP
www.ldscn.org/prep

Emergency Preparedness Manual www.mormon.com/epm Great links and resources on emergency preparedness. Includes materials on teachings of the Brethren, emergency preparedness recommendations, gospel principles, the plan, meetinghouse floor plan, emergency situations, 72-hour kit, food storage, water supply, first aid, heating, cooking and lighting, sanitation, childbirth, earthquake, winter storms, flood, structural fire, forest fire, damaging winds, chemical and radiological accidents, communications, emergency links, and links to other emergency preparedness sites. ★★★★★

Emergency Preparedness www.deseretbook.com/ldsinfo/emergency.html An almost inconsequential list of links. ★

Emergency Storage www.uvol.com/www1st/foodstor.html Latter-day Saints have been counseled to prepare to care for themselves and their families in time of need. Provident living involves being wise, frugal, prudent, and making provision for the future while attending to immediate needs. This site lists the amounts needed for one adult for one year, and provides a number of suggestions for effective storage. ★★★

Epicenter theepicenter.com/emerg.html A good collection of links to disaster relief, emergency preparedness, and even search and rescue resources. ★★★

FEMA www.fema.gov The Federal Emergency Management Agency. The site contains excellent information about emergency preparedness and disaster management. ★★★★★

Food Storage Online www.foodstorage.net/world.htm Mostly commercial, but the World Watch column is a pessimist's dream. ★★★★

Food Storage Planner www.revelar.com/fsp.html Software for estimating, budgeting, and planning your food storage. Between natural, political, and personal disasters, there's nothing but wisdom in storing food and fuel says the site author. A commercial site. $

Lamp Oil thelampoil.hypermart.net An LDS newsletter devoted to self-sufficiency and preparedness. Doesn't appear to be regularly updated. ★★

National Food Safety Database www.foodsafety.org Tips on food safety and home food storage. ★★★

Natural Disaster Program for Families www.ces.ncsu.edu/depts/fcs/disaster North Carolina program advocating emergency preparedness. Helpful information on preparing a family emergency kit and other emergency prep material. Not specifically LDS. ★★★★

PREP www.ldscn.org/prep Links, free food storage software, frequently asked questions, suggestions for 72-hour kits, and much more. Affiliated with the PREP e-mail lists. Discussions and information about disaster preparedness, home storage, and emergency planning, from an LDS perspective. Subscribe from the Web site. ★★★★

Talking About Disaster: Guide www.redcross.org/disaster/safety/guide.html By the National Disaster Education Coalition. The Red Cross' recommendation: Pack a 72-hour disaster kit. Sounds familiar. Lots of good info in this guide. It's worth printing out. ★★★★

13

THE GLORY OF GOD IS INTELLIGENCE

My first year of college was a tremendous lot of fun. I was finally beginning to comprehend the vast scope of the gospel: the discovery was hugely exciting. Fortunately, my college classes were easy that year, and my job allowed me time to study, because I barely had time for school.

Theology was the driving interest in my life. It seemed as though I couldn't learn fast enough. I signed up for classes at two different institutes of religion just so that I could inhale more knowledge, ask more questions, listen to more ideas. I was reading voraciously, getting up early to drive my sibs to Seminary, and attending Sunday meetings both in my own ward and with my grandmother in her ward.

After a few months of it, I realized I was never going to discover everything I wanted to know from the pint-sized library at my community college, so I sent in my application to Brigham Young University.

I was overjoyed when I got the acceptance letter. I continued throughout the summer in my mad pursuit of knowledge, determined that some day, I would know everything there is to know.

The final Sunday before I was to go to BYU, I attended Church with Grandma. Among the speakers that week was a sour, balding, middle-aged man, who stood up to the podium and began to drone. On and on he went, exploring the minutiae of some inconsequential subject of absolutely no interest to anyone other than himself. His talk was peppered with unexplained technical jargon and obscure scholarly references; heads throughout the congregation were bobbing and weaving as members of the ward fought off sleep.

My normally patient grandmother peered at him over the tops of her glasses, an inscrutable look on her face. I tried to listen, but between the monotony of the talk, and the expression on Grandma's face, I was able to absorb not a thing.

Mercifully, the talk finally ended, and the meeting closed.

On the way home, Grandma finally spoke up. "Did you find that interesting?" she asked me.

"Well, um, sort of," I hedged.

"Would you like to be able to speak that way?"

"Um, I guess."

"Promise me you won't."

"Why not?"

"That young man has spent the last twenty years doing nothing but going to college," she told me. "He doesn't work, he doesn't go out, he doesn't have any friends. All that education, and he still doesn't know the first thing about life." Then she paused.

"I'm proud of you for getting an education," she said slowly. "But honey, don't you ever lose sight of life."

So stand warned. Grandma's caution applies to all the carnage you'll tear through in this chapter. You'll find here research resources on every topic that's ever made you curious. Church History is treated in great detail. It's followed by sections on Research Projects and Research Groups, Science and Religion, The Church in Society, Doctrinal Issues, and Comparative Theology.

And to Grandma's caution, I add my own. If I've learned any wisdom in twenty years of serious gospel study, it's this: Prayerfully obtained knowledge is the only kind worth having.

CHURCH HISTORY

The Internet is awash in Church history—the whole Church, from its original establishment, to its reestablishment in each dispensation. You'll find there information about the Church's growth in the New World, as well as its modern manifestation in the latter-day dispensation.

In this section you'll find Internet sites tracing the Old Testament foundation of The Church, The Church in the New World, the Pre-Christian Era, The New Testament Church, The Interregnum, and finally, The Modern Church.

The Old Testament Church

Latter-day Saints have a profound love for the Church founded at the beginning of man's sojourn on earth, and carried on through a series of prophets and dispensations. The Saints also feel a deep appreciation for their brothers and sisters who maintained—in the face of great tribulation—the history, doctrine, records, and traditions that form the foundation of the gospel.

Latter-day Saints feel an even greater kinship with the children of Israel because of a heritage of shared experiences. The persecution, the pioneer exodus, the temple worship, the belief in Elijah, the faith in the Messiah . . . indeed, all of Mormonism shares a common heritage with the Church founded with Adam; the Semitic roots of the Book of Mormon bind those ties forever.

In this section, you'll find valuable resources for studying the history of the original Church, a key to comprehending the roots of Mormonism.

Additional Old Testament study materials focusing on the doctrine and the text of the book are located on page 144 in chapter 7 and on page 293 in chapter 12.

Adam-Ondi-Ahman www.gbwattorney.com/ADAM_ONDI.htm An examination of the name, location, and latter-day events surrounding Adam-Ondi-Ahman. ★★★

Ancient Evidence of Baptism for the Dead ourworld.compuserve.com/homepages/MGriffith_2/proxy.htm Excerpts from Michael Griffith's book, *One Lord, One Faith: Writings of the Early Christian Fathers as Evidences of the Restoration* (Horizon Publishers, 1996). 📖

ON KNOWING HISTORY

We feel that there is a crying need for the study of our own Church History, and for a better understanding of the revelations and commandments which have been given in this Dispensation for our temporal and eternal welfare. [T]he Church today, like the Church in the first centuries of the Christian Era, is constantly in danger. As it was in the first century, so now, we must guard against . . . those of an apostate spirit, who would lead away many after them. If we are informed as we should be, then these evil designing persons will have no influence upon the members of the Church.

Joseph Fielding Smith, *Church History and Modern Revelation*, Vol 1, p. i

---

HOTLINKS

Ancient Studies Page
members.aol.com/stclairst/studies.html

Old Jerusalem Temple
www.gbwattorney.com/Old-Temp.htm

Who is a Jew?
www.jewish.to/toc.htm

Works of Flavius Josephus0
wesley.nnc.edu/josephus

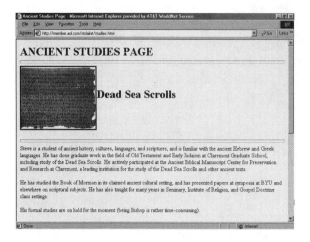

FIG. 13.1

Ancient Studies Page.

Ancient Studies Page members.aol.com/stclairst/studies.html Steve St. Clair's scholarly articles on ancient documents as they relate to LDS beliefs (see figure 13.1). Includes papers on Aaron's calling, loss of priesthood keys, eschatology, the stick of Joseph, and the name Nephi. ★★★★

Bible History www.bible-history.com Timelines, charts, articles, languages. Loads of information on Biblical history, including a separate section on intertestimental history. ★★★★

Celestial Ascent Homepage fhss.byu.edu/history/faculty/hamblin/celestial.htm Dr. William Hamblin of BYU teaches a class on "celestial ascent" in ancient writings; this homepage has his reading list and an outline of the class. Find here—in rough outline form—Temple parallels, deification, and much more. ★★

Comparison of the Babylonian and Noahic Flood Stories religioustolerance.org/noah_com.htm If you can get through the Biblical criticism that misunderstands prophecy without rolling your eyes, you'll be left with a strong witness that God has been around for a very long time, and has been trying to get through to his hard-headed children from the beginning. *Very* not an LDS site, very worth reading. ★★★

Derech Ben Noach www.noach.com Thought-provoking information on the Talmudic record of the covenant between Hashem (God) and Noach (Noah). See similar pages at www.fastlane.net/~bneinoah and www.jewfaq.org/gentiles.htm#Noah. ★★★

From Abraham to the Beginning of the New Testament www.lib.ricks.edu/reserve/ satterfield/history.html Brief, focusing only on the salient points necessary for understanding the Jewish world of the New Testament. From Bruce Satterfield at Ricks College. ★★★

Guide to Polygamy in the Bible and Jewish Law www.teleport.com/~arden/polyg.htm History, religion, and law. Discusses mostly ancient Hebrew polygamy. Useful background on the practice of plural marriage. ★★★

Guided Biblical Archaeology www.digbible.org/tour An online photographic tour of the Holy Lands. ★★★

Halakhah: Jewish Law www.jewfaq.org/halakhah.htm Explanation of the 613 Mizvot, and the Gezeirah, customs, and traditions. ★★★

HaLashon www.torah.org/learning/halashon What do you understand of the prohibition against evil-speaking? Read this rabbinical interpretation and see whether it changes your world view. ★★★

Hebrew Dictionary home.lv.rmci.net/jdstone/hebrew%20dictionary.html Basic words you should be familiar with when studying the ancient Church. ★★★

Herodotus' History of the Ancient World www.math.byu.edu/~smithw/Lds/LDS/ Ancient-history-items/Herodotus-History A lesson in ancient history. Thick. ★★★

Israel Revealed www.ysite.com/israelrona Holy Land Tours with Daniel Rona, the first and only LDS-licensed guide in Israel. $

Judaism www.teleport.com/~arden/religium.htm#jewish Arden Eby's list of resources on Judaism as it interests Latter-day Saints. ★★★

Kosher Nosh www.koshernosh.com/dictiona.htm Online Yiddish Dictionary. Oy. ★★★

Medieval Sourcebook www.fordham.edu/halsall/source/rambam13.html Thirteen Articles of Jewish faith and the resurrection of the dead. More incredible parallels—and differences—between Judaism and the original Church. Of particular note is the allusion to a premortal existence in the Garden of Eden. ★★★

Old Jerusalem Temple www.gbwattorney.com/Old-Temp.htm The least you should know about the history of the first and second temples. Heavily footnoted from (motly) LDS sources. ★★★

Old Testament Foundations of Contemporary Temple Liturgy www.cybcon.com/~kurtn/ottempl.txt S. Kurt Neumiller examines Old Testament precedents and evidences for the temple observance. ★★★

On Circumcision www.cybcon.com/~kurtn/circum.txt S. Kurt Neumiller's explanation of the token of the covenant between God and Israel. ★★★

Pharaohs and Kings www.knowledge.co.uk/xxx/cat/rohl Summary of a TV series tracing biblical history. ★★

Rediscovering the Lost Ten Tribes www.nazarene.net/brit-am Account of the dispersion of the tribes from the perspective of a Jewish writer. Interesting correlation with LDS teachings. ★★

Religious Parties During the Second Temple Period www.lib.ricks.edu/reserve/satterfield/bs1140r211.htm Bruce Satterfield has collected statements from various New Testament scholars concerning the religious parties during the Second Temple Period. 📖

Temple of Herod www.lib.ricks.edu/reserve/satterfield/bs1140a211.htm Bruce Satterfield, Ricks College, describes the second Jewish temple, and says the whole of the Law of Moses had the Temple at its core. 📖

Virtual Jerusalem www.virtual.co.il The Ask the Rabbi feature is particularly interesting. Worth a read. ★★★

Who is a Jew? www.jewish.to/toc.htm Thirty questions and answers. Fascinating parallels with the Latter-day church, particularly the requirement of baptism (T'vilah) for converts. ★★★★

Works of Flavius Josephus wesley.nnc.edu/josephus The complete works of Josephus, a historian who wrote at the end of the first century. A valuable source for early Jewish history, especially concerning the destruction of Jerusalem. ★★★★

The Church in the New World

Book of Mormon scholarship has undergone some significant advances in recent years. This section examines new physical evidence—so-called external evidences—for the Book of Mormon and discusses the historicity of the text.

Find additional Book of Mormon study materials in chapter 6 on page 99; in chapter 7 on page 143; and in chapter 12 in page 280.

Book of Mormon Archaeology FAQ www.teleport.com/~arden/mormfaq.htm Answers to frequently asked questions on the origin, geography, population, mythology, archaeology, language, and etymology of the Book of Mormon. Written by Arden L. Eby. ★★★

Brant Gardner's Self-Published Papers Page www.highfiber.com/~nahualli A collection of essays about meso-American issues (Quetzalcoatl's "Fathers" and "The Impact of the Spanish on our Record of Native Oral Tradition") and commentary on the Book of Mormon, along with other interesting essays. Lacks authority, but the thinking is worth a read. ★★★

Case for Lehi's Bondage in Arabia www.farmsresearch.com/jbms/6_2/brown.html S. Kent Brown argues that Lehi's family lived for a time in a servile condition. ★★★

HOTLINKS

Brant Gardner's Self-Published Papers Page
www.highfiber.com/~nahualli

FARMS Review of Books
www.farmsresearch.com/review/main.htm

Insights: A Window on the Ancient World
www.farmsresearch.com/insights/main.htm

Rabbi Yosef's Jewishness of the Book of Mormon
www.itstessie.com/jewishbom

Correlation www.farmsresearch.com/jbms/1_1/hilton.html John L. and Janet F. Hilton explain the correlation of the Sidon River and the Lands of Manti and Zarahemla with the Southern End of the Rio Grijalva (San Miguel). ★★★

Epigraphy Forum www.geocities.com/Athens/Aegean/6726 E-mail discussion of epigraphy, the deciphering of ancient languages, and cultural diffusion. Topics covered have included the Bat Creek Stone, the Newberry Tablets, and the Ogham Inscriptions. ★★★

External Evidences for the Scriptures www.cyberhighway.net/~shirtail/external.htm This panel discussion includes Paul R. Cheesman, Noel B. Reynolds, Arthur Wallace, and John Sorenson. The relationship with internal and external evidences for the scriptures is discussed, with emphasis on the Book of Mormon. ★★★

Eyewitness Descriptions of Mesoamerican Swords www.farmsresearch.com/jbms/5_1/roper.html Matthew Roper discusses Spanish accounts of those who encountered the macuahuitl in battle. ★★★

FARMS Review of Books www.farmsresearch.com/review/main.htm More than a decade of reviews of the most significant books in, and about, Mormonism. Covers everything from anti-Mormon literature to scientific analyses of Book of Mormon evidence and its relationship to the novels of Orson Scott Card. Several volumes are now online in their entirety. These in-depth reviews are often as thoughtful as the books that inspire them. Lacks a comprehensive table of contents. ★★★★

Historicity of the Book of Mormon   www.math.byu.edu/~smithw/Lds/LDS/Oaks-on-BoM-critics From a 1993 address to the FARMS annual dinner, by Elder Dallin H. Oaks. Another transcript is maintained at www.farmsresearch.com/transcripts/dho-93.html. 📖

Insights: A Window on the Ancient World   www.farmsresearch.com/insights/main.htm The regular FARMS newsletter, containing numerous articles on Mormonism and the ancient world in general. The newsletter is updated often and back issues are archived online. ★★★★★

Jewish and Other Semitic Texts Written in Egyptian Characters   www.farmsresearch.com/jbms/5_2/tvedrick.html John A. Tvedtnes and Stephen D. Ricks discuss evidence that at least some ancient Israelite scribes were, like the Nephite scribes, acquainted with both Egyptian and Hebrew. ★★★

Jewish Foundation of Christianity   www.religioustolerance.org/chr_jf.htm Interesting site supports religious tolerance with the argument that Christianity should recognize that Judaism and Christianity share the same foundations. Good, if sometimes doctrinally suspect, historical information. ★★★

Journal of Book of Mormon Studies   www.farmsresearch.com/jbms Five years' of FARMS scholarly journal for Book of Mormon research. This page lacks a table of contents, so you'll have to dig through each issue to find what you need. ★★★★

Lehi's Jerusalem and Writing on Metal Plates   www.farmsresearch.com/jbms/3_1/adams.html William J. Adams, Jr.'s report on the discovery, unwrapping, and translation of silver plates found in a Jerusalem burial site that dates just before the Babylonian captivity. Additional information is located at www.farmsresearch.com/jbms/4_2/adams.html. ★★★★

Maya Harvest Festivals and the Book of Mormon   www.farmsresearch.com/review/3/annual.html Allen J. Christenson's 1991 FARMS lecture draws parallels between Mayan traditions and Book of Mormon events. 📖

Metallic Documents of Antiquity   www.cyberhighway.net/~shirtail/hcurtis.htm H. Curtis Wright's astonishing demonstration of archaeological patterns confirming the Book of Mormon practice of writing on metal plates. ★★★

Nephi's Jerusalem and Laban's Sword www.farmsresearch.com/jbms/2_2/adams.html
William J. Adams, Jr., describes an archaeological find that supports the Book of
Mormon account of the use of swords. ★★★

New Evidence for the Horse in North America Before the Spaniards www.
cyberhighway.net/~shirtail/new.htm New data from the University of Illinois database available on the Internet shows evidence of modern horses having existed
prior to the Spanish arrival in the Americas. Data covers North America from the
Middle Holocene (3500–8500 years ago) down to the Late Holocene (450–4500
years ago). ★★★

Notes Concerning Mesoamerican Archaeology and the Difficulties Involved
www.cyberhighway.net/~shirtail/notes.htm Kerry Shirts responds to critics who asked
where the evidence is for the Book of Mormon in Mesoamerica. Perhaps, he says,
they need to understand the more complex situation that actually exists. ★★

Pre-Columbian Archaeology Links copan.bioz.unibas.ch/mesolinks.html Some 200
links covering pre-Columbian American history. ★★★

Proposed Book of Mormon Geography hometown.aol.com/jhardy355/bomgeog.htm
Joel Hardy's own proposal for Book of Mormon geography, in a large-scale setting. Needs explanation. ★★

Rabbi Yosef's Jewishness of the Book of Mormon www.itstessie.com/jewishbom
Page maintained by a Jewish rabbi who believes the Book of Mormon has
Semitic origins. The page demonstrates connections linking the Book of Mormon
and Judaism for Messianic Jews (see figure 13.2). ★★★★★

FIG. 13.2

Jewishness of the Book of Mormon.

Tel Arad www.cyberhighway.net/~shirtail/telarad.htm An archaelogical discovery for the Bible and Book of Mormon. Here scholars have found the Hebrew language written in Egyptian characters, demonstrating historically that as early as 600 B.C., some groups of Jews were bilingual in both Hebrew and Egyptian, a finding that supports the statement of Nephi, the Book of Mormon prophet, who said he was taught in the learning of the Jews, in the language of the Egyptians. ★★

Viva Zapato! Hurray for the Shoe! www.farmsresearch.com/review/6_1/sorenson.html John L. Sorenson's review of Deanne G. Matheny's "Does the Shoe Fit? A Critique of the Limited Tehuantepec Geography." Presents an updated look at the well-done 1985 research by Brother Sorenson. ★★★★

Were There Two Cumorahs? www.farmsresearch.com/jbms/4_1/cumorah.html No one doubts that the hill where Joseph Smith received the plates is known as Cumorah, but is the hill where the final battles between the Nephites and Lamanites took place another Cumorah? Sidney Sperry's thoughts. ★★★

When Lehi's Party Arrived in the Land, Did They Find Others There? www.farmsresearch.com/jbms/1_1/sorens.html John L. Sorenson considers other inhabitants of the Americas before Lehi. ★★★

Why [are] There No Archaeological or Historical Remains? www.cyberhighway.net/~shirtail/mesoamer.htm Kerry Shirts' discussion of Mesoamerican archaeology, metallurgy, and the Book of Mormon. ★★

Years of the Jaredites www.farmsresearch.com/transcripts/sor-69.html John L. Sorenson's 1969 thoughts on a possible Jaredite chronology. ★★★

Pre-Christian Era Apocrypha and Pseudoepigrapha

When the Prophet Joseph Smith was preparing to commence work on the Inspired Version of the Bible, he asked the Lord for instruction on the apocryphal portion of the text.

The revelation he received in response to his question was clear: Some is true, some is not true, and Joseph need not produce the translation.

It's the job of the reader, said the Lord, to seek individual understanding through the Spirit.

In this section we pull together references on pseudoepigraphal and apocryphal texts, along with a number of resources specifically focused on the Dead Sea Scrolls.

Apocrypha and Pseudoepigrapha www.mormons.org/
basic/doctrines/scripture/apoc_pse_eom.htm Background
and explanation of apocryphal texts. An *Encyclopedia
of Mormonism* article. 📖

Dead Sea Scrolls www.enoch.com/voicesfromdust/
deadsea/deadsea.html A commentary on why the
scrolls are of particular interest to Latter-day Saints,
along with a good link to information on their history
and geography. ★★★

Dead Sea Scrolls www.mormons.org/basic/doctrines/
scripture/dead_sea_eom.htm An introduction to the
Scrolls as they relate to the literary and sectarian diversity of Judaism at the time of Jesus, evidence relating
to the history and preservation of the biblical text,
advances in the science of dating Hebrew and Aramaic
documents based on changing styles of script, and valuable additions to the corpus
of Jewish texts and text genres. An *Encyclopedia of Mormonism* article. 📖

Forty-Day Teachings of Christ: A Gnostic Endowment webpages.marshall.edu/
~wiley6/40_days.pdf An investigation into possible
remnants of temple ceremonies in the Early Church.
In his article, *Forty-Day Teachings of Christ in the
Books of Jeu and Pistas Sophia: A Gnostic Endowment*, author David Wiley searches for parallels
between the writings of Joseph Smith and certain
Gnostic records. He finds evidence that while on
earth, Jesus taught the endowment to the apostles.
★★★★

Glossary of Kabbalah and Chassidut www.inner.org/
glossary/glossary.htm A tool for the study of Rabbi
Ginsburgh's works. May also be of service to students
of the Kabbalah and *Chassidut.* ★★★

Gnostic Christian Esoteric Rites www.vt.edu:10021/B/
bbickmor/ECGnTpl.html Rituals survived for a time in
various branches of "gnostic" Christianity. This article
also has a brief introduction to gnosticism. ★★★

HOTLINKS

Dead Sea Scrolls
www.enoch.com/voicesfromdust/
deadsea/deadsea.html

Forty-Day Teachings of Christ:
A Gnostic Endowment.
webpages.marshall.edu/~wiley6/
40_days.pdf

Scrolls from the Dead Sea.
lcweb.loc.gov/exhibits/scrolls/
toc.html

ON THE APOCRYPHA

Verily, thus saith the Lord unto you concerning the Apocrypha—There are many
things contained therein that are true,
and it is mostly translated correctly;
There are many things contained therein
that are not true, which are interpola-
tions by the hands of men.

Verily, I say unto you, that it is not
needful that the Apocrypha should be
translated.

Therefore, whoso readeth it, let him
understand, for the Spirit manifesteth
truth; And whoso is enlightened by the
Spirit shall obtain benefit therefrom; And
whoso receiveth not by the Spirit, cannot
be benefited. Therefore it is not needful
that it should be translated. Amen.

Doctrine & Covenants 91:1–6

Japan/Israel Folklore php.indiana.edu/dostlund/isuraeru.htm D. Glenn Ostlund's record of Japanese accounts linking the Japanese to the Lost Tribes of Israel. The author says: "This is a collection of stories I have gathered from Mormon missionaries, just one of the many groups who share these traditional stories." A related page, **Did Christ Visit Japan?** is located at www.geocities.com/Heartland/ Plains/4723/jesusjp1.htm. This page contains Spencer J. Palmer's record of a tale from East Asia of Jesus living in Japan. ★★★

Lost Books www.math.byu.edu/~smithw/Lds/LDS/Ancient-history-items/Early-Christian/Lost-Books-Early-Christian Lost Books of Early Christian Literature. A list without explanation. ★★

Messianism in the Pseudepigrapha and Book of Mormon www.cyberhighway.net/ ~shirtail/messiani.htm Duke University's James H. Charlesworth considers concepts associated with the Messiah from the ancient Jewish viewpoint. Printed in Truman G. Madsen, ed., *Reflections on Mormonism: Judeo-Christian Parallels*. The BYU Religious Studies Center Symposium held in 1984. ★★★

Noncanonical Homepage wesley.nnc.edu/noncanon.htm Apocryphal and pseudoepigraphal texts. These are documents that date from around the Christian period. Many are quite interesting from a Mormon point of view, particularly those—such as 1 Enoch, the Testament of the Twelve Patriarchs, and the Assumption of Moses—referenced, but not canonized, in the New Testament. ★★★

Religion davidwiley.com/religion.html An impressively comprehensive compilation of links to the religious and sacred texts of the world's major religious movements. Maintained by David Wiley. ★★★★

Scrolls from the Dead Sea lcweb.loc.gov/exhibits/scrolls/toc.html Very comprehensive collection of pages on the Dead Sea Scrolls. If you're at all interested in the subject matter, this is a can't-miss site. A similar site is located at sunsite.unc.edu/expo/deadsea.scrolls.exhibit/intro.html. Not an LDS page, but the Dead Sea Scrolls in general are of tremendous interest to students of Mormonism, for they cast light on some of the attitudes, practices, and beliefs presented in the Book of Mormon for a Semitic people prior to the coming of Christ. ★★★★

Some Archaeological Outliers economics.sbs.ohio-state.edu/jhm/arch/outliers.html One part "Believe it or Not," one part "In Search of . . ." A lot of digging and research are presented by J. Huston McCulloch. ★★★

Voices from the Dust www.enoch.com/voicesfromdust Writings on the Dead Sea Scrolls and Mormon's Story from an LDS perspective—and more. ★★★

Writings www.davidwiley.com/writings.html Author David Wiley offers his take on Christian polytheism, gnostic texts, Shakespeare, The Dead Sea Scrolls, and more. ★★★★

The New Testament Church

Focusing primarily on LDS-specific New Testament resources, the following sites provide a glimpse into the history of the New Testament period of the Church.

You'll find additional materials for studying the text, and the doctrine, of the New Testament in chapter 7 on page 144, and in chapter 12 on page 293.

Ancient Evidence of Baptism for the Dead ourworld.compuserve.com/homepages/ MGriffith_2/proxy-2.htm A study by Michael T. Griffith, from a newly published book. An excellent compilation. ★★★★

Apocalyptic Texts www.mormons.org/basic/ doctrines/scripture/apocalyptic_eom.htm C. Wilfred Griggs's introduction to the genre of literature that contains visionary or revelatory experiences. An *Encyclopedia of Mormonism* text. 📖

Barry's Early Christianity and Mormonism Page www.vt.edu:10021/B/bbickmor/ EC.html A very large collection with many essays showing that LDS theology is much closer to early Christianity than is modern orthodox Christianity. Addresses apostasy, cosmology, requirements for salvation, the Temple, references, resources, and more. ★★★★★ ☑

Bridges for Peace www.bridgesforpeace. com/library.htm An organization dedicated to the support of Israel. Includes information on archeology, politics, life in biblical times, and more. ★★★

HOTLINKS

Ancient Evidence of Baptism for the Dead
ourworld.compuserve.com/ homepages/MGriffith_2/ proxy-2.htm

Barry's Early Christianity and Mormonism Page
www.vt.edu:10021/B/bbickmor/ EC.html

Early Christian Temple Rites
www.mormons.org/basic/temples/ Early_Home.htm

Organization of the Church in New Testament Times
www.mormons.org/basic/ organization/Organization_ NTtimes_EOM.htm

Christian History Institute www.gospelcom.net/chi A nonprofit, nondenominational corporation dedicated to providing awareness of role of Christianity in Western civilization throughout history. Many links, *Pocket Classics*, and a "What Happened on This Day in Christian History?" calendar are among the many features. ★★★

Christian Polytheism webpages.marshall.edu/~wiley6/poly.html An interesting treatise on the notion of multiple gods. ★★

Early Christian Deification www.mormons.org/basic/godhead/Deification_EOM.htm The standard Christian term for salvation was *theopoiesis* or *theosis*, literally, "being made God," or deification. An *Encyclopedia of Mormonism* article by Keith E. Norman. 📖

Early Christian Temple Rites www.mormons.org/basic/temples/Early_Home.htm Scholarly articles on temple practices in the early Church. Includes information on Early Christian Temple Rights: Ancient and Modern Parallels; The Doctrinal Exclusion: Lesser Arguments; Baptism for the Dead in Ancient Times; and Ancient Sources for Baptism for the Dead. A Mormons.Org page. ★★★★

Early Christian Works www.math.byu.edu/~smithw/Lds/LDS/Ancient-history-items/Early-Christian Early Christian texts of interest to Latter-day Saints. Tremendous content (Augustine, Creeds, Gnostic-works, Lost-Books, Plotinus, the Problem-of-Evil, and Tertullian works), but it's not yet an HTML (Web) page. Takes some digging to find the information. ★★★

Early Christianity www.teleport.com/~arden/religium.htm#earlychrist A collection of essays and links from Arden Eby. Some bizarro links, but interesting if you've got nothing else to read. ★★

Early Church Fathers wesley.nnc.edu/noncanon/fathers.htm The writings of the Early Church Fathers—from the apostles through Augustine and Anastasius the Librarian. These writings are very early Christian documents dating from between 50 A.D. to around the third century. Many have very interesting items concerning Mormon doctrine. Lacks a search engine. ★★★★

EarlyChurch.com www.earlychurch.com The Dallas Early Christian Church is similar to Mormonism in that it views the majority of churches of the present day to be substantially different from the early Christian church of about 33 A.D. to 300 A.D. Contains many links to online resources as well as an online catalog for Scroll Publishing Company. ★★★★

From Jesus to Christ www.pbs.org/wgbh/pages/frontline/shows/religion The PBS series provides an intellectual and visual guide to "the new and controversial historical evidence which challenges familiar assumptions about the life of Jesus and the epic rise of Christianity." The level of scholarship is surprisingly casual. The historical information provides good background. ★★★

Israel Revealed www.ysite.com/israelrona By Daniel Rona, an LDS tour guide in Israel. A commercial site. $

Nature of the Spirit World www.vt.edu:10021/B/bbickmor/ECSpWrd.html Joseph Smith preached some strange things about the spirit world for his day, but these doctrines would have been right at home in the early Christian Church! ★★★

Organization of the Church in New Testament Times www.mormons.org/basic/organization/Organization_NTtimes_EOM.htm A brief but enlightening *Encyclopedia of Mormonism* article. ★★★★

Society for the Advancement of Nazarene Judaism www.nazarene.net "Jewish Christianity" was the most primitive form of ancient Christianity. Contains fascinating information on this ancient movement and its modern counterparts. ★★★★

True Church www.shire.net/mormon/church.html Allen Leigh's essay, *The True Church*, focuses on the organization of the true church, scriptural passages, and the links to revelations to the living prophets. 📖

Why There Will Never Be Another Bible webpages.marshall.edu/~wiley6/bible.html A slightly angry, but insightful, examination of the history of the canonization of scripture, from Dave Wiley. ★★★

The Interregnum

You'll find in this section a large volume of materials on the period following the death of the Apostles, tracing the religious movements that fostered the latter-day restoration of the gospel.

Anglicanism www.teleport.com/~arden/religium.htm#cofe Historical and modern documents on this branch of Protestantism collected by Arden Eby. ★★

Ante-Nicene Fathers ccel.wheaton.edu/fathers A 38-volume collection of writings from the first 800 years of the Church. This collection is divided into three series:

HOTLINKS

Apostasy Foretold
www.vt.edu:10021/B/bbickmor/
ECApFr.html

Apostasy Papers
www.math.byu.edu/~smithw/Lds/
LDS/Apostasy.html

Dissecting the Athanasian
and Nicene Creeds
millennium.fortunecity.com/
bertisevil/375/creeds.htm

Early Christian Online Encyclopedia
www.evansville.edu/~ecoleweb

Ante-Nicene, Nicene, and Post-Nicene. Not an LDS page, but of interest for its historical value. ★★★

Apostasy Foretold www.vt.edu:10021/B/bbickmor/ECApFr.html The apostles and prophets predicted a total apostasy from the truth. Barry Bickmore considers other aspects of the apostasy on these pages: **Apostasy: A History of Rebellion** www.vt.edu:10021/B/bbickmor/ECApRb.html. The apostles indicated that the predicted apostasy was happening even as they wrote! **Rebellion Continues** www.vt.edu:10021/B/bbickmor/ECApCon.html. Even after the apostles were gone, the rebellion against established authority continued. Eventually, the Church came under secular control. **Loss of Apostolic Authority** www.vt.edu:10021/B/bbickmor/ECLsAp.html. A defining characteristic of the true Church of Christ was lost by the end of the first century. **Gates of Hell** www.vt.edu:10021/B/bbickmor/ECGates.html. Response to a mainstream Christian who takes issue with Barry's interpretations. ★★★★

Apostasy Papers www.math.byu.edu/~smithw/Lds/LDS/Apostasy.html Traces the history of the early Christian apostasy, prophecies of a falling away, changes in doctrine, and early Church councils, and controversies. In an unattractive FTP format, but it's tremendously valuable nevertheless. ★★★★

Augustine on the Internet ccat.sas.upenn.edu/jod/augustine.html A comprehensive view of the life and times of Augustine of Hippo, who wrote extensively in defense of Catholicism, and the doctrines of infant baptism and the trinity. Text of Augustine's teachings, as well as commentary and historical background. ★★★

Canadian Society of Patristic Studies www.chass.utoronto.ca/~turcescu/patristic.html See what the professional theologians who study the post-New Testament Church are interested in. Not LDS. ★★

Christian Classics Ethereal Library ccel.wheaton.edu/cdrom/ccel/index.htm The library includes bibles, commentaries, sermons, devotional and theological books, and writings of the early Church fathers. ★★★★

Did the Ancient Church Fall Away? ourworld.compuserve.com/homepages/MGriffith_2/apostasy.htm Scriptural analysis and discussion demonstrating that an apostasy was prophesied, and that it did occur. Condensed excerpt from Michael T. Griffith's *One Lord, One Faith: Writings of the Early Christian Fathers As Evidence of the Restoration.* ★★★

Dissecting the Athanasian and Nicene Creeds millennium.fortunecity.com/bertisevil/375/creeds.htm By dissecting the Athanasian and Nicene Creeds, Michael D. Crowe examines the foundation of disagreements between Mormonism and modern Christianity. ★★★★

Early Christian Online Encyclopedia www.evansville.edu/~ecoleweb Texts, history, and writings of the Church from Adam through the 15th century A.D. Graphics, texts, and histories. Phenomenal resource. ★★★★

Falling Away and Restoration Foretold www.xmission.com/~health/mormon/apostasy.html A handful of illustrated quotes. ★★

Guide to Early Church Documents www.iclnet.org/pub/resources/christian-history.html This service of the Institute for Christian Leadership provides hundreds of links to New Testament canonical information, writings of the apostolic fathers, patristic text, creeds and canons, and much more. ★★★★

History of Christianity in Egypt interoz.com/egypt/chiste0.htm A nondenominational approach to the history of Christianity in Egypt. ★★★

History of the Church to the Eve of the Reformation abbey.apana.org.au/history/hughes/~Index.Htm By Philip Hughes. Very, very well-done history. The Roman Catholic view of how things wuz. Fascinating, particularly the first few chapters covering Christ's founding of the Church. ★★★★

Journal of Early Christian Studies muse.jhu.edu/journals/journal_of_early_christian_studies Scholarly input about early Christianity in a full-text e-journal. The book reviews are particularly interesting. ★★★

Medieval Christianity www.teleport.com/~arden/religium.htm#medieval Brief list of links from Arden Eby. ★★

Orthodox Christian Esoteric Rites www.vt.edu:10021/B/bbickmor/ECOrTpl.html Learn about these esoteric rites in the "orthodox" branches of early Christianity. ★★★

Orthodox Corruption of Scripture www.cyberhighway.net/~shirtail/orthodox.htm Review of Bart Ehrman's book by Kerry Shirts. Ehrman's book purports to show

how Christological controversies in early Christianity shaped the present form of the New Testament canon. Kerry Shirts's reviews this book and its implications for Mormonism and modern Christianity. 📖

Questions About the Restoration www.jefflindsay.com/LDSFAQ/FQ_Restoration.shtml Despite its name, this site focuses on questions about the apostasy. ★★★

Reformation Era Studies www.teleport.com/~arden/religium.htm#reformed Links to good historical information on the Protestant reformation. ★★

Upon This Rock www.vt.edu:10021/B/bbickmor/ECUpRk.html Did Jesus ever claim His earthly Church would survive? Barry Bickmore responds. ★★★

History of the Modern Church

From the Restoration to the international expansion, you'll find every "era" of the latter-day Church represented in this section.

This section begins with resources on the Restoration period of the Church, followed by materials on the Church in New York, in Ohio, in Missouri, and in Nauvoo. It continues with information on the pioneer period, the California period, the Deseret period, the Utah statehood period, and finally multiple periods in the expanding Church.

HOTLINKS

Need for the Restoration
www.new-jerusalem.com/
stumpus/restoration-need.html

Restoration of the Gospel
www.mormons.org/basic/gospel/
restoration

Restoration

These resources focus specifically on the pre-1830 history of the Church.

Need for the Restoration www.new-jerusalem.com/ stumpus/restoration-need.html A heavily footnoted discourse by the late LDS apostle, Mark E. Peterson, presented online by Gene Robbins. 📖

Organizational Chronology of the Church of Jesus Christ webpages.marshall.edu/~brown/chu-org.html A timeline describing the organization of the Church from 1829 to 1836. ★★

Prophet Joseph Smith's Testimony www.lds.org/library/the_pro_jos/the_pro_jos.html His own words, extracted from the History of the Church. 📖

Restoration of the Gospel www.mormons.org/basic/gospel/restoration A collection of articles on the history of the Restoration. Includes information on The Restoration of the Gospel of Jesus Christ, Why Did the True Church of Christ Need to Be Restored? Apostasy, First Vision, Joseph Smith—History, Visitations of Moroni, Faith Once Delivered to the Saints—What Happened to It? Cumorah, and Christopher Columbus. A Mormons.Org page. ★★★★

Review of David Whitmer Interviews: A Restoration Witness www.farmsresearch.com/review/5/dcp2.html The book edited by Lyndon W. Cook is reviewed by Daniel C. Peterson 📖

Review of One Lord, One Faith www.farmsresearch.com/review/9_1/tvedtnes.html John A. Tvedtnes reviews Michael T. Griffith's portrayal of the Writings of the Early Christian Fathers as Evidences of the Restoration. 📖

Three Witnesses www.lib.ricks.edu/reserve/AndersonR/HC1-56-Josephrelievedat3witnesses.htm His mother, says Joseph, was relieved at the appointment of three witnesses (HC 1:56). 📖

New York Period

This information concerns the Church from 1830 to the Kirtland exodus.

America's Witness for Christ www.ldscn.com/hcp All about the Hill Cumorah Pageant, with information on the history of various sites in the area, maps, and travel information. This was a better site before it had the LDSCN-sponsored banners filling half the pages. ★★★★

Hill Cumorah www.canaltown.net/hillcumorah Historic sites around Palmyra (see figure 13.3). Includes photos and histories. ★★★★★ ☑

Early New York History www.ldscn.com/hcp/nyhistory.shtml A very readable, very well written illustrated history of the Church in New York, originally from the Encyclopedia of Mormonism. ★★★★

ON WRITING HISTORY

Historians try to create a narrative, tell a story, and they base that story on the best evidence available to them, understanding that we can never know more than the tiniest fraction of what we'd like to know about any time in the historical past. To a historian, all evidence is valuable, and all evidence is flawed, and most of your time is spent weighing the relative value of this or that piece of evidence. And of course, the historical narrative comes from the historian's own prejudices and beliefs and ideology. It's simply not possible to let the facts speak for themselves, or to view any piece of evidence uncritically.

I am personally convinced that Joseph Smith saw God the Father and His Divine Son in the sacred grove. I believe as a matter of faith that that really happened. If I were to write about Palmyra in the 1820's, my interpretation of that time would necessarily reflect that belief. But does the evidence we have for that event support that conclusion? The answer has to be a strong maybe. As it would have to be for any assertion. Well, not any—lots of eyewitnesses say they saw John Wilkes Booth shoot Abraham Lincoln, and I think we can conclude safely that Lincoln really was assassinated. But I don't know that we can prove beyond a shadow of doubt much else about that event.

Eric Samuelsen
<ersamuel@byugate.byu.edu>, "Writing History," a thread on AML-list (August 12, 1999)

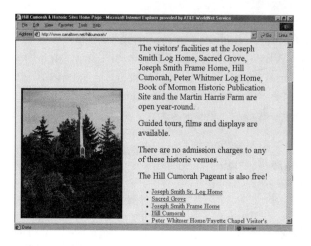

The visitors' facilities at the Joseph Smith Log Home, Sacred Grove, Joseph Smith Frame Home, Hill Cumorah, Peter Whitmer Log Home, Book of Mormon Historic Publication Site and the Martin Harris Farm are open year-round.

Guided tours, films and displays are available.

There are no admission charges to any of these historic venues.

The Hill Cumorah Pageant is also free!

- Joseph Smith Sr. Log Home
- Sacred Grove
- Joseph Smith Frame Home
- Hill Cumorah
- Peter Whitmer Home/Fayette Chapel Visitor's

FIG. 13.3

Hill Cumorah and Historic Sites.

History of the Mormon Church in New York City www.panix.com/~klarsen/nyc_lds_history New Yorker Kent Larsen has gathered a fine collection of information on the Church in New York. Includes a chronology, links, personal recollections and oral histories, and general New York City history. ★★★

New York Period www.indirect.com/www/crockett/newyork.html Part of Dave Crockett's magnificent suite of Church history resources. Links to articles on the Joseph Smith Home in Palmyra, Accounts of the First Vision, the Martin Harris Conversion, Book of Mormon Witnesses, Restoration of the Priesthood, the Urim and Thummim, Timeline for Restoration of Ordinances, and more. ★★★★

HOTLINKS

America's Witness for Christ
www.ldscn.com/hcp

Hill Cumorah
www.canaltown.net/hillcumorah

Ohio Period

The Kirtland, Ohio, history of the Church has little representation on the Internet. Fortunately, these sources tend to be of good quality.

Additional Historical Material on Ohio Revelations www.cybcon.com/~kurtn/ohiorevs.txt A white paper on the chronology of the revelations given to Joseph Smith in Ohio. ★★★

Josiah Jones www.math.byu.edu/~smithw/Lds/LDS/Early-Saints/jones,j Text of the document by Josiah Jones: "History of the Mormonites, Kirtland, 1831." *The Evangelist* 9 (June 1, 1841):132–36. 📖

Kirtland Elders' Quorum Record 1836–1841   www.math.byu.edu/~smithw/Lds/LDS/Early-Saints/Kirt-eq-rec Text of the historical record. 📖

Kirtland Temple   www.vii.com/~nicksl/kirtland.html From Nick Literski's collection of Temple dedicatory prayers. Tremendously interesting. ★★★

Kirtland, Ohio, Period   www.indirect.com/www/crockett/kirtland.html Excellent links. ★★

Literary Firm   webpages.marshall.edu/~brown/literfrm.htm A chronology of a method used to published Church books, newspapers, and other items in the 1830's. ★★★

HOTLINKS

Additional Historical Material on Ohio Revelations
www.cybcon.com/~kurtn/ohiorevs.txt

Kirtland Temple
www.vii.com/~nicksl/kirtland.html

Ohio   www.math.byu.edu/~smithw/Lds/LDS/Early-Saints/smith,j-ohio Text of The Ohio Experience And Joseph Smith And The Restoration. Remarks of Church Leaders Published in Journal of Discourses, 26 Vols. Liverpool, 1855–1886. 📖

United Firm   webpages.marshall.edu/~brown/UNTDFIRM.htm A chronology of business operations by Church leaders in the 1830's, which is often confused with the Law of Consecration (United Order). ★★★

Willard Richards   www.math.byu.edu/~smithw/Lds/LDS/Early-Saints/richards,w Text of Willard Richards: "History of Willard Richards" (1836–1839). The Latter-day Saints' *Millennial Star.* 📖

WW Phelps   www.math.byu.edu/~smithw/Lds/LDS/Early-Saints/phelps,ww Text of William W. Phelps: "Excerpts from Letters from Kirtland" (1835–1836). Microfilm, Family History Library. 📖

Zebedee Coltrin   www.math.byu.edu/~smithw/Lds/LDS/Early-Saints/coltrin,z The text from Recollections (1833–1836) of Spiritual Experiences in Ohio recorded in Minutes, Salt Lake School of the Prophets, Church Archives. 📖

Missouri Period

When I moved to Missouri for graduate school, my bishop called me into his office to give me the scoop.

"Welcome to Missouri," he told me. "The Extermination Order has finally been rescinded, and we aren't being treated so badly anymore."

Whew.

Expulsion of the Mormons www.math.byu.edu/~smithw/ Lds/LDS/Early-Saints/green.jp Text of an 1839 document describing the extermination order. 📖

HOTLINKS

Missouri Church History Foundation
www.ldshistory.org

Missouri Period
www.indirect.com/www/
crockett/missouri.html

Far West Cemetery www.sunflower.org/~ronromig/mmffpp.htm A project to locate the names of early members of the Church buried at Far West. ★★★

Headquarters of the Militia home.lv.rmci.net/jdstone/Boggs.html The letter issued by Governor Boggs of Missouri on October 27, 1838, to General John B. Clark authorizing the removal of the Mormons from Missouri. 📖

Historian Recounts Mormon Ouster examiner.net/stories/042597/boggs.html A recent news article on Missouri Governor Lilburn Boggs, published in the Jackson County, Missouri, *Examiner.* ★★

Missouri Church History Foundation www.ldshistory.org Really cool site sponsored by the Missouri Church History Foundation. Historical reviews, membership information, and links to LDS resources. You'll enjoy the story of Parley P. Pratt's escape from a Missouri prison. ★★★★★

Missouri Mormon Frontier Foundation oz.sunflower.org/~ronromig/mmffhp.htm A page of Restoration history. Fun. ★★

Missouri Period www.indirect.com/www/crockett/missouri.html First rate list of links. ★★★

Mormons and Danites: The 1838 Setting in Missouri www.jefflindsay.com/LDSFAQ/FQ_Missouri.shtml Additional information on the history of the Mormon War. A Jeff Lindsay page. 📖

Never Forsake: The Story of Amanda Barnes Smith and Legacy of the Haun's Mill Massacre www.lgcy.com/users/k/keeban Keeban Publications' life and times of Amanda Barnes Smith. 💲

Persecution www.math.byu.edu/~smithw/Lds/LDS/Early-Saints/pratt.p-prs Text of the document by Parley P. Pratt: History of the Late Persecution Inflicted by the State of Missouri Upon the Mormons. Detroit: Dawson and Bates, 1839. 📖

The 1838 Mormon War and Tales of the "Danites"
www.jefflindsay.com/LDSFAQ/FQ_Danites.shtml A look at the Danites and the circumstances surrounding the 1838 Mormon War by Jeff Lindsay. ★★★

Nauvoo Period

Nauvoo is a magical place for me. It seems almost insolent to drive through Nauvoo. When I go there, I park my car on the outskirts of town and walk.

I walk to the Temple grounds, wander through the streets, stroll down the hill, and out to the river. As I wander, I can almost hear echoes of voices, of children playing, long skirts brushing against the dust of the ground, laughing, and living. I sometimes think I hear more. Sometimes there's a hurrying of footsteps, an anger, a rushing about. There's weeping, a solemn quiet. I can hear whispers of a meeting in the bowery, a determined clanging of blacksmith iron, a creaking of wheels, then silence.

HOTLINKS

Joseph Smith Daguerreotype
www.comevisit.com/lds/
js3photo.htm

Nauvoo Temple History
www.ldsworld.com/gems/nauvoo

Nauvoo Temple Tour
www.indirect.com/www/crockett/
nauvoo.html

William Clayton Nauvoo
Diaries and Personal Writings
www.code-co.com/rcf/mhistdoc/
clayton.htm

Nauvoo leaves me in awe, it gives me a sense of reverence. It gives me hope.

If you can't be there yourself, the information on these Web sites might give you some of the same sense of history and wonder about that miraculous period in Church history.

Allyn House in Nauvoo www.outfitters.com/com/allyn/nauvoo.html A commercial site with some interesting Nauvoo history. ★★

Brigham Young Company www.cc.utah.edu/~joseph/BYCompany1847.html The first 2000+ pioneers who made the trip to the Salt Lake Valley. ★★

George Moore www.math.byu.edu/~smithw/Lds/LDS/Early-Saints/moore,g The text of George Moore: Diary excerpts in Donald Q. Cannon, "Reverend George Moore Comments on Nauvoo, the Mormons, and Joseph Smith." *Western Illinois Regional Studies* 5 (Spring 1982):6–16. 📖

Hosea Stout www.math.byu.edu/~smithw/Lds/LDS/Early-Saints/stout,h Text of Hosea Stout: Diary (1844–1846). Holograph, UHI. Typescript, BYU-S. 📖

In Search of Joseph home.fuse.net/stracy One man's project to find a correct image of the Prophet Joseph Smith. The subject is treated with reverence. A fascinating read with lots of good information about the interment of the Prophet, Hyrum, and Emma. ★★★

Joseph Smith Daguerreotype   www.comevisit.com/lds/js3photo.htm   The primary feature of this site is a photograph of a daguerreotype of Joseph Smith and a discussion of its authenticity. The photograph was presented to the Library of Congress in 1879 by Joseph Smith III. ★★★★

Josiah Quincy   www.math.byu.edu/~smithw/Lds/LDS/Early-Saints/quincy,j   Text from Josiah Quincy: "Joseph Smith at Nauvoo: Figures of the Past from the Leaves of Old Journals." Boston, 1883. 📖

Members of the Anointed Quorum   webpages.marshall.edu/~brown/aq-list.htm   Anointings and endowments performed in Nauvoo from 1842 to 1845. 📖

Nauvoo   www.nauvoo.net   A brief history of Nauvoo, a virtual tour, and the latest news releases. ★★

Nauvoo Expositor   www.sj-coop.net/~tseng/LDS/expositr.txt   The same document is also available at www.blueneptune.com/~tseng/LDS/expositr.txt. Partial text, transcribed from the only edition of the *Expositor*. Unformatted, difficult to read on screen. Unfortunately, the text does not include the inflammatory Prospectus. ★

Nauvoo Temple History   www.ldsworld.com/gems/nauvoo   Detailed history of the Nauvoo Temple by David R. Crockett, broken out into 10 sections. ★★★★

Nauvoo Temple Tour   www.indirect.com/www/crockett/nauvoo.html   Another site from Brother Crockett. Photos, history, diagrams, and descriptive tour. Completely fascinating. A valuable document. Worth revisiting. ★★★★

Nauvoo, Illinois Period   www.indirect.com/www/crockett/nauvoop.html   Some good links. ★★

Nauvoo Temple   people.delphi.com/deseret/home/homenauv.htm   A tour, and various articles related to the temple in Nauvoo. ★★★★

NauvooNet   www.nauvoonet.com   NauvooNet offer links to the history of Nauvoo, a family vacation planner and virtual tour, as well as information on shops, events, and lodging. ★★★★

Pioneer Story   www.lds.org/library/pio_sto/pio_sto.html   An interactive site that follows the pioneers from Nauvoo to Salt Lake. ★★★★★

Place to Visit www.outfitters.com/illinois/hancock/points_hancock.html Hancock County, Illinois, places of interest include Nauvoo and Carthage, the town where Joseph and Hyrum Smith were jailed on the night of their murders. This site features historical information, photos, other points of interest, and a directory of local services. ★★★

Preparing Early Revelations for Publication www.flash.net/~mdparker/Prep_Revelations.htm Melvin Petersen's 1985 Ensign article, which looks at the mechanics involved in writing a revelation. 📖.

Spirit of Nauvoo www.nauvoo.com/vacation A Nauvoo directory featuring information on vacationing, dining, lodging, and attractions. 📖

William Clayton Nauvoo Diaries and Personal Writings www.code-co.com/rcf/mhistdoc/clayton.htm A chronological compilation of the personal writings of William Clayton while he was a resident of Nauvoo, Illinois. A very, very good resource. ★★★★

Pioneer Period

Shortly after Pioneer Day this year, I took my oldest teenager and my baby to visit the This Is The Place monument in Salt Lake's Parley's Canyon—a place I haven't been since I was a teenager myself. There, after several hours in a cushy, air-conditioned van, we walked out under the blazing sun, hot and uncomfortable. The baby cried, my teenager was cranky, and I was irritable.

The place was a little different than it had been in the 70s. Just three days previously, a new monument to the handcart pioneers had been dedicated, and we stood there, in awe, reading plaques and looking at the dusty desert all around us. I read the names of the companies of handcart pioneers, saw the numbers of Saints who had died during their journey, and caught a glimpse of their faith. Then I understood. For the first time, I saw something of what it was those brave souls had undertaken in crossing the plains, lugging 300 pounds of their worldly goods across streams, mountains, and desert.

We left a little less cranky, and a lot more grateful.

After all the interest generated by the Pioneer Sesquicentennial and subsequent interest in Utah history, the Web is abuzz with pioneer sites. This has been one of the most popular topics for new LDS Web site builders.

HOTLINKS

Heritage Gateway Pioneer Page
heritage.uen.org

Mormon Pioneer Trail
www.omaha.org/trails/main.htm

Mormon Trail
www.esu3.k12.ne.us/districts/elkhorn/ms/curriculum/Mormon1.html

Faith of the Latter-day Pioneers   www.geocities.com/Heartland/Plains/6358/faithof.htm
Essays, personal notes, and inspirational writing of the early pioneers. ★★★

Gathering   www.deseretbook.com/gather Clips and excerpts from the book *Mormon Pioneers on the Trail to Zion*, by Maurine Jensen Proctor and Scot Facer Proctor. Commercial, but interesting. $

Heritage Gateway Pioneer Page   heritage.uen.org Pioneer Trail project sponsored by Utah State Office of Education (see figure 13.4). Historical diaries, excerpts from published books such as *I Walked to Zion*, articles, commentaries, maps, and video clips all reflecting the life and times of those early pioneers. Includes scholarly writings, links to other Internet resources, and a comprehensive bibliography of related writings, maps, and organizations all related to the study of the pioneers, as well as instructions on how to build an authentic handcart. A phenomonal site, worth bookmarking. The best site anywhere for learning about the Pioneer Trek. ★★★★★

Mormon Diaries/Journals and Biographies   www.indirect.com/www/crockett/bios.html
Another tremendous collection of historical links from Dave Crockett. Pioneer biographies and—most fascinating of all—links to some historical audio clips of Wilford Woodruff, Joseph F. Smith, and Heber J. Grant, maintained by BYU. ★★★

Mormon Pioneer National Historic Trail   www.nps.gov/mopi Sponsored by the National Park Service. History, reference materials. ★★★

Mormon Pioneer Story   www.uvol.com/pioneer Information on the Pioneer Trail State Park and the This is the Place Monument. Good history. ★★★

FIG. 13.4
Heritage Gateway: Stop by to see the Pioneer Trail Project.

Mormon Pioneer Trail www.omaha.org/trails/main.htm An unbelievably well-done page sponsored, interestingly, by the Douglas-Sarpy (Nebraska) Counties Mormon Trails Association. History of the trail, history of the Church, history of anything of interest, in an easy-to-navigate page. ★★★★★

Mormon Trail www.esu3.k12.ne.us/districts/elkhorn/ms/curriculum/Mormon1.html This site chronicles the Pioneer Trek westward and their stay at the Winter Quarters in Omaha, Nebraska. Sponsored by the Elkhorn, Nebraska, Middle School. Excellent collection of information. Kudos. ★★★★

Mormon Trail Discussion of the development and history of the Mormon trail and the celebration of the Mormon Trek. To subscribe, send an e-mail request to <*mormontr@unlvm.unl.edu*>. Sponsored by the University of Nebraska at Kearney. 📖

Parley Parker Pratt www.cswnet.com/~ramona/ppratt.html Picctures of Parley P. Pratt's grave site, with text from grave marker. ★★

Pioneer Cooking www.ldscn.com/pioneer-cooking Discussions, stories, recipes, and techniques related to all aspects of pioneer life, with an emphasis on pioneer cooking. Subscribe with an e-mail request to <*majordomo@ldscn.com*> with the message `subscribe pioneer cooking`. ★★★

Pioneer Moments www.desnews.com/cgi-bin/libheads_reg?search=%22Pioneer+moment%22&limit=999 A collection of inspiring pioneer stories from the *Church News*. Worth reading. ★★★★

Pioneer Period www.indirect.com/www/crockett/pioneer.html A very good list of links from David Crockett. Excellent sites, many of which were written by Brother Crockett. ★★★★

Pioneer Trail Journals www.sltrib.com/trek/journals A must see! The Salt Lake Tribune has collected journal entries from pioneers who walked to the Valley. 📖

Pioneer Trails from U.S. Land Surveys www.ukans.edu/heritage/werner A collection of information about the Western frontier in general, with several sites related specifically to Mormon experiences on the Pioneer Trail. ★★★

Trail of Hope www.trailofhope.com The story of the PBS broadcast on the Mormon Trail. Includes stories and photos. ★★★

California Period

A fascinating period in Church history, it's one only just coming to light. And these sites, prepared mostly by California-dwelling Saints, do a great job of pulling together some of the disparate pieces.

HOTLINKS

Mormon Battalion
people.delphi.com/deseret/home/
homebatt.htm

Mormon Battalion
www.mormonbattalion.com

Voyage of the Brooklyn
www.indirect.com/www/crockett
/brooklyn.html

Huntington Library huntington.org/ResearchDiv/AmHistRes.html A collection of Mormorabilia called "Latter-day Saints in El Dorado: The Mormon Presence in California, 1846–1856." Features letters, diaries, and drawings from California's first Mormon immigrants. The San Marino–based library owns and sometimes displays what it claims is the finest collection of Mormon manuscript diaries and journals outside of Utah. ★★

Jacob Micah Truman www.geocities.com/Heartland/Prairie/4501 Life history of Jacob Micah Truman and a history of the Mormon Battalion. 📖

LDS History in California www.templehill.com/history/sf_history_index.html The Voyage of the Brooklyn, Temple News, links, and more. ★★★

Mormon Battalion people.delphi.com/deseret/home/homebatt.htm Brion Zion's great collection of historical documents related to the Battalion. ★★★★

Mormon Battalion www.mormonbattalion.com The Official Homepage of the U.S. Mormon Battalion, Inc. features links to History, Calendar of Events, a newsletter, and others. ★★★★

Mormon Battalion Roster www.cc.utah.edu/~joseph/MBatallion.html Information on the Saints who made up the Mormon Battalion company. ★★

Mormon Colonization of San Bernardino covalt.ourfamily.com/mormon.htm Fascinating research on the history and results of California colonization. ★★★

Voyage of the Brooklyn www.indirect.com/www/crockett/brooklyn.html Amazing account of the Pioneer Saints who traveled by sea to California. By David Crockett. ★★★★

Deseret Period

It was one of those niggling little questions that has been worming its way up through my subconscious for several years now. Today, it ate its way through to the top, and when it did, I realized I had the answer.

Many years ago, my grandma told me that it's easier to learn things now, in mortality, than it will be in the future, when we don't have these bodies clothing our spirits.

My grandma's wisdom has generally proven sound, so I took her at her word. I never understood the concept, though. Why would learning now be *better* than learning after death? Why faster? Why easier?

Then this week, during sacrament meeting, I had one of those flashes of insight that suddenly make everything clear. The speaker talked about the United Order and the necessity of being willing to share all that we have with our brothers and sisters when the need arises. We will, he suggested, be required to live the United Order during the millennium.

And it occurred to me that sharing will be much easier when we don't worry about starving to death.

Then I realized that many of the things we struggle with here have much to do with bodies that die. We immerse ourselves in jobs to get money, to stave off starvation and homelessness. People get angry at being cut off on the freeway, develop unkind stereotypes about people they consider dangerous, overeat, over-worry, overreact—all because they have bodies that *might* die.

And so, when we inhabit bodies that might die, the lesson of charity is both real and lasting. Without the risk of death, the notion of charity is merely theoretical, and much more difficult to assimilate. Self-control, without a body subject to temptation, is easy in theory. But to incorporate it would be very difficult.

And yet, perfection requires learning—really learning, not just theorizing principles of godliness. Faith, charity, love, control of self, compassion, justice, mercy—it's in front of the veil that all these principles have reality.

And so, you see, my grandma was right. Now is the time, the best time, to learn and to exercise charity and compassion and all the other qualities necessary to live again in a United Order.

The following Web sites examine a unique period in Church history—that safe place between the Pioneer Trek and Utah statehood, when members had the peace and freedom to live a higher law.

HOTLINKS

150 Years Ago in Church History.
www.ldsworld.com/gems/150

Deseret Alphabet.
people.delphi.com/deseret/home/homealph.htm

Old Deseret Living History Museum.
www.uvol.com/pioneer/olddeshm.html

150 Years Ago in Church History   www.ldsworld.com/gems/150 Walking in the footsteps of the pioneers. After tracking the pioneer journey for two years, day by day, the series has now cut back to a weekly report. Very, very well done. ★★★★

Cove Fort   infowest.com/covefort History, photos, and maps of historic central Utah site. I'd visit. ★★★

Deseret Alphabet   people.delphi.com/deseret/home/homealph.htm Learn about the writing system that Brigham Young attempted to incorporate among the Saints. ★★★★

Deseret Alphabet   www.blueneptune.com/~tseng/Deseret/Deseret.html Proposal for making the Deseret Alphabet part of the Unicode. Very good historical information and background on the use of the alphabet. ★★★★

Deseret Alphabet   www.surfmadison.com/$webfile.send.FONTS./DESERET_.TTF Learn the Deseret Alphabet yourself. Great family activity. See also the site at ftp://voyager.cns.ohiou.edu/users/sadkins/truetype_fonts/deseret.ttf ★★★

Endowment Houses   www.mormons.org/basic/temples/endowment_houses_eom.htm History of the Endowment Houses and other sites used by the early Saints for temple ordinances. ★★★

Jacob Hamblin Home   www.infowest.com/Utah/colorcountry/History/JHamblin/JHHome.html A thumbnail tour, and history lesson, at the Jacob Hamblin Home in Santa Clara. ★★

Old Deseret Living History Museum   www.uvol.com/pioneer/olddeshm.html Pioneer life is recreated in Old Deseret, where 13 authentic pioneer homes and buildings combine with typical pioneer guides in authentic pioneer dress and animals. Old Deseret represents any of the hundreds of Mormon villages that popped up all around the State of Deseret between 1847 and 1869. An online guided tour. ★★★★

POLYGAMY   A mailing list for the discussion of the practicality of living the law of celestial plural marriage. Not a forum to debate the doctrine of Polygamy, or the apostasy of any particular church or group of churches. To subscribe, send an e-mail request to *<majordomo@lofthouse.com>* with the message `subscribe polygamy`. 📖

Questions to be Asked www.xmission.com/~dkenison/lds/lds_quo/ref_1856.html Historically interesting questions from the 1856–57 Reformation Movement. The precursor to temple recommend interviews. ★★★

Sons of the Utah Pioneers www.uvol.com/sup Thumbnail sketches of Mormon pioneer history, from the trail to the first years in the Utah Territory. Includes some worthwhile artwork, but otherwise not very substantial. ★★★

St. George www.so-utah.com/zion/stgeorge/homepage.html Photos and brief descriptions of historic sites in St. George, the Southern Utah headquarters of the Church during the administration of Brigham Young. ★★★★

What Is the State of Deseret? people.delphi.com/deseret/home/who-what.htm#deseret A map of the territory of Deseret. ★★

Utah Statehood Period

After a period of retrenchment, the collective Church was finally able to square its shoulders and take on the world once again. The period of Utah statehood covers the time frame from the completion of the transcontinental railroad to World War II.

HOTLINKS

Statehood for Utah
www.media.utah.edu/ucme/s/
STATEHOOD.html

Tour of Temple Square
www.uvol.com/www1st/tsquare

Mormon Meteor III www.ti.dixie.edu/meteor/meteor1.htm Racing aficionados will enjoy the story of the Mormon Meteor, driver Ab Jenkins, and the Bonneville Salt Flats. ★★★

Statehood for Utah www.media.utah.edu/ucme/s/STATEHOOD.html An encyclopedia account of the quest for statehood. ★★★

Tour of Temple Square www.uvol.com/www1st/tsquare Photos and descriptions of historic Temple Square in Salt Lake City. ★★★★

Utah History Home Page www.xmission.com/~drudy/histpage.html Links to information on Utah history. No original content. ★

Utah Period www.indirect.com/www/crockett/utah.html Another page of Utah history links, but these all have definite LDS connections: History of the Salt Lake Temple, Australian Saints Shipwreck, Godbeites, and more. About twenty in all. ★★

Zion National Park   people.delphi.com/deseret/home/homezion.htm   Author Brion Zion loves this place. Here's all you need to know for a great trip to Zion. ★★★

HOTLINKS

Dave Kenison's Church History Stories Collection
www.xmission.com/~dkenison/lds/ch_hist

Into the Western Country
www.lib.byu.edu/~imaging/into/poster.html

LDS Historical Information
www.math.byu.edu/~smithw/Lds

Utah History Encyclopedia
eddy.media.utah.edu/medsol/UCME/UHEindex.html

Multiple Periods

The following sites cover multiple periods of Church history and provide good overall historical links to online LDS resources.

Church History   www.mormons.org/daily/history Eclectic collection of articles on various Church history subjects. Includes Richard Ballantyne; Biography and Autobiography; Beehive; Ezra Taft Benson; Blacks; Building Program; Christus Statue; Colesville New York; Council Bluffs (Kanesville), Iowa; Nineteenth-Century Ecclesiastical Courts; Oliver Cowdery; and Joseph Smith. ★★★

Dave Kenison's Church History Stories Collection   www.xmission.com/~dkenison/lds/ch_hist A collection of over 400 stories, each chronicling events in Church history. Titles include Lorenzo Snow's Introduction to the Church, The Death of Alvin Smith, William Geddes—The Boy Preacher, Brigham Young Talks to Norwegian Oxen, and more. A remarkable collection. ★★★★★

Department of History   fhss.byu.edu/history Brigham Young University's Department of History home page. This is primarily a students' guide, although the resource links can be of interest to all. ★★★

Diaries and Biographies   www.math.byu.edu/~smithw/Lds/LDS/Early-Saints A dozen dozen journals, diaries, biographies, and autobiographies of some early Mormons and others who knew Joseph Smith, Jr. Prominent among the prominent are the record of the Kirtland Elders Quorum, Truman Angell, William Clayton, Mary Fielding, Heber C. Kimball, Amassa Lyman, William McLellin, Orson Pratt, Parley P. Pratt, Hosea Stout, John Taylor, John Whitmer, Wilford Woodruff, and Emily Dow Partridge Smith Young. ★★★

Did You Know? Hidden Treasures from Church History   nauvoo.byu.edu/Church/ChurchHistory/DidYouKnow/underside2.cfm Using Paul Harvey's *The Rest of the Story* as her model, Judy Fraser has put together stories about people who have had significant roles in the Church. ★★★

Gathering and Colonization   www.mormons.org/basic/organization/world/gathering
Histories of various LDS Pioneer settlements. A Mormons.Org page. ★★★

History   www.wnetc.com/resource/lds/history.html Very brief list of links. ★

Into the Western Country   www.lib.byu.edu/~imaging/into/poster.html A fantastic collection of photos and historical items related to Nauvoo, Iowa, pioneer companies, and the Utah Territory. Sponsored by BYU. ★★★★★

Journal of Mormon History   www.mhahome.org/mhajourn.htm The Mormon History Association's regular journal, dedicated to the study and research of Mormon history. ★★★

Latter-day Saints in Early Wisconsin   www.jefflindsay.com/WisconLDS.shtml Taken from a brochure by Dr. David L. Clark, this site provides some historical information about early Mormons who helped settle Wisconsin. ★★

LDS Historical Information   www.math.byu.edu/~smithw/Lds William Smith's excellent collection of papers, original diaries, and texts. Includes Teachings of the Prophet Joseph Smith, History of the Church, all the versions of the First Vision, and much, much more. Unfortunately, there isn't a search engine, but it is a very good—albeit unattractive—site. ★★★★★ ☑

LDS Resources   www.teleport.com/~arden/religium.htm#mormon Arden Eby's list of links to LDS historical resources. Includes other links. ★

LDS-HIST   www.kingsleymc.com/clark/Lists/lds-hist.htm A high-traffic list for the discussion of LDS history. Subscribe at www.egroups.com/list/LDS-hist/info.html, or send an e-mail request to *<lds-hist-request@mail.kingsleymc.com>*. Contact the list operator at *<Clark@mail.kingsleymc.com>*. 📖

Mormon Diaries/Journals and Biographies   www.indirect.com/www/crockett/bios.html
Over 20 journal and biography links, as well as several historical audio links. ★★★

Mormon History   fhss.byu.edu/history/resources/history/mormon.html A disappointing list of links to historical references from BYU's department of history. ★★

Mormon History & Doctrine www.code-co.com/rcf/mhistdoc/mhistdoc.htm An outstanding collection of historical analysis. Includes the William Clayton journals, a critical text of all variations of the Book of Abraham, and the Egyptian alphabet and grammar. ★★★

Mormon History Resource Page www.indirect.com/www/crockett/history.html Over 150 links covering all periods of LDS history. An outstanding, well-organized collection. ★★★

MORMON-HIST A discussion list for LDS historical subjects. To subscribe, send an e-mail request to <*majordomo@sara.zia.com*> with message `subscribe mormon-hist`. 📖

MORMON-J: The LDS Journal History Page www.writerspost.com/mormonj/mjhist The history page is part of the Mormon-J site for everyone who keeps a written record of Mormon history—public or private. This particular page lists links to journals and biographies, as well as links to a number of other historical documents available online. It was created by yours truly, so be skeptical of this rating. ★★★★

Prophecy, History, and Mormonism www.geocities.com/Athens/9975 Things as they were, as they are, and as they will be. Presented by Anthony E. Larson. ★★★

Timeline www.ricks.edu/Ricks/employee/CHECKETTSM/Church%20History%20timeline.htm Significant events in Church history from the apostles in the meridian to Brigham Young's calling as president of the Church. ★★★

True History www.homestead.com/truehistory A brief chronology of significant moments in Church history from the Council in Heaven to the Second Coming. ★★★

Utah History Encyclopedia eddy.media.utah.edu/medsol/UCME/UHEindex.html Everything you've always wanted to know about Utah from A to Z. Over 350 articles by over 200 contributors recount Utah history, past and present. ★★★★

Worldwide Church Period www.indirect.com/www/crockett/world.html A page of more than 20 links. The central theme is building Zion. Links include Postwar Europe, Africa, Mexico, and more. ★★

RESEARCH PROJECTS
AND RESEARCH GROUPS

LDS scholars, academics, and avocational historians join forces to undertake a number of research projects at these Internet sites.

Archive, an LDS Research Page www.homestead.com/thearchive Research data on virtually every subject of interest to Latter-day Saints. The material is plentiful and the links are relevant. ★★★★

Barry's Early Christianity and Mormonism Page fbox.vt.edu:10021/B/bbickmor/EC.html Dedicated to the comparison of Early Christianity and Mormonism. Dozens of Barry Bickmore's articles are referenced throughout this text. An excellent resource if you're studying the history of the Church. ★★★★★ ☑

Book of Abraham Links www.geocities.com/Athens/Parthenon/2671/Abraham.html Tremendous collection of articles and links. ★★★★

Book of Abraham Project www.boap.math.byu.edu/BOAP.html The nonprofit Book of Abraham Project includes scholarly analysis, documentation and supporting texts, and links to relevant sites. One of its best projects is the downloadable Joseph Smith Commentary on the Book of Abraham. ★★★★

HOTLINKS

Archive, an LDS Research Page
www.homestead.com/thearchive

Barry's Early Christianity
and Mormonism Page
fbox.vt.edu:10021/B/bbickmor/
EC.html

Book of Abraham Links
www.geocities.com/Athens/
Parthenon/2671/Abraham.html

Book of Abraham Project
www.boap.math.byu.edu/
BOAP.html

Foundation for Ancient Research
and Mormon Studies
farmsresearch.com

Insights: An Ancient Window
www.farmsresearch.com/insights/
main.htm

Mormonism Researched
www.cyberhighway.net/~shirtail/
mormonis.htm

BYU Studies: A Multidisciplinary Latter-day Saint Journal humanities.byu.edu/BYUStudies/homepage.htm "Dedicated to the correlation of revealed and discovered truth and to the conviction that the spiritual and the intellectual may be complementary and fundamentally harmonious avenues of knowledge." Whatever. There's not much material at this site. ★★

Center for the Computer Analysis of Texts ccat.sas.upenn.edu/teachtech/about-ccat.html The Center for the Computer Analysis of Texts is based at the University of Pennsylvania. Visit the home page to learn about scanning and analyzing old texts. ★★★

Center for the Study of Christian Values in Literature humanities.byu.edu/DeansOffice/CSCV.html Publishes *Literature and Belief*, a semiannual journal of scholarly critical articles, interviews, personal essays, book reviews, and poetry focusing on moral-religious aspects of literature. Sponsored by the BYU Humanities Department. Vanishingly little information here. ★

Chapman Research Group www.2s2.com/chapmanresearch A private effort to address many LDS topics. An eclectic mixture of subject matter. ★★★

DNABOM www.onelist.com/subscribe/Dnabom An examination of genetic evidence that Book of Mormon people originated from the Middle East. Microbiologists, geneticists, anthropologists, or any other "serious" pursuers of scientific evidence are invited to participate. List is closed to casual lurkers—even me. Members are expected to participate. For more information, www.latterdaylampoon.com/gazelem/dnabom.htm. 📖

Essays on the Gospel www.erols.com/crest/menu.htm An extensive collection of essays on a wide range of gospel topics, written by author Ron Cappelli. Contains more than 40 essays on the Foundation of Faith; the Plan of Salvation; the Nature of God, Man, and Heaven; and the Doctrines of Christ. Essays are thoughtful, but lack documentation. ★★

Foundation for Ancient Research and Mormon Studies farmsresearch.com FARMS is a nonprofit educational foundation that encourages and supports research about the Book of Mormon and other ancient scriptures independent of all other organizations. Research areas include ancient history, language, literature, culture, geography, politics, and law relevant to the scriptures. As a service to teachers and students of the scriptures, research results are distributed in both scholarly and popular formats. ★★★★★ ☑

Insights: An Ancient Window www.farmsresearch.com/insights/main.htm (See figure 13.5.) Information from the FARMS monthly newsletter. Book of Mormon research, scriptural history, Dead Sea Scrolls, much more. Excellent stuff. ★★★★★

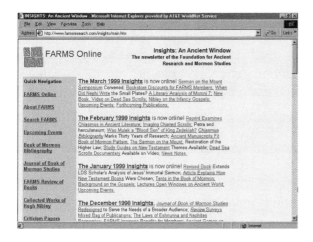

FIG. 13.5

FARMS: Ongoing research on Book of Mormon themes.

Is the Book of Mormon Derived from Modern Writings? www.jefflindsay.com/LDSFAQ/FQ_BMProb3.shtml Jeff Lindsay answers some of the more common charges made by anti-Mormon critics who insist that the Book of Mormon was a contemporary creation. ★★★

James E. Talmage Society—The Latter-day Saint Association of the Mathematical & Physical Scientists cpms.byu.edu/cpms/talmage The Latter-day Saint Association of the Mathematical and Physical Scientists (LAMPS). A group publishing information about LDS scientists and issues related to science and religion. Chatty. Science Departmental. Sometimes valuable. ★★★★

John Whitmer Historical Association www.sunflower.org/~tems03/jwhahp.htm An independent scholarly society housed at Graceland College, the RLDS educational institution. The Association is composed of individuals of various religious faiths who share "a lively interest" in the history of the Restoration Movement. Not much information available at this site. ★★

Marketplace of Ideas www.farmsresearch.com/transcripts/eyr-94.html On the work of FARMS and on the necessity of declaring the truth, by Elder Henry B. Eyring (October 13, 1994). ★★★

Mormon History Association www.mhahome.org An independent scholarly society composed of individuals of various religious faiths who share an interest in the history of the Restoration Movement. This page is small, but growing. ★★★

Mormonism Researched www.cyberhighway.net/~shirtail/mormonis.htm Kerry A. Shirts is the Samson of the Internet—long hair and all. How does anyone find the energy and strength to do this much research? Extensive materials on the Book of Abraham and the most comprehensive examination of the Facsimiles and their interpretations in the Book of Abraham on the Internet. You'll also find a large section of materials on the Book of Mormon, the Bible, and Church History. In all, about 11 gazillion scholarly research articles. One of the best places to learn about the LDS scriptures and the evidences for them. Some of the articles need editing. ★★★★★ ☑

Restoration in Light of the Testimony of History www.restorationhistory.com Researcher DaRell D. Thorpe discusses evidence for Christ's worldwide trek, and other items of interest to those who study the apostasy and the Restoration. The supposed trek is traced to early Christian beliefs that Christ went to other nations around the world. Considers other restored doctrines, rituals, and symbols through the centuries. Not tremendously scientific. ★★

SAMU-L This group is for more technical discussions about antiquities and how they relate to Mormonism. There are frequent discussions about the historical background of Mormon scriptures, archeology and the Book of Mormon, and historical symbols. Generally low in volume, and most posts contain quite a bit of information. To subscribe, send an e-mail request to *<pacal@bingvmb.cc. binghamton.edu>* or *<mraish@library.lib.binghamton.edu>* 📖

Second Coming of Christ Research Group users.aol.com/clintg777/private/ lastdays.html A cooperative Internet project working to develop a template, using LDS scriptures, for use with all last-day prophecies. The project is directed by Coloradoan Clint Gray and is presently rather difficult to read. ★★★

Works of Hugh Nibley www.math.byu.edu/~smithw/Lds/LDS/Hugh-Nibley Nibley's research on Book of Abraham topics. ★★★

SCIENCE AND RELIGION

For nearly 60 years, Dr. Richard T. Wootton (second president of the BYU-Hawaii Campus) has been researching Mormonism and scientists. In a recent "Life, the Universe, and Everything" presentation at BYU, Wootton, author of *Saints & Scientists* (EduTech, Mesa, Arizona, 1992), noted that on a per capita basis, Utah is the leading producer of scientists of any state in the Union and has been since at least 1938, when the statistics were first tracked.

In each case, Dr. Wootton found, Utah had more than double the average state production of scientists.

Dr. Wootton surveyed the Utah-produced scientists in 1955, and again in 1992, with the same questionnaire. Of the scientists produced in Utah, 76 percent were Latter-day Saints. Of that population of LDS scientists, 81 percent had "very strong convictions" of Mormonism (up from 38 percent in 1955).

The number of 1992 LDS scientists with No or Weak convictions was only a third of its 1955 percentage.

According to Dr. Wootton, almost all the recent group of Mormon scientists believe the Church was responsible for Utah's lead and contributed significantly to their own achievements. He said that 85 percent of self-described Strong Mormons believe they harmonize their religion and science.

At least two other studies have corroborated Dr. Wootton's findings. (Compiled from information provided by Lee Allred *<LeeX_Allred@ccm.ut.intel. com>*. Brother Allred, an organizer for the presentation, has just recently posted the data to his Web site at www.leeallred.com/utah_sci/utah_sci.htm.)

On the following Web sites, you'll discover what it is these LDS scientists and their armchair cheerleaders are doing:

HOTLINKS

EYRING-L
www.kingsleymc.com/Clark/Lists/eyring-l.html

FAQ: Evolution
www.frii.com/~allsop/eyring-l/faq/evolution

LDS Creation
members.aol.com/ldscreatio

Science and Religion
www.shire.net/mormon/science.html

Utah Produces More Scientists
www.leeallred.com/utah_sci/utah_sci.htm

Constancy in the Midst of Change   www.jefflindsay.com/entropy.html A discussion of entropy and the gospel, from Jeff Lindsay. Very thoughtful. ★★★

Creation   www.mormons.org/basic/gospel/creation All About Mormons' great collection of articles as diverse as Creation Accounts, Animals, Earth, Mankind, Matter, Origin of Man, Worlds, The Atonement, Evolution, and Kolob. ★★★★

Evolution: Introduction   www.cc.utah.edu/~skg5166/Contents.htm A tremendous collection of thoughts and analysis on a difficult subject. Well worth considering. ★★★★

EYRING-L   www.kingsleymc.com/Clark/Lists/eyring-l.html The Mormonism and Science List. Includes discussions on evolution, the ethics of various scientific techniques, and the interplay between scientific disciplines and religion. Subscribe with an e-mail request to *<majordomo@majordomo.netcom.com>* with the body `subscribe eyring-l` *<your@email.address>*. ★★★★

Faith and Reason—A Christian/LDS Perspective www.jefflindsay.com/Experiment.shtml Quotes and thoughts on how faith and reason mesh. Author Jeff Lindsay writes "Faith and reason need not be exclusive. Indeed, true faith is intelligent faith, and benefits from the intelligent application of the scientific method, in which hypotheses are tested and used as experimental stepping stones toward further knowledge." Worth considering. ★★★

Famous Latter-day Saint Scientists www.kingsleymc.com/Clark/Lists/Eyring/Eyring-l_Scientists.html Interesting commentaries on prominent LDS scientists. ★★★

> **ON SCIENCE AND RELIGION**
> My association with men of great learning in science and philosophy or in religion leads me to conclude that one's faith in spiritual matters is disturbed by his scientific or philosophical studies only because his knowledge in either or both science and religion is deficient.
>
> Harold B. Lee, Stand Ye In Holy Places, p. 74

FAQ: Evolution www.frii.com/~allsop/eyring-l/faq/evolution Frequently asked questions on the origin of man. An excellent resource for Saints who accept the theory of evolution and are attempting to reconcile it with faith and creation. Information collected by faithful members of the Eyring-L mailing list, a list for discussions pertaining to Mormonism & Science. See related FAQ on Science and Progress at www.frii.com/~allsop/eyring-l/faq/science. ★★★★

Great Quotes from Great Skeptics www.jefflindsay.com/SkepticQuotes.html "[W]hen the Paris Exhibition closes electric light will close with it and no more be heard of." Fifteen other equally insightful quotes to amuse you. ★★★

Is Human Population Really the Problem? www.jefflindsay.com/Overpop.shtml Jeff Lindsay's thoughts on the myth of the overpopulation crisis. ★★★

Lack of Design in Nature www.jefflindsay.com/DesignFlaws.shtml A response to those who would argue against a Creator based on the notion that organisms have design flaws. Well reasoned. ★★★

LDS Creation members.aol.com/ldscreatio For those who reject the theory of organic evolution and believe in divine creation. Regardless of where you stand on this particular question, this Web site will give you something to think about. Very well researched, very readable. ★★★★★

LDS Evidences www.geocities.com/Athens/Forum/5499/ldsstuff.html A collection of evidence supporting the doctrinal and historical claims of the Church. ★★★

LDS-PHIL   www.nd.edu/~rpotter An e-mail discussion group for the contemplation of philosophy of religion, philosophical theology, and others issues of religion and philosophy from within the context of Mormonism. Subscribe with an e-mail request to *<listserv@vma.cc.nd.edu>* and the message `subscribe lds-phil`. ★★

My Opinion: The Bursting of the Big Bang   www.jefflindsay.com/BigBang.shtml Jeff Lindsay's thoughts on the origin of the universe. Very brief. ★★

Physical and Mathematical Sciences: Quotes   www.byu.edu/tmcbucs/fc/ee/ds_pms.htm Part of BYU's Education for Eternity site, this page addresses questions of harmonizing science and religion, particularly with regard to the origin of man and the age of the earth. ★★★

Science and Religion   www.jefflindsay.com/MyLinks.shtml#scirel Jeff Lindsay's collection of links to great resources for believing scientists. ★★★

Science and Religion   www.shire.net/mormon/science.html Allen Leigh's new essay explaining why science and religion sometimes seem to conflict, and how Latter-day Saints should respond to apparent discrepancies. His views are worth understanding. ★★★★

Selected LDS Quotes on Evolution   www.cs.umd.edu/~seanl/Evolution.html A variety of quotes from official and semi-official sources supporting multiple points of view. ★★★

Utah Produces More Scientists   www.leeallred.com/utah_sci/utah_sci.htm Lee Allred has finally put this tremendous site on line. Read it and learn. ★★★★

THE CHURCH IN SOCIETY

The latter-day Church has had a tumultuous relationship with the world at large. At times, it's been a relationship of mistrust or worse. Other times, it's been entirely positive.

The Internet sites in this section examine politics and other social issues that receive a great deal of attention from Latter-day Saints.

Attitudes Toward Business and Wealth   www.mormons.org/daily/business Articles describing the Church's financial investments. ★★★

Attitudes Toward Health and Medicine   www.mormons.org/daily/health Articles describing LDS teachings about medicine and doctrinal issues. Includes

HOTLINKS

LDS-POLL.
<lds-poll@egroups.com>

Stop Dr. Death Home Page.
www.geocities.com/Athens/
Atlantis/8099

Teachings About Law.
www.mormons.org/basic/
doctrines/law

Teachings About Sexuality.
www.mormons.org/daily/sexuality

information on Attitudes Toward Health, Abortion, Abuse of Drugs, AIDS, Alcoholic Beverages and Alcoholism, Artificial Insemination, Autopsy, Birth Control, Blood Transfusions, Burial, Cremation, Hospitals, Organ Transplants and Donations, Materials for the Blind and Deaf, Maternity and Child Health Care, Medical Practices, and Word of Wisdom. A Mormons.Org page. ★★★

Congress   home.lv.rmci.net/jdstone/Congress.html A collection of contact addresses for the United States Congress. ★★★

Congress   www.erols.com/jdstone/Congress.html Online Contact Addresses for the United States Congress. ★★★

Congress Today   congress.nw.dc.us/rollcall Your congressman may not be in the yellow pages but he will be found here, as well as committee rosters, leadership, congressional officers, and Capitol Hill phone numbers. ★★★

Constitution and Mormonism   members.tripod.com/~runwin/gov.html Quotes from various Church leaders on the U.S. Constitution. 📖

False Gods We Worship   www.xmission.com/~dkenison/ lds/lds_quo/swk_fals.html An address by Spencer W. Kimball. 📖

LDS-POLL   www.egroups.com/list/LDS-poll/info.html The new address to join is *<lds-poll-subscribe@egroups.com>*. LDS Politics is a site to discuss politics and world events within the perspective of how faith as LDS and as Christians can and should be manifest in the public sphere. Very active. ★★★★

Military and the Church   www.mormons.org/basic/doctrines/military A collection of articles on the military and the Church, War and Peace, Chaplains, and Conscientious Objection. A Mormons.Org page. ★★

Mosiah 4:16–27   www.ricks.edu/ricks/employee/MARROTTR/Imparting%20Mosi%204.htm On imparting your substance to the poor. 📖

Politics   www.jefflindsay.com/MyLinks.shtml#pol Jeff Lindsay's collection of political links that will be of interest to many Latter-day Saints. A related link, Government, at www.jefflindsay.com/MyLinks.shtml#gov, is also worth considering. ★★★

Politics www.mormons.org/daily/politics Teachings of the Church with regard to political issues. Quotations, overviews, doctrine, and other resources on political issues and Mormonism. Articles cover D&C 134, Civic Duties, Church and State, Diplomatic Relations, Political Teachings, Political History, Political Culture, Contemporary American Politics, and The Council of Fifty. ★★★

Politics and the Church www.xmission.com/~dkenison/lds/lds_quo/fp_polit.html A 1996 Statement from the First Presidency. 📖

Relationships Between Man and the Earth www.shire.net/mormon/earth.html Thoughts on Environmentalism. ★★

Responsibilities of Citizenship, Provo 1994 www.xmission.com/~dkenison/lds/lds_quo/dho_free.html An address by Dallin H. Oaks. 📖

Social Issues www.jefflindsay.com/MyLinks.shtml#soc Jeff Lindsay's collection of links to resources on social issues—some of which are also doctrinal issues—that will be of interest to many Latter-day Saints. ★★★

Stop Dr. Death Home Page www.geocities.com/Athens/Atlantis/8099 An argument for life and against euthanasia. Includes bulletin board discussion areas. ★★★★

Teachings About Law www.mormons.org/basic/doctrines/law A collection of articles on LDS beliefs about civil law. Includes information on D&C 134, An Overview, Divine and Eternal Law, Constitutional Law, Constitution of the United States of America, Murder, Capital Punishment, and Civil Rights. A Mormons.Org site. ★★★★

Teachings About Sexuality www.mormons.org/daily/sexuality A collection of articles on various teachings about sexuality. Includes "Of Souls, Symbols, and Sacraments"; "A Parent's Guide"; Abortion; Adultery; Artificial Insemination; Birth Control; Law of Chastity; Homosexuality; and Sexuality. A Mormons.Org page. ★★★★

Thomas Legislative Information Online thomas.loc.gov:80 Find out about the current status of House Bills and what your favorite committee is doing about it. ★★★

U. S. Constitution and Mormonism members.tripod.com/runwin/gov.html An editorial on the role of the

---

ON POLITICS

Politics, as I have often said, are a great deal like the measles: The measles don't hurt very much, if you will take some saffron tea and keep them on the surface: but if they once set in they turn your hide yellow and you can't see straight. (laughter) And politics have more or less of the same effect. Let us keep politics on the surface, so far as any reformation is concerned, anything for the benefit of the people, for the advancement of the people, to help them to better serve God. We should not let politics interfere with anything of this kind.

Heber J. Grant, *Conference Report*, April 1911, p. 24

Church in the protection of the U.S. Constitution. Controversial, well-documented site includes links to talks and quotes from Church leaders and other sources of information. ★★★

We Will Still Weep for Zion   www.farmsresearch.com/nibley/v09.html A Hugh Nibley essay on serving man and mammon. ★★★

William H. King   eddy.media.utah.edu/ucme/k/KING,WILLIAM.html Biography of the leading organizer of the Democratic party in Utah. Biographies on other leading LDS Democrats, including Gunn McKay, Frank Moss, Governor Cal Rampton, Governor Scott Matheson, Abe Murdock, and William Orton. See index at eddy.media.utah.edu/ucme for other entries. See related site, **Mormon Democrats** at www.democratsabroad.org/oldnews/su98/editorial.asp, where Elder Marlin Jensen's call for political balance to ensure stability is lauded by the democrats. ★★★

Write   www.whitehouse.gov/WH/Welcome.html. Send an e-mail to the President of the United States at <*president@whitehouse.gov*>. Or visit the White House. ★★★

Yankee Go Home!   www.homestead.com/amerisaint This Latter-day Saint dislikes hyper-Americanism in the Church, and explains why. ★★★

DOCTRINAL ISSUES

This section examines most of the doctrinal issues that generate controversy among the Saints. For the most part, the content on these sites tends to be positive and thoughtful.

African Converts Without Baptism   advance.byu.edu/devo/98-99/LebaronF98.html E. Dale Lebaron talks about the Church history in Africa before the priesthood was granted to all worthy men. 📖

Arden's "Mormon Racism" FAQ   www.teleport.com/~arden/mormrace.htm A very intelligent, forthright response to questions about the priesthood issue. By Arden L. Eby. ★★★★

Baptism for the Dead   personal.pitnet.net/netty/scripturefiles/baptism4dead.html "Is vicarious baptism required to go from prison to paradise? This file addresses the question of whether or not a spirit currently in spirit prison must have vicarious baptism performed for him/her before they can enter into paradise, even if they have accepted the gospel as taught in the spirit world." ★★★

Blacks and the Priesthood   www.linkline.com/personal/ dcpyle/reading/Blksprst.htm An entirely different perspective on the priesthood issue, drawing parallels with ancient priesthood and proselyting prohibitions by D. Charles Pyle. Ain't free agency great? ★★★★

Bookman's Files on Mormoniana   webpages.marshall.edu/ ~brown/lds-lgb.html A large collection of articles on LDS history (succession in the first presidency, the endowment house, chronology of Church organization); doctrinal issues (fullness of the priesthood, calling and election made sure, second comforter, progression between kingdoms, the Father and the Son), study helps, talks (everlasting covenant, resurrection, begotten sons and daughters of God, Church of the First Born, women and the priesthood), and more. Author Lisle Brown seems to be the only Latter-day Saint undertaking the effort to post his talks. For the well grounded. Lots of meat, not much milk. ★★★★

Christ's Subordination to the Father in Early Christian Writings   ourworld.compuserve.com/homepages/ MGriffith_2/sonsub.htm "Christ's Subordination to the Father in Early Christian Writings" is an excerpt from Chapter 7 of Michael Griffith's book, *One Lord, One Faith: Writings of the Early Christian Fathers As Evidence of the Restoration.* ★★★

HOTLINKS

Arden's "Mormon Racism" FAQ. www.teleport.com/~arden/ mormrace.htm

Blacks and the Priesthood. www.linkline.com/personal/ dcpyle/reading/Blksprst.htm

Bookman's Files on Mormoniana. webpages.marshall.edu/~brown/ lds-lgb.html

Classics in LDS Doctrine. www.xmission.com/~dkenison/lds/ lds_quo

Question and Answer. www.mormons.org/qa

Relationship Between Us, Christ, and God. www.jefflindsay.com/LDSFAQ/ FQ_Relationships.shtml

Women Leaders and Priesthood Authority. coned.byu.edu/cw/cwwomens/ akapp.htm

Classics in LDS Doctrine   www.xmission.com/~dkenison/lds/lds_quo Collection of information from David Kenison. Includes various official proclamations, official statements, prophecies, apostolic addresses, and much more. Worthwhile reading. ★★★★

Creation   www.mormons.org/basic/gospel/creation Small collection of authoritative articles addressing Creationism. Includes information on Creation Accounts, Animals, Mankind, Worlds, and The Atonement. A Mormons.Org page. ★★★

Discussion of the Book of Hebrews and its Relationship to the Melchizidek Priesthood www.teleport.com/~arden/hebrews.htm Arden Eby's response to questions about transferability of priesthood. A bit obscure. ★★

Disputed Mormon Texts Archives www.sas.upenn.edu/~dbowie/dispute/dispute.html A depository for various texts that some have claimed are authentic Mormon texts and others claim are not. Mostly amusing. ★★★★

Doctrines of the Gospel www.mormons.org/basic/doctrines An eclectic collection of authoritative writings on popular gospel-related issues. Includes information on Accountability, Agency, Amen, Angels, Anti-Christs, Apostasy, Authority, Blasphemy, Calling and Election, Charity, Chastening, Commandments, Confession of Sins, Consecration, Contention, Covenants, Cursings, Source and History of Doctrine, Grace, Justice and Mercy, Teachings About Law, Martyrs, Military and the Church, Murder, Patriarchal Chain, Remission of Sins, Repentance, Revelation, Scriptural Writings, Sexuality, Soul, Spiritualism, Stillborn Children, Suicide, Temptation, Testimony, Testimony Bearing, and Unpardonable Sin. A Mormons.Org page. ★★★★★

Fall of Adam www.mormons.org/basic/gospel/fall An excellent collection of information related to the Fall. Includes articles on the Fall of Adam, LDS Sources, Ancient Sources, Adamic Language, Adam-ondi-Ahman, and the Atonement. A Mormons.Org page. ★★★★

FAQ: Medical Practices www.frii.com/~allsop/eyring-l/faq/med_practices Information collected by faithful members of the Eyring-L mailing list, a list for discussions pertaining to Mormonism & Science. ★★★

God the Father www.mormons.org/basic/godhead/father Doctrinal beliefs about God. Includes articles on An Overview of Beliefs About God the Father, Names and Titles of God the Father, The Glory of God, The Work and Glory of God, Mother in Heaven, and Ahman. A Mormons.Org page. ★★★★

God's Foreknowledge www.ricks.edu/ricks/employee/MARROTTR/God's%20Foreknowl %20etc%20wp35.htm Thoughts from Joseph F. Smith, Neal A. Maxwell. 📖

Grace, Works, and Eternal Life www.jefflindsay.com/faith_works.html The relationship among the principles. Well-written discourse with useful hyperlinked references. ★★★

Is Baptism Necessary for Salvation? ourworld.compuserve.com/homepages/ MGriffith_2/baptism.htm "Is Baptism Necessary for Salvation" is an excerpt from

Chapter 34 of Michael Griffith's book, *One Lord, One Faith: Writings of the Early Christian Fathers As Evidence of the Restoration.* ★★★

Issue of Race   www.jefflindsay.com/LDSFAQ/FQRace.shtml History of the priesthood issue, responses to questions about racism. Lots of documentation, but Arden Eby's "Mormon Racism" site (page 360) is a bit better. ★★★

Mansion House Library   www.nauvoo.com/library Author Orson Scott Card holds forth on homosexuality, the historicity of the Book of Mormon, the problem of evil, prophets, and the origin of pre-Columbian people. The essay on Consecration will undoubtedly cause you to rethink your mortgage. These essays, along with the contents of Brother Card's irregular *Vigor* e-zine (www.nauvoo.com/vigor/index.html) ought to be required reading for every Latter-day Saint. ★★★★★

Masonry and Mormonism: The Differences   www.teleport.com/~arden/mason.htm A respectful discussion about how the endowment differs from the Masonic ceremony, with an examination of the root of similarities. Includes a good reading list. ★★★

Michael Griffith's "Real Issues" Homepage ourworld.compuserve.com/ homepages/MGriffith_2 The LDS Information link contains numerous essays, including Which Church is Right? Basic LDS Doctrines and History, Evidences of the Restoration, and more. Also on the Real Issues page find information on creation vs. evolution. ★★★

> And the disciples came, and said unto him, Why speakest thou unto them in parables?
>
> He answered and said unto them, Because it is given unto you to know the mysteries of the kingdom of heaven, but to them it is not given.
>
> Matthew 13:10–11

Mormon Origins   www.xmission.com/~research/about A collection of controversial historical documents maintained by H. Michael Marquardt. (Find responses to Marquardt's several books at FARMS www.farmsresearch.com.) Documents found here include a bibliography; Books Owned by Joseph Smith; Egyptian Alphabet and Grammar; Family of Joseph Smith, Sr.; Family of Joseph Smith, Jr.; 1823 Assessment Roll; 1826 Bill of Justice; Albert Neely; Affidavit of Isaac Hale (1834); Interview of Martin Harris (1859); Joseph Smith Jr.'s first recorded revelation (1828); Independence Temple of Zion; *Inventing Mormonism: Tradition and the Historical Record;* Journal entries of November–December 1832 by Joseph Smith; List—Early Documents Relating to Joseph Smith, Jr. (1825–1831); News items; Patriarchal Blessings; Some Interesting Notes on Succession at Nauvoo in 1844; Visual Images of Joseph Smith; and Writings of Joseph Smith. Sorely lacks images or other documentation that would lend credibility. ★

Necessity of Priesthood Authority ourworld.compuserve.com/homepages/MGriffith_2/priest.htm "Necessity of Priesthood Authority" is an excerpt from Chapters 19 and 20 of Michael Griffith's book, *One Lord, One Faith: Writings of the Early Christian Fathers As Evidence of the Restoration.* ★★★

On Dealing with Uncertainty www.lib.ricks.edu/reserve/coatesl/bx8613h87.htm What historians should understand when writing histories. A Brigham Young University devotional address, by Bruce C. Hafen, president of Ricks College, delivered January 9, 1979. ★★★

Prophetic References to the Signs of the Last Days members.xoom.com/mdalby This site by Mark Dalby features many links highlighting the signs of the last days. Included are links to headlines, prophecy photos and maps, last-days parables, and more. ★★★

Question and Answer www.mormons.org/qa Real questions about problematic and difficult doctrines, posed by members and nonmembers. Growing. ★★★★★

Questions about the LDS Temple and Masonry www.jefflindsay.com/LDSFAQ/FQ_masons.shtml Very long, very thorough investigation into similarities between Free Masonry and the LDS endowment. By Jeff Lindsay. ★★★

Relationship Between Us, Christ, and God www.jefflindsay.com/LDSFAQ/FQ_Relationships.shtml Answers to common questions about the LDS understanding of God. Responds to: Do you believe that Jesus is your elder brother? Do you believe that Christ and Satan are brothers? Was God once man like us? Did God once have a heavenly father like we have him now? Do you think God and Christ are different beings and that Christ "progressed"? Aren't God and Christ one? If you believe the Father and the Son are separate beings, doesn't that make you polytheistic? Do Mormons believe they will become perfect and that they will be gods? Didn't Joseph Smith even say that he was greater than Jesus? Isn't belief in an anthropomorphic God unchristian? Do Mormons worship Adam? Have they ever? Did Brigham Young deny the miraculous birth of Christ? Quality of responses is generally, but not always, pretty good. ★★★★

Teachings About Children www.mormons.org/basic/family/children Articles about children and the Church. Includes information on Caring for the Souls of Children, The Role of Children in the Church, Born in the Covenant, Adoption of Children, Blessing of Children, and Salvation of Children. A Mormons.Org page. ★★★

Teachings About the Holy Ghost   www.mormons.org/basic/godhead/holy_ghost A collection of articles on the subject of the Holy Ghost. Includes information on Always Have His Spirit, His Peace, The Holy Ghost, An Overview, The Holy Spirit of Promise, The Gift of the Holy Ghost, Gifts of the Spirit, Baptism of Fire and the Holy Ghost, Spirit of Prophecy, Confirmation, and The Sign of the Dove. A Mormons.Org page. ★★★★

The Mormon God and the Problem of Evil   www.teleport.com/~arden/evilfaq.htm Brother Eby posits that only Mormonism has a valid response to the fundamental question of why God permits bad things to happen. ★★★

The Unwritten Order of Things   www.geocities.com/Heartland/Acres/1756/packer.html Elder Boyd K. Packer's well-known talk. Are you familiar with the ordinary things about the Church that every member should know? Here is the information you won't find in a handbook. 📖

True Church and Additional Scripture   ourworld.compuserve.com/homepages/ MGriffith_2/addscrip.htm "The True Church and Additional Scripture" is an excerpt from Chapter 28 of Michael Griffith's book, *One Lord, One Faith: Writings of the Early Christian Fathers As Evidence of the Restoration.* ★★★

What We Believe   advance.byu.edu/devo/97-98/MilletW98.html Robert L. Millet was dean of Religious Education and professor of ancient scripture at BYU when he gave this devotional address in the Marriott Center on February 3, 1998. In it, he explains the Latter-day Saint position on additional scripture, men and women becoming like God, salvation by grace, and Mormons as Christians. ★★★

Women Leaders and Priesthood Authority   coned.byu.edu/cw/cwwomens/akapp.htm Ardeth Greene Kapp's 1998 Women's Conference address. ★★★

Work on the Sabbath   www.cybcon.com/~kurtn/sabbath.txt Quotes and scriptures addressing keeping the Sabbath day holy. 📖

COMPARATIVE THEOLOGY

In the following list you'll find a number of resources comparing Latter-day Saint beliefs with the beliefs of other faiths. As in the previous section, authors of these sites tend to be positively enthusiastic about the gospel.

Adherents www.adherents.com Preston Hunter's AMAZING collection of comparative figures for nearly every religious movement on—or off—the planet. This is the Louvre of religious stats. (And here's an eye-opener: Feeling patriotic? Maybe a little TOO patriotic? The entries under Americanism and Amway should brighten your day.) ★★★★★ ☑

Arden Eby's Religious Studies Center www.teleport.com/ ~arden/religium.htm A phenomenal collection of links, categorized into Philosophy, General Christianity, Early Christianity, Medieval Christianity, Reformation Studies, Anglicanism, Mormonism, Judaism, Islam, World Religions, General Religion, and Anti-Religious Servers. Brother Eby is a Latter-day Saint, and this collection is world class. Unfortunately, it's not maintained as frequently as one would like, and several of the links have expired. ★★★

Are You Saved? www.jefflindsay.com/grace_def.shtml A well-written discourse on LDS belief in the New Testament doctrine of salvation. ★★★

Buddhism millennium.fortunecity.com/bertisevil/375/buddhism.htm An LDS perspective on Buddhism by Spencer J. Palmer. ★★★

Church of Christ, Restored members.aol.com/hopeofzion The Church of Christ Restored, Lawton, Michigan, traces its authority back to 1830. ★★★

Church of Christ, Temple Lot church-of-christ.com The Church of Christ (Temple Lot) Independence, Missouri. These are the folks who presently own the patch of land in Independence that the Prophet dedicated for a temple. ★★★

Confucianism millennium.fortunecity.com/bertisevil/375/confcnsm.htm Confucianism article by Spencer J. Palmer. 📖

Faith, Grace, and Works www.vt.edu:10021/B/bbickmor/ECFGW.html The similarities and differences between LDS doctrine and the beliefs of most Protestants. Evidence that the earliest Christian writers unanimously supported the LDS view. 📖

Frequently Asked Questions www.mormons.org/faq Addresses questions about basic beliefs of the Church, as compared to teachings of other religious traditions. Responds to What is "Mormonism"? What does LDS stand for? Are Mormons Christian? Do Mormons believe in the Bible? Do Mormons believe in the Trinity? How is LDS theology different from that of other Christians? What are some distinctive LDS teachings? Do Mormons believe in the virgin birth? Why don't Mormons have crosses on their buildings and temples? What is the LDS conception of Hell? Also responds to Who was Joseph Smith? Who are your present Church leaders? Can you help me with Family History (or genealogy) research? What are some common policies, practices, and procedures of the Church? Do Mormons worship Joseph Smith? Why did the true Church of Christ need to be restored? Can Mormons have more than one wife? Why is a temple recommend necessary to enter the temple? What is the role of women in Mormon society? Do Latter-day Saints date outside the faith? Do Mormons celebrate holidays and birthdays? What are the Church's policies on divorce? Are Church leaders considered infallible and free from error? Do Mormons wear special undergarments? Do Mormons believe that God is married? ★★★★

Interfaith Relationships www.mormons.org/daily/interfaith A collection of articles on the Church's relationship with other faiths. Includes articles under the headings of Christianity, Judaism, and Other Faiths. Very extensive, and covers most prominent religious faiths. A Mormons.Org site. ★★★★★

Questions About Salvation and Exaltation www.jefflindsay.com/LDSFAQ/ FQ_Salvation.shtml Responds to questions about commandments and works, Mormon exclusivity, attaining godhood, and instant salvation. Fair amount of documentation. ★★★

Relationship Between Faith, Works and Salvation www.jefflindsay.com/ faith_works.html A supplemental list of related scriptures is located at www. jefflindsay.com/faith_works_list.html. Are biblical and LDS views compatible? A well-documented discourse on the subject. ★★★

Religion www.davidwiley.com/religion.html Great list of links to religious and sacred texts. If someone considers it sacred, it's probably here. ★★★

Religious and Sacred Texts webpages.marshall.edu/~wiley6/rast.htmlx A collection of links to religious texts for all major world religious traditions. ★★

Reorganized Church of Jesus Christ of Latter Day Saints www.rlds.org The more Trinitarian form of Mormonism. A well-done page explaining RLDS theology. ★★★★

Restoration Theology   www.sas.upenn.edu/~dbowie/restore/restoration.html A guide to churches claiming Joseph Smith as founder. A bit out of date, but site author David Bowie did his homework. An excellent compilation. ★★★

Restoration.org   www.Restoration.org Good site with a wealth of early LDS history, as well as history from other Restoration groups (see figure 13.6). Excellent resources, many of which take a perversely Strang-ite point of view. Take a deep breath and plunge in. ★★★★

True and Living Church of Jesus Christ   www.tlcmanti.org The Manti, Utah, breakaway sect. Once a source of good documents, this page now contains just a warning. ★★

Which Is the "True" Christian Church?   religioustolerance.org/chr_true.htm This very popular, very much NOT an LDS site, questions which Church, if any, is true, and logically examines all the possibilities. Interestingly, it arrives at no conclusion. More interestingly, it leaves open the very real possibility that the correct answer is Mormonism. ★★★

Who Holds the Keys? (Pope or Prophet?)   www.vt.edu:10021/B/bbickmor/rc_dex.html Barry Bickmore takes on Steve Clifford, a Roman Catholic (and former Latter-day Saint), on the issue of the apostasy. Did the authority of the Apostles continue in Catholicism or did a total apostasy occur, necessitating a Restoration through the Prophet Joseph Smith? Both LDS and Roman Catholic readers will be encouraged by the friendly tone of the debate. ★★★★

FIG. 13.6

Restoration.org: God Be with You 'Til We Meet Again.

14

ENDURE
TO THE END

When I first discovered the World Wide Web, I thought it would be a fine thing to build a Web site on Mormonism. But as I began gathering a few links, I soon discovered that all the simple things I'd originally thought to include on my site had already been done—and done much better than I ever could have done myself. As I continued to explore, though, I found that the topics of most interest to me personally—journalism, LDS journal-keeping, and personal histories— weren't represented at all. I limited my site building strictly to information on these closely related topics, and quickly filled several pages.

Want to build a Web page of your own? As an online community, Latter-day Saints do some things very well, as this book has shown. When it comes to building Church-related Web sites, we're particularly good at the Book of Mormon, genealogy, the Young Women's program, Single Adults, and Scouting. We don't lack Web sites that respond to critics, that promote commercial products, or that describe the fundamentals of the Church. Sites on the better-known aspects of Church history abound. Those tend to be the easy topics, the ones that get rebuilt by every new, enthusiastic Webmaster.

> Wherefore, if ye shall be obedient to the commandments, and endure to the end, ye shall be saved at the last day. And thus it is. Amen.
>
> 1 Nephi 22:31

Unfortunately, we're not quite so prolific about some other aspects of the gospel that really need to be represented.

WHAT'S MISSING

Here's a quick list of subjects that are under-addressed by LDS Web site builders. If you have a personal interest in any of the following areas, you'd do the online world a good turn by building a Web site addressing the topic.

Jesus Christ
Atonement
Plan of Salvation
Role of Christ
Life and Mission of Christ
Nature of God
Godhead

Worship
Tithing
Individual temples
Prayer
Baptism
Personal Revelation, the Gift of the
    Holy Ghost
Service
Repentance
Faith
Priesthood

History
Conversion stories
History of the 20th-century
    Church
Journal-keeping, personal family his-
    tories
Ohio period of the Church
Restoration—tracing prophecies,
    apostasy, enlightenment, Restora-
    tion
The Endowment House

Visitors' Centers/Church Historical
    Sites

Missionary
Interfaith Relationships—sites
    describing the similarities of belief
    between the restored gospel and
    other religious traditions.
Crisis of Faith—prayerful, loving sup-
    port for Saints dealing with issues
    that weaken their faith. Anytime
    we bear one another's burdens, we
    follow the Lord's admonition to
    "feed my sheep."
Order of Services—how Latter-day
    Saints meet, what to wear, a begin-
    ner's guide to being a Latter-day
    Saint.

Auxiliaries
Helps for ward music people—how to
    conduct choir
Young Men's Program
Helps for stake missionaries

Leadership
Church welfare program/Bishop's
    storehouse, etc.
Leadership in-service
Public information from the General
    Handbook of Instructions

Teacher development

Families

Family Activities

Marriage Issues—support for Saints dealing with spousal inactivity, interfaith marriage, spousal substance abuse, and other difficulties

Family Histories—beyond genealogy, the online community is the perfect place to share stories of faith, conversion stories, family photos, and other information that can build family ties for far-flung families

Advice Pages—for parents of infants, children, teens

Resources for Men—fathering, employment

Provident Living—financial tools, paying tithing

Guidelines for Families

Practice

Roadshows and other nonbasketball programs for youth

Senior Saints—including Missions for retired Saints

International, Non-English-Language Sites

Ward Activities

Fellowshipping

Health and Fitness

Professional advice for Latter-day Saints: medical and dental, legal, financial, counseling, educational, career, relationships

More Volunteer Opportunities

Primary/Secondary Schools

Role of the Book of Mormon

If you're ready to build a site of your own, here are suggestions for how to proceed. First, talk to your Internet service provider—whether it's a commercial provider such as America Online, or a dedicated Internet service provider—to find out how much disk space is available to you on your provider's server. Typically, if you're an individual user, you'll be allowed about five megabytes of storage space at no charge. If the disk space allowance is considerably smaller, you'll need to plan the material you'll include on your site carefully. With less than, say, one megabyte of storage space, you'll really feel the pinch when it comes to space-consuming graphics and audio files.

If your own Web space is limited, if you don't have an ISP, if you're considering changing ISPs, or if you don't have the tools or experience to build your own Web site yet, you'll want to consider one of the hundreds of free Web space services on the Internet. Many of them come with built-in Web-building tools, some provide unlimited Web space, and others provide e-mail and other services.

Free Web Sites

Here's where you should go to find free Web space.

Build Your Own Web Site www.writerspost.com/testify/buildit.htm Reviews of various free Web space tools. ★★★

Free Webspace.Net www.freewebspace.net Searchable guide to more than 300 free Web space providers. If you want a free Web site or more free space for your homepage, this is the place. The providers listed on this site will host your site absolutely free or give you a free e-mail address. You will also find reviews of some of these sites. ★★★★★

Once you know your limitations, consider your commitment. If you're really dedicated to maintaining the site, you'll want to contemplate getting a dedicated domain name. The domain is your location on the World Wide Web. For example, in the Church's address, www.lds.org, the "lds.org" portion is the domain name. When you have a name of your own, you're not stuck with your Internet service provider for life. If you ever change Internet service providers, you can take the name with you and your readers won't have to hunt for you. It's entirely optional, of course, but at a cost of about $70 to start, and $35 a year to keep, the domain name can be a permanent home for your Web site, even if you change service providers, or move to the other side of the world. You can do a search for available domain names, and find more information about naming, at www.simplenet.com/ whois.html.

Third, create a rough plan for your site. Think in terms of a hierarchical structure, with a top, or "cover," page. This top page is a combination magazine cover and table of contents, with links to all the other pages on your site. As you develop additional areas of interest over time, the new pages will retain a central link, keeping it all in the family.

Finally, start with what you know. The first page on your Web site, after the top page, should be your personal and family pages. Involve the entire family. Encourage each family member to contribute to a family page. If you have access to a scanner (they can be purchased for as little as $70 if you shop carefully), scan in the artwork of your younger children. Use your site as a place to build a family history. Scan in vacation pictures, keep a family journal, create a family logo. Let every family member keep separate pages. Have fun with it.

Build separate pages where you record information of a more solemn, sacred nature. Describe your conversion to the gospel of Christ. Share the joy you've found in your membership in the Church. Tell visitors to your page about how the gospel affects your life. When you're ready, consider building a page that focuses on your favorite gospel topics. Be careful not to violate copyright law, but do include summaries of and reports on doctrinal material.

Avoid the temptation to produce nothing but a list of links to other sites. Instead, add some original content.

When you're finished with your site, be sure to submit it to several search engines so that other Internet users will be able to find it.

And of course, don't forget to submit it to the *Mormons on the Internet* submission site! Go to www.writerspost.com/mormonnet/submit.htm to add your own site to the list.

Submission Services

Manually adding your site to the hundreds of search engines on the Internet can be extremely time consuming. Instead, use one of these great tools to submit simultaneously to multiple search engines.

Addme!   www.addme.com Submit your Web site to more than 30 search engines for free. ★★★

Easy Submit   www.scrubtheweb.com/abs/promo.html Submit to 28 engines. The helpful instructions and explanations here make this my favorite. ★★★★

Mormons on the Internet **Submissions**   www.writerspost.com/mormonnet/submit.htm Add your own LDS site and see it appear immediately. ★★★★★

PostMaster 2   www.netcreations.com/postmaster/registration/try.html Post to two dozen popular sites. ★★★

Site Owner   www.siteowner.com Submit to seven search engines with a single query. ★★★

Submissions.com   businessweb.com.au/add-it/free Trial software adds your site to more than 1000 search engines. But you've got to download and install the software first. Overly complicated. ★★

Now you've done it. A Web site of your very own. Welcome to the LDS Internet!

BEST LDS RESOURCES ON THE NET

This book wouldn't be complete unless we provided a rundown of the best LDS sites on the Internet. The top 20 list from the last edition has grown to 25 can't-miss sites, plus a list of honorable mentions.

Two super-sites are not even on the list because they're such obvious keepers. Number one, the **Church's official Web site** at www.lds.org, where you'll find a growing collection of resources for missionary work, family history, and Church publications.

The other is the **Mormons on the Internet Web site** at www.writerspost.com/mormonnet. There you'll get access to all the Web sites listed in this book, as well as a search engine, and a newsletter that describes new additions to the site.

Here, in order, are the 25 best sites on the LDS Internet:

Top Twenty-Five Sites

The 25 Best LDS-oriented sites on the Internet, in order are the *rest* of the top LDS:

1. **FamilySearch** www.familysearch.org Who ever thought this day would come? The site is incredible, and it is, I suspect, the real reason we humans have made any technological progress in recent years. Nah, I don't just suspect it. You can quote me! Go here, find your ancestors, learn what your third cousin Beulah discovered about your Grandpa Wild Bill. Now you know how to contact Cousin Beulah, and you know where to get started finding Grandpa Bill's wild father. Did I mention that this is now the best site on the Internet? The numbers back me up. You'll also find a free copy of the new Windows edition of Personal Ancestral File www.familysearch.org/OtherResources/paf4, which makes the site particularly attractive. (See related sites in chapter 8: "Genealogy.") FamilySearch is the new Only-Site-On-The-Web-To-Receive-This-Rating site. ★★★★★★ ☑

2. **All About Mormons** www.mormons.org John Walsh's very large site containing texts on virtually anything anyone has ever wanted to know about Mormonism. It's, ahem, encyclopedic in its coverage. In fact, it makes extensive use of the *Encyclopedia of Mormonism* and a few other classic Mormon texts. Good information. I'd be happy to see it stay around. (See related sites in chapter 4: "Links to Links"; chapter 6: "Items of Interest to Investigators and New Members"; and Chapter 7: "Texts.") ★★★★★ ☑

3. **LDS-SEMINAR** www.cybcon.com/~kurtn/exegesis.html Commentary on each week's Gospel Doctrine lesson. The posts are open to exegesis, textual analysis, historical issues pertinent to the context or application of the scriptures, life applications, and "likening the scriptures unto us" issues. Includes regular columns, plus postings from other participants. To subscribe, send a message to <*majordomo@LDSchurch.net*> with the message subscribe ldss

<yourname@your.email.address> or the digest version `subscribe ldss-d` *<yourname@your.email.address>*. (See related sites in chapter 9: "E-mail Lists"; chapter 10: "Sunday School Resources"; chapter 11: "Teacher Resources"; and chapter 12: "Study Resources for Multiple Books of Scripture.") ★★★★★ ☑

4. **Nick Literski's Latter-day Saint Temple Home Page** www.vii.com/ ~nicksl From the opening hymn ("The Spirit of God Like a Fire Is Burning") to the closing links, there's not a better place in the world for understanding the temple. The site includes temple dedicatory prayers, photos, plans for new temples, and talks and documents related to LDS temples. Be sure to read Nick's newest link: Letters from Visitors to the Home Page. (See related sites in chapter 8: "About Temples.") ★★★★★ ☑

5. **LDS-GEMS** www.lds-gems.com The best mailing list on the Web. If you have e-mail access, you need to sign up. Daily traffic is about five messages, which includes 150 Years Ago Today, LDS news, stories from Church history, messages from general authorities, and inspiring subscriber submissions. Recently introduced commercial bits make it slightly less valuable, but the content is excellent nonetheless. (See related sites in chapter 7: "Inspiration"; and chapter 9: "E-mail Lists.") ★★★★★ ☑

6. **FARMS** www.farmsresearch.com FARMS is a nonprofit educational foundation that encourages and supports research about the Book of Mormon and other ancient scriptures, independent of all other organizations. Research areas include ancient history, language, literature, culture, geography, politics, and law relevant to the scriptures. As a service to teachers and students of the scriptures, research results are distributed both in scholarly and popular formats. (See related sites in chapter 6: "Response To Critics of the Church"; and chapter 13: "Research Organizations.") ★★★★★ ☑

7. **SEMINARY** www.listservice.net/seminary Lesson ideas for teaching seminary, institute, or any other level. Inspiring. A really first-class, useful list. Send your subscription request to *<majordomo@listservice.net>*. (See related sites in chapter 9: "E-mail Lists"; and chapter 10: "Seminary Resources.") ★★★★★ ☑

8. **Affinity LDS Chat** affinity.faithweb.com Graphical, interactive Web site. This is the community of the future. Go swimming, dance, play laser tag, have pizza; Monthly socials; Youth Den with music and munchies; and lots more. Java-enabled browsers are OK. I'm very impressed. (See related sites in chapter 9: "Chat Areas"; chapter 10: "Young Single Adults"; chapter 11: "Youth"; and chapter 11: "Dating Resources for Single Adults.") ★★★★★ ☑

9. **Mormon Town** www.mormontown.org It takes a village . . . to justify spending hours on the Internet. Here's your village. Larry Barkdull's site is a

must-mark. The commercial bits are a disappointment, but if they fund the rest of the site, they're worth putting up with. It's the Church Lessons that propel this into the top ten. (See related resources in chapter 4: "People Finders"; and chapter 11: "Teacher Resources," plus links throughout this text to various Mormontown sub pages.) ★★★★★ ☑

10. **Testify!** www.writerspost.com/testify Conversion stories. Arranged by contemporary individuals, historical individuals, contemporary collections, and historical collections. It's my own page, but I'm tremendously fond of it, and give it a correspondingly high rating. (See related sites in chapter 6: "Testimonies"; and chapter 8: "Temple Experiences.") ★★★★★ ☑

11. **Seniors** www.lds.net/ldslife/elderly An LDS community for senior Saints. Dating ideas, grandparenting, volunteering, share your testimony, resources and links for seniors, and a senior chat room. (See related sites in chapter 11: "Resources for Seniors.") ★★★★★ ☑

12. **GospeLibrary.Com** www.gospelibrary.com Search the scriptures online, along with the Topical Guide and the Inspired Version of the Bible. The Topical Guide makes this site a treasure, as do the Gospel Classics and the seven-volume history of the Church. (See related sites in chapter 4: "Links to Links"; chapter 7: "Online Texts"; and chapter 7: "Scriptures Online.") ★★★★★ ☑

13. **HTVT Web Site** members.tripod.com/~hometeaching Dedicated to improving home and visiting teaching. Mailing list, resources, links, ideas, and experiences. Submit ideas of your own. Phenomenal. (See related sites in chapter 10: "Priesthood"; and chapter 10: "Relief Society.") ★★★★★ ☑

14. **MORMON-NEWS** www.panix.com/~klarsen/mormon-news A mailing list for news of the Church. Average daily volume: eight messages. Digest version available. Subscribe by sending an e-mail request to <*majordomo@mailinglist.net*> containing the message `subscribe mormon-news`. (See related sites in chapter 9: "E-mail Lists" and chapter 9: "Recent News of the Church.") ★★★★★ ☑

15. **BYU Continuing Education** coned.byu.edu Home study, travel study, education week, bachelor's degrees, conferences and workshops, more. An excellent resource. (See related sites in Chapter 7: "Continuing Education.") ★★★★★ ☑

16. **Nauvoo** www.nauvoo.com Once upon a time, Nauvoo was a forum on AOL. Now everyone can participate—and should. This is easily the best discussion place on the World Wide Web. Orson Scott Card's sponsorship gives it cachet; his *Vigor* newsletter gives it substance. Follow the links to the kids' forum, the Red Brick Store, the Mansion House library, and more. It's the *Vigor* publication, along with the great bulletin board, that make this an

especially memorable site. (See related sites in chapter 4: "People Finders"; and chapter 9: "Web Discussion Areas.") ★★★★★ ☑

17. **Jeff Lindsay's Cracked Planet** www.jefflindsay.com Scores of articles responding to critics of the Church, examining science and the gospel, and more. This is a phenomenal effort. (See related sites in chapter 4: "Links to Links.") ★★★★★ ☑

18. **Barry's Early Christianity and Mormonism Page** www.vt.edu:10021/B/ bbickmor/EC.html A very large collection with many essays showing that LDS theology is much closer to early Christianity than is modern orthodox Christianity. Addresses apostasy, cosmology, requirements for salvation, the temple, references, resources, and more. (See related sites in chapter 13: "The New Testament Church"; and Chapter 13: "Researchers.") ★★★★★ ☑

19. **Mormonism Researched** www.cyberhighway.net/~shirtail/mormonis.htm Kerry Shirts' apologetics site. It ain't pretty, but it's smart. (See related sites in chapter 6: "Responses to Critics of the Church"; chapter 12: "Responses to Critics of the Book of Mormon"; and chapter 13: "Researchers.") ★★★★★ ☑

20. **AML-List** cc.weber.edu/~byparkinson/aml-list.html List of LDS and LDS-affiliated publications. The Mormon literature mailing list. View a list of newspapers at cc.weber.edu/~byparkinson/aml-list.html#newspapers. A list of LDS journals is maintained at cc.weber.edu/~byparkinson/aml-list.html#journals. Webmaster Benson Parkinson does a great job of keeping these lists up to date. (See related sites in chapter 9: "Print Publications"; chapter 9: "E-mail Lists"; and chapter 12: "Mormon Arts and Letters.") ★★★★★ ☑

21. **LDS Deaf Connection** www.gutches.net/ldc A tremendously well-done site with helpful resources for deaf members. Features include a message board, news, visitors center, and mission information. (See related sites in chapter 11: "Disability, Medical and Counseling Resources.") ★★★★★ ☑

22. **Christy's Primary Art** www.crosswinds.net/~christy/New_Main_Page.html Phenomenal. There's nothing missing. Art, lessons, sharing time, games, international stuff, coloring pages, primary nursery, songs. . . . This site is amazing. It seems to have two home pages, though, so try pw2.netcom.com/ pesukone/primary_art.html if you have trouble. (See related sites in chapter 10: "Primary, Relief Society, and Young Women's Resources"; and chapter 11: "Ward Newsletter Editor.") ★★★★★ ☑

23. **Women's Conference** coned.byu.edu/cw/womens.htm Transcripts from recent BYU Women's Conferences. Addresses by prominent women in the Church. Very nicely done. (See related sites in chapter 7: "Talks"; and chapter 11: "Women's Resources.") ★★★★★ ☑

24. **BYU Devotional and Fireside Speeches** advance.byu.edu/devo.html A listing of the devotional and fireside speeches available at this Web site.

Includes talks by President Hinckley, Elder Packer, LeGrand Richards, Elder Holland, Hugh Nibley, Elaine Jack, and many more. (See related resources in chapter 7: "Talks.") ★★★★★ ☑

25. **Mormon's Story** www.enoch.com/voicesfromdust/mormonstory/mormonstory.html
The text of the Book of Mormon in a simpler English. While I'm a great fan of reading scriptures in their original form, I'm an even greater fan of understanding the scriptures—in whatever form generates understanding. Timothy Wilson's rewrite of the Book of Mormon is beautifully done, and it's all available online, at this Web site. If this is the kind of simplification it takes to get a child or a new reader through the Book of Mormon, it's a worthwhile venture. (See related resources in chapter 7: "Book of Mormon Online"; and Chapter 12: "Book of Mormon Study Tools.") ★★★★★ ☑

Honorable Mentions

The next-best sites on the Internet, all of them keepers. Here are the 15 *Mormons on the Internet* honorable mentions.

Adherents www.adherents.com Preston Hunter's AMAZING collection of comparative figures for nearly every religious movement on—or off—the planet. This is the Louvre of religious stats. (And here's an eye-opener: Feeling patriotic? Maybe a little TOO patriotic? The entries under Americanism and Amway should brighten your day.) (See related resources in chapter 13: "Comparative Theology.") ★★★★★ ☑

Cyndi's List of Genealogy Links www.CyndisList.com Perhaps the best-planned, most thorough noncommercial site on the entire Internet. More than 22,000 genealogy sites categorized into 70-some categories, including adoption; biographies; books; microfilm and microfiche; cemeteries; funeral homes and obituaries; census-related sites worldwide; events and activities; family bibles; handy online starting points; heraldry; historical events and people; hit a brick wall?; how to; LDS and family history centers; medieval; genealogy home page construction kit; photographs and memories; preserving your family's treasures; stories and genealogical research; professional researchers; volunteers and other research services; software and computers; terms, phrases, dictionaries, and glossaries; and sites for every region; country; and U.S. state. (See related sites in chapter 8: "Genealogy.") ★★★★★ ☑

FAIR www.fair-lds.org The Foundation for Apologetic Information and Research. FAIR is a nonprofit apologetic organization formed in late 1997 by a group of

LDS defenders of the faith who frequented the America Online Mormonism message boards. The group is dedicated to providing solid, well-documented answers to critics of LDS doctrine, faith, and practice. Provides front-line apologetics and answers to anti-Mormon attacks on the doctrine of the Church. The "About Us" section at www.fair-lds.org/AboutUs/AboutUs.html alone is worth memorializing. (See related sites in chapter 6: "Responses to Critics.") ★★★★★ ☑

Gospel Doctrine Class members.tripod.com/~beardall/gospdoct.html Notes and quotes from the Gospel Doctrine class taught in Sunday School. Handouts, lesson schedules, history, and more for a ward in Federal Way, Washington. Tremendous! (See related sites in chapter 10: "Sunday School"; and chapter 11: "Resources for Teachers.") ★★★★★ ☑

Hill Cumorah www.canaltown.net/hillcumorah Historic sites around Palmyra. Includes photos and histories. (See related resources in chapter 13: "History of the Church in New York.") ★★★★★ ☑

Home and Visiting Teaching Resource Page www.absolutesaint.com/resources/htvt.html Absolutely great. Mailing list. Talks. Scriptures. Tips. Resources. Daily reminders. This one's a keeper. (See related sites in chapter 10: "Priesthood, and Relief Society Resources.") ★★★★★ ☑

Ideas for Young Men Mutual Activities nauvoo.byu.edu/Church/Teaching/ymma/underside2.cfm This book helps keep mutual activity ideas flowing for both youth and their leaders. Use the ideas found in this book to plan fun, meaningful, mutual activities of many kinds. Wow. (See related sites in chapter 10: "Young Men's Resources"; and companion sites in chapter 10: "Young Women's Resources.") ★★★★★ ☑

LDS Historical Information www.math.byu.edu/~smithw/Lds William Smith's excellent collection of papers and original diaries and texts. Includes Teachings of the Prophet Joseph Smith, History of the Church, all the versions of the First Vision, and much, much more. Unfortunately, there isn't a search engine, but it is a very good—albeit unattractive—site. (See related resources in chapter 13: "Multiple Periods of Church History.") ★★★★★ ☑

LDS Home www.ldshome.com A really incredibly well-done magazine for LDS women. Includes a mailing list, many tips for home management, helps for callings, storage, recipes, and much more. (See related resources in chapter 9: "Online News"; chapter 10: "Homemaking"; and chapter 11: "Resources for Women.") ★★★★★ ☑

LDS Scouting Resources www.gemstate.net/scouter/ldsplus.htm Quotes from general authorities, training and orientation topics, LDS units/resources, LDS patches, LDS/BSA history, articles on Scouting, and more. (See related resources in chapter 11: "Scouting.") ★★★★★ ☑

Mission.Net www.mission.net Find your mission on the Internet. The Mission.Net site lists mission home pages, information about many countries, and help for new missionaries. For alumni of various missions of the Church of Jesus Christ of Latter-day Saints. This site facilitates e-mail, reunions, and snail-mail contacts. Also, young men and women who are called on missions may find the information on these pages useful as they prepare to enter the mission field. How do you choose from among so many fine sites? (See related sites in chapter 6: "Missionary Resources"; and chapter 9: "International Sites.") ★★★★★ ☑

My Beliefs www.osmond.net/donny/beliefs Donny Osmond explains his beliefs. Actually, a very thoughtful page. Worth a read. (See related sites in chapter 6: "Testimony.") ★★★★★ ☑

Standard Works 208.201.207.12/scriptures Gregor McHardy's very nicely done site for reading the scriptures online. You can also download the entire collection for free so that you can read the scriptures on your own computer, offline. No search tool, but the indexed tabs are familiar and easy to use. (See related sites in chapter 7: "Scriptures Online.") Affiliated with Brother McHardy's Gospel Doctrine Weekly Reader at www.dancris.com/~gregor/gdlist. ★★★★★ ☑

Standard Works www.deseretbook.com/scriptures Scripture search site from Deseret Book. Beautifully done. (See related sites in chapter 7: "Scriptures Online.") ★★★★★ ☑

The Wasp www.xmission.com/~estep LDS journal of news, reviews, and commentary published by Christopher and Deanna Estep. Humor, opinion . . . not nearly as biting as its Nauvoo-period namesake. (See related sites in chapter 9: "Online News"; and chapter 12: "Humor.") ★★★★★ ☑

INDEX

P age numbers in **bold** type refer to Internet sites, newsgroups, and e-mail lists. A more complete index, with all the Internet sites listed in this book, is available from the *Mormons on the Internet* Registry at www.writerspost.com/mormonnet.

Excite, 66–**67**
Eyre, Linda, 138
Eyre, Richard, 138
Eyring, Henry B., 253, 353
EYRING-L, xiii, 11, **201, 355–356**

FAIR (Foundation for Apologetic Information and Research), **105, 107, 378–379**
Faith, **97, 110, 124, 356**
Faithful Fathering, **136**
Families, **201**
Family/families
    forum, **138, 139**
    history, 160–161, **162, 165–167**
    importance of, **135, 138**
    marriage, resources on, **141–142**
    parenting resources, **134–138**
    records, publishing, 167
    recreational resources, **138–140**
    topics covering, 371
Family: A Proclamation to the World, 33, **99, 147, 148**
Family Based Internet (FBI), 77
Family.Com, **139**
FamilyFellowship, **202, 274**
Family First, 92
Family Guidebook, 33, 136
Family History Center (FHC), 132–133, 162, 164–165
Family Home Evening, **138, 139**
Family Tree Maker, **166–167**
FamilySearch, **160, 161, 162–163, 167, 374**
FAQ, **103–104, 108, 356, 367**
    Answers to, **101, 102**
FAQ About Lists, **56**
FARMS (Foundation for Ancient Research and Mormon Studies), **105, 106, 107, 108, 113–114, 281, 285–286, 288–289, 352, 375**
    book reviews by, 192–193, 290–291, 323–324
    Insights: An Ancient Window, 193, **352**
    Journal of Book of Mormon Studies, 193
Fathers/fatherhood, **135, 136, 137**
FatherWork, **135, 136**
Faust, James E., 30, 147
FEMA (Federal Emergency Management Agency), **315, 316**
FHUnion, 132–133
Filtered Internet service providers, 75–80
First Presidency messages, 147
First Vision, **109**
Fletcher, Harvey, 352
Flood stories, **320**
Folklore, 119, **328**
Food Safety. *See* National Food Safety Database, **316**

Forte Free Agent, **44**
Forty-Day Teachings of Christ . . . A Gnostic Endowment (Wiley), **327**
Forward, Dan, 94
14 Fundamentals, 150
Fowkes, Kathy, 32
Franceschini, Massimo, 303
Freedom of speech issues, 80–81
FreeSaints, **202**
Free Webspace.net, **372**
Frequently Asked Questions. *See* FAQ
Friends, **58, 217, 250**
FTP (file transfer protocol) designation, 45, 46
    sites, 48

Gainsayers, **113**
Galletly, George, 80
Games, **234**
Gardner, Brant, 283, 323
Gardner, Brent, 308
Gates, Debbie, 53
GAYMORMON, **202, 274–275**
Gazette, 195
Gee, John, 301, 302
Gendex, **163**
Genealogy
    helplist, **132, 133**
    Lady, 163
    online, **163–164**
    oral, **167**
    research, 20, **160–165, 378**
    software, 167
    tracing pioneers, **167**
General Conference, **148–149**
Germany, churches in, 182
Gileadi, Avraham, 297
Gileadi, Cathy, 16, 24
Glass, Roxanna, 258
Goble, Clark, 198, 201, 293
God
    the Father, **362**
    foreknowledge and, **362**
    and man, relationship between, 111
Godhead, 97, **99**
GodMakers, 108, 109, 110
Gods, Mormons as, **109**
Goin' to Zion, **187**
Gonder, Pam, 9
Goode, Stephen Rex, 273, 276
Google, **67**
GOSHEN (Global Online Service Helping Evangelize Nations), **297**
Gospel
    classics, **151**
    doctrine, **128, 151, 238, 263, 362, 379**
    essays on, **352**

UKLDS, **216**
U.S. Air Force Academy, **155**
U.S. Constitution, **358, 359–360**
US GenWeb, **165**
University of California (Stanford), **154**
University of Missouri, **155**
University of Utah, **157**
URLs (Uniform Resource Locators)
    copying, 44–45
    entering, 45–46
UseNet newsgroups, 48
Utah Contemporary Dance Theatre, **309**
Utah Historical Quarterly, 194
Utah History Encyclopedia, **350**
Utah statehood period, **347–348**
Utah State University, **157**
Utah Valley State College, **157**

Valletta, Thomas R., 17, 21
Venturing programs, 255
Vigor, 196
Visitations, 168

Walsh, John, 50, 101, 151, 374
Ward Scouting Job Descriptions, **255**
Wards, 19, **197**
    activities committee, **260**
Washington, Kirkland, 230
Wasp, The, 195, **380**
Watchmen Institute, **309–310**
Watson, Wendy L., 251
WebCrawler, **70**
Weber State University, **157**
Weissman, Hartmut, 193
Welch, John W., 292
Welfare, **133–134**
Whalen, Curtis (Jewel), 55, 252
Whitmer, David, 335
Whitmer, John, 151, **353**
Wilcox, Brad, **306**
Wilde, Arthur L., 16, 42, 220
Wiley, David, 171, 327, 328, 329, 331
Williams, Andrea, 306
Wilson, Keith J., 121
Wilson, Timothy, 284
Winship, Jeffrey B., 10–11
Wirth, Diane E., 290
Wisconsin, **349**
Wolverton, Dave, 52
Woman's Perspective, A, 233

Woman's Touch, A, 233
Women, **216, 307**
    on the Internet, **53**
    LDS_OR_SIS, **204**
    LDS-Youngwomen, **210**
    LDS-YW, **210**
    LDS-YWLIST, **210**
    leaders, **365**
    lesbian, **206, 275, 276**
    magazine, 196
    resources for, **264–266**
    sexual abuse, **276**
    Sisters, **215, 231, 266**
    Sister-Share, **231, 266**
Women's Conference (1999), 124, 150, 266, **377**
Woodhouse, Gregory, 52, 215, 239, 304
Woods, Debra, 242
Wootton, Richard T., 354–355
Word of Wisdom, **96, 99, 313**
Work, on the Sabbath, **365**
Works, standard, **146–147, 380**
World Wide Web, x, xviii
    discussion areas, 220–221
    First Ward, **58, 59**
    free sites, 371–373
Worship, topics covering, 370
Wright, H. Curtis, 324
Wright, Newell, 200
WW-LDS, **185**
WW-LDS, **216**

Yahoo!, **x, 70, 156**
YCHAT, **218–219**
Yeager, Derryl, 309
Yosef, Rabbi, 325
Young, Brigham, 295
Young men, **239–240, 379**
Young women, **240–242**
Youth/teens, **196, 213, 216, 217, 218**
    dating and courtship, **248–249**
    magazine, 196
    resources, **244–247**

Zephaniah, **292–292**
Zielinski, Stan, 168
ZION, xiii
    fiction, 196, **310**
Zion, Brion, 344, 348
Zion National Park, **348**
Zion Search, **71**

Religion and Business Do Mix!

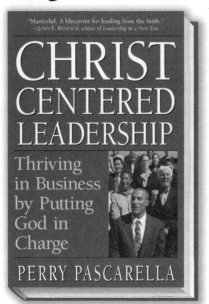

"Masterful. A blueprint for leading from the faith."
—JOHN E. RENESCH, editor of *Leadership in a New Era*

CHRIST CENTERED LEADERSHIP

Thriving in Business by Putting God in Charge

PERRY PASCARELLA

For a growing number of corporate executives, religion and business do mix—powerfully and effectively. Faith in the boardrooms is changing the face of some of today's most successful companies. In *Christ-Centered Leadership*, top Christian business leaders show you how such biblical principles as servant leadership and the Golden Rule can turn your workplace into an environment that nurtures extraordinary success based on timeless values.

"This book is must reading. In compelling language it explains Christian truths and their application to modern commercial enterprises. Pascarella understands his Christian faith and the difficulties of successfully guiding a corporation in global competitive markets. This book will help many executives achieve more congruency between what they believe and how they lead."

—Bill O'Brien, former president and CEO of Hanover Insurance Company and partner of Centre for Generative Leadership

ISBN 0-7615-2106-2 / Hardcover
288 pages / U.S. $22.95 / Can. $33.50

Kids Say the Darndest Things—Especially About God

Out of the mouths of babes come words of wisdom. Author Dandi Daley Mackall asked children across the country why they believe in God. Their heartwarming—and often hilarious—answers will charm, inspire, and delight you. Inside, you'll discover such gems as:

- I believe in God, but I still wonder about a lot of things. Like I wonder how He made eyeballs.

- God is very powerful. He made the whole world in six days. It takes me that long to clean my room!

- There are so many people talking to God at the same time. He listens to every one of them and doesn't even have call waiting.

- And many more!

Why I Believe in God

And Other Reflections by Children

Dandi Daley Mackall

ISBN 0-7615-1649-2 / Hardcover
112 pages / U.S. $10.95 / Can. $16.00

PRIMA

To order, call (800) 632-8676 or visit us online at www.primalifestyles.com